WHATEVER IT TAKES

1·11·94

WHATEVER IT TAKES

Graham Richardson

BANTAM BOOKS
SYDNEY • AUCKLAND • TORONTO • NEW YORK • LONDON

WHATEVER IT TAKES
A BANTAM BOOK
First published in Australia and New Zealand
in 1994 by Bantam

National Library of Australia.
Cataloguing-in-Publication Entry.
Richardson, Graham, 1949– .
Whatever it takes.

ISBN 1 86359 332 2.

1. Richardson, Graham, 1949– . 2. Australian Labor Party – Biography. 3. Politicians – Australia – Biography. 4. Australia – Politics and government – 1965– . I. Title.

328.94092

Bantam books are published by
Transworld Publishers (Aust) Pty Limited
15–25 Helles Avenue, Moorebank, NSW 2170
Transworld Publishers (NZ) Limited
3 William Pickering Drive, Albany, Auckland
Transworld Publishers (UK) Limited
61–63 Uxbridge Road, Ealing London W5 5SA
Bantam Doubleday Dell Publishing Group Inc
1540 Broadway, New York, New York 10036

Edited by Jacqueline Kent
Cover and text design by Reno Design Group 14193
Cover photograph by Arunas
Typeset in Berling Book by Midland Typesetters, Victoria
Production by Vantage Graphics, Sydney
Printed by Griffin Paperbacks, South Australia
10 9 8 7 6 5 4 3 2 1

To Fred, Peg and Marje's

ACKNOWLEDGMENTS

I'd like to thank my agent Jill Hickson for getting me so much money, Brian Johns, Robert Ray, Peter Barron, Geoff Walsh, Simon Balderstone and Laurie Oakes for reading the manuscript and assisting with accuracy, Michelle Macaulay and Brett Gale for research and manuscript preparation, my wife Cheryl for typing it and my family for enduring the countless hours of disruption that its writing entailed. Thanks are also due to my editor Jacqueline Kent for giving order, form and structure to the mayhem with which she was presented and to Transworld's Judith Curr for her faith during the long periods when nothing was being produced.

CONTENTS

Preface

No one writes books about the Liberal Party. The real inside story of how John Hewson defeated Peter Reith or how Alexander Downer rolled John Hewson doesn't interest anybody much, including the participants. In the conservative parties, colourful characters are rare indeed, and anyone possessed of a real personality obviously doesn't bother to join them.

This is undoubtedly why more media attention is paid to the Labor Party, in or out of government, than is ever given to our opponents. Only the laziest of journalists could fail to get a good yarn out of any of our conferences, whether state or federal. Contrast this with Liberal Party conferences, whose purpose is solely to guide the parliamentary party and whose decisions bind no one. They usually provide a platform from which a leader might speak, but they never give a platform for their party. The contest for the Liberal Party's national presidency has no meaning, though it may result in the odd hurt feeling; for Labor the election of the national president is a test of strength. Either the position goes to an acceptable high flier who can add to our election hopes, or the factions slug it out toe to toe.

In the Labor Party the game is played hard. The Marquis of Queensberry's rules never applied to Labor, or maybe we never bothered with them. Whether deciding who is to run for alderman or who will be prime minister, almost everything the Labor Party does to itself is naturally ferocious.

Over the last decade, this ferocity and its results have hit the national headlines time and time again. And several books have already been written about many of the events chronicled in these pages, as well as TV documentaries. These books have in common that they have been written by people who observed those events from the comfort of positions far behind the lines, usually in the well-protected haven of the press gallery. The authors of such books have never taken part in the battles, never risked their present, let alone their future—and none of them has been steeped in the values and traditions of the Australian Labor Party or in the intensity of the personal and factional rivalries that have beset the party since its inception. No matter how hard their noses are pressed against the window pane, those outside the processes find difficulty in understanding the personal dilemmas of so many players who have had to reconcile personal and factional loyalties, weigh up conscience against threat, personal integrity against the welfare of the party and of course the public lie against the private truth.

By a combination of luck and misfortune, well directed and misdirected effort, I was there when many significant decisions were taken. I was on one end of hundreds of the thousands of telephone calls made to bring about the birth and death of the Labor leadership on two occasions. Labor has governed for fourteen of the last twenty-two years, and when Labor made an important decision, I was in there somewhere. So I am uniquely qualified to give not just an account of what really happened but to convey a sense of the human drama involved, as well as the real flavour of two leadership campaigns that had the remarkable similarities of first-challenge failures, six months of intrigue and strife, and eventual success.

The book is not an exercise in self-justification: that would be pointless.

Graham Richardson

Part 1

LEARNING THE TRADE

CHAPTER 1

First Steps

By the time I was sixteen, I had learned more about politics from my parents than most politicians learn in a lifetime.

I was born in Sydney on 27 September 1949, and was hooked on politics from a very early age, coming to it through the union movement. My father Fred was the New South Wales secretary of the Amalgamated Postal and Telecommunications Union (APTU), the most internally divided union in the New South Wales labour movement. He had been involved in industrial relations in the Postmaster-General's Department and had gone to the union as an industrial officer. He later joined it and took it over, and the process of gaining power and hanging on to it enthralled and fascinated me. Kids whose families are in politics or trade unions sometimes grow up hating their parents' passion and principles, but I was fascinated by both. And this total family involvement in the union meant that union and Labor politics were always the main topics of conversation in the Richardson household.

Every two years there was a ballot for APTU office bearers. For two or three months beforehand, our home was a place of frenzied activity. Mum, who worked as Dad's secretary, would address thousands of envelopes to union members by hand; pamphlets would be designed and redesigned; the makeup of the ticket that Dad would lead would be decided. My strongest memory of this period is the telephone: it never stopped ringing in our place.

I learned about strength and weakness, about betrayal and courage, about loyalty. Dad always said you could always tell who your friends were—they're the ones who vote for you when you're wrong. But most of all, I learned about persuasion. I'd have loved a dollar for every time I heard my father ring a waverer and shore him up. On one such call that Dad was making in the bedroom, Mum was listening from an extension in the lounge room, and gave me a message for Dad: 'Ask him if he's with us or with them.' It's a question I've been asking people ever since.

The big umbrella that is the Labor Party, under which shelter so many different shades of opinion, had to be pretty big in the 1960s. When I was growing up Australia still had an active Communist Party, especially in the trade union movement. I learned very early that 'the comms' were the world's No. 1 enemy, the root of all evil. Furthermore, my father confirmed what Sister Annette told us in second class at St Raphael's School, South Hurstville: the communists were coming to get us. In those days, there was much talk of fellow travellers, those who were members of the Labor Party but who ran on unity tickets with the communists. I was never sure who was voting with whom—whether the communists voted with the fellow travellers or vice versa. But I was certain that they voted with each other on the executive of Dad's union week after week, year after year.

If communists and fellow travellers were evil, my young mind quickly got the impression that Masons weren't real flash either. They were the ones who conspired to keep good decent Catholics out of good decent jobs. Fortunately, neither of my parents was a militant Catholic so I was never taught to hate Masons, just to be very wary of them. None of Mum and Dad's best friends was a Mason.

The communists' arch enemies were supposed to be the National Civic Council (NCC) and the Democratic Labor Party, that curious bunch of Catholics who had split from Labor when

I was five years old and who kept it from governing until I was twenty-three. Labor's years in the electoral wilderness allowed that most dreadful of luxuries to be enjoyed to the full: Left and Right, Catholic and Mason hoed into each other with glee and gusto. Bob Hawke claimed that he had great faith in the intelligence of the Australian people because they would always make sure that the right people were elected. He never said this because he was trying to suck up to his audience. Rather, these words were an admission that Labor had not been fit to govern during the two decades to which I have just referred. All those election losses under Evatt and Calwell, with the possible exception of 1961 when Labor came within two seats of governing, were simply examples, as Hawke saw it, of the people making the right decision.

I was too young to judge this, but from all I can recall of what my parents told me, Hawke was spot on. The union movement was the assembled foes' favourite arena, and the APTU had the reputation of holding the record for militancy and infighting. Some particularly nasty strikes, especially at the Redfern mail exchange, occurred during the 1960s. It was a work environment that degraded its employees, whose resentment was never far below the surface, so Dad's predictions of an industrial relations nightmare came true. During these strikes the treatment of scabs attracted the most publicity, and I'm not sure the papers ever knew the full story. Women workers who crossed picket lines had their heads pushed into toilets that were continually flushed. At the time it seemed that the women were particularly vicious towards members of their own sex who transgressed. Tyres were slashed, windscreens shattered, and more than once physical violence was used. This was always justified on the grounds that scabs were subhuman anyway, so it didn't really matter.

Contrary to popular belief, this kind of violence was not organised by union officials. I can recall Dad many times spending hours on the phone, pleading with workers to go easy on offenders. My father's defence of these actions was never delivered with real passion, but it was delivered none the less; the working class of thirty years ago demanded solidarity among themselves. Many of his pleas fell on deaf fists.

But there was also a glamorous side to union politics, and we knew who our heroes were. When I was about ten, the biggest deal in my life was to be taken to dinner at the old St George Leagues Club. It was great even to be left in the TV room with some other lucky kids while our parents played the poker machines. One evening I was told to be on my best behaviour because we were having dinner with Frank Waters. The federal president of the APTU, Frank had represented the Labor Party in the Queensland Parliament during the 1930s. To meet such a famous man, I was determined to be perfect.

My first memory of union power was old Frank's head sinking slowly into his oyster soup. I'm sure he'd have been the first man ever to drown in a bowl of it if my father's hand had not pulled his head to safety and plucked the oysters from his eyes. Frank's cerebral capacity was to brains what Phar Lap's coronary equipment was to hearts. Though he was one of a coterie of infamous drinkers who surrounded the legendary Jack Egerton during his days as the ultimate power in Queensland Labor politics, no matter how many brain cells had been destroyed by his alcoholic excesses he remained an astute judge of people and tactics, and I never met anyone who was better read.

Success in trade union politics has always involved a capacity for bastardry. When I was about sixteen something happened to my father that I thought raised bastardry to new heights. The National Civic Council and the communists combined to try and defeat him. He stuck it out, and eventually won. But he had to face a hostile state executive for two years and, despite the fact that he was state secretary of the union, the executive voted to take away his car and his phone. Worse than that, they sacked my mother.

When Mum was sacked I saw for the first time how the media can completely destroy a relatively peaceful suburban existence. Our three-bedroom fibro house, tastefully painted lilac, with an outside toilet on the classic quarter-acre block, suddenly received the attention normally given to houses of a much grander nature. For days we were front-page news in the papers and we headlined the television news. Leaving the house five minutes after my father Mum was photographed, according to the caption 'leaving by another entrance', a pretty spectacular effort given that we had only one way in or out. This was the first time I witnessed media distortion. I thought the whole episode was incredibly unfair, and it created great family upheaval. My mother even stopped going to church for a time in protest at the involvement of some priests in the union elections. The NCC still had tentacles everywhere, presenting formidable opposition.

Although the crisis came and went—my father triumphed in the next union election and my mother got her old job back—peace never really returned to Oakdale Avenue, Kogarah. My father always believed that some officials of the New South Wales branch of the APTU actively supported those who were against him. And while a gentle man in every respect, he never relented to the point of employing an enemy. To have opposed him once was to be counted as an enemy forever, at least if that opposition had come in the form of betrayal. 'If they rat on you once, they'll rat on you twice,' he would say. But those who remained loyal were always rewarded. No one ever complained that Dad had not kept his word when he gave it to a friend. It is hardly surprising that in this household, loyalty was everything. I learned that 'ratting' was the lowest act of all, and more importantly, that no act of betrayal could ever be forgiven or forgotten.

Dad was never a member of a particular faction; he didn't follow the line, which made him a bit of a maverick. Postal Workers delegates always supported the Right at Labor Party state conferences, but in 1969 Dad departed from the true path at the ACTU conference by supporting Bob Hawke as president against the Right's candidate Harold Souter. Hawke had the backing of Ray Gietzelt, the most powerful union left-winger in the country. My father supported Hawke against the wishes of John Ducker, who was the New South Wales ALP senior vice-president at the time. Dad reckoned Harold Souter was a good bloke but he was never going to set the world on fire, whereas like a lot of others, Dad kept looking at Hawke and seeing prime ministerial potential. He prevailed on his delegation, most of whom were right-wing ALP people and part of Ducker's team, to vote for Hawke. I don't think this impressed Ducker, and Dad had to suffer some enmity from the Right in New South Wales. It wasn't a real problem, but he had to suffer it nevertheless. When you're impregnable, your opponents either deal with you or watch you vote against them. Given that I've never seen a case of the latter, I guess the New South Wales Right did the former.

I had suspected that my mother was a bit tougher than my father and in the years that followed her sacking my instincts were proved correct. She was more practical and harder-headed than Dad, less sentimental perhaps.

While my fascination with my parents' involvement in union affairs grew at a furious pace, and as an only child I was roped in to help many times, I began to discover debating and public speaking at school. I won the public speaking cup at Marist Brothers Kogarah in 1965. If one considers that there were only two competitors, the significance of the victory is somewhat diminished. It was, however, the first time I had spoken in front of a large audience—500 people gathered at the Hurstville Civic Centre for the school prize-giving night. The subject of the speech was the anti-worker governments of Menzies and Holt and their miserable record. I was embarrassed by a lengthy silence in the middle of my speech when I forgot my lines, but the contentious nature of this speech didn't faze me at all; I loved the fact that some thought it wicked and some thought it wonderful and they all kept talking about it. It is probably safe to confess now, some thirty years on, that I did not write the speech. It was written by my parents' closest friend, Des Barney, a union colleague.

I showed my flair for drama in another way on 1 November 1965, the evening of my first exam in the Leaving Certificate, when I was involved in a near-fatal car crash close to Tom Ugly's bridge at Dolls Point, Sydney. I was thrown from the passenger seat to the roadway, my torso having hit the dashboard and my face having gone through the windscreen. My spleen was removed and, 200 stitches later my only memory was being given the last rites twice, which is pretty disconcerting when you're sixteen.

When one of my school friends visited me in hospital after my ten days in intensive care, he saw my badly smashed-up face and muttered the immortal words, 'Oh, shit!' This did not do my confidence a great deal of good. Three operations over the next few years gradually reduced the scarring, but I became a bit depressed and passive. The whole episode screwed me up for quite a few years. It was the Labor Party that restored meaning and purpose to my life.

During most of his career as a union official, Dad was not a member of the Labor Party. When I joined in November 1966 at the age of seventeen, I was the first member of my family to do so. My father joined some months later, but would not have attended half a dozen party meetings in his life. Frederick James Richardson had not the slightest interest in power or influence beyond the small world of his union activity.

Although convenient, it is probably also accurate to put down my abysmal academic performance over the next few years to my state of mind induced by the accident and its aftermath. Two successive enrolments in arts at the University of Sydney were doomed to failure because I rarely went near the university. I spent six months working in the Auditor-General's Department, discovering that this was not to be my lot in life. In 1969, at my parent's urging, I enrolled in law and passed the first two years more by divine intervention than consistent effort. Having good friends who were conscientious students meant that I could borrow their notes on the night before exams and just scrape through.

During these years I became one of the world's greatest bludgers. Sure I had part-time jobs to keep a few dollars in the pocket, but the art of carousing all night, sleeping all morning and waking only to catch the midday movies became one in which I excelled. Indolence is habit-forming and, had it not been for my growing interest in the Labor Party, I would have continued to be its victim.

During the late 1960s, my interest in the party rapidly increased. The Monterey branch of the ALP, which I joined late in 1966, was a small right-wing branch in the marginal federal seat of Barton in Sydney's southern suburbs, won by Gary Punch in 1983. The branch was small because of Labor's great debacle in the 1966 election, which saw Barton and many other seats lost. The party took a principled stand against the war in Vietnam and was slaughtered for its trouble, so morale was low and enrolments were down.

My father frowned on my attendance at protest meetings against the war, which were very big in 1966 and 1967. He was never one of the world's great radicals, and he believed that nothing was worth an arrest and conviction, but attend I did. I also became involved with Young Labor. There was a branch in Barton, which was largely organised by Frank Walker, later attorney-general in the Wran Labor government and already a leftie of note. A few people on the Right looked at me askance because of my association with Walker, and I sensed that Dad was rather doubtful about it. But at the time, I associated Young Labor with car rallies and barbecues rather than ideology, so Dad did not consider that contact with Walker would contaminate me too much. He did take me aside and tell me I could never join the Left because they were no good, but I never seriously contemplated it anyway.

In 1967, I went to a conference that the Australian National University in Canberra held to explore the possibility of forming a national Young Labor association. That was where I met Paul Keating. The meeting with Keating was less than earth shattering. I shook hands with him and then he was gone. (In fact it was another four years before I had a conversation with him. Appropriately for the times and what we then represented, Garry Johnston introduced me to him at the Catholic Club in Sydney where I was having a drink with Leo McLeay. This was a real thrill. He had only been in Parliament for two years but Keating was someone that was unmistakable.)

At the conference I had my first experience of Left–Right party combat and it was heady stuff. My parents' union wars were carried on in rooms barred to my entry, and I could only learn about them by listening to my parents' phone calls. Now there I was in person, watching the venom fly. It was great.

Keating rapidly got into the centre of an argument with Frank Walker and Bob Hunt, one of Walker's henchmen. Their conflict demonstrated one indisputable fact: no matter what differences they had, all the people I was beginning to meet in the party—Garry Johnston, Leo McLeay, Laurie Brereton—had one thing in common, a prodigious and inventive capacity to use four-letter words. For Keating, therefore, the temptation to use rhyming slang in choosing a nickname for Hunt was irresistible, and Mr Hunt was obviously none too pleased with the result. Although he had no power to do so, Keating had expelled Hunt from Young Labor because he hated him, and in those days Keating really knew how to hate. Acting as chairman for one of the sessions, he simply refused to recognise Hunt and would not let him speak. The ensuing fiasco taught me two things: you could bounce rocks off Keating and only the rocks would be damaged, and the rest of the party in Australia regarded the New South Wales Right with a barely disguised loathing. Like the rest of the Labor Party, Young Labor was split between Right and Left, both sides taking their views to extreme. Young Labor was very Right in New South Wales, very Left in Victoria.

Having seen a bit of party warfare first hand, in 1968 I was elected as a delegate to the Barton Federal Electorate Council, the party body dealing with federal affairs in the Barton electorate. It was here I learned another important lesson. In the Barton branch I moved what I thought was an obvious motion, condemning the 1968 Russian invasion of Czechoslovakia, confidently expecting it to be carried unanimously. Here it was that whatever shred of political innocence I still possessed disappeared forever. A Scotsman named Harry Wilson boldly informed us in his heavy brogue that Russian intervention had been necessary to prevent 'CIA infiltration'. His only evidence for this assertion was Dubcek's decision to allow the sale of *Time* magazine in Prague.

This was the first time I had heard mass murder defended, and however I thought such a defence might be mounted I had never contemplated anything like this. I was appalled to see this disgraceful effort compounded as the loyal comrades rushed to defend the legitimacy of the invasion. The uglier side of Australian communism, which had supported Stalin through tens of millions of murders, obviously had its share of supporters in the Labor Party. The Left was shockingly hardline in those days. Then and there I decided not simply to be a right-wing member of the ALP, but to become a tough and active one. My anti-communist resolution was eventually carried, but I had seen firsthand the tyranny of the Left which my father had fought all his life.

In 1970, I made one friendship that was to prove pivotal in climbing Labor's ladder of success, which I had now firmly decided to do. To climb such a ladder, you first have to know where it is, and there was no one better to point the way than Laurie Brereton. I met him in about mid 1970, and he impressed the hell out of me. It was in the old Randwick Labor Club, which was a real dump—I think they have pulled it down now. I was there with a bunch of students and in he walked, a young man in a magnificent suede coat. I'd never seen anything like Laurie. And in the year I met him, he was elected to the State Parliament, at twenty-three the youngest MP in New South Wales history.

This was the first time we had met, though we'd come across each other a couple of years before, when Laurie challenged my right to vote at the 1968 Young Labor elections. This apparently happened because I was suspected of having uttered friendly phrases in the direction of Frank Walker, and Laurie, who was pretty hardline Right, had never heard of my branch. In those days, Young Labor Council ballots were held in a dingy basement in Sydney's dingiest building, the Sydney Trades Hall. Laurie's intervention caused me to vote for Left candidates in some positions—the only time in my life I have been guilty of so heinous a crime. For the next few years Laurie and I did not cross paths and when I was finally introduced to him by Garry Johnston, then secretary of Young Labor, Laurie had forgotten our inauspicious first meeting.

Laurie knew everyone: unless you do, your capacity to go nowhere is greatly enhanced. Not only did he know everyone, but they listened to him. And because Laurie and I became firm friends, very slowly doors began to open. At the ALP office I met Kerry Sibraa, the office's liaison man with Young Labor, and even Geoff Cahill the assistant party secretary in New South Wales. This was all pretty heady stuff.

I have never been politically ambitious and I certainly wasn't in 1970. Like so many of my colleagues who will appear later in this book, I was a political addict. If I couldn't get enough politics any other way, I'm sure I'd have injected it. So meeting the right people in the Labor Party was not part of a brilliant strategy carefully constructed by a youthful political genius. I wanted to meet them because everything they did fascinated me and I could get another fix of the stuff that was beginning to give my rather indolent life some purpose. And, while most people who attain positions of power may be reluctant to say so in these terms, the prospect of people deferring to me one day—in the way they deferred to the 'right people' I was beginning to meet—was pretty attractive.

Laurie Brereton was the first person I met who had real power. Our friendship developed quickly and became permanent. Laurie taught me all there was to know about fine foods, fine wines and winning ballots. These lessons came from a man who, by the age of twenty-six, had been elected to State Parliament, had his seat abolished, been defeated in a preselection for a redrawn seat, worked in the union movement for a few years and then won the seat back after several years of basic branch organisation. These were pretty impressive credentials. I also came to the gradual knowledge that, as with most of the powerful figures I was to encounter, Laurie did not forgive easily. Once crossed he became the most unrelenting of pursuers.

He and Paul Keating had one very important thing in common: they could count. They shared the view that if you took all those who swore their allegiance on the heads of their children then deducted 20 per cent, you would be pretty close to right. It takes a special talent to read body language, to pick the truth in the eyes while the mouth utters the lie: to know whether, when the absolute promise of support is made, it is worth anything.

But Brereton and Keating were much more than just nuts-and-bolts numbers men deciding positions and policies. They always had other interests, and conversations with them were rarely mundane, since they were voracious readers. They brimmed with insights and ideas, and listening to them was seductive indeed. In politics a talent for numbers operations, for persuasion, for acquiring power, is not always accompanied by intellect. When you see people with both, as Brereton and Keating had, there is an inevitability about their success.

During the next two years, my preoccupation with the ALP continued to grow. While I worked in a solicitor's office by day—it was there I met my wife Cheryl—at night I attended more meetings and began to speak more often. I became more active in Barton and I began to deliver delegates to state conferences from my local area. In the party nothing is noticed more quickly than delivering numbers, and so in late 1970 or early 1971 I met John Ducker. This was a really big deal. Although he was senior vice-president of the state ALP, not president, his sheer personality and political skill had gained him much more power than the mere title suggests. Not long after I met him, he took over the presidency from Charlie Oliver.

Ducker and I met at a Young Labor function for members of the Right faction, exchanged a few words, shook hands, and that was it. The meeting was very formal, no relaxed humour or banter, strictly business. Over the years I discovered that Ducker is a very formal man indeed. He is the only man I know who could turn up to a barbecue at the Trades and Labour Council camp at Currawong on Pittwater with 200 trade union colleagues wearing shorts and thongs, in a shirt, tie, sports coat and leather shoes. This was no accident: Ducker belonged to the school that says a leader should always look like one. It was all part of the game.

But around this time I learned what 'the game' can do. Stress and extended periods of constant confrontation with the enemy do take their toll. My parents died young, frighteningly so: my mother in 1969 at only forty-two, with no history of illness. My father had two heart attacks and died on the third three years later, alone, while I was away at a party meeting in southern New South Wales. Mercifully, they both died in their sleep.

In material terms, they left me with a home unit and a few thousand dollars. But they left me with other legacies that were priceless: a magnificent obsession with the Labor Party and a code to live by. Dad always believed you could sort out the problem in private, retreat and alter course if necessary. But you must never show the enemy any semblance of disunity in the forces representing all that was good and holy, which naturally enough were those grouped around you.

As I've already mentioned, my father often said that there was only one certainty in life: anyone who will rat on you once will rat on you twice. In the twenty-two years since his death, I have seen nothing to alter that truth. When George Georges, who had crossed the floor to vote against legislation deregistering the Builders Labourers Federation, shed tears at the national executive while promising not to do it again, I pleaded with the executive to show no mercy. The usual New South Wales hardline gibes were thrown at me and the prodigal senator was welcomed back to our bosom. To me it was as certain as night follows day that he would rat again, and of course a few months later that's exactly what he did. From the countless battles fought in and by the Postal Workers Union during my childhood, I had learned the true value of forgiveness in politics: nil.

Perhaps most important of all, Dad taught me the inestimable value of admitting your errors quickly, something almost totally absent in today's politicians. You can only compound an error by sticking to it, but you can cloak yourself in virtue by admitting it and taking a different tack. I also learned how to know my weaknesses every bit as well as my strengths. Politics is full of people whose ambition outweighs their talent. Knowing your place, even if it is not the top rung on the ladder, is not being humble or putting yourself down. It's just being smart.

CHAPTER 2

Climbing the Ladder

In September 1971, Kerry Sibraa rang to tell me that an election for ALP state organiser was coming up at the state council meeting, and that I should consider standing for the position. This meant I had to get right-wing support and that meant John Ducker. Ducker's endorsement was probably a foregone conclusion, as Sibraa and Brereton were already pushing for me. But I had negative backing as well: state assistant secretary Geoff Cahill could be counted on to support anyone who wasn't the candidate favoured by Peter Westerway, the then general secretary. Westerway was a university lecturer and television host whom Ducker had engineered into the state party's top administrative job. He was a cleanskin, untainted by the brawls that had marked the state party when it was run by Bill Colbourne and Charlie Oliver. Sibraa arranged for me to meet Cahill, Westerway and Ducker in that order. I rushed out, bought a new suit and prepared for what turned out to be the only job interviews I had ever attended.

Geoff Cahill was a big man, never as big as he thought he was, but big nonetheless. His office was next door to Westerway's and I was determined to impress them both. During my chat with

Cahill I even smoked a cigarette, though I hadn't smoked for some years, just because he offered it to me. The interview went well and Cahill promised his support. He also made it clear that he would deliver John Ducker's support, giving the impression that the New South Wales labour movement was run by two people, not just one as the rest of the world believed.

I wandered into Westerway's office feeling pretty buoyant, only to be instantly deflated. Westerway declared his support for Dorothy Isaksen (later a member of the New South Wales Legislative Council), informing me that a change in image would be good for the Right and it was time for a woman to hold elected office in the party. He added that he would be calling senior party colleagues to express this view. The journey from the ninth to the tenth floor at 377 Sussex Street now seemed inordinately long and I trudged into Ducker's office, fearing the worst.

I told Ducker what Westerway had said and his reaction demonstrated the absolute power he wielded. He was immediately dismissive, almost contemptuous, of Westerway's view. I was told that Dorothy Isaksen would not nominate, that Westerway would make no more calls and that I should proceed to contact every union secretary who supported the Right and tell them I had Ducker's imprimatur. My realisation that the current general secretary enjoyed less than total influence was an important lesson.

True to Ducker's word, I heard no more of Dorothy Isaksen, and the trade union secretaries treated this very young man with great kindness. I rang as many delegates as I could (out of the 410 delegates to state council I personally spoke to more than 300) and when the state council met in the Teachers Federation Hall, Kent Street, Sydney on 6 December 1971, I received 235 votes in a field of twelve candidates. Any supposition that I achieved this high vote because I impressed all the delegates I contacted should be immediately dismissed. My efforts might have added a half dozen votes to the officer's ticket, as the Right's 'how-to-vote' has always been termed, but the rest were strictly hardliners who would have voted for anybody whose name appeared beneath the photograph of John Ducker on the how-to-vote card.

I learned that, even at the New South Wales state conference, the biggest political gathering in Australia with 820 delegates, you can pick any result within 10 votes. Each of my rival candidates was given five minutes to address that state council and each of them knew the speech would mean nothing to their prospects in the ballot. Some hoped their contributions might be noted for the future, some just liked to hear themselves talk. (None of the other eleven candidates, by the way, ever achieved high party or parliamentary office.)

Being elected to the organiser's position at twenty-two is not all you might think. Firstly, there is the problem of overcoming the gibes from the Left that you got there only because you sucked up to the power elite. Given that there is more than a hint of truth in this, it is difficult to rebut. Secondly, virtually everyone with whom you deal is older than you. When you are barely out of adolescence, it is pretty hard to develop the instant wisdom and experience to impart to the party, to exert authority, simply because the returning officer declares you have won a ballot. The benefit of all this is that you grow up very fast, and the 1970s presented me with opportunities to mature beyond my wildest dreams.

Having now found the ladder, the process of climbing it became my focus. As I have said, I had not made a careful plan to rise through the ranks, and in fact subsequent events proved the truth of the saying that while talent is a bonus, to succeed you need lots of luck above all else. Being in the right place at the right time and having the person above you promoted or sacked is much more a function of luck than of skill. So is having the chance to learn the finer points of the game at the feet of a master.

In John Ducker, I observed the master player of the New South Wales Labor Party. Ducker was an uneducated migrant from Hull, with the accent to prove his ancestry. From a boilermaker's shop he became an official of the Ironworkers Union, a protege of Laurie Short who had fought the good fight and won. Not tall or imposing, no Robert Redford to look at, with a wardrobe that was strictly working class, slightly deaf from his years in a boilermaking shop, he was one of the most unlikely leaders I ever knew. And yet he knew more about real leadership and power than anyone I have ever met. He embodied something he once said: 'The best way to understand hunger is to be hungry. The best way to understand power is *not* to have it.' And he showed me that leadership has less to do with good looks and dulcet tones than what is in the mind and heart.

Ducker had kept the New South Wales Right alive when the national executive decided to intervene in New South Wales party affairs because the left wing complained they weren't getting a fair go from the Right. They made some pretty serious allegations about financial mismanagement, saying that money for party purposes was going to a company with links to some party officials. Ray Gietzelt, the most powerful left-wing union figure in state politics, saw this as the opportunity to bring down the Right.

Lionel Murphy, a leading left-winger, thought he had organised a much more complete intervention, which would have seen the Right all sacked and the Left take over. On behalf of the national executive, Tom Burns had investigated a series of allegations of improprieties in preselections, favoritism in decisions taken on branch rorting and flagrant breaches of standing orders at party conferences. His report was more than enough to justify the national executive putting the New South Wales Right out of business. With John Ducker at work, however, a dozen Burns reports would not have been enough. Ducker forged alliances with Clyde Cameron, later Minister for Labour in the Whitlam government, and Jack Egerton, the leader of the Left in Queensland. Had he not done so, the Right would have been slaughtered. By June 1971 it was obvious that the Right wouldn't be crushed by federal intervention, though some kind of power sharing would have to be conceded.

The man who did this wasn't the John Ducker who issued orders and established his superiority—it was the friendly, amiable Ducker, who got what he wanted by drinking with Egerton and flattering Cameron. I knew that Ducker could cajole, but what intrigued me the most was his use of temper. Losing your temper was a waste of time and effort, he said, unless you could use it as a weapon. He never ranted and raved at ceilings or open spaces in some solitary gesture of defiance: he chose to explode only in the company of people from whom he wanted something. He would go from a murmur to a session of screaming and shouting within a millisecond, and could make the toughest cringe.

John Ducker was a man to be thoroughly respected, neither loathed nor loved, always to be reckoned with. I saw him use the weapon of his temper time and time again, I watched him plot and plan to get his way and I remembered everything. I was privileged to be his friend and ally for most of the 1970s, and the things he taught me gave me some unique qualifications for mounting numbers operations against two Labor leaders some years later.

My election as organiser was a real thrill, as were my subsequent elections to a whole range of party and government positions. Whether it was to the position of general secretary, to the Senate, the ministry or the Cabinet, every step was satisfying, with a feeling that I had finally made it. But no personal milestone was ever as important as being allowed into Ducker's kitchen cabinet that ran the party and the unions in New South Wales.

During 1972 and 1973, I watched Sibraa, Cahill, Brereton and Keating make the trip from the ALP's head office on the ninth floor of the Labour Council in Sussex Street, Sydney, to John Ducker's office one floor above. Ducker was also assistant secretary of the Labour Council and every Thursday afternoon a selected group of colleagues called into his office to discuss issues of party importance. The organiser of the Labour Council Barrie Unsworth attended, as well as Peter McMahon, now a New South Wales industrial commissioner but then the secretary of the Municipal Employees Union, Joe Thompson, the then secretary of the Vehicle Builders Union, John Morris, secretary of the Liquor Trades Union, and his henchman Michael Whelan. Barry Egan, the very strange secretary of the Shop Assistants Union, was another regular attender.

To be invited to that room on a Thursday afternoon was a recognition I craved. When the invitation finally came, I was the proudest apparatchik in Christendom. The surroundings were ordinary, the hospitality even more so—beer and a very occasional Scotch were the order of the day. But the dramas played out in that room were among the greatest of Labor politics. There were discussions of support for Neville Wran as premier against Pat Hills, decisions about Whitlam's future after the Iraqi loans affair and the 1975 electoral disaster, decisions on party matters that would bring bitter confrontation with the Left—that room was an epicentre for quakes that shook the party, the state and the nation.

John Ducker was a prominent player in all of them. Not that his power went unchallenged: power is attractive and absolute power irresistible. It was therefore inevitable that Ducker's power would be contested by members of the inner circle in that room. Not one, but two among the tried and trusted were of the view that the interests of the party would be best served by transferring all power to them. The saga of the Geoff Cahill sacking and the defeat of Barry Egan in the Shop Assistants Union were proof of Ducker's absolute power and the folly of challenging it.

Kerry Sibraa's elevation to the Senate in 1975 led to my promotion to the position of assistant general secretary in March 1976. Peter Westerway had been replaced as general secretary at the state conference in 1973, and for the next few months I worked closely with his successor, Geoffrey David Llewellyn Cahill. He had taken to criticising Ducker to quite a few people in the party. If you are wondering whether he was courageous or stupid in so doing, think only of the latter. Like everyone else to whom he made these criticisms, I dutifully reported every one of them back to Ducker. My loyalty was not up for grabs, nor, apparently, was anybody else's.

At the 1975 conference, Cahill proposed to abolish the 800-strong conference and replace it with one extra meeting per year of the 400-strong state council. Asking people to abolish themselves is a tall order, and in Cahill's case it couldn't have been taller. The proposition had the support of the faction leaders: Ducker and Geoff Cahill on the Right and Arthur Gietzelt and assistant secretary Bruce Childs on the Left, but a revolt was breaking out in both camps.

The New South Wales conference is held on the June long weekend each year. The Rules debate, during which this proposal would be discussed, was to be held on the Sunday morning. By Saturday evening, having wandered the floor talking to delegates, I knew that Cahill's plan had no hope of success. Given that the Right don't get defeated at the New South Wales conference, I took my opinion to the only man who could stop this madness. With all the respect I could muster, I advised Ducker to back off. Ducker's response—'We won't be defeated, Geoff will be'—

suggested to me that there was a whiff of tension in the air.

Following a debate in which such prominent right-wing identities as former state president Charlie Oliver and John Johnson, now a Labor MLC, opposed the resolution, Cahill had the right of reply. No right-wing party officer has ever made a poorer effort. Presumably intending to recall past party glories, he shrieked the first words of his speech into the microphone: 'Things worth fighting for . . . ' No one could remember anything else he said as his speech trailed off into an embarrassing, weak-minded mishmash. Ducker sat impassively through Cahill's speech and through the entire debate, after which the motion was duly defeated. He voted with Cahill but failed to do the one thing that could have turned the tide or at least made the size of the loss more respectable—leave the chair and lend his authority to Cahill's proposition.

Most of us would have learned something from the humiliation; Cahill learned absolutely nothing. His criticisms of Ducker to an ever-widening team of insiders continued undiminished. When Neville Wran won the state election in May 1976, Geoff dragged himself from the sick bed to which he had taken as soon as the election was announced to claim victory for a great campaign. Party officials from all over Australia were flown in at great expense to hear and see how Geoff had won the election for Labor. What Neville Wran thought of this remains unclear, but to say that he and Geoff were never close may sum up their relationship. This period heralded Cahill's export of his criticisms of Ducker to Labor figures in other states, and here he sowed the seeds of his own destruction.

At the national executive meeting in July 1976, Ducker stood for the position of senior federal vice-president. He was defeated by Bart Lourigan, the Queensland secretary of the party (shortly thereafter booted out of the Queensland branch for incompetence) by 10 votes to 8. This was politics at its worst. The majority of delegates to the national executive wanted anybody but Ducker. The desire to get square with him far outweighed any acknowledgment of his talent or ability.

Jack Ferguson, Tom Uren, Arthur Gietzelt, all the old war horses of the Left came onto the battlefield to ensure Ducker's defeat for this relatively unimportant post, and they had been busy. Bob McMullan, then a young Left secretary of the West Australian branch, and Mal Bryce, who went on to become the deputy premier of Western Australia, were visited at their Sydney motel by Jack Ferguson on the night before they flew to Canberra for the conference. No vote was taken for granted.

On the night after the ballot, Ducker and I sat in a suite at the Carlton Rex Hotel in Canberra and proceeded to drink copious quantities of alcohol. This pastime was by no means exclusive to us, for at midnight a senior party official visited us to swear allegiance to Ducker. Having so sworn, he proceeded to vomit all over the bathroom floor before an abrupt departure. His career never did take off after that night. Ducker was convinced that Geoff Cahill had played a role in his defeat—he believed Cahill could have persuaded Bart Lourigan not to run—and had therefore broken the bond of loyalty. This required action, and Ducker told me what it was. He was going to remove Cahill; no mean feat considering that the general secretary was elected from the floor of the conference.

Even though Ducker and I had consumed almost two bottles of Scotch between us, I was eerily sober. 'You can't sack the general secretary!' I said.

'Just watch me,' said Ducker, not with the false bravado of drunken camaraderie but with chilling purpose.

It was arranged that Geoff would be persuaded to leave voluntarily, and that I would replace him. Naturally, I would have to sing for my supper. I was told to go through all the party's records and prepare a case that would encourage Geoff to accept his fate. During the next few weeks, Ducker consulted those who attended the Thursday afternoon sessions in his office, and a few others as well. The State Administrative Committee approved a twelve-week trip to the United States for Cahill, an odyssey planned to end in organised tragedy. While the preparations for his demise continued, no one sought to warn him. Whenever I have been challenged from within, I have been fortunate enough to have plenty of people prepared to bear witness against the miscreant. Cahill had no one.

In accordance with accounts published in the press and in several books, Barrie Unsworth, wearing a raincoat, met Geoff at Sydney airport when he returned from the United States on

1 September at 6.30am and took him home. He asked Geoff to come into the city for a short meeting. Cahill was whisked into Ducker's office, where he was confronted by the upper echelon of most of the party and the union movement. A sombre Ducker told him that he had lost the confidence of his colleagues and presented him with the letter of resignation I had already drafted. He had the option of going quietly or running for his position at the 1977 conference. A job was to be found for him within the New South Wales public service. Cahill was given an offer he couldn't refuse, and he went quietly. He found himself in the New South Wales bureaucracy, being appointed first as the Counsellor for Equal Opportunity and later as one of four chairmen of the New South Wales Government and Related Employees Appeal Tribunal.

While these events were taking place upstairs I was at a meeting of the party's finance committee, waiting for the phone to ring. I knew Cahill had no alternative but to accept Ducker's offer and resign, but when the call finally came I was greatly relieved.

By the time Geoff had come down to the party office a locksmith was at work on the door and I was sitting behind the desk Cahill was just about to clean out. This was a tad awkward, but with practised politeness and hypocrisy an ugly scene was avoided. We were all so friendly. A few nights later, Cahill was given a send-off after an administrative committee meeting. New heights of hypocrisy were reached as Cahill and Ducker agreed how saddened they both were by Geoff's decision to seek a job where he could work 'more closely with the community'.

Ducker's first rival had been routed, but there was no time for complacency. The strange and awkward Barry Egan, who had come to prominence as the secretary of the Shop Assistants Union, had for some time been showing all the signs of a man about to establish a more independent position for himself and his union. Neither John Ducker nor I was keen on independence.

I first met Egan in 1971, when Laurie Brereton introduced us in Egan's office. Behind his desk was a photograph of Lionel Murphy at which darts were regularly thrown by Egan and his officials. Egan spearheaded a campaign in the Miscellaneous Workers Union, the key left-wing union in New South Wales, which had come very close to defeating Ray Gietzelt in 1971.

He was regarded as being on the far Right already but he decided to become an independent, at first almost imperceptibly to the rest of us and later at a frightening pace.

At the 1973 state conference the Right was at the height of its dominance. In ballots conducted under proportional representation (introduced as a result of the 1971 federal intervention to ensure that the Left got some sort of say in party decision-making) where there are two positions to be contested, a vote of 66 per cent is required to win both. On a national executive constantly voting 9–9 and 10–8 on the big factional divisions, the prospect of winning two positions in New South Wales was a wet dream for us and a recurring nightmare for the Left.

The New South Wales representatives on the national executive were John Ducker and Arthur Gietzelt; in 1973, John Benson from the Seamens Union was running for the executive as a candidate for the Socialist Objective Committee, who had split from the Left. (The Socialist Objective Committee was mainly drawn from those who have since bemoaned the dismantling of the Berlin Wall.) Ducker learned early in life that the Left's tendency to split should always be encouraged, even if those doing the splitting had views with which he could never be comfortable. At the ACTU he had little difficulty in dealing with the likes of Pat Clancy, Australia's foremost Stalinist, provided the deal was in their mutual interest, so dealing with Clancy's mates in the ALP provided no problem whatsoever.

For the Left, the loss of Gietzelt on the national executive was a disaster and they needed to change some votes to win. To do so they found the most unlikely bedfellows: Barry Egan and Paul Keating. The latter's defeat by only one vote in the ministerial ballot when Whitlam came to government in 1972 had soured Keating's relations with Ducker and the machine. He had always suspected that Cahill, with Ducker's permission, had supported Bill Morrison instead of him, and in the aftermath of that defeat Keating had started to talk to Arthur Gietzelt. By nature and temperament Egan was an outsider, no matter how close to the inner circle he might have been—perhaps he and Arthur Gietzelt were attracted by each other's sense of humour.

For Keating, opposition to the likes of John Benson came very easily, simply justifiable on ideological grounds—Benson represented everything Keating had fought against all his life. The Gietzelt line to Keating was, of course, that only by maintaining a representative of the real Left on board could stability in the party be guaranteed. From there the obvious port of call was Egan, who by that time was employing Laurie Brereton as an organiser. The opportunity for demonstrating independence of thought was not lost on Egan, and the necessary votes for Gietzelt, some twenty of them, were found from the Right's heartland.

Into this unstable situation strode Charlie Oliver, already in his seventies and the veteran of decades of Australian Workers Union infighting. Charlie was a hard man who had never quite gotten over being pushed out by Ducker as party president. The opportunity to show the new machine a thing or two was not lost on Charlie.

The amalgamation of the Shop Assistants Union with the Australian Workers Union in New South Wales surprised everyone. What shearers had in common with shop assistants was a mystery to most of us, and presumably to most of them as well. And this union of unions had drawn together the ambitious Egan and the old warhorse Charlie Oliver—a very dangerous combination.

After that conference, difficulties began to occur more frequently with Egan and Oliver. It was a certainty that when the opportunity came for retribution against Egan (or, as Bob Carr always described it, 'the doctrine of massive retaliation') it would be eagerly accepted. My father's belief that you should be more aware of your limitations than your strengths would have been a more than useful credo for Barry Egan to adopt. The extraordinary decision by Egan and Oliver to unite an already unlikely mix of shearers and shop assistants with building and construction workers was always likely to bring about their demise, particularly when the Building Workers Industrial Union, as it was then called, was the breeding ground for Australia's Stalinists. To imagine that the Shop Assistants federal hierarchy would wear this, let alone an incredulous rank and file, was an incredible assumption on Egan's part.

The speed of the reaction to the proposed amalgamation staggered me. The Shop Assistants federal body, headed by Jim Maher, arguably the hardest anti-Left union official since Laurie Short, had also been waiting for a shot at Egan's title. The blows rained on Egan would have sunk Muhammed Ali in the first round. Store after store held rank-and-file meetings to declare their abhorrence of the amalgamation and a former Egan acolyte, Brian O'Neill, signed them up in the federal union. Within a few months Egan presided over an empty shell and even that was cracked by the courts over the following year. By 1978, Barry Egan was out of business. The AWU, free of his yoke, went back to supporting the Right and the BWIU returned to the building sites. Ducker had seen out another rival from within the inner circle.

CHAPTER 3

The Whitlam Rollercoaster

Given my view that keeping the Left in a minority position was vital in giving the ALP a real chance to win elections, whatever was left of my time was spent in beating Liberals.

By the beginning of 1972, it was pretty certain that Labor would win the next federal election. I spent the year clocking up 80 000 kilometres in my battered Falcon as I ran around New South Wales shoring up branches and generally getting support in country areas. In country towns there were usually Labor people among council and postal workers, forming the basis of country branches. Because I used to travel around the bush with my father on organising trips, I knew quite a lot of postal workers anyway. Teachers were the other Labor voters but they were usually Left supporters, so I didn't often go and see them.

These were heady days; for the first time in my life we were looking at victory. During that year, one of my duties as an ALP apparatchik was to act as Bob Hawke's driver, which meant going wherever he went to campaign, in the city and the country. This began an association that served both of us pretty well over almost twenty years.

Peter Westerway dragged the New South Wales branch out of the dark ages in campaign techniques. A great student of communication, he was a lecturer in politics at the University of Sydney, and he had a TV current affairs program on Channel 7 called 'Seven Days'. He laid the foundations for the New South Wales branch being the party's best campaigners for quite some time.

The campaign opening at Blacktown Town Hall in 1972 will always be remembered by a generation of Labor supporters as the greatest political meeting the country had ever seen. Gough Whitlam's opening phrase 'Men and women of Australia' was an inspired choice by his chief speech writer Graham Freudenberg because it had been used by John Curtin, Labor's wartime Prime Minister and a sentimental icon of the faithful. Whitlam's brilliantly crafted speech brought an enthusiastic crowd to the edge of ecstasy more than once.

I stood in the wings watching Freudenberg smoke a hundred cigarettes as Gough performed in his best regal mode. The front rows of the auditorium were filled with singers, actors and Labor luminaries. It was a public relations extravaganza on a scale Australia had never previously seen. Labor's advertising campaign saw the dawn of another new era as our material got closer and closer to American trends. This was the first campaign where leadership was featured as much as the party—a trend that has developed strongly ever since. Many Labor diehards, always more concerned about the party than the individual, were very wary of a series of newspaper advertisements that featured Whitlam. The party's name was not even mentioned, setting a precedent that is still followed two decades later.

This campaign, then, saw Labor put all its faith in the leader to deliver electoral success. It was the beginning of the end for ideology predominating over electoral victory, and the Left whinged loud and long about this dangerous new trend. Focusing on leadership is only a good idea, however, if you have the best person on your side and, once this trend had been established as the norm in election campaigns, any party whose leader was a dud would struggle. The focus suited Labor at the time and with Neville Wran poised to take the reins in New South Wales in 1976, we would have been crazy to fight it. Labor's capacity to produce better, more attractive and more glamorous leaders than the conservatives has generally served us well. The problem that Labor faced was that by the time the 1977 election came around Whitlam, who was still being featured in the campaign, was on the nose. The trend was only worthwhile while the leader was popular.

But as the man who swept us to power in 1972, Gough Whitlam made us all proud to be in the Labor Party. He was so much better than anyone on the conservative side of politics, he looked and sounded so good. Gough was the first Labor leader to look like a winner in more than twenty years. His dominance of the politics of his era was absolute and complete. Coming after Evatt and Calwell, this was a whole new feeling for the party. Not only did we know our cause was right, we knew it was irresistible. And the 'It's Time' campaign perfectly expressed the mood sweeping Australia. The use of virtually every famous Australian involved in the arts, in sport and on stage and screen was a dramatic statement of superiority. If everyone who was anyone supported us, how could we be beaten? No matter whether people dug ditches, painted pictures or pushed a pen, they knew Labor's time had come.

These were heady days indeed. But as well as glossy TV ads and jingles, we were still using the more traditional methods of campaigning, including good old-fashioned public meetings. In town halls all over Australia, the faithful gathered to hear the message. I was responsible for organising the itineraries for the party heavyweights and in all the meetings I attended I can't actually recall encountering anyone who wasn't a Labor supporter, apart from the odd heckler bent on disruption.

Whitlam was the star of the show and the fan club had no shortage of recruits. Gough could attract anything between 500 to 1500 people, depending on the venue, and as an orator on the stump he had no peer. Like hundreds of thousands of Labor Party members and Labor supporters, I was in awe of him. Our chests swelled with pride every time he got up to speak and he never failed to deliver that special combination of knowledge, wit, sarcasm and above all vision. Until Gough came along, Labor had not had a visionary in decades. He dared to take on the forces that had shackled Labor for years, and the more he dared, the more he won.

The public perception of the party no longer included the 'faceless men' of the executive who had decided policy. Gough Whitlam never did like factions and consequently never joined one. He did not mind, however, being the constant beneficiary of the Right's support. When he attended a state council meeting at the Teachers Federation Hall in Kent Street, Sydney in the early 1970s, he told Ducker this was the day he would sort out the brothers Gietzelt. To the 400 assembled delegates, Gough then gave the Gietzelts a terrible serve.

He was able to preserve his independent image by making great public play of having journalists excluded from the meeting. But he arranged with John Ducker to ensure that the microphones that broadcast to the foyer where the journalists had reassembled were left on. The journos heard every word. By sheer force of personality and because of the rapidly growing public support that surrounded him, Whitlam rolled back years of policy neglect. State Aid and the White Australia policy were issues he confronted, and decades of policies that had kept Labor in Opposition were swept away.

Gough had a vision of every Australian having a right to a tertiary education, of a nation where first-class services were extended to those who lived on the exploding fringes of our great cities, where the arts flourished as they hadn't since Renaissance Europe, where truth and justice were placed firmly on the everyday agenda of a classless society. The enormity of the vision captured a breathless nation. The drastic increase in interest rates blurred the vision for some.

The campaign for the election in 1974, however, gave me an insight into the problems Labor would encounter over the next eighteen months. A national campaign committee meeting was held in the Sussex Street offices. On Monday 6 April a cast of thousands turned up for this crucial meeting, virtually all of whom gained admittance at one time or another during the day. Each senior minister who came along brought staff with him. It was soon obvious to me that a great many people who were in that room and giving us the benefit of their wisdom were not even members of the ALP.

The thought that virtually anyone could wander off the street into such an important meeting caused me real concern. At least some were entitled to be there, including Phillip Adams, invited to the meeting by Mick Young to talk to us about advertising. He came up with the best commercial of the 1974 campaign, showing a schoolmasterly Gough indicating the inflation rates of the countries with which we would normally be compared, all written down on a blackboard. Whitlam had been resisting the need to make inflation a central issue in Labor's campaign, despite the fact that the Liberals' Billy Snedden was causing us considerable damage on this point. Though Bob Hawke had been urging Whitlam to change tack on this issue, he had been rebuffed. Finally, however, a combination of Hawke, Mick Young, David Combe and John Ducker forced Whitlam to yield. Once the change in the campaign had been accepted, Phillip Adams and a hastily convened group from around the table actually started to write copy for the ad at the meeting. Whitlam wasn't even there—it was quite extraordinary that a major change in the party's campaign could be agreed in his absence. Given the attention paid to Whitlam as leader during the campaign it still seems unthinkable that its whole direction could be altered while the star was in Brisbane.

Towards the end of the 1974 campaign there was a huge meeting at the Sydney Opera House. Again, it was a gathering of stars with most of the old faces who had sung 'It's Time' reinforced with some extras. Neville Wran introduced one such star with a flourish usually reserved for Whitlam. Patrick White, who had won the Nobel Prize for Literature the previous year, had volunteered his services early in the campaign and had recorded a radio message that was never used because it was considered too long. With a close election certain, however, that mistake was not to be repeated and White was given star billing. To tumultuous applause he walked onto the Opera House stage and acted as if he had been performing there for years. Whitlam really inspired White, and the Nobel laureate's distaste for Hawke in particular during the 1980s suggests that Whitlam attracted support that relied entirely on him and his vision.

To this day, the party has a percentage of members who remember all of Whitlam's greatness and none of his weaknesses, chief among which was his inability to manage his team in government. Its disintegration in a series of ministerial scandals and sackings left a sour taste in the minds of most and a tear in the eye of the true believers. (Robert Ray has said that many Labor supporters could not bear to read the front part of newspapers in 1975, so the party has many experts on that year's Australian sporting achievements.) A hostile Senate might have given Kerr an excuse to do what he did in 1975, but Labor's failures were much more of its own making than anything the Senate, Kerr or the conservatives contributed.

Jim Cairns, who had come within six votes of defeating Gough Whitlam for the leadership in a Caucus ballot in 1968, led the way. This grand figure of the Left, who personified whatever civil libertarian, humane streak there was in our society, who was treated as a saint at Vietnam moratorium meetings, fell from grace so quickly that even those on the Right, who had always opposed him, were stunned. He was never the same after being bashed at a party in Melbourne's Hawthorn in 1971, certainly, but that his fall could be accelerated by a relationship with a beautiful woman was amazing. Jim Cairns was no playboy and his very public relationship with Junie Morosi seemed to mesmerise him. He became a shell of what he had once been and drifted off into some kind of hippy heaven.

Make no mistake about it, Junie Morosi was a beautiful woman. I can remember walking into the foyer of the Florida Hotel, Terrigal, New South Wales, for the national conference in February 1975 and seeing her in a plain white cotton dress fairly floating down the stairs. Whether or not she was bright as well as beautiful I am in no position to say. It would appear, however, that she was privy to a range of discussions that had a real bearing on how our nation was run. But it wouldn't have mattered if she wasn't too smart; plenty of not-too-bright people were in similar positions. That Jim Cairns would end by running against the party in a Senate election in Victoria, in which he attracted only a handful of votes, is a tragic reminder of how fragile political success can be.

The respite given to Labor by the double dissolution election of May 1974 was quickly forgotten. The welter of scandal, the rocketing rate of inflation and the continual sacking of ministers left Labor right across the country with a feeling probably not unlike that of those who went down on the USS *Indianapolis* in

1945. If you were lucky enough to survive the sinking, you had to face the sharks that were working themselves into a frenzy at the prospect of ripping you apart. And watching the hopes and confident expectations of millions of Labor supporters being put to death, slowly roasted over a constant flame, one by one, remains one of my saddest memories.

The Whitlam rollercoaster was a great ride, but it was no way to run a country. Great advances were made in urban renewal, education and funding for the arts, but twenty years on, it's time for Labor to remember the dark side of 1972–75.

My obsession with the Labor Party robbed me of my youth. This obsession meant that I went from boyhood to manhood without the normal period in between. It's hard to be a normal, fun-loving Australian youth when your life consists of going from one party meeting to the next. It's hard to fit in a personal life, and by the end of 1972 I had to make up for lost time. As soon as the Whitlam victory was confirmed on 2 December, I flew to meet my future wife, who was then in England. Cheryl had embarked on the trip to Europe and the working holiday in London which were then almost compulsory for young women of her age. I chased her, persuaded her to come home, and we were married early in 1973.

The following year she and I, with our very young son Matthew, went up to Darwin during the Northern Territory election campaign, to help the local party. My first problem was finding it. I discovered that the party consisted of about 150 members, there were practically no records, very few functioning branches, if any, campaign experience was nil and at least four of our eleven candidates had serious drinking problems. Furthermore, two weeks before the election the candidates were yet to have a meeting, no campaign literature of any kind had been prepared, let alone distributed and the party was stone motherless broke. When a policy speech was delivered it was in fact given by the then secretary of the party in the Northern Territory, John Waters, because none of the candidates could possibly be used as a spokesperson.

Being an optimist by nature I organised a meeting of candidates at the Don Hotel where we were staying. It was agreed that I would prepare a newspaper, to be entitled the *Northern Territory*

Times, which I would have distributed throughout the Territory. Having met all the candidates for the first time, I knew after a few seconds that no election of a leader was possible; the new trend in campaigning wasn't going to hit the Northern Territory ALP. After the meeting we adjourned to the bar, a practice I noted a number of candidates had obviously followed before. This jolly gathering was rudely interrupted by one of our candidates being thrown through the glass door of the hotel by one of his colleagues. Concepts of party unity had not permeated the Northern Territory either.

On a Sunday morning I headed out to the home of Jim Bowditch, a candidate who was the former editor of the Territory's main paper and who could help me get this newspaper together. Jim turned out to be extremely enthusiastic about alcohol. Sitting in an area designated as his office underneath his typical Territory home on stilts, the floor covered in bottles, we prepared our newspaper, the only real campaign tool used by the party in this election. During the day, Jim consumed one and a half flagons of white wine and yet remained lucid enough to write some florid criticisms of his opponents and some rather inventive praise for Labor's policies. There was no properly constituted body to approve policies, so quite a few were created underneath his house.

That Labor failed to win one seat in this election cannot be blamed entirely on me. I did learn that outside the big cities, campaigns were different. This should have prepared me for the federal by-election held in the Tasmanian seat of Bass—my other worst campaigning experience. But it didn't.

By the time I arrived in Launceston to assist in the Bass by-election campaign in July 1975 I knew, as did almost every Australian except apparently Gough, that we were in deep trouble. We hadn't made things any easier for ourselves by our choice of candidate. Lance Barnard, the Deputy Prime Minister and a real Tasmanian hero, had retired to become Australia's ambassador to Sweden (letting him go was another example of the appalling political judgment that bedevilled the Whitlam government). To replace him we had selected a teacher who was no great advertisement for the state education system and whose capacity to string two coherent sentences together was in considerable doubt. Brian Harradine, a former member of the federal executive, had recently been expelled and the old Right machine that had ruled the party that governed Tasmania for more than three decades had disintegrated faster than any of us had believed possible.

Outsiders have always been viewed with suspicion in Tasmania, and anyone from the New South Wales Right in 1975 was regarded with outright hostility. Many party locals received me with the same degree of warmth as Launceston's weather. The party campaign was being run from the office of Senator Don Grimes, a medical doctor who had been elected to parliament by means of a preselection deal between the factions, and no one was quite sure where he stood factionally. That question mark hung over Don Grimes for the next fifteen years as he rose to be a senator and a successful minister in successive Hawke governments.

For ten days I worked out of the office but mainly I went out door knocking, being quite deliberately excluded from real campaign planning. Those next few days proved to me just how badly the Whitlam government was travelling. All the wrath of a very angry nation was concentrated in the Bass by-election. Launceston had been a textile town, very significantly damaged by the 25 per cent tariff cut announced in 1974. The people who answered doors to me were mostly polite, but that lack of warmth that I now thought distinguished Launceston was everywhere. A tiny percentage of those who were willing to commit themselves said they would vote Labor; many, many more were prepared to declare themselves against us.

While the impending disaster was obvious to anybody who went out into the streets, the party heavies continued to look for secret weapons. Like Hitler promising his boy soldiers new rockets, plans were hatched in great secrecy for the president of the local chamber of commerce to declare his support for Labor. When he finally did so, the party's national secretary David Combe and the Whitlam staffers were jubilant, and they all adjourned to a restaurant in the village of Evandale outside Launceston for a celebration. Amidst the singing of 1950s rock songs and rivers of red wine, Labor's campaign strategists revelled in self-delusion. While in public it may always be necessary to lie about the party's prospects, erring of course on the positive side, private assessment should always be rigorous. In the dismal climate of the Bass by-election, the belief that a pro-Labor statement from a single small businessman would swing the result in any way was an indication of the depths to which we had sunk.

Around that open fire at the end of June 1975 I learned at first hand what was wrong with the party. If there was anyone around who would tell Whitlam how deeply hated he already was, that person did not turn up in Bass. And if that person did exist, after two and a half years as Prime Minister Whitlam probably wouldn't have listened to him anyway. Something happens to the men we make prime ministers. A few years in the job and they change, always for the worse, always irreversibly. When finally pushed from the job, either by their ungrateful party or an ignorant electorate (it being taken for granted that only the unenlightened could oppose them), they wander the world searching for a kind word, a standing ovation and a place in history that recognises their greatness. Maybe Curtin was different, maybe Keating will be, but being PM, receiving all the kudos, the bowing and scraping, being the focus of a nation's attention has proved too much for most who have held the job.

All those who came to support Labor's doomed campaign in Bass stayed in a pretty ordinary pub called the Cornwall. Back in 1975 there was no Launceston casino and country club, and if there had been, I doubt if we would have stayed there anyway. In those days the experience of the Terrigal conference plagued our minds. The memories of bikini-clad women surrounding a number of our delegates by the pool had caused many Labor people to question the working-class roots of the party, apparently best demonstrated by our staying in very ordinary hotels.

My experiences of the party in other places was certainly expanding. In the dining room of the hotel I had the pleasure of dining with John Dawkins and Peter Walsh. They were new to parliament and were not in the Cabinet, but they were regarded as up and comers. Both were pretty bright, except that they seemed to suffer from the same disease that afflicts many people from outside the borders of my state—they made it very clear that the New South Wales Right was not among their favourite organisations. While Dawkins later mellowed, Peter Walsh never warmed to us.

The actual election day was one of the worst of my life. It absolutely poured with freezing rain all day, and from 8am to 8pm I stood on various polling booths with no umbrella, no food and no hope. One booth was located opposite the Cornwall Hotel and I had the privilege of seeing the great white chariots carrying the great white hopes (otherwise known as the Whitlam staff) off to lunch. I had nothing to eat all day, not a sandwich or a cup of tea. I finished the day at a local school on the outskirts of Launceston. Seeing me totally drenched and forlorn, not to mention drooling at the goodies she was giving her colleagues, a Liberal lady took pity on me and gave me a hot apricot pie and a cup of coffee. By that stage if I had a vote I'm not sure what I would have done.

Having been Labor's sole scrutineer at that booth, I walked out into the rain, found a telephone box that worked and rang for a cab to take me to the party's party. This was predictably held at the Trades Hall and I stood pretty much alone all evening, mainly because nobody wanted to talk to me. That by-election was a disaster for Labor, right across the whole of Bass. I flew out to Sydney the next day with my mind firmly made up about two things: one, Australia couldn't wait for a chance to throw us out at the next election, and two, it would be a long, long time before I returned to Launceston.

I was too junior in the party to be privy to the Khemlani loans affair, and I found out that Kerr had dismissed Gough Whitlam on 11 November only after I returned from lunch in Dixon Street. (I ascribe my present girth to the ALP office's proximity to a large number of excellent Chinese restaurants as well as to chronic weakness of character.) But I was actively involved in the 1975 election campaign, which turned out to be the most exciting of all those I have witnessed.

The quixotic nature of this campaign, our feeling that Labor had been robbed and cheated of office, largely allowed us to ignore the views of a pretty substantial number of Australians. Cloaked in righteousness, surrounded by an army of supporters at every rally in numbers unheard of since the days of Jack Lang, many Labor people were happy to believe that Australians would see that Whitlam hadn't been given a traditional fair go and would respond accordingly at the ballot box.

The campaign committee meeting held at the New South Wales branch office at the start of the campaign followed the example of its 1974 counterpart, though only in its worst features. At one time during the afternoon I was sure that if there had been a head count, including the hangers-on, members of the party would have had a bare majority. The attack on Fraser and Kerr in the slogan 'Shame, Fraser, shame' was eagerly adopted.

I will always retain one memory from that meeting. I walked past the glass-partitioned office of Dorothy Isaksen (who was secretary to committees for the New South Wales branch) and saw an extremely odd gathering. The branch office was home to every star in Labor's galaxy, so Whitlam's presence was to be expected. In the frenzied few days of a campaign, it would scarcely be worthy of comment—but seeing him in a small room with David Combe and Bill Hartley was pretty special. Whitlam had hated Hartley for years; Hartley had threatened to defy the party on State Aid while secretary of the party in Victoria, had supported Cairns in his challenge to Whitlam for the leadership, had voted to lock Whitlam out of executive meetings and even supported various attempts to discipline him—and Whitlam did not have a forgiving fibre in his body.

My only thought was that perhaps this time of great trial and tribulation was bringing the party together. This was true only up to the point that desperate times can bring about desperate deals and the most improbable of suggestions can be accepted without proper analysis in the heat of the moment. I had no idea that at that very moment Bill Hartley was offering to organise a donation of $500 000 from Iraq's Ba'ath Socialist Party to offset the huge debt the ALP knew would follow the 1975 campaign.

How either Whitlam or Combe, then federal secretary, could ever have considered this lunatic idea has remained a mystery to me. That the Iraqi loans affair has been totally forgotten by the generation of Whitlam supporters still around is even more amazing. Real heroes, of course, can be forgiven almost anything by those who regarded them as heroes in the first place. When a leader such as Whitlam falls from grace, most people outside the party decide that the mantle of hero has been wrongly bestowed, but the generation who worshipped Whitlam for all his vision and for leading Labor out of the wilderness never quite accepted his failures. To this day, criticisms of Whitlam still draw cries of 'foul' from some of his diehard supporters.

While Hawke was treating me as a brother during the period from 1972 to 1975, E. G. Whitlam probably never knew my name. Talking to the unimportant was never his strong point. Gough only wanted to talk to people who were as intelligent as he was, and given that there weren't any, he had no one to talk to. But during the 1975 election campaign, I was given the great honour of meeting him and was actually asked for my advice about whether a major rally in the Sydney Domain would be (a) sufficiently huge and (b) whether having a rally at all was a good idea anyway. His office in the old Reserve Bank building in Martin Place was dark; my mood should have been lighter than it was. I was certainly excited by the thought of meeting the person whom I'd regarded as the nearest thing to God. By then, however, his faults were all too obvious and I knew that on election day slaughter was inevitable. Gough had been, if not our God, then certainly our Moses. He had parted the Red Sea, we had all followed him in, but the sea drowned us all before we reached the Promised Land. And unlike the Israelites, we didn't have the pleasure of watching our evil pursuers drown—they were sitting on the banks watching us.

Nonetheless, even if he was a bit tarnished, on the day I met him Gough had great presence. Anyone who met him then had to be impressed. He was tall, imposing and intelligent, and had an aura that invaded the space of all who got near him. I told him quickly and succinctly that he would get a huge crowd no matter where or when he appeared, and that displays of mass support were about all he had going for him. This was of course the line followed by the New South Wales branch, though I had every reason to agree with it. Gough didn't say much, just asked a couple of questions, listened to the answers, thanked me for coming up and off I was whisked.

That rally in the Domain was the largest political gathering I have attended and I very much doubt that I'll see a bigger one. It took place on Monday 24 November. As I looked over the Domain from the stage, it seemed that every single bit of it was chock-a-block with people. The crowd estimates at the time ranged from 50 000 to 100 000. They had come to pour out their rage at the Kerr decision and at Fraser, the man who had benefited from it, and also to show their love and praise for Whitlam. This enormous crowd gave him an ovation, a roar, I will never forget.

As Whitlam spoke, plenty of tears were being shed to go with the rage and the love. I couldn't cry for Gough. I just stood at the side of the stage and wondered what had happened to the hope and confidence of the Blacktown Town Hall in 1972. The Domain crowd was at least ten times bigger, but its size couldn't make up for the difference. I had also stood at the side of the Blacktown stage but then I knew we couldn't lose. Now I knew we couldn't win.

I organised for a team of people to move among the crowd with plastic buckets seeking donations, no matter how small, from ordinary Labor supporters. They responded magnificently and thousands of dollars were collected. I drove back to Sussex Street with a fortune in the boot of my car. John Johnson, the patron saint of the New South Wales Right and a former president of the Legislative Council, counted it: $23 000, a king's ransom. It is worth noting that rallies in all other states reported a similar phenomenon. Robert Ray says he drove back to the Victorian ALP office after a huge rally with $22 000 in a garbage bin.

Three weeks later, on the last day of the campaign, Friday 12 December, Labor conducted a rally at the southern end of Hyde Park which drew almost 10 000 people. This meeting took placed on a wet and miserable day proving that, even if Labor voters were in a minority, their outrage at the sacking was such that they would turn up to wave the flag and support their cause.

At that Hyde Park rally, Senator Jim McClelland made quite a brilliant speech. His command of the language was second only to Gough's and in those days he was more of a realist than many of his Cabinet colleagues. He didn't make cheery claims about Labor's prospects but contented himself with the line that while Labor had begun the campaign a mile behind, he could sense that a real turnaround had occurred during the campaign. 'People are coming back to Labor,' he declared, to appropriate applause. This was the only time in the campaign that I can recall a senior Labor figure being halfway honest at these gatherings that were taking place every single day around the country. Gough had become a Billy Graham-type figure for many, and the faithful drew comfort from just being together in great numbers.

The Hyde Park rally was another tremendously successful fundraiser. The troops were again prepared to put their hands in their pockets for their hero, for their party and for the destruction of the bastards who had robbed them of their government. We couldn't keep up with the demand for supplies of badges and stickers such was the desire of Labor supporters to stand up and be counted. Everyone wants to be identified with success, yet I find it hard to believe that many of these supporters thought we had a hope in hell. They were prepared to be identified with Labor, even if we were to be massacred. This was what Whitlam had created—a mass following prepared to go anywhere with him. Australian politics has seen nothing like it in my lifetime, and probably never will again.

C H A P T E R 4

Wran's Our Man

From the day after the 1975 election, a terrible air of doom and gloom descended on the party. The conservatives had been voted in with 91 of the 127 seats in the House of Representatives and 35 in the Senate. The only states where Labor was in power were Tasmania and South Australia; the great bulk of Australia's population and wealth were now presided over by the conservatives. Labor didn't matter, and some held the view that this could become permanent.

Fortunately, Neville Wran was not among them.

Because of the emphasis on leadership during the Whitlam years, assessing leaders had become a serious party pastime, and nowhere more so than in New South Wales. The golden boy of the Labor Right for some time had been one Patrick Darcy Hills, Leader of the Opposition against Sir Robert Askin. But as the boy had gotten older, he hadn't gotten any golder. A brilliant behind-the-scenes manipulator, he was a very bad front-line performer, and his performance in the 1973 state election campaign was a case in point. In his opening speech he promised workers more holidays and more of everything else; it was real old-style politics. After yet another lacklustre campaign and deserved defeat, Ducker knew that something drastic had to be done. But the New South Wales Caucus didn't exactly have a lot of talent to choose from.

The Left's Jack Ferguson after some initial reluctance seized upon Neville Wran, a barrister who had become Labor leader in the Legislative Council in 1971. Jack was always ready to support anyone who could defeat a candidate from the Right. Ducker could see that Wran was a good choice, and we all thought that he was our best chance. But Ducker knew most of the Right would stick with Hills, so he and Ferguson decided to do a deal. In return for Wran as the leader, the Left would be given the deputy leadership for the first time in their lives.

Getting the Left to deliver a bloc vote was made easier because Wran had close friends on that side, especially Lionel Murphy, then federal Attorney-General. But the big problem with Wran was that he was a member of the Legislative Council, the Upper House, and he would have to move down to the Legislative Assembly in order to become the party leader. The hunt for a suitable Lower House seat for him was on in earnest.

The seat of Bass Hill in Sydney's western suburbs and in Paul Keating's electorate of Blaxland was chosen. Clarrie Earl, an old and undistinguished party stalwart, was retiring and all that was required was Keating's decision to abandon a local supporter who had lined up the seat for himself. After some angst, Keating agreed. It was rumoured that the unsuccessful candidate would be given an Upper House seat if he withdrew (if this promise were given, it was never honoured) and the party's administrative committee took the unusual step of declaring Neville Wran as the candidate without a local rank-and-file ballot. While this pleased the Left, a precedent was being set that could be used against them on other occasions. As Hills's representative on the administrative committee, Kevin Stewart opposed the resolution. His opposition alerted Ducker to the difficulties that would lie ahead: the Left's bloc vote could not provide Wran with a majority, and winning any Right votes for Wran in Caucus was going to be a considerable struggle.

The Left–Right deal was duly done, the Wran/Ferguson ticket established. The leadership ballot was taken at the first Caucus meeting after the 1973 election, with contenders Neville Wran, Pat Hills and Kevin Stewart. Most of the Right duly stuck by Hills, so Wran needed every vote he could muster from the Left, plus a few rebels from the Right. Ducker picked off a few of Kevin Stewart's votes as preferences to Wran. Stewart got 9 votes, and when he was out of the ballot all his preferences didn't go straight to Hills as everyone expected: 4 went to Wran. Ducker's action affected only three or four votes, but they were the ones that counted. As it was, the final result was 22 votes all, but Wran had 18 first preference votes to Hills' 17, so Wran was declared elected. If Hills supporter Michael Cleary had not been absent, Wran would have been defeated.

I hadn't even met Neville Wran at that stage, but I got to know him very well in the years that followed. Once elected he quickly established his authority, and before long even his opponents realised he was a star. His quality was really shown when a state election was called in 1976. From the beginning of the campaign Wran set a pattern that ought to be a compulsory study for anyone seeking election. He understood that every single message has to be repeated ad nauseam. When you are getting sick of it, the mob may just begin to listen. That means of course that the same trick can be repeated many times over. Time and time again, Wran climbed aboard a bus or a train to the clicking of cameras. Every ride was worth another headline and he regarded public transport as just about the most important issue.

I had become the assistant secretary of the New South Wales branch in March 1976, so I was heavily involved in the state election campaign. I couldn't claim to have influenced its style or content, but I did get to attend the meetings where the decisions were made. Neville was always the master of proceedings. While a campaign committee consisting of the party officers and several senior Cabinet ministers might have been set up, nothing could be approved without him. Wran knew how to win because he understood people better than anyone around him. He read the electorate with unerring instinct.

I have already said that talent will take you a long way in politics, but it won't take you to the top unless it is combined with luck. Neville Wran was lucky enough to lead Labor when the Liberals were falling apart. Sir Robert Askin, probably the toughest politician the Liberals had ever signed up, had retired in 1974 and while Eric Willis, a dour dull man well suited to conservative politics, was his chosen successor, the party room had other ideas. They elected as premier Tom Lewis, a relative unknown. This was good news for Wran. Not only was Lewis no match for him, but some of the Liberals were restive, with quite a few influential figures working to undermine their new leader.

While any Opposition leader could have made headway in these circumstances, Wran relentlessly exploited his superiority. This was where he laid the foundations for the absolute focus on him as an individual that in later campaigns would produce overwhelming victories and huge majorities. If you wanted to know how to beat Liberals, you couldn't do better than to watch Neville Wran, and I watched till my eyes ached. Everywhere he went, he got people not just to respect him but to like him. He could turn on the charm tap and men, women and children fell under his spell. Rich or poor, bright or stupid, it didn't matter; when Neville Wran was out winning votes, he was in a class of his own. The intellect and the charm were matched by a fairly simple philosophy—occasionally guide them in a direction you think appropriate, but always be prepared to give them as much as possible of what they want.

One of the most attractive things about him he kept firmly in the background. He had an elderly brother in Balmain whom he visited virtually every Sunday morning. Armed with seafood purchased at the fish markets on the way, Wran never missed seeing his very much older sibling. When the old man died, Wran was deeply affected. The consummate politician with the silver tongue was still a Balmain boy who never forgot his roots.

His performance at a national campaign committee meeting a few days after Bob Hawke became Labor leader in 1983 best sums up his philosophy. Hawke was telling all and sundry how his vision of recovery, reconstruction and reconciliation would be the basis of the forthcoming election campaign, and the committee were earnestly discussing how these noble concepts might best be broadcast to the nation. A silent Wran observed patiently at first, but then his patience wore thin. Finally he could take no more. 'This sounds like a meeting of the fucking Hare Krishnas,' he rasped. 'Give them something to vote for. These greedy bastards want a quid in their pockets.' And, while the three Rs were used as a campaign theme, Labor did start to think about putting a quid in people's pockets.

This is not to say that Wran had a jaundiced view of the electorate. He had never forgotten his humble origins and believed that when you have the arse out of your pants, you are entitled to want more. Labor, he believed, was there to provide people with more, and he was never going to allow high-minded rhetoric to get in the road. He was there to deliver to Labor's voters, the most disadvantaged in the community, more of whatever it was they needed.

The charm and the intellect made the electorate warm to him, but it was his other side that made the party sit up and take notice. He had a fearsome temper and the capacity to use the word 'fuck' more often than anyone I have ever known, and among my friends and acquaintances are swearers and blasphemers of Olympic class. This darker side was, when used as a weapon in line with the Ducker theory, quite devastating. It could also occasionally be used to further his prejudices.

The close tussle for his leadership with Hills and his years in parliament had bred in him distrust and dislike for those around Hills. Two of Hills's cronies bore the brunt of what was to become an all-too-obvious hatred. In the Labor Party you are able to hate, some would say even encouraged to do so. You are expected to be able to continue working with the people you hate, so commonsense dictates that you keep your feelings to yourself. Civility is all that is really required. This was just not possible for Neville when he dealt with Ron Mulock and Bill Haigh, both Cabinet ministers and therefore, one would reasonably assume, entitled to some respect. Neville regarded both with contempt he never bothered to conceal.

Whatever Ron Mulock's sin was, it must have been mortal. Even as far back as 1976 when talking to Malcolm Macfie (the head of Labor's advertising agency Mullins, Clarke and Ralph) about the shape of Labor's campaign, Neville couldn't help himself. Macfie had dared to suggest that Mulock, whom he had considered a reasonably good-looking and impressive performer, should take a bigger role in the campaign and perhaps even appear in some of the advertisements. Wran blew up in the style for which he was to become infamous: 'He's a fucking boneheaded middle-class suburban solicitor and he stands for everything I despise. He gets a role in this over my dead body.' Thereafter, whenever Wran referred to Mulock, he always called him 'the fucking bonehead'. There was never any need to use Mulock's name; Wran's inner circle always knew to whom he was referring. Ron Mulock went on to become Neville's deputy, and despite Neville's views, wasn't a bad minister. As a former mayor of Penrith and a practising Catholic with seven children, he was pretty good at reaching a constituency that was important to Labor's survival.

It was a bit more difficult to dispute Neville's view of Bill Haigh. Admittedly Haigh, as Minister for Justice, had been given the job of looking after prisons. These are places where thousands of bad guys sit around all day working out how to escape. The odds are that some will succeed and for the hapless Bill Haigh, they seemed to attain their highest success rate during his stewardship of the portfolio.

On one Sunday night, after a series of escapes had been covered in graphic detail by the media, followed by the usual silence from the minister, the Premier could stand it no longer. He picked up the phone to talk to Bill Haigh to discover that Bill had taken the phone off the hook, either to maintain the customary media silence or to avoid another tirade from his boss. Wran had no intention of being defeated by such an obstacle on this occasion, and his next call was to Maroubra police station not far from Bill's home.

The sergeant in charge came on the line, and the Premier said: 'That fucking Bill Haigh has got his phone off the hook, and I want you to take a message to him for me.'

Naturally the sergeant agreed and took out his notebook. 'Okay,' said Wran, 'this is it. "If you don't call me within one fucking hour, you won't have a job tomorrow." Would you read that back to me?' The missing minister was very soon on the Premier's line.

Wran was an interventionist Premier with no qualms about sawing off the tree branch on which a minister was precariously balanced. If a policy was causing trouble—defined as receiving bad publicity and hence losing votes—Wran had no difficulty in ditching it. It didn't take very long for his Cabinet to work this out, and consequently they learned very quickly to check with the premier's office. The alternative was incurring Wran's wrath, which most of them were extremely reluctant to do.

When all his skills were combined, Wran was the perfect campaign machine, as shown by the results he achieved. His first win was perhaps the most unexpected: he won the 1976 election by just one seat, against all the odds. The Labor Party was generally on the nose after the Whitlam years and with the Liberals in power everywhere, Wran was expected to lose. At least by those who didn't know him.

He worked incredibly hard; I have no doubt that his personal appearances in key seats increased Labor's votes. Rural areas were worked as hard as city ones and we just squeaked over the line, with the last seat to be decided—Hurstville—actually determining the result.

Sir Eric Willis's resignation as Liberal leader and from State Parliament two years later provided a test of Wran's popularity. The timing was perfect; the by-election for Willis's seat of Earlwood took place on 15 July 1978, leaving just enough time for Wran to establish complete parliamentary dominance over his opponents and to establish himself as the master of the thirty-second grab on the television news. The Liberal candidate was none other than Alan Jones, later Australia's Rugby Union coach and a radio commentator, then an adviser to Malcolm Fraser and a complete unknown. Our candidate Ken Gabb, a quiet lawyer, was a leftie, which could have been a problem except that in keeping with Neville Wran's luck, Gabb was a practising Anglican so he was never going to frighten the horses. Earlwood had not been a Labor seat in living memory and, given that by-elections generally deliver swings against the government, we approached the campaign with both trepidation and determination. The residents of Earlwood couldn't walk out their front gates without tripping over a Cabinet minister or a shadow minister.

The campaign quickly became a test of who had the better leader, and the results were phenomenal. The swing to Labor was 9 per cent, an absolutely unheard-of result. Wran had created the first of a series of electoral precedents in an incredible career. When I rang him from our campaign rooms to give him the result, it was one of the few times when the Balmain boy actually cried. I didn't see it, but I could hear the emotion in his voice. For all his confidence in himself, Wran had not even contemplated such a terrific result. While our research had indicated how popular Wran was and had suggested that a Labor win was possible, the swiftness of the rise in Labor's stocks and Wran's personal popularity had been too rapid for the polls to measure.

The Earlwood result meant we decided to go to an early election, in 1978, and it made inevitable the tone of Labor's campaign. 'Wran's Our Man' was born. No other slogan, no other campaign, was ever so directed at charisma and personality, and no election has ever seen a bigger win for Labor. The result wiped out the Liberals for a decade and the bad times of December 1975 could be put behind us. Just as well. By that time we had little rage left to maintain.

The party allowed Wran a free rein to a degree undreamed of by any other leader. His 1979 decision to give Lotto to a consortium involving Kerry Packer and Rupert Murdoch would have caused the downfall of any lesser man. Murdoch was a hated figure—we had not forgotten the savagery with which he pursued Whitlam in 1975—and the hatred was not confined to those on the Left of the ALP. Many on the Right of the party, including people who recognised the support Murdoch's papers had given the Wran government in 1978, baulked at the notion of giving to Murdoch what was wrongly considered a licence to print money. Even if Murdoch had not been involved, there would have been strong opposition to the notion of handing over Lotto to a private company, since the move was seen as contrary to the party's support for state-owned enterprises. The party conference did pass a resolution condemning the decision by two votes, despite the efforts of people like myself to prevent it being taken. But apart from a few spontaneous resolutions from rank-and-file branches, the opprobrium that would have been heaped on the head of any other leader never came. The Left had no heart for a campaign against Wran and unless they were prepared to orchestrate a real factional effort in the branches, electorate councils and unions, his survival was assured.

The indulgences that the Left were prepared to extend to Wran no doubt came from the friendships he had cultivated during his time at the bar, as well as from the friendship he developed with Jack Ferguson during his term as premier. And like Bob Hawke, Neville Wran had found an invaluable ally in Ray Gietzelt, secretary of the Miscellaneous Workers Union, the most important in the Left apparatus, and brother of Senator Arthur Gietzelt, leader of the New South Wales Left who went on to become a minister in the Hawke government. Wran had often represented the union in the industrial courts and Gietzelt recognised his undoubted talents. The other barrister who had so often represented the union was Lionel Murphy, and Wran's friendship with him was almost fanatical.

If Jack Ferguson had ever been reluctant to embrace Wran as leader, his reluctance was well and truly overcome. Ferguson and Wran became incredibly close and Ferguson was always defending Wran from the accusations of his more doctrinaire colleagues. The friendships Neville Wran made with non-traditional colleagues were real, not part of an organised plot to protect himself. I don't believe he could have ever faked friendship—he was far too direct in letting everyone around him know exactly what he thought of them. None of his best friends was on the Right, but in the earlier days of his premiership he was still close to Jim McClelland, who had nominally been on the Right, and he remained close to Paul Landa who, while a member of the Right, was never quite considered a part of it. Landa had an amazingly quick wit and a tremendous sense of humour, but his capacity to verbally brutalise lesser mortals ensured he was never popular in the party. Lesser lights, particularly older lesser lights, were often humiliated by Landa and they never forgave him. That he could survive while being disliked by so many in the party gives some inkling of how clever he was. Landa could count Ducker and myself among his friends, but he could never be counted as of the Right.

Neville Wran never joined any faction, but as the leader of the state parliamentary Labor Party he was able to vote for internal party positions at state conferences, and he always voted with the Right. Later, as national president, he could be counted on every time. State governments can't change the economic performance of the nation and so their capacity to give their electorate a better lifestyle can only be measured by improvements in the services they provide. Wran's ten years as premier certainly delivered better transport, health and education. He also introduced landmark electoral reforms to make gerrymander virtually impossible, to bring in public funding of election campaigns and a democratically elected Upper House. Those inside the party and out who sought to criticise him can't point to any particular failure. No public institution went broke, the state was not driven into debt and the record of industrial peace was second to none. One minister was found guilty of corruption, although sinister allegations were continually directed at the government and the party. It must be said that many of these allegations were directed at me.

The faction had a bad year in 1979. I had left on a trip to the United States in April and while I was away a number of rule changes were agreed that created very considerable strife in the party. We had all agreed in a Thursday night meeting in Ducker's office to change the Rules of the party to allow Upper House members a vote in the ALP Caucus. Caucus was the body that elected the leader and the Cabinet and, as the Upper House was centrally preselected, the Left feared that this would give the dreaded party officers, in particular Ducker and myself, too big a say in who was chosen. Given that this was the very reason we were seeking the Rules change, you could hardly blame them. I knew that this power grab would cause trouble and strife but I believed we would see it through at a conference where we enjoyed a big majority, and that time would heal the wounds. When you are grabbing power, you have to believe at least that.

While I was away, however, two elements were added that gave great force to the campaign of hysteria that the Left were whipping up in the party. Under pressure from the Municipal Employees Union, John Ducker and Leo McLeay, the assistant secretary of the party, agreed to submit to conference a rule change that would permit a form of central preselection for the Lord Mayor of the City of Sydney and the aldermen. This was justified on the grounds that this council received much greater publicity than any other in the state and so deserved our most special consideration. The fact that the Right had lost control of many of the inner city branches who had a vote in these preselections was not lost on anyone, especially the Left.

The right of rank-and-file preselection was near and dear to the hearts of every member of the party, and this very minor attempt to change that right, even for one local government area, was exploited brilliantly by the Left. The cry went up that this move was the thin end of the wedge, the beginning of the end for the rank-and-file system. Branches everywhere were up in arms.

When all this was combined with another rule change that would allow me as general secretary to impound branch books without a resolution of the administrative committee, the recipe for party mayhem on the grandest of scales was taken up by thousands of left-wing chefs. With the cauldron well and truly boiling, Paul Landa rang me in America to come home urgently.

I had just visited eleven out of the thirteen cities I was to see in the United States in the space of four weeks, and on this particular early morning, Paul Landa found me in the Desert Inn in Las Vegas. The fact that this was my only day and night of relaxation on a hectic trip was of no concern to him. I picked up the phone to a typically warm Landa greeting: 'What the fuck are you doing in Las Vegas when the party is blowing itself apart in Sydney?' he roared. He explained to me the seriousness of the situation and, being quite committed to the Rules change as leader of the Legislative Council (and as a person who wanted to be in the full Caucus as a step on the road to eventually replacing Wran), Landa could see the unthinkable happening—the Right might be defeated at a state conference.

When I reached Los Angeles two days later, ready to leave for Sydney, I was preparing to ring Leo McLeay when he saved me the trouble. He didn't want to talk about the Rules change, however. He had a very simple message for me: 'Frank Stewart's dead, I'm running.' This wasn't the most sensitive way of breaking the news of the death of the former Whitlam minister or of Leo's intention to contest preselection for the seat of Grayndler which Frank had now vacated. Still, sensitivity was not Leo's strong suit.

I did manage to get him to focus a little on the problem of the Rules changes and he told me that the City of Sydney preselection change had gone through, even though I had told him to make sure it failed to get on to the conference agenda because John Ducker had insisted. Ducker had told him 'Leave Graham to me'. Graham boarded the plane for home wondering how we could get out of this mess. Within twenty-four hours of reaching Australia, I knew that everything Paul Landa had told me on the phone was spot on, including his warning to 'Watch Neville'. By that time, Wran had made some public comments indicating he was opposed to the joint Caucus proposal.

It's worth noting that this proposal, power grab that it actually was, would simply have put New South Wales in the same position as every other state branch of the party. Just as the rank-and-file preselection system is used only in New South Wales to ensure there is no central influence on the selection of candidates, and hence to ensure that the Right can't gain the same advantage as the Left has in Victoria, so it was also true that only in New South Wales was an Upper House member considered unworthy of full entry into the state Caucus. Power was fine as long as it wasn't exercised by the New South Wales Right.

John Ducker, like my father, knew when he had erred and knew that it was better to retreat at the earliest possible moment. As soon as I told him that the City of Sydney proposal had to be withdrawn, he agreed. There was no argument, just an acknowledgment that whatever had to be done to preserve the main game (i.e., the joint Caucus proposal) should be done immediately. He also agreed to see Neville Wran with me in an attempt to gain his support. I then announced publicly that two of the three proposals that were causing such concern were to be withdrawn and that the joint Caucus proposal would proceed to be debated at the state conference, the only body with the power to change the Rules.

With every day that passed during May 1979, more and more party units committed themselves to oppose the Rules change. It became clear that the Right would have to struggle to get this proposal through and that defeat was a real possibility.

Obviously, a white knight was needed to ride to the rescue and given that white knights were an endangered species, only one came to mind. Neville Wran had to be won over to our cause and to guide us through a difficult debate at conference. I arranged for John Ducker and myself to see Wran on a Sunday morning in Wran's Macquarie Street office. Pleasantries were dispensed with in half the normal time, and we got down to business. Jack Ferguson had successfully stoked the fires within Wran and the

Premier opened the proceedings by announcing that he 'wouldn't fucking wear it'. He lectured Ducker and me about the evils of fanning party disunity and about the sorry spectacle that a bitterly divided state conference would provide.

Ducker sat in silence during the lecture, then he began to speak, the words just exploding from his mouth. 'I'll tell you what you'll fucking wear,' was how he began, and it got harder from there. Ducker bored in heavily by reminding Wran that a stable party run by himself had provided the base from which electoral successes could be built, the base about which Wran never had to worry. While the need for Neville to be persuaded to enter the debate had been discussed for some weeks by Ducker and myself, Ducker's bold, blunt assertion took me by surprise and left Wran momentarily speechless. 'Not only will you wear it, you'll fucking move it,' thundered Ducker.

Wran's capitulation was quick and complete. Nobody could have rejected Ducker in similar circumstances and, despite his previous public utterances and the close relationship he enjoyed with Jack Ferguson, Wran committed himself to moving for the change at the conference. This meant that the Premier and the Deputy Premier would be the principal speakers pitted against each other at the conference. Jack Ferguson was the only Left personality with real standing who could make a decent conference speech—a unique and dangerous situation.

As the showdown grew closer, the factions counted heads, the argument grew more and more public and the newspapers were playing up the issue for all it was worth and then some. A young Left activist, Rodney Cavalier, became the Left's public champion, giving interviews to anyone who would publicise his case. Cavalier could make little impact as a conference speaker but his skill as a publicist for the Left cause was such that later I tried to muzzle him by threatening to expel him for bringing the party into disrepute. Fortunately these threats were never carried out, and Cavalier went on to become a successful minister in the Wran and Unsworth governments.

By the Saturday morning of that conference, Cavalier had brought the issue to a fever pitch exceeding all my worst fears. He then compounded this crime by being the only Left person in the party to completely outwit and outsmart me.

Cavalier had been deputed by the Left to organise the debate with me: while this might sound anti-democratic, it was just pragmatic. With 800 or more delegates, a debate like this could see a rash of rank-and-file delegates seeking the call, especially those from the Left. If they were all given a go the debate would last an entire day, not just the couple of hours allotted to it, and the Left's main speakers might fail to get the call. While the Left were sticklers for democracy, this was taking democracy too far. The rank and file hit the fence and the Left heavies had their day.

Cavalier and I negotiated an arrangement whereby the debate would be conducted in sections. While this seemed to be a sensible outcome, I had not realised that this arrangement would enable Jack Ferguson to speak in a different section of the Rules report from Neville Wran. The great advantage of Wran advocating our position against Ferguson and the Left was lost, and I had made a tactical blunder of quite some magnitude. Whether this would have changed any votes in such a highly charged atmosphere, where every delegate had already been subjected to considerable pressure, is hard to say, but getting outmanoeuvred was a new and unwelcome experience for me.

The conference debate was acrimonious in the extreme. With 800 delegates on the floor and at least as many more in the galleries above, the Sydney Town Hall had all the atmosphere of the old Sydney Stadium before a championship fight. The publicity war had done the Right's cause a great deal of harm and, from the moment Jack Ferguson strode to the microphone and said: 'Jack Ferguson, Building Workers Union' (he had been an organiser of this union before entering parliament and represented the union at conference) I knew we had a very serious problem. Ferguson would use phrases expressing the defiance of the gallant underdog fighting the good fight, and the crowd would erupt with prolonged applause. The Left have always been superior to the Right when it comes to cheering and jeering, and at that conference their capacity to drown out their opposition reached new heights. Ferguson the working-class hero received a greater ovation than Gough Whitlam's when he attended the 1973 conference as the first Labor prime minister in almost a quarter of a century.

Try as they might, none of our speakers in reply could hope

to have anything like the same impact. The only one who could have matched him was Neville Wran, and my error ensured that he wasn't directly pitted against our most dangerous opponent. When the vote came, the Right survived by 56 votes: loyalty was just enough to get us through. This was the only time a serious proposal by the Right at a conference came close to defeat. Shock waves reverberated through the conference, the party and, most importantly, the party officers.

As we closed on Monday afternoon, John Ducker told me this was his last conference. He had not been well for quite some time and his disappointment at the way the conference had gone had not done anything to improve his outlook. Not only had we come close to defeat on the Rules change motion, but the votes for our officers' positions had not been much better. That Ducker would resign in August 1979, at the nadir of the faction's fortunes, was unjust. He had ensured our survival and yet resigned at a low point in our history. His resignation brought about a radical transformation in our faction, and it was just as well. The Left probably hadn't realised how close they had come to an historic victory.

In the inner-city suburbs of Sydney, the Irish Catholic traditions of Labor had been breaking down for a long time. The older working-class people, who had voted Labor for generations and had been the backbone of the party, were seeing the 'gentrification' of their area, with a lot of professional people moving in. These had flocked to Labor's colours when Whitlam was in power and many had joined to support the party after the dismissal. They were the new face of the Labor Party, and it was soon clear that confrontation between old and new was inevitable. This took the form of brawls—sometimes physical, sometimes intellectual—between the varying factions at branch meetings, but it came to a head over the question of branch stacking and the rorting of branch books.

The rorting of branch books in the Labor Party goes back to its formation. In the inner city, it was an expected and unchallenged reality for decades. Many inner-city branch areas covered only a few streets, and whoever controlled the branch made certain that every resident was able not just to be a member of the Labor

Party but to vote in a preselection for public office. So attendance books were hawked around from house to house and people who had never been near a branch meeting voted in every important ballot.

Most of the glue that bound these operations together was found in local government. Getting a job 'on the council' was the payback by the local party boss for favours done. The family of the council worker would all join the party and vote for their benefactor, no matter what. Add this to religion (Danny Minogue, an old Irish politician, used to sign up the Irish migrants as they got off the boat) and the ways of the old inner-city Labor Party were set in concrete, and would take quite an explosion to blow away.

This tradition had been around long before I was born, but I was unlucky enough to be the New South Wales branch secretary when it became a matter of public scandal. While it is certainly true that the old Left enclaves in these areas could rort with the best of them, the changing nature of inner-city residents, indeed the changing nature of the inner city, was bound to destroy a tradition to which I was instinctively attracted and which I felt bound to protect. This was a very big mistake on my part.

The error I made in not using the strength of my position in the party to stamp out this rampant cheating in branches was not mine alone. In the preselection for the seat of Sydney when Les McMahon was chosen to replace Jim Cope, a thousand party members voted. Barely half of these people would have been eligible if honesty had been a prerequisite for qualification to vote. There were, however, no serious protests because both sides had been out there, rorting as hard as they could.

On the Right, Rozelle East and Redfern East were the big crook branches, with hundreds of members eligible and very few fair dinkum. But to paint themselves as innocent, the Left would really have had to battle. Surry Hills and Waterloo were their two rotten boroughs. At the credentialling of the books for the ballot between McMahon and his Left opponents, Jack Ferguson and I agreed to allow substantial numbers of members in the big four crook branches to vote. The big battalions of the Left and the Right, irrespective of their entitlements, voted in the Sydney preselection. It was always difficult to credential the books of the

Surry Hills branch, which had a way of disappearing at crucial moments. During the credentialling for the McMahon ballot in Sydney, the problem was that some of the branch's older records in a cupboard of the secretary's home had been eaten by rats. When we formed a high-ranking body to credential all the books of the branches in the inner city after Peter Baldwin was bashed, the new secretary of the Surry Hills branch—none other than Robert Tickner, later Minister for Aboriginal Affairs in the Keating government—tragically lost all the branch books after leaving them in a pub on the way to the ALP office in Sussex Street.

From 1975 to 1980, the Left cleaned up their act in the inner city and we didn't. They eliminated much, but not all, of the rorting on their side and began to recruit the new residents of these changing areas. The gentrification of some of these suburbs brought academics and professionals to the party, very different from the people they replaced. For the Left branch stackers, they were manna from heaven.

Things came to a head in mid 1980. Peter Baldwin, one of the Left's most successful branch stackers and a member of the New South Wales Legislative Council, had wanted to switch to Federal Parliament and decided to run for preselection in the seat of Sydney against Les McMahon. He started to investigate the membership of Enmore, a branch held by McMahon's right-wing supporters. The secretary of the Enmore branch was Joe Meissner and one of his offsiders was Tom Domican. Meissner's girlfriend was Virginia Perger, later famous for alleging that she entertained various parliamentary luminaries on board a 'love boat' on Sydney Harbour.

After he looked at the books, Baldwin challenged the preselection voting eligibility of about half the Enmore branch members, including Meissner himself. Baldwin's report contained so much evidence of rorting that it could not be ignored. With some reluctance, I ensured that the party endorsed his report. As a result, the Enmore branch was dissolved in July 1980. Late on the night of the sixteenth, Peter Baldwin was severely bashed when he returned to his home after a left-wing meeting.

Despite a long and intensive police investigation, the perpetrators have never been identified. A number of people were charged with falsifying branch records, including Tom Domican and Joe

Meissner (still referred to as 'former ALP identities'), Virginia Perger and the late John Harrison, the then mayor of Marrickville. With allegations of massive branch rorting, earlier uncovered by Peter Baldwin himself, this was a journalist's heaven. John Harrison, who had lived in the same home for many years, was arrested there early in the morning; naturally the media had been told, so photographers were on hand to graphically record the event. Hundreds of charges relating to Joe Meissner's alleged failure to pay parking fines were laid at the same time as the Enmore charges, enabling anyone on the Liberal side of politics to argue that 600 charges had been laid in relation to the Enmore case.

Also charged in what became known as the Enmore conspiracy case was a 'garbo' at the council whose name I can't even remember and whose crime appears to have been giving some 'lip' to the investigating policemen. Allan Johnson, a war veteran who still carried shrapnel in his body and who suffered from emphysema, was also charged. As the former president of the Enmore branch this was probably inevitable, but poor Allan didn't know what had hit him. He was a mail sorter who had been vice-president of the Postal Workers Union when my father was secretary. I had known him since I was ten years old and found it tragic to see this great Labor stalwart, so typical of people who participate in the party at branch level, being caught up in a criminal proceeding. I would have done anything to help him, but there was precious little I could do.

With Peter Baldwin in hospital, the Left clamoured for vengeance against the Right, whom they held responsible for the bashing. They wanted a public inquiry into the bashing and into corrupt elements in the party. As party secretary, I was in the eye of the storm. There had been other, less dramatic, incidents of violence—at two meetings of the Balmain branch where a huge stacking war was going on, at a meeting of the Sydney Federal Electoral Council and at a meeting of the Redfern East branch—and had I clamped down earlier on all of the above, perhaps Peter Baldwin would never have been bashed. The world, however, is not built on perfect hindsight or 'what if'. You live with your mistakes just as you live with your successes. It was a long time ago, I didn't know then what I know now, and if I was wrong, I had plenty of company.

The case was heard by the then deputy chief magistrate Mr Brown, who eventually dismissed the charges. This was the right decision: an extraordinary precedent would have been set if they had proceeded. If any other decision had been made, the police budget would have been stretched to breaking point for all time, looking not only at Labor Party branch books but the records of all kinds of clubs and associations. But in this particular case there was an element of righteousness and punishment: nobody had been charged over the Baldwin bashing and someone should pay a penalty. Thousands of people in the party felt that, and they probably still do. They were wrong then and they are wrong now. If such a precedent had been applied, new prisons would have had to be built to accommodate the victims.

These victims would not have been criminals, simply party members who went too far in chasing their version of the dream of power. They might have been running as delegates to Youth Council, or more likely running for local government preselection. Whatever they were doing, they wouldn't have deserved to go to gaol and the party would never have survived the eruption of publicity that occurs when police surveillance of anything happening in a political party is even hinted at.

Rumours, allegations and innuendos about the case persisted for years. The police brief allegedly fell into the hands of the accused: I was supposed to be the person who dropped it there. The prospect of my asking Peter Anderson, then the police minister in the Wran government, to hand over the brief to me was nil; the prospect of his agreeing was even less. This rumour probably started because some of the witnesses' statements got into the hands of the accused: given that quite a few of the prospective witnesses were close relatives of those accused, this was hardly startling.

The magistrate was rumoured to have been influenced, which was even more stupid than the allegation about the brief. The only person who could have spoken to him was Frank Walker, the then New South Wales Attorney-General. Given that Frank and I hadn't spoken for years and that anything he could do to add to my discomfort would have been too difficult to resist, the proposition was preposterous. Apart from that, Magistrate Brown had an impeccable reputation which was never even slightly tarnished.

The only 'crime' to which I could plead guilty was to writing to the premier and all state ministers to tell them that I, the administrative committee and the New South Wales conference all thought the charges should have been dropped. The terms of the resolutions I conveyed received considerable publicity at the time, as I gave out their text in a press release. My letters were politely ignored by all those to whom they were sent because acting upon them at the time would have been politically impossible. The truth was that a good barrister—Brian Donovan, now a QC—argued a good case, and the charges were dismissed.

Lessons were learned from this whole sorry episode, especially by me. The inner city was cleaned up, with control eventually going to the Left. More importantly, though, tolerance for 'cooking' the books disappeared and is no longer a regular feature of preselections in New South Wales. It happens, but less often and less spectacularly.

The great danger to the rank-and-file preselection system in New South Wales will not be rorted books but branch stacking. The party's numbers in Victoria have doubled since the 1993 election as a result of ethnic groups being organised to join the party en masse to support particular candidates, and in Victoria, branch votes count for only half the selection panel. In New South Wales, where branch votes count for everything, the next few years may well see party stalwarts replaced by 'stackers' with no party history. It won't matter who wins this war—and if Victoria is any guide it will be the Right—because the Labor Party will be the ultimate loser. The party must expand again to become a mass party and this can never truly happen, irrespective of the numbers of its members, if this expansion occurs only in a few ethnic groupings.

Part 2

HAYDEN VERSUS HAWKE

CHAPTER 1

Hayden

Factional strife persisted throughout 1979 and 1980 in the New South Wales Labor Party. They were ugly times, and the difficulty for me as general secretary was that, while fighting this war, I still had to help ensure that the party was ready to fight and win elections at the national level. When I looked nationally, however, the certainty that yet another bitter Labor Party war would be fought was obvious. I didn't know anyone who thought Bill Hayden could win an election, but I knew plenty who had found their saviour. Bob Hawke was coming.

The Labor Party, the Caucus, probably the entire nation knew that a confrontation between Bill Hayden and Bob Hawke was inevitable. And when the complexities of the contenders were thrown in, the fight for Labor's leadership was guaranteed to be spectacular. I can say, in fact, that the few years after 1980 were the most intriguing I have spent in the party.

Whitlam finally bowed out following the party's rout by Malcolm Fraser in 1977. This had been doubly humiliating as some elements in the party had expected to make a substantial comeback after two years of Liberal rule. However, if they believed that the Whitlam experiment had meant the dreaming of great dreams from 1972 to 1975, the electorate could remember only nightmares. Whitlam was a hated figure, and the electorate was in no mood to forget. One chance to let him know how they felt wasn't enough, and in 1977 the electorate took advantage of their second go. It had never been easy to tell Gough anything, but this time the message stuck. I can still remember the cameras catching Whitlam as he entered an elevator explaining that he would call the Caucus together in the next week to elect a new leader. 'I myself will not be a candidate,' he said.

Why has practically every Labor leader been able to make this statement, or something like it, only when it's too late? When either the party or the electorate has forced them to utter words of defeat without honour for themselves or for the party they lead? Whitlam, Hayden and Hawke just didn't know how to go when their time had come.

Whitlam's successor, Bill Hayden, should never have accepted the position of leader. His personality was never suited to the role. He was the classic loner in a job that required a gregarious nature. The piano tuner's son from Ipswich in Queensland, whose childhood had obviously been poor and deprived, was by nature wary of all those with whom he came into contact, and he had very few friends. And while it has been said that the meek shall inherit the earth, they are unlikely to do so while leading the Australian Labor Party, which—I think it can safely be said—is no place for the meek.

In the last decade I have developed a really good relationship with Hayden, and he is someone I respect. He is a calmer, warmer person now, and he has learned how to mix. In a Labor Cabinet his counsel was always invaluable. He genuinely cared about the little people, and he knew at least as much about economics as Hawke or Keating, possibly more, but compassion has to be communicated, and that he could never do. He was always hamstrung by his upbringing and his naturally suspicious nature.

Hayden was one of the most unlikely leaders the party has had in my lifetime. He didn't look like a leader: the clothes were never quite right, the bearing was that of a corporal rather than a general. Leaders know how to mix, they stand out in the crowd, they are people whom everyone would like to meet. The sad fact is that nobody much wanted to meet Bill Hayden, and he wasn't keen on meeting them anyway. He never sounded like a leader, he lacked the capacity to inspire. If Hayden had delivered the Gettysburg address, the Confederacy would still have been in the hunt. He never acted like a leader: when in the throes of a crisis, he spent the weekend at home in Ipswich tiling his bathroom. Leaders don't tile their bathrooms; they let their fingers do the walking.

Relations with business are critical for any Labor leader, and his were lousy. The necessity for getting on with the private sector was highlighted in the 1975 Terrigal conference, where despite uproar from the traditionalists in the party, Whitlam had forced recognition of the role of the private sector and the need for profits in the party platform. Conspiracy theories flourish in the Labor Party, and many preferred to believe that a 'capital strike' had, at least in part, been responsible for the economic conditions that brought about Whitlam's removal from office. Any conspiracy theory based on the premise that the captains of industry had acted badly was bound to be swiftly and widely accepted. I don't believe that Hayden ever treated such nonsense seriously; in fact, during his period as leader he worked flat out, and with considerable success, to restore Labor's economic credibility with the *Financial Review* set following the fiasco of the Whitlam period. But he never liked talking to business. He spent so much time looking for the traps they were laying for him that he could never really listen. So when Labor was campaigning for victory in 1980 and beyond, business was definitely going to be in the Liberals' camp, when pushing them into a neutral corner should have been relatively easy for a smart Labor leader.

Naturally, when Hayden became leader, John Ducker and I extended the hand of friendship, hoping he might be interested in a civilised and constructive working relationship. I arranged for the three of us to have dinner together not long after his accession. We met at a ritzy noshery called Le Cafe at the farthest and most fashionable end of Sydney's Oxford Street in the old rectory of St Matthias Anglican Church. It is a heritage building and the two restaurants that have traded there have been among Sydney's finest and most expensive. Nouvelle cuisine was just becoming the rage in the trendier Sydney restaurants: while you were never guaranteed to come away with your hunger sated, the cultural experience of seeing a plate placed before you on which the food appeared to have been painted by Michelangelo always made you feel as if you were going somewhere special. Still, in those days our suits had wide lapels and we wore garish open-necked shirts over the collars of our jackets—what did we know?

Having spent a reasonable amount of time acting out the preliminaries, John Ducker got down to business. He told Hayden that in the New South Wales Right, the new leader had an experienced team of operatives who were interested in Labor being in government. On policy issues we appeared to have very few differences with Hayden and therefore, said Ducker, the New South Wales Right was offering itself as an ally in Hayden's quest for electoral victory.

Naturally, Ducker added, we were concerned that the Left should not be given too prominent a place at the leader's table, but we had no doubt Hayden would be sensible about such matters. Hayden was well aware that the New South Wales machine had not been close to Lionel Bowen, his rival for the leadership, so what Ducker was putting to him could have been taken at face value. Against that, of course, he knew that both Ducker and I were close to Bob Hawke, who would one day enter parliament, and that a Hayden–Hawke challenge was only a matter of timing. Whether he thought that our support for Hawke was a certainty or not, we could reasonably expect him to play along with us for a while, or at least appear to do so. After all, Hawke did not look like being in parliament for a few years, and that's an awfully long time in politics.

If that was what Ducker and I expected, we were destined for disappointment. Hayden just said 'no'. He had no love for the New South Wales branch; we were close to Hawke and had been close to the machine in Queensland, led by Jack Egerton, that had fought Hayden for most of his political career. He had no love for Paul Keating, nor did he trust him, believing that after encouraging him to run against Whitlam for the leadership Keating had voted for Whitlam (Hayden was wrong about this too). Given the lack of support he had received from the better known New South Wales Right supporters in the Caucus, Hayden saw no reason to expect any improvement. So he said no, he would not be getting any closer to the New South Wales branch. He would be co-operative, but any thought of an alliance was just not on.

The significance of this response should not be underestimated. While it was quite reasonable for Hayden to believe that when push came to shove we would support a Hawke challenge against him, he failed to understand the rules of a challenge coming from a faction with a real sense of the party's future as the government of Australia.

Even before Hayden had left the restaurant's grounds, Ducker told me that this was one leader who would always lean further to the Left than to the Right. And once Hayden had rejected our blandishments, my conscience was quite clear about whatever had to be done over the next few years to achieve a victory for Hawke.

The 1980 election, in which Hawke entered parliament, probably summed up Hayden's problems. Our research had shown that doubts about Hayden were widespread in the electorate. Not that we needed a poll to tell us that; I cannot recall another election campaign in which Labor's leader had to be surrounded by other leaders to convince a sceptical public that our leader could lead. Creating a 'triumvirate'—a nice word to describe Bill being surrounded by Neville Wran and Bob Hawke whenever we showed an advertisement—was a public admission of lack of faith in our leadership. If the people don't believe you can lead, you really are wasting your time and the party's as well. Unfortunately, as the Labor leader is elected only by the party Caucus—a select group of insiders who, when in Opposition, often come from safe seats where the will of the people is not much of an issue—the problems acknowledged by this advertising campaign were ignored by those who could have fixed them.

It was on the issue of a capital gains tax that the weakness of the Hayden leadership was most effectively demonstrated.

The 1980 campaign pitted two relatively unpopular men against each other. Malcolm Fraser was an austere patrician, a wealthy grazier possessed of absolutely no charm and even less warmth. He had been elected to the job by the electorate unelecting Whitlam, and was therefore the Liberal equivalent of the drover's dog. There were no ecstatically cheering crowds for him, just the gentle, smug applause of the well bred ladies and gentlemen who might have been delighted that one of their own had landed the job, but whose breeding dictated that showing emotion in public was bad form.

Against him was our Bill—brilliant, compassionate, isolated, friendless and suspicious.

On the face of it, this would not appear to promise a very exciting contest. But to Hayden's great credit, he made a real fight of it. The Liberals' advertisements in 1977 had promised health, wealth and prosperity for all who voted Liberal, symbolised by fistfuls of dollars. Only three years later, this was widely regarded as a sham, and the government never had the credibility it should have built after five years in power. To fight this, Hayden had real intellect—an extraordinary mind, in fact—and the ability to apply it single-mindedly to the task. He was one of the few Whitlam ministers to emerge from the debacle of 1975 with his reputation intact, if not enhanced, with a record of achievement as the architect of Medibank, our first universal health scheme, which he doggedly and repeatedly used to good effect. It is probably true that if Gough had made him Treasurer after coming to power in 1972, the government would not have been in anything like the mess it was. Bill's 1975 Budget was the only sensible one in the three Whitlam years; it was one reason why Fraser had to move to block supply. That Budget could have put things back on track, and Bill's approach could have given Labor a show of survival if the parliament had gone its full term.

As the 1980 campaign developed, the public, who didn't really like either leader, was actually beginning to examine issues. But it was a pretty staid campaign until Fraser, picking up a throwaway line of Ralph Willis's, challenged Hayden to rule out a capital gains tax.

Given that a capital gains tax is now a fact of life in Australia, causing practically no comment, such a challenge would seem to have been a non-event. But in the climate of the 1980 election, in a country with a proud tradition of home ownership going back generations, anything that even looked like threatening the great Australian dream of the three-bedroom brick veneer on the quarter-acre block was set to be a big issue. We knew this, and some of us thought the whole thing should be defused. Among others, Hawke, Keating and I urged Hayden to say 'no' to a capital gains tax and to get back to fighting the election on our turf. However, Hayden believed—and quite rightly—that a capital gains tax was an absolute necessity, even though it had never been spelled out in any party manifesto. At the very least, he believed this tax had to be maintained as an option that could be examined properly in government. This was all very well, but the campaign was drawing to a close and we had no time to explain. This was, we knew, a time for discretion, not for valour.

Our Bill didn't think so. He was determined to show himself as the honest politician who would not back away from what he believed just to make himself popular. Nobody could sway him. Even Hawke, waiting in the wings, to whose advantage a defeat for Hayden would be, fought hard to persuade him to back off. (It's an absolute rule of logic that Opposition leaders are much easier to challenge than prime ministers, as I was to discover some ten years later). Seeing the writing on the wall Paul Keating, who was champing at the bit to become a minister, was furious.

Bill Hayden's integrity won. So did Malcolm Fraser.

Nobody can prove conclusively that the capital gains issue cost Labor victory in what turned out to be a relatively close election. Maybe the memories of the Whitlam years had not yet dimmed sufficiently; perhaps Bill's lack of popularity might still have denied him office. But victory had been so close I could smell it, and that one decision was enough to cost us the votes we needed in the vital seats.

Bob Hawke, the man who faced Bill Hayden after the 1980 election, was everything Hayden could never be.

By the time he entered parliament, Bob Hawke was already a folk hero. His years as president of the ACTU had given him popularity on a grand scale. No union leader in our history has ever had anything like his degree of public acceptance. His talent for entering big industrial disputes at the last moment and forging agreements to end strikes meant that he was always seen as doing something positive. The public lapped up his successes, ignored his failures, and admired him all the more for his flaws.

Hawke had seen what the union movement in Germany and Israel had done and he wanted our own movement to supply workers' needs, from housing to health insurance, from petrol in their cars to fridges in their houses. Armed with these great ideas, he blundered into their implementation. The ACTU forays into travel agencies, petrol retailing and discount stores were all flops; high hopes were never realised and the perfect score of failures just kept mounting.

The labour movement and the party, as well as the public, allowed for these mistakes as they have never done for any other political figure on the national scene. All those allowances were made because they liked Hawke. Respected and admired him, sure, but most of all liked, even loved him. The willingness to forgive a loved one is common enough among humankind, and an entire nation chose to forgive Bob Hawke. If he appeared in public after a few too many, his standing actually seemed to be enhanced, largely because he was the perfect blend of all things Australian and all things people hoped would one day be so. He hadn't just been a bright student, he had been a Rhodes Scholar; not just a drinker but the holder of a world record for downing the largest amount of beer in the smallest amount of time, not just popular with the boys but very appealing to the girls. He was the extraordinary Australian whom most ordinary Australians would either love to have been, or at least would love to count among their friends.

Hawke was a stranger to self-doubt. While this sometimes showed up as colossal ego, it was also demonstrable inner strength under pressure. If you could bottle whatever his parents instilled into him as a child, you would make a fortune. Hawke always believed it was his duty to lead Australia to the Promised Land, for his parents had given him a belief in his own star. His admission to Perth Modern School, his selection as a Rhodes Scholar and his opportunity for an Oxford education did nothing to dim his vision of his destiny, and his road was studded with success. Even when I drove him to a thousand functions in the city and country in 1972 and 1974 he was a commanding figure. For the best part of fifteen years he was the embodiment of charisma and he knew it.

Popular appeal, of course, does not always accompany great intellect. Having at different times heard Hayden, John Button, John Dawkins and Paul Keating deriding Hawke as a second-rate thinker, I looked closely at him to try and form my own judgment. While you could never accuse Hawke of being an original thinker, there is no doubt he had a first-class mind. He could master a brief quickly and completely, argue a case in the most heated of debates and had an uncanny knack of listening to conflicting advice from ministers and public servants and then knowing the correct decision to make.

Admittedly, he wasn't a visionary. When he became Prime Minister, two of his most senior staffers, Peter Barron and Geoff Walsh, always knew that they could calm him down by sending him home to the Lodge for the weekend with instructions to write down his vision for the country so that it could be translated into policy. The words to describe this vision just never came. Hawke wanted a more egalitarian and better-off country but he could never express just how this was to be achieved. However, it is trite to write him off because of this. Leadership is more about making the right choices than creating new agendas and Hawke's record at the ACTU, the party's national executive and then for almost a decade as Prime Minister confirms that on this score he had a real skill.

In contrast to Bill Hayden, he was pragmatic when it came to dealing with business. In fact, he was always comfortable with businessmen, no matter how big and powerful. His role as ACTU president had seen him dealing directly with every captain of Australian industry, and many genuinely liked him. Even those who didn't, the committed Liberals and refined gentlemen who regarded hard-drinking, hard-swearing men like Hawke with the same suspicion as Hayden had, recognised the need to be on civil terms with him. Whether Labor's Caucus realised it or not, very few captains of industry doubted that Hawke would lead Australia in the very near future. With him as leader, business would certainly be in a neutral corner, and some businessmen were seriously thinking about supporting us.

Not that some party members thought they should. Hawke's friendships with the likes of Peter Abeles were seen as proof of his untrustworthiness by many in the Left of the party and beyond. Some, the zealous guardians of the party's conscience, accused him of being a class traitor. While the climate is a little better today, the Labor Party has long suffered from reverse snobbery when it comes to wealth and success in business. From our earliest days, we have tended to consider that the rich have achieved their wealth on the backs of the poor and probably on the wrong side of the law as well. If they are powerful as well as rich, so much the worse. Even today, a statement criticising Kerry Packer, regardless of its accuracy, is bound to get a cheer at any Labor gathering.

Hawke's view was that among those who made it to the top in business were some brilliant people whose ideas were worth hearing. Today if a senior minister wants an idea of how the economy is going or where it is heading, he can call upon a vast array of experts from the economic departments. A hundred MBAs will rush forward to give their learned views and from among those, you would assume, plenty of information can be gleaned. Just imagine how much better governments of any political persuasion would be if a successful businessman such as Kerry Packer were asked his opinion. If you can turn millions into billions and keep doing it, your opinion should perhaps count for more than the army of MBAs.

Hawke could also be a good hater. In his battles to gain supremacy, he always had to dislike an opponent in order to fight him properly, but a feature of his character that intrigued me was that, once he had won, he couldn't do enough for the person he had defeated. A perfect example of this was his treatment of Gerry Hand, the member of the Socialist Left who opposed him for preselection in the Victorian seat of Wills in 1979. Hawke worked himself up into nothing less than a frenzy over Hand's alleged misdeeds. According to Hawke, Hand's only claim to fame was that he had 'run a provincial Trades and Labour Council for a bunch of commo unions', and Hawke scathingly described the Socialist Left as a 'telephone box minority' even though they had captured the party apparatus in Victoria. But once Hawke had defeated him, and Hand had been elected first a member of Hawke's government, then of his ministry and finally his Cabinet, in Hawke's eyes he became 'a really decent bloke', who was given more latitude as a minister than were any of those aligned with Hawke.

Whether Gerry Hand ever deserved Hawke's original opprobrium will never be known, but in Bill Hayden's case the issue was much simpler. Hayden worked hard to give Hawke plenty of reasons to dislike him and so to justify in Hawke's mind the steps he would need to take to overthrow him. A good example of this was seen at the 1979 federal conference in Adelaide.

The party's industrial relations policy was at issue and the Left, with Jim Roulston, the late joint secretary of the Metal Workers Union at the helm, were planning a series of amendments that Hayden and Hawke (as president of the ACTU) considered unworkable. Hayden asked me to assemble as many delegates as possible to enable him to explain the problems and, he hoped, to support him in the coming battle against the Left.

The next morning, a tentative step was made in the formation of an anti-Left grouping. We assembled in a small conference room at the Adelaide Convention Centre, close to the main conference venue. Coffee and tea were supplied to a group of people who were cautiously eyeing each other across the room. It was an interesting group. There were Opposition leaders such as Ron Davies from Western Australia and Ed Casey from Queensland; Clem Jones, the flamboyant long-time mayor of Brisbane, mixed with Mick Young and those South Australians he thought he could trust. John Ducker, Paul Keating, ex-Senator Tony Mulvihill and I represented New South Wales, while Neil Batt and Frank Wilkes represented Tasmania and Victoria. There was one absentee of note, Bob Hawke himself. Never one to pass up an opportunity to save the world, he was off settling some great dispute of national importance, having told me he wasn't sure whether he could make the industrial relations debate, even though he had chaired the committee that had prepared the recommendations Roulston was seeking to amend.

Hayden put his point of view to this meeting and, with very few questions, the meeting resolved to oppose Roulston's amendments. Feeling pretty pleased with the way things had gone, I rang Hawke's personal assistant Jean Sinclair to ask her to give Bob the good news. With Hayden about to lead the charge against the Left, the possibilities of new alliances were obvious: this was going to be a great day. The morning debates were hurried through without passion as we all prepared for the one big, fierce battle. I had a light lunch with Ducker, who was keen to prepare what would be his last major speech at a national conference. We returned from lunch ready for the fray, hoping to get a nice surprise—the arrival of Bob Hawke to at least share in the glory of the moment.

The surprise was there all right, but not one either of us had hoped for. Bill Hayden sauntered over to tell us what he had been doing at lunchtime. He had gone off for a quiet chat with Jim Roulston during which, Bill blithely informed us, he and Jim had come to an arrangement. This made redundant the decision taken at our morning meeting and, with only the most minor alterations, Hayden would now be supporting the Roulston position.

Up to that moment, our concern about Hayden's leadership had focused on our doubts about his popular appeal. But this revelation opened up a whole new area of worry. Now we had no faith that Hayden could handle sensitive electoral matters, policies that could influence voters when the crunch came. Ducker didn't try to argue with Hayden beyond informing him of our disappointment, as well as briefly attempting to explain the public difficulties Hayden would have by being seen to back down to the Left.

When the debate took place, only three votes were recorded against the Roulston amendments: Keating's, Ducker's and mine. Ducker formally opposed the motion in a very short speech but he couldn't conceal the anger he felt. In fact, around the room anger was growing at what was a pretty appalling breach of faith on Hayden's part.

But what we thought was anger was nothing to Bob Hawke's fury when he reached Adelaide later that afternoon. For the next few hours he went troppo—completely out of control. His already prodigious capacity for alcohol reached new heights and, having taken on enough fuel, and witnessed by the obligatory crowd of journalists with whom he had been drinking at the Ansett Gateway Hotel, he launched into his famous description of Hayden—'a lying cunt with a limited future'.

When this was reported all over Australia during the next few days, many were prepared to say that Hawke had been more damaged by the incident than Hayden and that this further demonstration of Hawke's lack of control under pressure, particularly when coupled with alcohol, would undermine his campaign to unseat Hayden. But this comment was largely confined to Hawke's opponents in the media and the party; it had no effect whatsoever on his popularity. If anything, his ratings went up over time, proving that, if people really like and admire you, forgiveness is not difficult to find. The art lies in not going to the well too often.

As far as Hawke was concerned, he now had right on his side. All the moral justification he needed for the tough decisions to follow—leaking damaging information to the press, mercilessly bagging Hayden to anybody who would listen for the next three years—had now been acquired. Truth and justice, then, would triumph over evil.

It is, however, worth noting that once Hawke had won, Hayden, the evil bastard who had been the 'lying cunt', was the wise head to be consulted, the revered name to be invoked. This wasn't only so in obvious matters—Hawke appointed Hayden Minister for Foreign Affairs and then Governor-General—it was everything in Hawke's demeanour in speaking to him or of him. Hawke always felt guilty over what was done to Hayden—not while it was happening, of course, only when it was over.

As I have said, this aspect of Hawke's personality has intrigued me. It seemed to me that once you made up your mind that somebody had to go in order to be replaced by someone better, it didn't matter at all whether he was a decent, caring person on the verge of canonisation or an absolute arsehole completely devoid of saving graces. If the king has to be brought down for the good of the party, then so be it. Any time spent worrying about the cruelty of executing such a nice fellow is time wasted. Any time feeling guilty about what you've done is even worse.

CHAPTER 2

Hayden and Hawke

After the 1980 election, it must have been blindingly obvious to the most amateurish political observer that Bob Hawke, the most popular person in the country, a hero in a nation desperately searching for one, was the only answer to Labor's leadership problem. The Caucus hated Fraser lording it over them and the thought of three more years of it was unbearable. They thought Hayden would probably win the next election; they knew Hawke would.

For those on the Left who viewed Hawke with hostility and saw Hayden as a safe buffer against the Right, the inevitability of Hawke's leadership didn't matter a damn. Many on the Left have fought a losing battle against the inevitable all their lives without flinching. To fight Hawke, they felt, would be a matter of pride. After all, they had managed to insulate the party from even a whiff of sanity during the 1950s and the 1960s, they had fought Whitlam for daring to bring some popular ideas into policy-making, so attempting to keep Hawke from the leadership was a crusade for most of them. Hell hath no fury like a faction scorned, and Hawke could never be forgiven for achieving the presidency of the ACTU with Left sponsorship and then proceeding to move steadily away from them over the next decade. The Left have always been good haters, and the hatred they developed for Hawke was especially bitter.

For the strange team assembled round Hayden, the nucleus of what later became the Centre Left, a fight against a populist such as Hawke suited their egos and their personalities. If the Left were the self-appointed guardians of the party's conscience, Hayden's group saw themselves as the brains of the party, the intellectual elite. Given that they knew better than the great majority of Australians, they would have no difficulty in overlooking Hawke's phenomenal personal ratings.

If the Left and Hayden's people saw themselves as the conscience and brains of the party, the Right were the self-appointed guardians of its fortunes. Hawke's arrival was the big chance to deal the Liberals a massive electoral defeat and to see Labor govern for a long period. So for the party's Right, bolstered by the inclusion among their ranks of the greatest convert since St Paul, this was the opportunity to do some good.

As far as I was concerned, the prospect of Hawke becoming leader, as well as what could be achieved by the campaign to capture the leadership, was just what my faction needed. At the beginning of the 1980s the Left was the only national faction. They occasionally held national gatherings to include leading party figures who were not in the Caucus, their national Left caucus in the union movement never stopped meeting, and in Federal Parliament they already had a disciplined system in operation. This meant that in every Caucus ballot members of the Left would vote in pairs to ensure that no individual broke the collective line.

There was very little to counterbalance this kind of organisation. The New South Wales Right had built an almost impregnable fortress around its home state, but no grouping in any other state called itself the Right. In each state, however, there was an anti-Left group, and the task as I saw it was to form a loose amalgam of these disparate groups. Some tentative steps in this direction had been attempted at the 1977 and 1979 conferences, but they never amounted to much. The one issue that united most of the anti-Left groups was the leadership. Hawke could be the rallying point for a national Right faction. The messiah had arrived. We just had to stop the party from crucifying him.

People like Paul Keating and Lionel Bowen had drawn together like-minded souls in a number of ballots during the late 1970s in particular, and as the 1980s dawned their efforts at drawing support for a national Right faction began to pay off. Even though it was the only organised faction, the Left could not guarantee to win any Caucus ballot for one of their number and the Right couldn't either. So in the Caucus after the 1980 election, we would obviously have to convert some people who didn't like Hawke or those behind him.

To break down some of these barriers, we needed someone outside New South Wales who could spread the message. And we had someone whose friendship with Hawke made him the ideal candidate for this job: Mick Young, the Member for Port Adelaide. While Mick had never been on the Left, and during his period as national secretary and in the Caucus had often done them injury, he was universally liked. Mick Young could make anyone laugh; he was always first with the latest joke. This was a very useful talent in the Caucus, where tensions were high, as well as in the national parliament when Labor wanted to make light of Fraser and his ministers, and of course in the pubs and restaurants where Mick Young was at his best.

Over a long lunch, Mick Young could convince you to do almost anything, and he was very close to Hawke. Hawke and Young worked on a time-tested formula: the family that plays together stays together. During the 1972 election campaign, the two men shared a flat in Sydney's Park Regis building, Mick as the campaign director for the party and Hawke as the ACTU president and political aspirant whose assistance every candidate was requesting.

Young and Hawke were committed to Hawke's destiny long before Hawke entered parliament—indeed, long before Hayden became leader. Hayden must have known that many senior figures in the party saw his tenure simply as a holding operation until Hawke could take over. With Young and Gareth Evans, his other strong Caucus supporter, working steadily for him, Hawke could afford whatever time it took for Keating, who saw Hawke's accession as a threat to his own leadership ambitions, to be won over to his cause. That was something I was to handle.

I have always taken the view that, when planning a challenge, you have to allow for the possibility of failure. You must undermine the leader enough in the eyes of the Caucus to unseat him, but not so much that the electoral damage is irreparable and he cannot win an election against the Liberals if your candidate fails. From time to time this means you have to lower the temperature in the challenge, much to the ire of the challenger. At other times you have to give the appearance of having called off the challenge altogether. This, of course, is a last-resort policy, but if you seriously believe your horse cannot win you have to call off the race. (Challengers never accept this philosophy; both Hawke and later Keating accused me of treachery when I appeared to be doing this.) The art of destroying a leader in the eyes of his Caucus but keeping him alive in the eyes of the electorate is an almost impossibly difficult balancing act. Maybe it explains why I went grey so early.

Our strategy was to keep the public perception of a popular Hawke, the one man who could be guaranteed to defeat Fraser, in the sharpest focus possible. No matter how much Members of Parliament might have wanted to ignore the wishes of the majority of the rank and file or of the electorate, any strategy that emphasised the certainty of a Labor win under Hawke, as against an outside chance of victory under Hayden, would eventually wear down the Caucus. We would eventually get a majority for Hawke. And momentum had to be maintained because that is what produces the state of inevitability that is the precursor to a successful challenge.

In practical terms, this meant that stories highlighting Hayden's weaknesses and Hawke's strengths had to be fed to any journalist who was willing to listen. Guerrilla warfare was to be the order of the day. Everybody knew it, everybody would dutifully deny that it was happening, everybody prepared for the next raid in support of their champion. With all sides snugly cloaked in the best interests of the party, everybody could get up to all sorts of bastardry with a clear conscience. So all of us embarked on campaigns to see the success of our candidates. Anything goes in these circumstances, and anything went.

When the goal is to have so much pressure put on Caucus

members that a change of heart is secured, the search for the right levers to exert that pressure is on in earnest. Hawke's trade union contacts were numerous and overwhelmingly friendly, which meant that whenever a Labor branch meeting took place, somebody would be pushing his cause. The influence of the trade unions was significant because they own 60 per cent or more of the stock in the party (as measured by the percentage of delegates directly elected by the trade union movement to state conferences). These state machines conducted the preselection system, so if you could get the state machines on side the chances were pretty good that the Caucus members could be influenced through them. This is not to infer that Caucus members would necessarily take their orders from the state machines, but undoubtedly a few extra votes could be picked up in this way.

Mick Young was the key influence in South Australia, and clearly we would do well with the Caucus members from that state. However, two factions had intervened to prevent us from getting anything like a clean sweep. Firstly, a Left group centred on Peter Duncan, who had been an attorney-general in the South Australian Dunstan Labor government and who went on to become a minister in the Hawke government, was seeking to gain ascendancy. Furthermore, intellectuals such as Neal Blewett and such mavericks as Ralph Jacobi (an unaligned old-style Labor man representing the vast rural seat of Grey) had been elected to parliament, and they wouldn't be following anybody's directions. So in the end it was doubtful whether the unions could deliver us much in South Australia.

In Western Australia the Left had been dominant for decades; only the odd non-Left person could sneak through. Kim Beazley Jr, however, had been too good to keep out. His father had been a successful minister in Whitlam's government and, along with Don Willesee, had been almost the token moderate preselected to go to Canberra. After the 1977 election we held very few seats in Western Australia—Kim lost preselection for his father's seat of Fremantle to John Dawkins and didn't get into parliament until 1980.

I already knew that to be seen with anyone from the New South Wales branch was a risk no West Australian, moderate or not, was prepared to take. As far back as the 1977 national conference, held in Perth and the first to which I was elected, the fear of being discovered talking to John Ducker or myself was quite remarkable. Brian Burke, then a young member of the Western Australian Parliament, had moved a series of amendments to the industrial relations report presented by John Ducker. After Burke's amendments had been defeated, Ducker returned to his seat muttering dark things about that 'fucking lunatic' from Western Australia. Later that day, in whispered furtive asides, I arranged with Beazley to have lunch with him and two other Western Australians who were as concerned as he was about breaking the stranglehold of the Left in their state. The rendezvous was to be in a restaurant well away from the conference, where we were unlikely to be seen.

Ducker was somewhat taken aback when I revealed to him that our two luncheon guests would be John Wheeldon, a Western Australian senator with a long history on the Left (but who as a Whitlam minister had grown apart from them) and the 'fucking lunatic' Brian Burke. Lunch was a furtive affair, much like those recorded in John Le Carré novels. We arrived separately, cased the joint to make sure no other Labor identities were present, then proceeded to talk.

The only clear undertaking Ducker and I received from these three fearful Western Australians was a promise to begin talking to others who seemed like-minded to gradually form a faction. It took quite some time for this to happen, but the genesis of the faction was at this lunch. Wheeldon, somewhat marginalised by the party, left the scene shortly thereafter, and it was left to Beazley and Burke, especially after the latter had become Premier, to formalise a new grouping. All of this came too late to help Bob Hawke in his quest for more Caucus votes. So that no one can be in any doubt about my views of Brian Burke, I am proud to count him among my friends, he is a great politician and I believe him to be incapable of stealing from anyone.

The Queensland branch was a logical place to seek out supporters, as Jack Egerton had been so close to Hawke. Egerton had run the Queensland branch with a rod of iron for many years. The branch was notoriously hardline when it came to allocating seats in parliament, and their treatment of dissidents made the New South Wales branch look weak by comparison. With Bill

Hayden harbouring grudges against them and the Left eager for an opportunity to increase their influence, the Queensland branch was a perfect target for intervention.

The pathetic sight of Jack Egerton kneeling before John Kerr and arising as Sir John had ended Egerton's reign in the party, and without his guidance the Queensland branch was obviously going to struggle. All that was needed was an excuse, and when threats were made to expel a group of rank-and-file members from Toowoomba, the national executive meted out swift and rough justice. In a matter of days charges were laid, carried by the executive, the old administration replaced with a new one and a new slate of candidates was selected for the Queensland Senate ticket.

Paul Keating joined me in defence of our mates in Queensland. Simon Crean attended the meeting in place of Bob Hawke (another part of the world urgently needed salvation) and we proceeded to a gallant but expected 10–8 defeat. While the result might have been disappointing from the losers' point of view, the relationships cemented under enemy fire stood the Hawke challenge in good stead. Every one of the old guard, as the Egerton remnants came to be known, became a strong Hawke supporter.

Even though I valiantly opposed Queensland intervention at the time, there was no shadow of doubt that it was the right course to follow—and, yes, I did realise that at the time. The long, unbroken period of rule by the National Party and Joh Bjelke-Petersen had roughly corresponded to the period in which Egerton and his cronies ruled the Queensland Labor roost. The transformed party that Wayne Goss now leads would not have existed without the decision for intervention. Talent had been stifled by the old regime as often as possible, lest it bred revolution. Nonetheless, the events after intervention never followed the script laid down by the Left or indeed by Bill Hayden.

The Australian Workers Union (AWU), by far the largest in Queensland, had long been estranged from the party, and the executive was in no position to continue to keep them out. Consequently, a union big enough to command one-third of the Queensland conference was admitted, and its leadership was friendly to the New South Wales branch and to Bob Hawke. Because of laws agreed to when I was too young to tie my shoelaces, the AWU controlled all union membership north of Rockhampton. Bolstered by this quirky arrangement, the AWU hordes descended on the Queensland branch of the party, and they control it to this day.

Hawke did very well out of his association with the AWU in Queensland. For some time he had been a friend of the retiring secretary, the ageing Edgar Williams. He was a typically hard Queensland AWU official and his replacement, Errol Hodder, a brash, cocky and confident younger version, was an even closer ally of Hawke's. Hodder strode into the Labor Party making damned sure that everybody knew it.

Even as late as 1991, Bill Ludwig, Hodder's successor as Queensland AWU secretary, pulled out all the stops to keep Bob Hawke in power. I still think Keating is disappointed at the treatment he received from the Queensland old guard in 1991, particularly since he had worked so hard for them when they were under threat, and I guess this goes back to the whole Hawke phenomenon. Those who really liked Hawke, such as the Queensland trade unionists I have just mentioned and their allies in the parliamentary party, were always going to opt for their oldest friend. And Tom Burns, the deputy premier of Queensland, demonstrated how old and true was the friendship with Hawke by attacking Keating very strongly in 1991. In the Labor Party, the only thing that dies harder than old friendship is old hatred.

However, our defeat in preventing intervention had cemented some alliances in Queensland; there can be value in defeat and from every defeat you must salvage whatever you can. We milked our Queensland defeat for all it was worth, and a Hawke victory came that little bit closer.

In New South Wales, two trade unionists of the old school continued to give Hawke great support. Ray Gietzelt of the Miscellaneous Workers Union, the heart and soul of the trade union Left and its influence in the party, had sponsored Bob Hawke in his drive to become ACTU president and, unlike his other colleagues on the Left, he seemed to forgive Hawke for shifting his allegiances to the Right after he had obtained the position. Ray was a pretty decent bloke, of whom my father had been quite fond. He always told me that Ray was on the Left more by accident of birth than by design, and warned me not to get too involved in machinations against him.

Ray Gietzelt provided counsel to Hawke through all the years when the Left had exiled him, and was rewarded by becoming a member of the board of Qantas once we had been elected. Ray could always ensure that the trade union dogs of war were never let slip against Hawke.

The other Gietzelt brother, Arthur, was a leader of the parliamentary Left, to the point that the mention of his name was enough to cause discomfort at any Right meeting. He was a different person altogether: while Ray could stand in the bar of a pub or a club with a glass of beer in his hand and enjoy it, Arthur always looked as if he were holding a turd instead of a glass, and his attempts at socialising suffered accordingly. Besides, Ray had a sense of humour and even Arthur's closest friends could never have accused him of possessing such a thing.

Charlie Fitzgibbon, the national secretary of the Waterside Workers Federation, was another Hawke ally. An ACTU vice-president, his voice was always raised in defence of Hawke and, while Charlie's voice wasn't the biggest, the respect it commanded assured that it was often heeded. The ACTU executive remained a very handy base of Hawke loyalty, despite the inroads the Left had made into it.

In Victoria, the party machine was so dominated by the orthodox Hawke-hating Left that talking to them was a complete waste of time. Bill Hartley, possibly the only man Hawke hated at that stage, still retained very considerable influence. His team, with people such as George Crawford of the Plumbers Union and Jean McLean, repeatedly made statements at national conferences that inflamed debate and turned Hawke into an unguided incendiary device. Hartley's hardline anti-Israeli position would send Hawke, the great defender of the state of Israel, absolutely berserk. Several attempts to expel Hartley were considered, but were usually abandoned when somebody lost courage. It took us until 1986 to get rid of him from the party and given that he had cost the ALP so dearly in electoral terms for almost three decades, this was far too late.

However, 1970 intervention into the Victorian branch had given a ray of hope that the Left's domination might be broken,

As a baby with Mum and Dad

My parents Peg and Fred

My father as he appeared as secretary-treasurer in 1967 on his how to vote ticket for the Postal Workers Union ballot.

Escorting Christine McLachlan to the school dance.

First Holy Communion

Queensland holiday 1960

Above, Christmas, and below outside our house in Kogarah, the proud owner of a rather large Malvern Star which I won in a raffle. As you can see, pretty much a standard fifties childhood.

AMALGAMATED POSTAL WORKERS' UNION
1967 ELECTION

Australian Labor Party

THE ONLY LABOR TICKET

REMINDER: HAVE YOU VOTED?

Hon. G. WHITLAM
Federal Labor Leader

F. J. (Fred) RICHARDSON
Secretary-Treasurer
N.S.W. Branch
Re-elect Him
(Member Monterey Branch A.L.P.)

Elect The Richardson Team

D. P. (Des) ROCHFORT
Assistant-Secretary N.S.W. Branch
Elected for term 1965-1969
(Member Central Executive A.L.P.)
says . . .
I strongly recommend to members that they vote exactly as indicated on this genuine A.L.P. "How-to-Vote"

VOTE A.L.P.
Keep Your Union Clean,
Strong and Progressive
UNITE YOUR UNION
by
Voting Exactly as Indicated Inside

T. A. (Tom) McLACHLAN
State President
N.S.W. Branch
Re-elect Him
(Member Manly Branch A.L.P.)

KEEP COMMUNISM OUT OF OUR UNION — VOTE FOR THE RICHARDSON TEAM

Follow Exactly this How-to-Vote Ticket. Mark Your Ballot Paper with an X — as shown Below — Do Not Use Figures

VOTE ONLY FOR THE REQUIRED NUMBER OF CANDIDATES; OTHERWISE YOUR VOTE WILL BE INFORMAL

PRESIDENT
McCaighy, H.
Lynch, J. N.
☒ McLACHLAN, T. A.

VICE-PRESIDENTS (2 required)
Dark, K. L.
☒ SAINT, A. W. R.
☒ JOHNSON, A. R. (Tingha)
McCaighy, H.
Griffiths, E. J.
Coughlin, M.
Reasbeck, L.
Hopkinson, L.

SECRETARY-TREASURER
Brook, K.
☒ RICHARDSON, F. J.
Dowdell, A. A.

ORGANISERS (3 required)
Harrison, E.
☒ CASSIDY, D. (Doug)
Skelton, L.
Underhill, N. J.
☒ BARNEY, Des
Ashe, B.
Carey, B. T.
Brook, K.
☒ EVANS, P. J. (Peter)

ELEVEN DELEGATES TO A.L.P. CONFERENCE
☒ McLACHLAN, T. A.
☒ SULLIVAN, J. W. R.
Underhill, N. J.
Brook, K.
☒ CASSIDY, D.
Dark, K. L.
Coughlin, M.
McCaighy, H.
☒ O'CONNOR, A. J.
Finneran, J. N.
☒ JOHNSON, A. R.
☒ HASTIE, N.
Harrison, E.
Dowdell, A. A.
☒ MUSTO, Thomas J.
☒ ROCHFORT, D. P.
Berg, R. R.
Porter, A.
Sharp, G.
Skelton, L.
Ashe, B.
Stenning, S.
Hopkinson, L.
Oram, A. R.
☒ BARNEY, Des
Lindsay, P. A.
Fitzgerald, J. L.
Smythe, E. W.
☒ STANDEN, G.
☒ LUXFORD, D. (Des)

TWO ALTERNATE DELEGATES TO A.L.P. CONFERENCE
Skelton, L.
☒ GILKS, K.
Sharp, G.
☒ MICKLEWRIGHT, M.

FIVE DELEGATES TO N.S.W. TRADES AND LABOR COUNCIL
☒ LUXFORD, D. (Des)
Finneran, J. N.
Lynch, J. N.
Ashe, B.
Poulton, F.
Lindsay, P. A.
Green, R.
Fitzgerald, J. L.
Wrigley, F.
☒ JOHNSON, A. R.
☒ HERRING, D. J.
☒ STANDEN, G.
☒ BROWN, C. (Peter)
McCumstie, A.
Walters, N.

TWO ALTERNATE DELEGATES TO N.S.W. TRADES AND LABOR COUNCIL
☒ COUGHLIN, M.
Phillips, B.
Hammond, L.
☒ UNDERHILL, N. J.

THREE DELEGATES TO A.C.T.U. CONGRESS
Hodges, L.
Johnson, A. R.
Dowdell, A. A.
Cassidy, D.
Lynch, J. N.
☒ MUSTO, Thomas J.
Stenning, S.
McCaighy, H.
☒ HERRING, D. J.
☒ SULLIVAN, J. W. R.

THREE REPRESENTATIVES ON STATE EXECUTIVE LINESMEN'S GROUP
Vodicka, J.
☒ HASTIE, N.
Sharp, G.
☒ HOPKINSON, L.
☒ O'CONNOR, A. (MICK)
Eades, K. H.
Berg, R. R.
Cosgrove, J.
Algie, R.

ONE REPRESENTATIVE ON PROMOTION APPEALS LINES GROUP
Kemp, D. K.
☒ McGRATH, M.

THREE DEPUTY REPRESENTATIVES ON PROMOTION APPEALS LINES GROUP
☒ HOPKINSON, L.
Cosgrove, J.
☒ STAKER, F.
☒ CHURCH, J.

THE RICHARDSON TEAM supports these Candidates for Federal positions and Competent Representation on the Federal Executive and Annual Conference of the Union.

FEDERAL POSITIONS

GENERAL PRESIDENT
Downard, Alan C.
☒ WATERS, F. J.

GENERAL VICE-PRESIDENT (One required)
Allen, D. J.
Hopkinson, L. W.
☒ CASSIDY, D.
Ashe, B.

ASSISTANT GENERAL SECRETARY-TREASURER
Kelly, D. P.
☒ O'GRADY, William

COUNCILLOR ON FEDERAL EXECUTIVE
Brook, K.
☒ RICHARDSON, F. J.
Dowdell, A. A.

ALTERNATE COUNCILLOR ON FEDERAL EXECUTIVE
Cassidy, D.
Lynch, J. N.
Skelton, L.
☒ ROCHFORT, D. P.

TWO DELEGATES TO ANNUAL CONFERENCE
Sharp, G.
Hammond, L.
Dowdell, A. A.
☒ RICHARDSON, F. J.
Cassidy, D.
Lynch, J. N.
☒ McLACHLAN, T. A.
McCaighy, H.

TWO ALTERNATE DELEGATES TO ANNUAL CONFERENCE
☒ ROCHFORT, D. P.
Reasbeck, L.
Underhill, N. J.
☒ BARNEY, Des
Coughlin, M.
Algie, R.

VOTE LABOR

A. R. (Tingha) JOHNSON
Mail Officer, Vice-President N.S.W. Branch
(Vice-President Enmore Sub-Branch A.L.P.)
Re-elect Him

P. J. (Peter) EVANS
Line Foreman
Candidate for State Organiser
(Member Wollongong Branch A.L.P.)
Elect Him

DES BARNEY
Motor Driver
Candidate for State Organiser
(Member Haberfield Branch A.L.P.)
Elect Him

Don't be a Personality Voter; Vote this Ticket in its Entirety — UNION BALLOT, 1967
KEEP OUT EXTREMISTS FROM THE LEFT AND FROM THE RIGHT
DON'T DELAY — VOTE TODAY — Your Vote Is Vital — Post It Now — Ballot Closes 12 Noon Thursday, September 21st, 1967

The front and inside of my father's election ticket for the Postal Workers Union. The inside of the ticket shows the rampant fear of communists, 'fellow travellers' and the Left that was a feature of unionism then.

My first date with my wife Cheryl. Typically, it was a Labor Party ball.

The start of Whitlam's 1972 election campaign and I was thrilled to be involved. It was the first time we could really smell victory and the atmosphere was unforgettable. From left to right: Tom Uren, myself, Allan Mulder, Michael Whelan, John Kerin, Gough Whitlam, Kerry Sibraa.

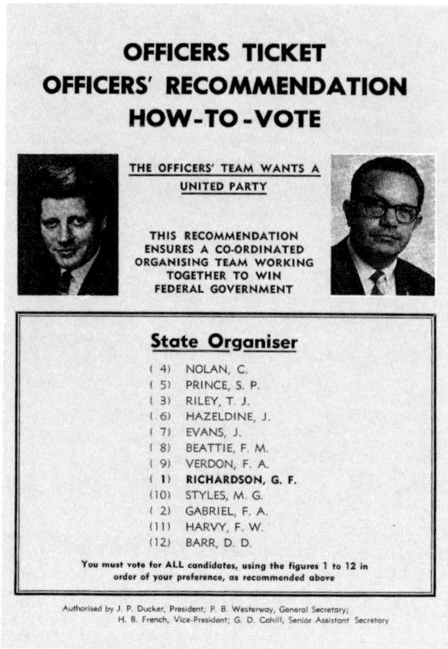

OFFICERS TICKET
OFFICERS' RECOMMENDATION
HOW-TO-VOTE

THE OFFICERS' TEAM WANTS A UNITED PARTY

THIS RECOMMENDATION ENSURES A CO-ORDINATED ORGANISING TEAM WORKING TOGETHER TO WIN FEDERAL GOVERNMENT

State Organiser

(4) NOLAN, C.
(5) PRINCE, S. P.
(3) RILEY, T. J.
(6) HAZELDINE, J.
(7) EVANS, J.
(8) BEATTIE, F. M.
(9) VERDON, F. A.
(1) **RICHARDSON, G. F.**
(10) STYLES, M. G.
(2) GABRIEL, F. A.
(11) HARVY, F. W.
(12) BARR, D. D.

You must vote for ALL candidates, using the figures 1 to 12 in order of your preference, as recommended above

Authorised by J. P. Ducker, President; P. B. Westerway, General Secretary; H. B. French, Vice-President; G. D. Cahill, Senior Assistant Secretary

My election as NSW state organiser in 1971 was the beginning of my move up the ladder. Pictured on the ticket are John Ducker, president (right), and Peter Westerway, general secretary (left).

At home on the day I was elected general secretary in 1976.

Neville Wran (centre back) was elected Premier in 1976 under the slogan 'Wran's Our Man', and revitalised Labor's image in NSW. Left to right: Fred Waller, Mayor of Randwick, Pat Hills, Stella Hills, Bob Carr, Jill Wran, Neville Wran, Lionel Bowen MP*, Pauline Johnson, John Johnson, Bill Haig* MP*, Edna Rodner* MLC*, Clare Bowen.*

At a fundraiser in 1977 at the Carrington Hotel, Katoomba with Bob Hawke then head of the ACTU, and Ross Free MP.

With Paul and Anita Keating in 1977. My first meeting with Paul Keating was in 1967. The thing I noticed about him was that you could bounce rocks off him and only the rocks would be hurt. On the far left is Vince Martin MP, *and John Ducker is on the right.*

Receiving a cheque for the 1977 election campaign with Gough Whitlam and David Combe. It was hard to rekindle the optimism of 1972.

Bill Hayden became leader in 1977. Although a clever man with an excellent intellect and numerous political skills, he lacked the essential qualities for strong leadership. Bob Hawke with just those skills was waiting in the wings.

and electoral success in Victoria became a possibility. First Jean Melzer and then a moderate called Bill Tracy ('Cyclone' to his friends) became the secretary of the party and Peter Redlich, a well known Melbourne lawyer and Hawke ally who was later Hawke's legal adviser, even served a term as president. As the 1970s drew to a close, however, 'Cyclone' had blown out and the Victorian branch was returning to hard Left domination. Bob Hogg became the secretary of the Victorian branch in 1976, which most of us saw as a leap backwards. We were wrong about that. Hogg can take most of the credit for making John Cain the Leader of the Opposition and for then running campaigns well enough to win a historic victory in 1982. Whatever may be said about Cain's government now, its election in 1982 meant a great deal to Labor's chances federally.

Hawke's factional colleagues in Victoria still regarded the New South Wales Right with great suspicion. The Labor Unity team (as the Victorian Right were known) had been built around the Storemen and Packers Union, which was led by Bill Landeryou, a pugnacious man whose reputation for toughness was well known to us all. During the 1975 election campaign, Landeryou and one of his burly union officials flew around Australia making sure that Hawke was protected during the most highly charged campaign most of us had ever known. Landeryou was more prepared than many of his colleagues to embrace the New South Wales Right, and Hawke's campaign drew the two groups closer anyway.

By this time Robert Ray was emerging from the pack to take over as faction leader from Landeryou, who was heading into State Parliament. Robert is the hardest person I have known in politics and, given some of the people with whom I have mixed, that is really saying something. With brains to match his considerable bulk, his 1981 entry into the Senate made it possible to turn the campaign against Hayden into a real national alliance. I never doubted that Robert would be able to hold the line and to convince even the most troublesome of his mates that an alliance with the New South Wales Right was the sensible way to go.

By the time of the special national conference in 1981, the growing friendship between Ray and me, as well as the unifying factor of people from all states wanting to support Hawke, was making the task of national union easier. Now, however, we had to undergo an exercise in academic politics, as distinct from the practical sort.

This special conference had been called to examine the report of a committee, set up by the national executive, to examine our electoral failures over the past few years. After a long period of the gravest consideration, this high-powered committee determined that, if we had a bigger national conference and proper affirmative action rules, Labor could win elections. Of course, if they had just agreed to call on Hayden to resign and give Hawke his chance, a great deal of time and expense could have been saved. Still, many members of the Left and the (later) Centre Left were determined not to lose the chance for another conference. I have never understood why they like meetings so much. Judging by the number of times their factions have to meet in order to make any decision, even in time of crisis, this love of talking amounts to group therapy.

As such, I'm sure the 1981 conference lived up to the expectations of all those who wanted to talk for three days about why we couldn't win elections, without even mentioning the problem. Doubling the size of the national conference, of course, did nothing to improve the quality of its decision-making. In fact, because virtually every delegate is part of a factional caucus, you could have quadrupled the numbers with nil effect. As one who expects the party to make those kinds of decisions, occasionally I was irritated, but not to the point of despair. That was to come in the debate on affirmative action.

The need to get more women involved in a man's party in a man's profession was obvious. The most casual observer of any party gathering could see the gender bias, but the prescription being put forward to remedy the problem was in line with the worst excesses of mindless trends. I began to realise that something special was happening when every state delegation started putting in female proxies for the men who had been elected as delegates. And when people from all factions began to agree, the special nature of the occasion aroused suspicion. Speaker after speaker committed themselves to rules that, we were told, would guarantee that one-third of our parliamentary party representation would be female. Just which male members of the parliamentary parties would commit political harakiri to enable this remarkable change to occur was never stated.

Two brave souls were prepared to speak out against this nonsense—Bill Hayden and myself. During this debate, Bob Hawke sidled up to where I sat as part of the New South Wales delegation. This was not the cocky, aggressive, abrasive Bob Hawke whom I had come to know and love, but a subdued little man, his head bowed, his voice lowered. 'Mate, can I have a dispensation on this one?' he said. 'The sheilas are giving me a hard time.' What could I say to this pathetic plea? Given the fact that those who supported affirmative action were absolutely guaranteed victory, I could only nod sagely and sadly.

The amendment was duly carried, but the change in rules has had little or no effect on the percentage of women in state and federal Labor Party caucuses and is now once again on the party agenda. It has been used quite cunningly by the Left in Tasmania and the ACT to ensure greater representation at national conference, but it hasn't changed anything. The ratio of men to women in the House of Representatives on the Labor side is about twelve to one, and I cannot recall one member standing aside to assist the cause of getting more women into parliament. There is one woman in the Senate team from each state except Western Australia and the New South Wales Right now has two.

Of course, affirmative action programs have resulted in more women attending national conferences and in increasing their numbers on policy committees, and I have no quibble with this. But the memory of delegate after delegate assuring us of the historic breakthrough we were making has never left me. Sometimes the force of a trend is so strong that normally sensible delegates are swept along with it, but if deeds are ever to match words on issues such as these, compulsion must be used. And, though the Left were paying lip service to the affirmative action trend as hard as they could, they had no intention of backing their words with any action that would bring about the forced resignation of one of their parliamentary colleagues to allow a woman through.

The twelve months that passed between the special conference of 1981 and the next full conference the following year were not triumphant for Bob Hawke. In parliament his star failed to shine. Parliament was never his arena; his inability to dominate its proceedings was evident from the beginning, and Keating and Young continued to be the stormtroopers.

For reasons I could never quite fathom, the charm that had won over an entire nation had little effect on the Caucus. Perhaps Hawke's overnight abandonment of alcohol after the 1980 election inhibited him socially, or perhaps his new surroundings, which allowed for immediate scrutiny of every word uttered and yet failed to produce national media coverage, had a soporific effect on him. For a while, Hawke seemed to coast, and Caucus recruits to his cause were few and far between.

All political parties know how to waste time, but in 1981 the ALP brought this skill to the status of a fine art. Labor's failure to gain ascendancy in the opinion polls meant that talk of a Hawke challenge was bound to continue, and a sense of drift was pervading the Caucus.The only realistic course of action for myself and those I represented was to suck up to Bill Hayden as best we could, while waiting to see whether the Great White Hope would get a shot at the title. So I summoned up all my saliva and went to work. This was neither difficult nor particularly unpleasant as, much as he would have hated to admit it at the time, Hayden was in most respects a political conservative in Labor terms. In private he was witty and intelligent, so spending time with him was never a hardship.

In any case, no definite timetable had been set for a Hawke challenge; I had always envisaged that Hawke would have to sit back and bide his time. This was a forlorn hope, as patience has never been Hawke's long suit, and as 1982 began, it became obvious that Hawke's was running thin. However, there seemed little he could do to lift himself out of the Caucus ruck.

The New South Wales branch were concerned to remove the electoral baggage of the capital gains tax which, we were convinced, had cost Labor a real chance of victory in 1980. A good opportunity to make that change soon appeared. It was clear that a by-election would soon have to be called for the seat of Lowe, held by former prime minister William McMahon, who was shortly expected to retire and resign from the parliament. Lowe was one of the most marginal seats in the country; a swing of just over 1 per cent would see it change hands. This made a change in capital gains tax policy even more imperative and Hayden, sensing that the party needed a good result there as a prelude to a successful federal election campaign, was a willing ally.

However, Ralph Willis was pushing for even greater opposition to a capital gains tax, and to the consternation of him and his supporters, they found Hayden opposing it. They could only watch in horror as Hayden showed that he was more than prepared to challenge his own support base in pursuit of electoral success. Furthermore, as 1982 unfolded, Hayden acted in concert with the Right on a range of issues. I was never certain whether this demonstrated nobility and courage, or whether it showed fundamental faith in the capacity of the Left to hate the greater enemy.

Either way, the record is clear—Hayden had little in common with the Left politically and much more in common with us. Besides, early in 1982 he was supremely confident that he would maintain his Caucus lead over Hawke. The debate on the capital gains tax issue was quite a robust one, with the normally staid Ralph Willis quite prepared to criticise Hayden. But as the big guns did battle over a crucial policy issue, Hawke stayed silent.

Over the holiday period at the beginning of 1982, McMahon duly gave the scribes something to write about by announcing his intention of leaving politics. This gave me the opportunity to work closely with Hayden, making sure he understood that the New South Wales branch would do everything in its power to achieve a handsome victory at the forthcoming by-election. There is a hint in Paul Kelly's *The Hawke Ascendancy* that in some way Hawke was distressed at the co-operation achieved between Hayden and the New South Wales branch in the Lowe campaign. I have never known Hawke to be anything but desperate about the need for Labor to win (at least until Keating defeated him in Caucus), and while he might have been frustrated about what that co-operation could mean in the longer term, he campaigned enthusiastically in Lowe.

At the 1980 election, Labor's candidate in Lowe had been Jan Burnswoods, a left-wing teacher who had failed to reach great heights as a candidate but who retained the fierce loyalty of her faction. Hayden was unimpressed with her credentials, and his failure to insist on her right to be Labor's candidate again further strained his relations with the Left. It was obvious that Hayden had reached the win-at-all-costs position that most leaders find very early. Bearing that in mind, Keating and I were able to convince him pretty quickly that a rank-and-file preselection ballot should take place, even if it wasted precious days. The wait would be worthwhile because we were convinced that the preselection system championed by the Left would see Ms Burnswoods defeated by Michael Maher, state Member for Drummoyne, an electorate entirely within the boundaries of Lowe.

Michael Maher had a reputation in state politics as the perfect local member. He had the second highest recognition rating of any ALP state member, trailing only Michael Cleary, who had represented Australia in three sports as well as being a commentator on TV wrestling and a minister in the Wran government. Well known and well liked, and a very nice man, Michael Maher was a member of the old school who campaigned by attempting to know the name of every voter and the names of their dogs as well. His opponents within his own party could find no way of attacking him; even his political enemies in the Liberal Party all wanted to claim him as a friend. (Perhaps the real measure of just how popular Michael Maher had been was the swing of almost 20 per cent recorded against the Wran government when the Drummoyne by-election was held some months later.)

Maher was duly preselected for Lowe and, with a popular candidate and the capital gains monkey removed from his back, Hayden threw himself into the campaign with considerable gusto. The more obvious the signs of recession had become, the more difficult it was for Malcolm Fraser to claim the mantle of economic competence and, as the Whitlam government faded further in people's memories, it was easier for Hayden and Labor to dismiss the tag of economic mismanagement.

The result was never in doubt: an excellent campaign, a confident leader and an extremely popular candidate was an irresistible combination. A two-party-preferred swing of 9 per cent saw Labor hopes for federal victory rise, and Hayden's newfound confidence was bolstered even further.

I must now concede that in the weeks following the Lowe victory, no thought of a challenge to Hayden entered my mind; I could see no way for Hawke to become leader before the next election. The only real expectation I had was that Hayden would seize the chance to dominate Australian politics. With a prime minister on the defensive and a decisive by-election win under his belt, he could not have been presented with a better opportunity to establish the inevitability of a Labor victory.

The period after the Lowe by-election in March 1982 was absolutely critical for Hayden, being perhaps the only time after the 1980 election when there was no momentum behind the Hawke bandwagon. But at the very time when Hayden's leadership should have been invincible, he showed us once again why he couldn't feel safe in his job and how vulnerable he really was.

In June some American ships possibly carrying nuclear arms were about to visit Australia. Without consulting Lionel Bowen, his deputy and shadow minister for foreign affairs, Hayden announced that a Labor government would not permit US vessels carrying nuclear weapons to enter Australian ports.

I suspect he had two reasons for this. Firstly, he had been disappointing the Left for some time and, as John Cain had shown by telling Malcolm Fraser that Victoria would not accept ships carrying nuclear weapons, this was an issue dear to the Left. If Hayden could stand up to the mighty United States on an issue of such magnitude, the Left might forgive him his sins on capital gains. Besides—perhaps it was the last hangover of his days in the Left—Hayden had never been totally convinced about the US alliance. He and Bowen had opposed Australia's participation in a Sinai peacekeeping force and on issues such as B–52 bombers visiting Australia and the sovereignty of US bases on Australian soil, Hayden's commitment to the alliance was shown to be soft.

The independent Australian foreign policy that Hayden and Bowen had been carving out for the Labor Party would probably never have been viable in the electorate, but as long as it posed no threat to the US alliance it could be overlooked. This time, however, Hayden had gone too far, and the US State Department basically said that the ANZUS treaty would not be viable if Hayden's policy were enforced. The US policy of not saying whether or not vessels carried nuclear weapons would certainly not be changed to suit the Leader of the Opposition in Australia.

While hysterical anti-Americanism had been deeply embedded in the lunatic elements of the Socialist Left in Victoria and beyond, the party's Right and most of its Centre found the Hayden line unacceptable. An indication of this was that Lionel Bowen, until then the most loyal of deputies, was prepared to publicly dump on his leader. Having stretched the lexicon in search of words that sounded as anti-nuclear as possible but still allowed for visits of US ships, he was furious that his leader had changed the policy without any reference to him. Hayden's ineptitude was magnified by an ANZUS meeting in Canberra late in June that made a humiliating backdown imperative. When it came, the fallout for Hayden could best be described as nuclear. By publicly retreating from his position, he was seen to give way to American pressure and the demands of the ANZUS alliance, and he also enabled Malcolm Fraser to emerge as a strong leader.

The whole saga served to remind the Caucus and the party at large that Hayden lacked whatever it was we needed, but more importantly, it confirmed to an already wary electorate that he just couldn't be relied on. There was still no perception of Hayden as a winner, apart from the Lowe by-election and a Caucus victory or two. The polls, which never quite gave Labor the lead many felt it deserved as the economy jerked to a screaming halt and the Costigan Commission mauled Fraser by pointing to the phenomenal growth of tax avoidance, just weren't good for Bill Hayden.

The nuclear ships affair, of course, was grist for the Hawke mill. Talk of a challenge was again heard in the corridors, and while Hawke was still not wearing warpaint in public, he was definitely back on the warpath. Fairly chafing at the bit, in fact.

On 25 June, three days after Hayden's backdown, Hawke came to see me in my office in Sussex Street, Sydney, to let me know in no uncertain terms that his time had come. My period of rapprochement with Bill Hayden had not escaped his notice, but it was time to forget all that and get down to the business in hand. He had been encourged by his Melbourne coterie of supporters (Evans, Kelty, Crean, Holding, Ray and Landeryou) but he needed to cement the New South Wales alliance before announcing the challenge, since that state would provide most of the votes. I had already been informed by John Brown and Doug McClelland that many federal members in New South Wales were anxious for a challenge to take place as soon as possible, and I knew that they and their colleagues would vote for Hawke. But Paul Keating was never one to be led. Besides, he was quite certain that Hawke was doing poorly in Caucus and would certainly be defeated if a challenge were mounted against Hayden.

Keating's reading of Hawke's Caucus standing was, of course, highly subjective. At the age of thirty-eight, Keating had already been in parliament for thirteen years and he considered himself our best parliamentary performer, policy-maker, reader of public sentiment—and very definitely our best for the leadership. He had never liked Hawke and was less than enthralled when Hawke entered parliament in 1980. In private conversation he was already using phrases about Hawke that he would later make famous when challenging him for the top job: 'show pony', 'lightweight' and 'hasn't paid his dues' were used in every conversation. Clearly, Keating would be no pushover to convert.

I was very reluctant to commit support to Hawke until I was convinced that he would come close to victory, even if defeated. To be beaten badly would damage Hawke greatly, but I also feared what an angry and ascendant Hayden might do to New South Wales at the national executive. With Hawke it never really mattered how negative you were in refusing him; I doubt he ever left a room believing he had no chance of receiving support, despite the vehemence or certainty of his rejection. All I could do was to plead with him to be patient until the numbers became clearer. I was pretty naive in those days.

The plot thickened as the national conference loomed in July 1982. It was held at the Lakeside Hotel in Canberra, where room service could take one and a half hours to deliver a toasted sandwich and where the bar was conveniently located in the foyer in full view of the hotel entrance. (At the conference Robert Ray introduced a fake notice of motion to the effect that: 'A Labor government will ensure that a hotel is built on this site.') What business observers and members of the public must have thought about the way in which Labor luminaries conducted themselves in the bar still makes me shudder. This can be taken as a criticism of practically everybody; our public displays of drunken excess knew no factional or territorial boundaries. But whatever was happening in the bar was nothing to what was about to happen in the suites, the rooms and then the conference floor, as the party prepared for a public blood-letting the like of which had not been seen since the 1955 split.

Because of the ever-present spectre of a Hawke–Hayden showdown, the conference was always going to be tense. But add to that explosive mix a move to change the party's policy on the mining of uranium and we all knew that the bitterness that had existed for years would bubble over into the public arena. And because this was the most public of party arenas, with every single political journalist in Australia present plus an arsenal of cameras, the ugliness of the most bitter factional division ever seen at a national conference would be carried into every living room in the country.

The Left's passion about uranium was utterly genuine and, to me at least, utterly incomprehensible. Sure there was some hypocrisy on the Left, with the Miscellaneous Workers Union members mining the stuff, Transport Workers Union members getting it to the ports and Waterside Workers Union members loading it onto ships for export, but such people as Stewart West, Tom Uren, Gerry Hand and Jeannette McHugh seemed to consider the anti-uranium policy as precious as life itself. Their commitment, together with the unlikely conversion of Don Dunstan, had resulted in one of the most successful ambushes I had ever seen. Paul Keating, John Ducker and I had arrived at the 1977 conference in Perth to find that practically every delegate had been sewn up to vote for a complete ban on uranium mining, with no compensation to be paid to the mines that would be forced to close down.

This was a totally unrealistic policy, one that no Labor government could ever have implemented. Banks from all around the world who had backed these mines would never have stood for it, and Australia's international reputation as a reliable supplier of raw materials would have suffered grievous if not terminal damage. The wide-eyed idealism that produced this policy, however, was maintained with such conviction that by 1982 its architects and promoters were referring to it as 'traditional Labor policy', meaning that anyone who sought to change it could be considered a traitor to Labor's heritage. As the 1982 conference approached, idealism and realism were set for collision.

Hayden had already solved the capital gains problem and robbed Fraser of any chance to use that policy as an electoral weapon against Labor. His backdown on the ships issue had been the wrong way to continue this cleansing process, and so he chose a more enlightened way of ridding the party platform of what he saw as the last impediment to a successful election campaign. In the months leading up to the conference, he cautiously sounded out potential allies in changing the uranium policy to allow for mining and export. In May the national executive set up a subcommittee to examine the ramifications of a Labor government implementing its current uranium policy. Those in favour of change had a majority on the executive and gave themselves a majority on the committee.

Hayden was unflinching in taking the fight on this issue to the Left. Knowing how strongly Tom Uren, undoubtedly the most powerful Left parliamentarian of the time, was committed to retaining the platform as written, we admired Hayden's gutsy performance. He knew that in the corridors of the Lakeside Hawke was openly lobbying for support, but this in no way deterred him from staying the course. If he could ever have conveyed to the public the strength he showed in the lead-up to the conference, let alone at the conference itself, the opinion polls would certainly have recorded better results for him.

The issues of Hawke and uranium soon came into conflict, even though both Hawke and Hayden were supporting a more rational approach to uranium mining. Tom Uren was furious with Hayden about his attitude and began saying that the Left would switch to Hawke, the Left's Bob Hogg began to see the need for change in both uranium policy and the leadership and the Victorian Right looked like voting with the Left on uranium to protect their position in Victoria, where uranium was a much bigger issue than it was anywhere else.

During the conference, there was no doubt in Hawke's mind that Uren had turned and would bring the Left with him. Had he not been certain of this, he would never have moved as quickly as he did. Hawke's tendency to search desperately for approval or agreement in even the most negative of circumstances sometimes led him into grave error, but by the end of that fateful week both Bob Hogg and Paul Keating were able to confirm all that Hawke had claimed. I remained deeply sceptical, feeling that Uren had as much chance of delivering the Left for Hawke as Keating did of delivering the Right for Hayden.

Achieving a change in uranium policy was always going to be difficult, though I had hoped that Hayden's adoption of the cause would bring us enough delegates to ensure success. But when it came, that ray of hope arrived from the most unlikely of sources.

Bob Hogg, the secretary of the party's Victorian branch, had been a discovery of Bill Hartley's, and ten years earlier he would have been considered the most radical member in the most radical branch. However, being secretary had given him a taste for government; unlike Hartley, he graduated from the school of the Left that was comfortable in Opposition and came to believe that his job as secretary was to help Labor win. (Hartley had used his time as secretary in Victoria to do his very best to maintain Labor in Opposition and to keep control of the party.)

Hogg knew that the current uranium policy was untenable, and when he had come to that conclusion he showed courage, a commodity in very short supply when it came to the uranium debate. He drafted a resolution to allow Labor to let the existing mines continue. It didn't matter that the resolution contained internal inconsistencies, was nowhere near as clear as Hayden or any of the pro-change people wanted and was couched in anti-mining language, or that, as Stewart West said to Hogg: 'It's not even credible, mate.'

Credible or not, we grabbed the Hogg amendment with glee. Speech after speech was made in support of a resolution that gave every reason why uranium should not be mined or exported during the body of its wording, but contained an out at the end which could get us through an election.

Given that the hysteria about exporting uranium is dead in the party and is never mentioned now except in the loonier Left branches of the ACT—where, incidentally, Castro is still spoken of in heroic terms—it is difficult to imagine the agony that the party and individual delegates were going through. As a party we were determined to save the world from its own ignorance, and in hindsight the self-righteousness of our position was pretty preposterous. And now that the party is again debating this issue, it is interesting to watch the Left desperately trying to whip up an argument and failing dismally. A change in policy was absolutely vital for the South Australians and their pursuit of the massive investment required to develop the Roxby Downs deposit (then the biggest uranium mine in the world), so there was never much doubt about where most of them would stand.

For some, the dilemma was a bit different. The Victorian Right was under very heavy pressure from the Left. All kinds of threats had been made against preselections of Right members and their delegation of fifteen, including proxies, was to take a vote on their stance in the debate. This vote was going to be close and the Hawke push, about which the Victorian Right were so enthusiastic, proved to be a useful lever in ensuring that they made the right decision. The Victorian Right caucus had some pressure coming the other way. I made it perfectly clear in a meeting with Hawke, Holding and Crean that it would be a 'fucking outrage' if the Victorians decided to vote against the Hogg resolution, and that New South Wales would not support Hawke if this occurred. Evans, Holding and Crean were all personally committed to Hawke and always intended to do the right thing. With an eye to a future national alliance between the Victorians and ourselves, Robert Ray was another who worked to convince the more nervous of his colleagues to resist the Left line.

It has been suggested that John Cain and John Button were given dispensations to vote with the Left because we believed we had the numbers even without them, but this was not entirely true. John Button had come under enormous pressure, and we agreed with Hayden that no one could expect to put at risk his Senate preselection, which depended on support from the Left in order to increase our majority, even if it was a narrow one. It is interesting to note that in twenty years in the Senate, John Button never had the numbers to be selected in his own right. He always had to rely on the Left for preselection, but, on the occasions when the Left were proving fractious on the national executive, he occasionally resisted their threats and voted for the forces of truth and justice. (The Left rewarded Button by stripping him of his preselection in favour of John Halfpenny just four years later.) But I cannot think of a time, except during the uranium debate, when he allowed the ever-ready guns of the Left to influence his voting record on policy matters.

The position with John Cain was vastly different. I cannot recall that he ever approached us. Hawke, Keating and I (and I suspect Hayden as well) expected Cain to do what he always did—vote with the Left. And so he did. But this should not be interpreted to mean that Cain had any principled attachment to the anti-uranium cause. While he revelled in the cheers that the very large gallery at the national conference gave him, he took a different private position at the 1984 conference when the issue came up for debate again.

In 1984, there was also considerable controversy about a proposal to admit four right-wing unions that had been refused application by that bastion of democracy, the Victorian branch of the Labor Party. With that proposal causing great concern for the Left, Cain met three of us (Hawke, his chief adviser Peter Barron, and myself) in Hawke's suite at the Lakeside Hotel. Cain said he was quite prepared to vote for us in the uranium debate if we would agree to defer considering admitting two out of four unions. How he proposed to reconcile this position with his actions two years previously was never explained; the man who had accepted the extra loud applause in 1982 was more than prepared to sell out his supporters for a quick fix.

The 1982 conference debate on uranium saw the only division (that is, those voting for and against the resolution standing on opposite sides of the room and having their names called out in a bizarre rollcall) that I have experienced outside parliament. There are no divisions at ALP conferences because the votes are counted by tellers representing Right and Left and the opportunity for cheating is virtually nil. The reason for this one was presumably to 'shame' those of us who were voting for a change in policy by forcing us to publicly declare our vote. The heroes were applauded loudly by a group called MAUM (Movement Against Uranium Mining), who had managed to stack the gallery with their members, mainly distinguishable by their twisted and contorted mouths from which came a continuous torrent of abuse. Some were dressed in the 'grim reaper' outfits which our AIDS advertising some years later would make infamous. The villains were hissed and booed and, in at least one case, spat upon. Most of us were proud to vote the way we did, so there was no thought of backtracking and definitely no embarrassment. With the national executive virtually certain to restore the preselection of anyone disendorsed because of the uranium vote, the division was a real fizzer in terms of fulfilling its purpose.

The Hogg amendment had been carried by 53 votes to 46, and for years afterwards people at branch meetings said that we had abandoned traditional Labor policy by our change on uranium mining. While this totally ignored the fact that even Jim Cairns tried to sell uranium while he was a Labor minister and that opposition to uranium mining was only in our platform for five of our hundred years, it demonstrated the almost spiritual quality with which this issue was imbued.

The real victim of the debate, and of the conference, was Bob Hogg. He was jeered, hissed and booed by the Left much more than were any of us on the Right, and his long-time friendship with Gerry Hand was shattered, never to be renewed. The Left have never forgiven those who stray from the true path, and Hogg had strayed on an issue that the Left turned into holy writ. He had supported Hawke, aided and abetted Uren's temporary conversion and had got up the trifecta by drafting the uranium resolution; he had therefore committed all the crimes for which the Left equivalent of capital punishment was the prescribed penalty.

I was not close to Bob Hogg—at the time I didn't like him much at all—but I couldn't help feeling sorry for him. He was banished from the Left and as far as factions are concerned, he has wandered across the Labor landscape a stateless soul. Never trusted by the Right, never again trusted by the Left, unable to embrace the Centre Left once it was formed, Hogg never again found a home. It is a high price to pay for taking a principled stand and being right, but politics has never been the arena where anyone should seek justice. However, though Hogg must have been badly wounded in personal terms, the episode did very little harm to his career. Credited as the mastermind behind the Cain victory in Victoria in April 1982, he joined Hawke's staff in March 1983 and moved on to become ALP national secretary a few years later.

The uranium debate was held on Thursday 8 July. For the whole of the conference week the corridors were simply places where huddles of Hawke and Hayden supporters could corner journalists and push their line. The polls kept giving Hayden more and more bad news, particularly because they were still responding to his handling of the nuclear ships issue. During the conference, with so many policy issues to be decided, Hayden couldn't take his eye off the ball. But Hawke had no such constraints and, apart from the odd foray onto the conference floor, he spent most of his time talking up a challenge.

Hawke was delighted at the publication of every poll and began to believe that they would make a real difference in Caucus. He had little understanding of Caucus; his own membership of it for nearly two years had yielded few friends. Uren's promises were only serving to feed this false bravado and Hawke, within earshot of Alan Ramsey, not only Hayden's press secretary but a real Hawke hater, was selling his cause to anyone who would listen. He wasn't doing too well with the journalists: whatever popularity he was later to enjoy with the press gallery, at the time Hawke had relatively few friends there, and those who were prepared to support him had been largely delivered by Mick Young. Gallery leaders such as Peter Bowers and Laurie Oakes were unabashed Hayden supporters. But while the Hawke charm wasn't working on them, the public was coming to him in droves.

Hayden could only sit and watch this challenge to his authority, but his team couldn't allow the undermining of their leader to continue, and it was certain that Hayden would call the Caucus together at the earliest possible opportunity to settle the matter of the leadership. He called the meeting for Friday 16 July.

It was all happening too fast; nobody, especially Paul Keating, really thought that Hawke could win at this stage. On the Friday of the conference, a week before the challenge was due to take place, Keating and I left early and drove back to Sydney. From the moment Hayden had announced his intention to call the Caucus together to bring about the challenge, Paul Keating had been a worried man. He was in a no-win situation. Either he stuck with most of his colleagues in New South Wales and voted for Hawke, thus postponing his own leadership ambitions for a considerable period of time, or he voted with Hayden and risked alienating the base he would need if he ever wanted to challenge for the top job. The long trip to Sydney was not a joyous one, and at its end it was the last time I saw Keating at his Condell Park home. He didn't see much more of it either, as it happened.

Hundreds of party activists spent the weekend on the telephone, issuing clarion calls for their comrades to come to the aid of their champion. The champion, however, delayed ringing Caucus colleagues until the Tuesday, almost five days after Hayden announced the ballot. Telecom's profits soared as we all sought to gain an advantage. No one was ringing the Left; the conference had barely finished before they met and a big majority declared for Hayden. This did not mean that Uren had sold out or committed an act of treachery. He had simply misread his own standing and the depth of hatred that so many of his colleagues felt towards Hawke. Uren couldn't convince the Left even to seriously entertain the idea of supporting Hawke, and the Victorian Left, led by Brian Howe, were never going to move from Hayden. With so many Left members anxious to scuttle the Hawke campaign, the details of the Left meeting leaked quickly. There is no such thing as a secret in the Left, and in this case that was even truer than usual. By Saturday morning we were in no doubt about their position.

A negotiating committee was set up to talk to both candidates, but this was no more than a sop to Uren and the press. Taking the optimistic line, Hawke continued to believe that he had a real chance of winning the Left by convincing the committee that he should be supported. Keating and I couldn't accept this for a moment.

As the Keating fingers cramped up in reaction to all the dialling, the numbers were starting to add up—the wrong way. On the Sunday night, Keating rang to tell me that Hawke couldn't win. He could get Hawke to within one or two votes, but then, if he applied his formula of reducing by 15 per cent the number of those who had solemnly promised support, it was clear that Hayden had enough votes to hang on.

On the morning of Tuesday 13 July, like a million other Australians, I awoke to the dulcet tones of John Halfpenny bucketing Bob Hawke on ABC Radio's 'AM' program. Halfpenny had resigned from the Communist Party of Australia only a short time before, and he and Laurie Carmichael (probably Australia's most prominent communist at the time) opened up the argument that had destroyed Labor's electoral chances for the past thirty years—that of 'outside influence', a beautifully emotive phrase used to conjure up the dungeons of the Lubianka and the screams of its unfortunate guests. This proved useful in influencing Keating's position, but it is also worth noting that these two old war horses of the Left proved uniquely consistent. While almost all of their Left colleagues were embracing Hawke and slamming Keating as evil incarnate a decade later, Halfpenny and Carmichael chose to make public their support of Keating. But the well publicised death of communism meant that the second time around, 'outside influence' was a phrase long out of vogue.

The same day saw the Left formalise what had been obvious at their meeting on the previous Friday—they would caucus and vote for Hayden.

The game was over for the time being, and at least from my point of view, the real job at hand had altered. We now had to make sure that Hawke got close enough to make another challenge possible, and for that to happen we needed a declaration of support from a very reluctant Keating. Hawke and his troops—Mick Young, Gareth Evans and Clyde Holding—jumped on a plane and headed for Sydney. For Keating, the imagery could not have been better; the supplicants were on their way. While at this stage he had not conceded to me, let alone to Hawke, that he would come on board, I'm quite sure he knew there was no escape.

The meeting that took place at the Boulevard Hotel was a classic. The Boulevard was owned by Frank Lowy and John Saunders, close friends of Hawke's and prominent members of the Jewish community, who were constantly agitating on Hawke's behalf. Sydney had more upmarket hotels, but it was unthinkable that Hawke would stay anywhere else. He always took the Lady Nelson suite, which had the advantage of two entrances in different corridors. When necessary, one visitor could be pushed out one door and another admitted through the front without ever seeing each other. It always struck me as an unusual place in which to determine Labor's leadership.

Over bacon and eggs (this was prior to Hawke's unfortunate conversion to the Pritikin diet), the hard politicking began. There was little time for pleasantries. The most amusing part of the morning was the attempt by Evans and Holding to convince Keating that his count .was wrong. Keating is the best counter the Labor Party has ever seen, bar none, and his two accusers wouldn't rank in the first thousand. Mick Young was uncharacteristically quiet, not even joining this attempt. He and Keating had never been close and, no mean counter himself, he probably shared Keating's disdain for the exercise.

Hawke rammed home his view that many in New South Wales would come with him anyway. All that was needed was Keating's declaration for a flood—or even a vital trickle—of defections to begin from the Hayden camp. Never one to miss an opportunity, Keating repeated his anger at the challenge being called without proper consultation, and the foolishness of relying on Uren to deliver the Left. He was honest enough to tell the Hawke team that victory would prove elusive, no matter what he did. The argument lasted for several hours before Keating finally conceded. Evans, forever the master drafter, put pen to paper, and Keating prepared to deliver his dictum.

He and I took the lift down to the foyer and, as soon as the doors opened, he was enveloped by the waiting throng of journalists. Whatever doubts were going through his mind, I saw Keating the warrior in action. With just a hint of menace, he told the journalists that the interference by Halfpenny and Carmichael had been 'totally unacceptable'. Further, the New South Wales Right would be supporting Hawke. He never flinched, and a casual observer would have thought this was what he had wanted all along. It was a magnificent performance and I couldn't help thinking that if ever the opportunity presented itself, Keating would make a great leader. Every time I fought with him over the next ten years I banished this thought from my mind, but it had a nasty habit of finding its way home from exile.

After his press conference, Keating and I strolled through East Sydney to Mario's restaurant in Stanley Street. As usual, he ate a little and I ate a lot. His mood was sombre. Keating knew Hawke would be defeated, and he knew he would bear the brunt of the aftermath. His forebodings were correct; having leapt into the fray, he tried everything he knew to turn the doubtful Caucus members, but to no avail.

On Thursday, the evening before the ballot, Richard Carleton told the ABC TV audience on 'This Day Tonight' that he had spoken to an unnamed leading Hawke supporter who had said: 'Hawke definitely has the numbers, I think'. As the author of this comment, I can now reveal that, while I exuded the confidence expected of me, I wanted Hawke to know that in New South Wales we had the gravest doubts about the whole exercise. On the morning before the ballot, Keating rang me and confirmed all my worst fears, though he said it would be a very close vote.

The meeting began at 11 on Friday morning. Hayden immediately declared the leadership vacant without debate, and the vote took place quickly. The result was 42 to 37 in favour of Hayden. He looked to John Button and asked him whether his five-vote majority was enough to stave off a further challenge. Button shook his head. However, in the euphoria of the moment, Hayden could convince himself that Hawke was permanently routed, and Hawke could promise eternal allegiance.

I was not despondent. The final tally left me in no doubt that Hawke could come again.

CHAPTER 3

Hawke

For about three months, Hayden and Hawke conducted a chummy relationship, beginning with a press conference in which they gave one of those false displays of bonhomie that all politicians must endure from time to time. This new rapprochement defied gravity and the rules of common sense, but eventually the combination of polls and ambition caused its demise.

The published polls, and Labor's own, confirmed that Labor was in the lead, as was to be expected in the middle of a recession. And in the Budget session of parliament, Labor was also boosted by the release of the Costigan Report on 27 July. The Royal Commission, set up under Frank Costigan QC to investigate the Ships Painters and Dockers Union, had done what all Royal Commissions do: got sidetracked. Set up to embarrass Labor by demonstrating that an affiliated union was run by gangsters, it had stumbled across a trail of tax evasion it was determined to follow.

Costigan's first report stunned Malcolm Fraser because it amounted to a damning condemnation of his government's administration of the tax laws. In parliament, it was for Labor almost what the Khemlani affair had been for the Liberals in 1975: Hayden, Keating, Dawkins and Young had a field day every day that the parliament sat, and Labor's star continued to rise.

But Hayden's ratings remained in the doldrums, and once again Hawke was getting restless. He kept whispering that Labor should be much further in front, and that it would be if the party made him leader. I made it very clear to him that no challenge would be supported in the future if he failed to consult widely about its timing. Keating and I remained adamant that no challenge was possible at this time, and the whispers never grew too loud.

The Flinders by-election put Hayden to the test once again. In October, Liberal deputy leader Phillip Lynch retired, a move that virtually nobody had expected or predicted. The contest for his seat of Flinders, on the outskirts of Melbourne and on the shores of Port Phillip Bay, would serve as an experiment for Fraser, who had been toying with the idea of an early election. Of course, it was also an opportunity for us to test the water.

Just as the Flinders campaign got under way, however, Hawke let his ambition overrule his judgment; on Michael Schildberger's ABC Radio program in Melbourne he opened up leadership speculation once again. None of us knew anything of this preemptive strike before it happened, and the party was in no mood to wear this brand of adventurism at the beginning of a tough and vital campaign. Even Hawke acknowledged that he had made a major error, but the public accepted it as an indiscretion that could be forgiven in any man of destiny. As far as the party was concerned, within a few days Hawke had sent a letter to all Caucus members, reassuring them of his honourable intention to serve his leader dutifully until the next election, and telling them that he had never intended to reopen the leadership issue.

No one who read that letter—and certainly not the person who signed it—ever believed that one word of it was sincere, but it was the kind of comment that, once put on the record, could be used to help turn black into white. The lessons I learned from this exercise came in very handy when the plot had been reversed and Hawke was the victim in 1991.

On Sunday 7 November, Hawke and I had dinner in Sydney's Coachman restaurant in the inner-city suburb of Redfern. Hawke thought it was time to introduce me to his closest friend Sir Peter Abeles.

There was a genuine affection between these two men that surprised me, even though Hawke had repeatedly talked about Abeles, who was his mentor and adviser on almost every aspect of his life. I had believed that the rich and the wealthy, particularly those knighted by Sir Robert Askin, the former Liberal premier of New South Wales, were most unlikely companions for Labor heavyweights. My ingrained reverse snobbery, which still affects too many in the Labor Party, took a battering on that Saturday night. Abeles had ideas and would obviously delight in Hawke's coming to power. He remained Hawke's real backstop throughout his prime ministership.

While many sought to draw sinister conclusions about this relationship, particularly as the Cabinet often discussed issues in which Abeles would have an abiding interest, I could see nothing improper. If every minister had to absent himself from Cabinet debates in which the interest of a close friend might be involved, Cabinet meetings would be left without a quorum. When tariffs were being discussed, those of us with close friends in affected unions would be the first to leave the room. But debates on industry, media, resource development, health and virtually every other subject involve ministers who have the interests of friends at stake.

Hawke was attracted to the US system of Cabinet members being appointed from outside the parliament and frequently mused about what a great transport minister Sir Peter would make. Of course, to make Cabinet appointments of this kind you would have to be president, a constitutional change with which Hawke would have been very comfortable indeed.

I did not come away from the Coachman empty-handed that evening. Within a few days a very senior executive of Ansett visited me and presented me with a pass to enter Ansett managers' lounges whenever I flew. These were places where politicians, pop stars and captains of industry mingled. I was pretty chuffed with this gesture and, while the price was no doubt cheap, I was even more indebted to Bob Hawke.

The phenomenal Hawke luck, which failed to run out for another nine years, was in great shape at this time. His stupidity in opening leadership speculation at the start of a hard and vital by-election campaign was quickly forgotten as first Fraser, then Hayden, did his best to erase its memory.

Fraser suggested a wages pause, the kind of concept previously confined to the octogenarian membership of the Melbourne Club. Instead of being immediately rejected by a hostile nation, it was seriously considered, even in Labor circles. The Labor premiers, who were already struggling to find sufficient revenue to fund their programs in the middle of a recession, couldn't bring themselves to reject the idea out of hand, and even the ACTU had its share of people prepared at least to consider the Fraser initiative. Federal Labor, already committed to negotiating a prices and incomes accord with the ACTU and having difficulty in finalising any firm arrangement, were caught totally unprepared by this new suggestion and tried desperately to reach agreement.

Hayden knew that Flinders would be hard to win. We were already aware from preliminary research that Labor candidate Rogan Ward, a local government politician and real estate agent, was decidedly unpopular in the electorate. Hayden believed the Victorian Labor Unity faction ran a dud candidate on purpose, giving Hawke supporters more ammunition, which in fact was not true: Ward had been endorsed several months before the by-election was announced. We had triumphed in Lowe with a swing of 9 per cent, but the local candidate had been excellent. Flinders was right on the borderline of the normal anti-government swing of 6 per cent in a by-election, where one of only 5.5 per cent was needed for a Labor victory. If we couldn't get the normal by-election swing and win the seat, the party would draw the obvious conclusion—Hayden couldn't win a general election. Rumours persisted that Fraser was desperate for an early election, so Hayden could afford no errors. While the polls continually showed Labor to be three or four points in front, the nagging doubts about Hayden's capacity to win meant that every test was vital, every one final.

Hawke was in the happy position of watching from the sidelines and playing the game only at the moment of his choosing. Now his years at the ACTU were about to pay a handsome dividend.

At a series of meetings between Hayden, Bowen, Willis and Hawke from the Labor Party and members of the ACTU executive,

Hayden couldn't come to any agreement on the prices and incomes accord, so no joint response to Fraser's wage pause idea was forthcoming. Hawke sometimes described these meetings before they occurred. The three senior officers of the ACTU—Cliff Dolan, Bill Kelty and Simon Crean—were all committed to the Hawke cause, and the consultations with Hawke took place before the official party meetings. Hawke was absolutely confident that the ACTU would not come to any quick agreement over the accord or the pause. But he could never have imagined just how badly Hayden would handle these problems.

Just two days before the by-election, and after yet another stalemate, Hayden gave a press conference to highlight his differences with the union movement. While agreement with the union movement was always derided by Fraser (and has been by every other Liberal leader, past and present) and considered as abject cowardice before union power, any disagreement is either an example of inability to negotiate and compromise or, even worse, an example of weak leadership that even the base will not follow. This truth was proven yet again: virtually every paper in the country gave Hayden a terrible hiding.

To make matters worse, Labor premiers Wran, Cain and Bannon refused to rule out some sort of deal with Fraser over the wages pause. Hayden's inability to produce a deal made him look weak and reinforced the opinions being formed over his negotiations with the ACTU.

In the end, the ACTU told the government they would recommend to unions that they consider a wage pause, on certain conditions: that the pause be limited to six months with some sort of catch-up period to follow, that all parties consent to return to centralised wage fixing and that the government would move towards a more expansionist economic policy—otherwise the ACTU said it would continue its campaign for a 6 per cent wage rise.

Hayden was furious that the ACTU had outflanked him and that the following day the headlines shouted the ACTU's willingness to negotiate with the federal government on a wages pause. No matter that the states would have been crazy to rule out a deal with the national government that controlled the purse strings. The King Midas-in-reverse touch that Hayden developed over this period ensured that not even a hint of reasonable excuse for failure found its way into print.

At the by-election for Flinders, there was a 3.5 per cent swing to Labor. This was a truly dismal performance; at the height of a recession, Labor's swing should have been in double figures. Every senior person in the party knew it, though not all could bring themselves to say so. But Labor candidates all over Australia began to make their feelings known, and every rank-and-file member of the party just about screamed it from the rooftops.

In New South Wales the candidates in marginal seats in particular gave full vent to their feelings at a candidates' seminar. Nobody from the Left opposed their position, and not from lack of courage. No matter how hard Gietzelt or Uren wanted to hang onto the anti-Hawke line, no matter how much Carmichael and Halfpenny wanted to describe Hawke's failings to an ever-diminishing audience, the rank-and-file Left had gotten the message. Left candidates are just as susceptible as anyone else to candidates' disease—they wanted to win, and that meant a change of leader.

Unfortunately, the swing to Labor was just enough to convince Hayden that he had some pulling power, and nowhere near enough to convince anybody else. The expressions of loyal support for Hayden that had flowed into my office during the July leadership challenge were not in evidence this time. Without the unions or the party, no leader can survive.

It was time to turn up the temperature.

This time, however, we all believed that Hayden would do the decent thing and resign. A friend had to deliver the message and help him make that decision, and he had no better friend than John Button. Button was pivotal because he had been close to Hayden in every fight he ever fought; he wasn't just a trusted ally, but a psychological prop. If that prop were whisked away, Hayden would fold. Over the next few weeks, I repeatedly tried to commit Button to persuading Hayden that he ought to resign. In any event, after the Flinders by-election Button knew the game was up. He didn't like it, but he knew it.

During December a number of useless national campaign committee meetings were held, useless because they could do nothing about the issue central to any successful campaign: the viability of the leader. As talk moved from early elections to shadow cabinet reshuffles and to new and better campaign management systems, the real issue was constantly avoided.

Just before Christmas at a two-day meeting of the committee, I told them I would handle the biggest campaign issue by changing leaders. I also told those assembled that Hayden's staff, and one member in particular, was an impediment to a Labor victory. Alan Ramsey, now of the *Sydney Morning Herald* but at the time press secretary to Bill Hayden, had antagonised almost the entire press gallery. Murdoch journalists were complaining that there was no room for them in itineraries, as any journalist with the temerity to criticise Hayden found a permanent 'no room at the inn' sign waiting whenever he or she needed to speak to the leader. From Paul Kelly and Lauric Oakes onwards, the list of journalists complaining bitterly had grown to alarming lengths.

Hayden put no real effort into defending Ramsey beyond indicating that loyalty dictated he could not abandon him. He said he would speak to Ramsey about his performance, and all would be well. No apparent improvement could be detected from that day, and Ramsey has made sure I have paid a very high price for my comments about him ever since.

At least these meetings gave me extra opportunities to talk to Button, and I took full advantage of them. Button, who was about to depart for a well earned Christmas break in Fiji, agreed to approach Hayden as soon as he returned and to attempt to persuade him to resign. The news that Button had finally agreed to this ensured that Hawke would get the present he wanted—if not for Christmas, then very shortly afterwards.

In the days that followed that meeting with Button, I managed to make a mistake that could have jeopardised the whole operation. At a supposedly off-the-record lunch with a former workmate who had gone on to become a journalist, I blabbed out the story of Button's commitment. Perhaps it is true that long-term friendship can never survive journalism, and from the moment that I saw this story in the *Financial Review*, my friendship with the person concerned was never the same again. I was terrified that Button would read the story and back away from his agreed course. At the time I didn't know he had taken the kind of holiday that eliminates the possibility of hearing a radio or seeing television or a newspaper. He didn't find out about the story until he was on the plane returning to Australia, and he stuck to his word. Hayden, of course, did not take too kindly to the story and set about digging in for a fight.

We still needed to make an important convert to our cause. While Lionel Bowen was unlikely to deliver numbers in a formal party room challenge, or no more than a couple, as deputy leader he would be very useful indeed in making Hayden agree to step down voluntarily. Though as a professional of many years' standing he knew that the Flinders result spelled trouble, Bowen was never going to be easy to convince; he had been particularly scathing about Hawke during the first challenge, perhaps because he had leadership ambitions of his own.

If not part of the factional machinations, Bowen was a popular individual who had spies everywhere. One had been present when I took Hawke to a meeting of the New South Wales Right's most trusted younger souls in early December. At that meeting I had said quite openly that Labor could not win the next election with Hayden as leader, and someone left the meeting and rang Bowen immediately with the story. (This person was not difficult to identify and he was never sent another invitation.) Bowen unhesitatingly told Hayden and the story soon found its way into the press. But Keating did spend some time talking to Bowen, and by the time Button was heading off to see Hayden in early January 1983, Keating reported that Bowen was coming closer and closer to throwing in his lot with us.

So Button and Bowen were talking together, a very good sign. By the time I got on a plane for a two-week trip to Israel with Cheryl, Bob and Helena Carr, John and Pauline Johnson and John and Gail Macbean (John Macbean was secretary of the Labour Council and president of the party), I had no doubt that change was coming soon. Button was also talking to other traditional Hayden supporters and, by the middle of January when we returned, the whole party seemed to be buzzing with the expectation that the agony would soon be over. Only Hayden couldn't hear the buzz, and his position hardened against resignation.

On 20 January, yet another meeting of the national campaign committee was being held. Just before it took place, Hawke, Mick Young, Stephen Loosley and I returned to the Lady Nelson suite at the Boulevard Hotel for a last meeting, over the now-obligatory plotters' meal of bacon and eggs. On the previous day the shadow cabinet had finalised the economic policy the party would take to the next election. Its release was imminent, but Hawke wanted it delayed at any cost until he had been installed as leader. We decided that the only way to get the necessary delay was to ask the ACTU to demand of the party that details of the accord could not be released until the special unions' conference had approved them—and this would not happen for at least another month. Hawke immediately rang Cliff Dolan, his friend of many years' standing, and informed him of the delay and the preferred method of achieving it. Dolan readily agreed and Mick Young went to the campaign committee meeting knowing that he would throw a very large spanner into the campaign works.

Young's announcement at the meeting sent Hayden scurrying to see Dolan in a futile attempt to get him to back down. The ACTU officers, who had been pretty well handpicked by Hawke, repaid whatever debts they owed him in one hit. Hayden obviously knew he was being handled, but having once abused the ACTU executive for having misrepresented his position on the wages pause in November, and having suffered grievous damage for having done so, there was nothing he could do about it. The decision stood, allowing the victorious Hawke to announce the policy a few weeks later—when he had become leader and before the special unions' conference was held.

By the end of January the tension was getting too much for all of us, and we couldn't wait any longer. I told Button that there had been significant changes in party and Caucus opinion over the past few months, which could no longer be bottled up. If Hayden refused to resign in the next few days—the logical time being the shadow cabinet meeting set down for Brisbane on 3 February—the more drastic course of a formal challenge would have to be taken.

Button then wrote to Hayden, putting in black and white all the things it was difficult for friend to say to friend. He told him he remained personally loyal to him, but he believed Hayden would not win the election. He said his own ultimate loyalty was to the party, and he believed Hayden should stand down as leader.

Though in July the party had been divided over the leadership issue, the majority view was in favour of a change. The party would have a much better chance electorally under Hawke, and we were desperate to win the coming election.

At the end of the Australia Day weekend Button flew to Brisbane where he had his final meeting with Hayden. Hayden's conditions for relinquishing the leadership were set down—they included non-victimisation of his most prominent supporters, a guarantee that he would become shadow foreign minister and foreign minister if Hawke won the election and the option of becoming Australian High Commissioner to London. Within a few hours, Hawke had agreed to the lot.

In one of the supreme ironies of Australian political history, Malcolm Fraser went to Yarralumla on Thursday 3 February 1983 to call an early double dissolution election on 5 March, sure that a quick campaign would lock Hayden into the Labor leadership. In an almost divinely inspired demonstration of Hawke's luck, the Governor-General Sir Ninian Stephen was too busy to see Fraser in the morning, and by the time Fraser received the Governor-General's consent at 4.55pm, the situation was very different.

At an ALP executive meeting in Brisbane at 11.40am, Bill Hayden resigned as leader of the Labor Party. Apart from his remark that a 'drover's dog' would be capable of winning the forthcoming election, he behaved with commendable restraint. He ended with: 'As recently as Sunday I was still determined to fight the matter out, but it was increasingly clear to me that if I did I would be guaranteeing great damage to my own party and the return of the Fraser government at the cost of my own personal interest, and I'm afraid my motivation goes beyond that.'

When people are faced with impending doom or acknowledging humiliating defeat, it is quite extraordinary how they can almost always find hitherto unknown reserves of dignity. As well as Bill Hayden in 1983, Paul Keating in mid 1991, John Howard in 1987 and Bob Hawke in December 1991 all demonstrated this. All were vintage performances, exuding dignity and generosity, when resort to a variation on the time-honoured phrase 'youse can all get nicked' would best sum up the speaker's feelings.

When, on the night of his accession to the leadership Hawke

denied to ABC TV's Richard Carleton that he had 'blood on his hands', this served to underline his ability to absolve himself of responsibility for any acts that history might not record as wholly desirable. Being prepared to deny Hayden the right to announce the economic policy he had laboured over for so long was certainly the correct political decision for the challenger—it was also one of the most ruthless political acts I have ever witnessed. There was a smell of blood about it.

Some six months earlier, he had conspired with Bob McMullan and me to ensure the release of poll information damaging to Hayden. Right down to the timing during a national executive meeting when I would ask McMullan to pass on the details of Rod Cameron's latest research, Hawke was involved. When stories were to be leaked to journalists, he often chose which one would be the beneficiary of the leak. So, while much of the blood was seen to be on my hands, you may rest assured that I was in the best of company.

From the moment he heard that Bill Hayden had resigned, Malcolm Fraser must have felt like a prize dill. Things could have so easily swung the other way for him. If Bill Hayden had listened to the last-minute advice of Laurie Oakes to resist the pressure to get him to resign because Fraser was about to call an election and changing leaders during a campaign would have been well-nigh impossible, Fraser's decision might well have been considered a stroke of political genius. Sometimes the line between being a mug and being a hero is gossamer-thin.

It should be noted that Laurie Oakes proved to be a pretty loyal friend to Hayden. The fact that as late as February 1983 he was still ringing him and urging him to fight should be seen in context. At about the time of the national conference in July 1982, Oakes had picked up the story that Tom Uren had been talking to Bob Hogg about switching the Left's support to Bob Hawke. He decided to base a 'Hayden leadership in danger' story on it for Channel Ten. A couple of members of Hayden's staff saw it and told Hayden what Oakes had said. Hayden sought Oakes out, angrily demanding his source for this, and Oakes reiterated that Uren was moving. Hayden didn't believe him and Oakes was in the doghouse until Hayden checked out the story and found out he was right.

The whole campaign added to my growing suspect reputation. As Hayden recounted stories that I had admitted lying to him on certain occasions and exaggerated some of the moves I had made on others, I became infamous outside New South Wales as well as within, and the list of my enemies reached gargantuan proportions. But I point out here that I was responsible for very few Caucus or shadow cabinet members actually changing their minds and switching allegiance from Hayden to Hawke.

While I would submit that the few for whom I was responsible had a devastating impact, it should be understood that managing a challenge is about much more than that. Many people contributed to the Hawke success. His Victorian colleagues always kept up the pressure on us, Paul Keating ensured that he got close enough in the July challenge to remain a threat, Bob McMullan was a close and willing ally throughout, and at the end John Button, Hayden's close friend, proved pivotal in getting the baton to change hands peacefully.

Part 3

THE HAWKE GOVERNMENT

CHAPTER 1

The Path to Victory

As soon as Hayden resigned, the Hawke juggernaut began to roll. By lunchtime on Saturday 5 February, we were a national campaign committee deciding upon the slogan and themes we would be using for the election campaign. The slogan 'Bringing Australia Together' was adopted, and the campaign themes were Reconciliation, Recovery and Reconstruction. The meeting also agreed on a TV advertisement featuring a challenge to Malcolm Fraser to debate Hawke. If Fraser refused, of course, we could say he was afraid.

This was a great ad for its time, but it became a problem later. As the 1980s wore on, it became apparent that a debate was not always a good idea from the incumbent's point of view. It's always a good idea for a challenger, and with American presidents debating all comers in every presidential race, what began as a tendency or trend has become firm political practice.

Labor showed how easy it is to run a campaign when you know you are going to win. There was no need for gimmickry or even great drama; at the campaign opening, all that was necessary was a speech from Hawke that promised hope, and that's exactly what was delivered.

Admittedly, the Liberals made it easy for us; in fact, the 1983 election marked the beginning of a decade of hopeless campaigning by them. They had emerged from the 1970s with campaign reputations high. While it might be reasonable to claim that anyone could have beaten Whitlam in 1975, particularly when Labor's slogan was 'Shame, Fraser, Shame', the Liberal campaign was slick and it certainly contributed to making Fraser's majority as large as possible. In 1977 the Liberals used advertisements seeking to convince the electorate that tax indexation would put more money into their pockets. The ad, showing a hand clutching a fistful of dollars, was crass and unsophisticated. It was also incredibly effective because it did what all good political or other advertising will do: offer viewers something with which they could identify, in this case greed. No matter that tax indexation was withdrawn a few months after the election: the image of that fist grabbing the dollars assured Fraser of a better-than-expected result. Again, in 1980, the Liberals were flexible enough to capitalise on a Labor error. In the last two weeks of that campaign, they belted Labor over the potential of a capital gains tax and just managed to beat Hayden.

So by 1983 Labor had come to expect that the Liberals would put up some sort of fight at least. But from the first time I heard that the Liberals' campaign slogan would be 'We're Not Waiting for the World', I knew we had the chance not just to beat Fraser but to slaughter him.

Malcolm Fraser's daring gambit of calling an early election to ensure that he was fighting Hayden, not Hawke, was now a sick joke. Every day the headlines of every newspaper, even those that had been traditionally anti-Labor, showed a triumphant Hawke striding into battle against a Prime Minister who seemed less prepared than we did, even though it was he who had called the election.

Whatever the Liberals' polling showed or whatever strengths they had were never apparent to me. Their advertising couldn't seem to develop a theme, let alone stick to it, and the four elections since 1983 have shown that little has changed. It now seems that nobody much in the Liberal Party, from the full-time officials to the parliamentary leadership and their staff, to the pollsters and advertisers, has any idea where mainstream Australia is and what it is thinking about. With each new election I have expected to see some kind of dramatic improvement, but it just doesn't happen.

With a dud slogan, not one memorable advertisement and a complete lack of new policies to break the recession, as well as being faced with a highly popular Opposition leader, February 1983 must have been a hard month for the Liberal Party. Nothing could give their campaign momentum and their policy speech that opened the campaign served only to set them back further. Not even the Liberal faithful could put their hearts into it, and Fraser's performance was one of the worst in living memory. They were facing a vibrant and resurgent Labor Party determined to win at all costs, one with a leader who gave every appearance of knowing precisely what Australia thought.

Hawke had still not been elected by Caucus, but it was as if he had always been leader. No Labor leader has ever had an easier accession to the throne; from the very beginning it was obvious that there was no room for anyone else in the campaign. Hawke was the totally dominant figure from beginning to end and shadow ministers were mainly relegated to the dingy town halls of a hundred electorates around the country. There was only one star in the spotlight—and didn't he love it.

The polls put Hawke in front, the business community queued up to promise support and in the streets and shopping centres the people of Australia couldn't get enough of him. If Fraser ventured into a public place, barely a ripple went through the crowd; a Hawke appearance provoked a tidal wave of interest. This phenomenon was still evident in Hawke's last year in office: in 1983, it was new, exciting and absolutely compelling.

Of course there were problems, and Hawke had contributed to some of them. On the night of Hayden's resignation, Hawke faced Richard Carleton on the ABC's '7.30 Report' and Carleton asked the immortal question: 'Mr Hawke, what does it feel like to have blood on your hands?' In an instant the Hawke temper was at flashpoint, and the result made headlines. It was probably conscience that made him react so badly, because there was no doubt that he had more blood on him than the entire stage at the end of *Hamlet*. To change the metaphor, while Hawke might not have fired all the bullets, he knew when every shot was to be fired, by whom and to what effect. Every blow that had rained down on Hayden for the previous six months had been reported to Hawke in advance.

Of course, this is not the way Hawke looked at it. Now he was on top he could embrace the man who had formerly been his enemy. The emotional side of Hawke—that characteristic that has always made him forgive and embrace every enemy in an attempt to assuage his own guilt—meant that he had access to the sacrament of confession without having to adopt the discipline of religion. Embracing Hayden meant that all the hard, tough decisions of the previous twelve months could be forgiven, and then some. The Hawke memory would be reprogrammed so that many of these incidents were erased. Whole chunks of political history simply ceased to exist in the Hawke psyche. He was clean. He was ready.

But not everything could be forgotten all the time. Whenever Hayden was around there were unpleasant reminders of truths that wouldn't go away. At that very first campaign meeting, Malcolm Macfie from the party's then advertising agency began to tell us all how great it was that at last we had a product we could sell. With exquisite timing, Hayden entered the room at precisely this point. A pall of guilt hung over the room for several minutes before the business of winning quickly re-established itself.

While Hayden's senior staff either stayed with him or drifted off to wherever displaced staffers go, some of the junior staff simply moved over to Hawke. Geoff Walsh, a former journalist who had been working with Bob McMullan at Labor Party headquarters, joined him immediately. I insisted that Hawke take Peter Barron on board as senior adviser. Hawke knew Barron from the latter's days as a journalist in the Canberra gallery, but had had little to do with him for a number of years. Barron had been working with Neville Wran and both Wran and I regarded him as the best campaign brain in the business. His instincts were superb, his antennae acute. Whatever difficulties Walsh might have had with a stranger being put in over him were quickly forgotten, and the two of them combined to give Hawke first-class advice.

Given that Peter Barron is my closest friend I can be accused of bias in his favour, but the record speaks for itself. Even today his advice is sought by prime ministers and would-be Labor premiers. However, it is worth noting that Hawke hardly knew Barron, agreeing to take him on simply because I insisted. Geoff Walsh was also wary of the Barron appointment, but like all smart operators he, too, could see that it was for the best.

When we added Bob Hogg, then secretary of the Victorian ALP, the staff looked formidable indeed. While Barron, Walsh and Hogg were later dubbed the Manchu Court by a frustrated Paul Keating, they formed the best team of campaigners I had ever seen. Hawke would be brought back to earth as often as necessary, and those policies that were likely to cost us votes were to be put under the microscope to be modified and diluted whenever necessary.

Labor would have a new way of campaigning called playing to win. When the campaign team was added to Bob McMullan at the ALP's national office and a team of dedicated officials around the states, Labor quickly took on an invincible appearance. And, while appearance might not be everything, it counted for a great deal when faced with a confused and clearly rattled government who had no idea how to stop the Hawke juggernaut.

The first policy meeting showed the calibre of the new Hawke advisory team. Present were Barron and Walsh, as well as Ralph Willis, Paul Keating and John Langmore (now a federal MP), who was then a member of Willis's staff. Tax policy was high on the agenda. The ALP had a policy of increasing taxes for all those on incomes of $60 000 and above. Given that the Fraser government already had these tax rates at more than 60 cents in the dollar, such an increase was of dubious economic merit, let alone plain political common sense: Barron insisted that these plans had to be thrown out. Hawke, he said, must campaign free of the old suspicions of high-taxing Labor governments, particularly as Hayden had refused to put down the capital gains tax during the 1980 campaign. Hawke had to be different, a leader for everyone. Willis was sceptical, Langmore antagonistic, Keating supportive. The decision was quickly made, and very early Barron had asserted that he was a force to be reckoned with.

The primacy of the Hawke leadership was established. He became known as someone who could ditch any policy he didn't like. This meant that there was little room for bit players.

Leadership is always stressed by both sides in political campaigns, and leaders dominate campaigns, but on this occasion the dominance was total. Keating, Willis and everyone else was ignored as photographers clambered all over each other to get the best Hawke angle and crowds clamoured to see their hero. At the launch of the party's economic policy at the Wentworth Hotel, the press conference was held jointly by Hawke and Keating, but Hawke fielded every question.

After only three days on the road with Hawke, Peter Barron rang me, utterly convinced that we could not lose. The first public rally of the campaign had just been held in a Launceston theatre, chaired by former Whitlam minister Ken Wriedt. A huge crowd turned up and Hawke was determined to give them a great performance. Unfortunately, Hawke usually equated greatness with length. Fully aware of this, Barron had arranged to signal to Hawke by running his hand over his throat when forty minutes had passed. This was duly done, but Barron and a host of other staffers he subsequently sent down the theatre aisles were totally ignored.

Finally after seventy-five minutes Hawke finished to sustained applause from the crowd who had stayed right to the end. After Ken Wriedt had thanked him, Hawke got up and gave them a second burst. He drew on Mao's exhortation to the people that if every citizen got ten of his friends to kill ten flies each, China would have no more flies. Hawke said that if everybody in the audience spoke to ten of their friends, there would be no more Fraser. The effectiveness of this suggestion can be gauged from the fact that there are still plenty of flies in China, but Malcolm Fraser has long since disappeared from politics.

Having given Launceston the benefit of his wisdom in such copious detail, Hawke knew he should return to Tasmania later in the campaign. So he dutifully returned to the island state, this time to favour the good citizens of Hobart with his presence and views. Hawke spoke from 12.15pm until 2pm. Lunchtime workers flocked to hear him, taking it in shifts according to their lunch hours.

All this talk, all this effort, all this adulation had absolutely no effect in Tasmania. Labor failed to win a single seat. In fact, except for Denison which Duncan Kerr won for Labor in 1987, seats in Tasmania were always beyond our reach in the 1980s. The Whitlam legacy, particularly the effect of heavy tariff cuts on local industry, lasted long after the great man had gone.

Any Hawke appearance in any electorate in any state was guaranteed to attract thousands of people. This drawing capacity, previously matched only by Whitlam in his heyday, continued for the best part of a decade. Australia loved Hawke: he was never going to lose that election. That, of course, was the reason why he was the leader. The national leader of the ALP is the party's most important position. Premiers and Leaders of the Opposition can all claim their places on the ladder of the Labor hierarchy, but the top rung can only be occupied by the Leader of the Federal Parliamentary Labor Party, as our Rules affectionately describe the position.

Even in 1983, some people in the party worried about the cult of the personality as against the promotion of party policies. This ignores the fact that many voters place their faith in an individual; if they like or respect the leader he or she will get their vote. The only time a modern party will want to concentrate on policy and seek to prevent the leader's profile from dominating the campaign is when the opponent looks more popular.

Leadership is everything in a campaign. Sure the campaign itself must go well, your policies must be saleable, discipline must hold and it helps if you've got a Fightback to shoot down or a remote aristocrat like Fraser to fight, but in the end if the people won't cop your leader you won't win.

So Hayden's remark that a drover's dog could have won in 1983 probably isn't accurate. Hayden himself had a first-rate intellect but, for whatever reasons of weakness in his presentation, he just couldn't convince Australia to like or respect him enough. On the other hand, the Hawke of 1983 was everything that the Australia of 1983 wanted.

The glamour of the leader shouldn't be underestimated either. Any party member lucky enough to have met our party gods will always be able to tell you how and when he or she met Whitlam or Hawke or Keating. It is a moment to be treasured and remembered. I recall the first time I met Whitlam. It was in 1972, a mere shaking of the hand that Gough would not have remembered five minutes later, but I never forgot it.

It was Whitlam, indeed, who proved to the Labor Party the real value of a leader who had all the attributes needed to win. Labor needs leaders who have the same capacity to inspire. When they come along the incumbent must understand that nobody holds a mortgage on Labor's leadership. When the new messiah has arrived the incumbent should gracefully retire: if not, he should be dragged down.

The campaign was surprisingly sedate as its inevitable conclusion drew near. It was the other side who panicked. The only memorable thing that Fraser said during the entire campaign was that people would be better off taking their money out of the banks and putting it under their beds, so Labor wouldn't steal it to pay for their extravagant election promises. He made this announcement at a Melbourne rally; Hawke was nearby at the time, having morning tea with John Cain. Richard Farmer, the journalist who worked on many Labor campaigns and a great admirer of Hawke's, swiftly came back with a suitable retort: 'He's getting a bit desperate, isn't he? You can't put your money under the bed because that's where the communists are.'

When Hawke delivered the line on the six o'clock news, the damage to Fraser was devastating. For the first time, Labor had made him look like a fool. Though in politics people can laugh with you, you can never afford to have them laugh at you. The 'Reds under the bed' joke rolled on and over any hopes the Liberals might have had. Two days later, when Hawke visited Radio 2MMM in Sydney, a bed was set up in the foyer of the station with bottles of Grange Hermitage stacked under it.

The only mistake our side made in the campaign came from Paul Keating. On Sydney radio's John Laws show, he said he couldn't be sure the Accord would work. Hawke was travelling in Queensland at the time and didn't find out what his shadow Treasurer had said until 6pm, when ABC journalist Russell Barton told Geoff Walsh. Peter Barron rang Keating, who was apparently very upset at his performance. Not upset enough to apologise mind you—that upset he has never been. Hawke didn't go feral. His simple reply to the media: 'Paul doesn't understand this like I do', gave an inkling of his dominance and confidence.

Our efforts to hose down the problem received great assistance from a wholly unexpected source. The next morning Andrew

Peacock played down Keating's comments for us by saying you could never be sure that anything will turn out the way you'd like it. By losing this golden opportunity to hammer Labor, Peacock demonstrated that his hatred of Fraser knew no bounds. Though common enough in politics, as it is in love and life, hatred is supposedly set aside during election campaigns while the greater enemy is being fought. But for some, the personal transcends the political; the greater enemy will always be the personal one, not the opposing party. By the extraordinary lengths to which he went to damage Fraser and then in later years John Howard, Peacock demonstrated his membership of this group.

I have to say that the Hawke and Keating governments have been especially fortunate in avoiding this kind of unpleasantness. Retired ministers, defeated preselection candidates and disgruntled backbenchers have generally refrained from bucketing their party and supporting our opponents during election campaigns. Government, it seems, is too precious to the modern Labor Party to be put at risk cheaply.

But the most notable feature of the campaign had little to do with politics and everything to do with the fickle nature of the elements in our beautiful but harsh land. The Ash Wednesday fires in mid February 1983 destroyed more than 2000 homes, 300 000 hectares of land and killed seventy-five Australians. The disaster was on such a scale that any attempt to campaign was immediately dismissed; despite the fact that Labor's campaign opening took place on the day when the fires really turned nasty, we stopped campaigning for two full days. And rather than visit the fires themselves, which might have looked like campaigning under the guise of compassion, Hawke merely visited the centres where the victims and evacuees were being looked after. Malcolm Fraser observed the same rules: for two days in the middle of an election campaign all politicking ceased. Hawke was a man of real compassion: politicians need to look compassionate, of course, but in Hawke's case the compassion was always real.

So, for the first time in nearly a decade, Labor had someone to cheer and something to cheer about. The campaign really hadn't mattered much, the decision to change leaders made it almost irrelevant and its result inevitable. And when the great day came—5 March 1983—the 4 per cent swing to Labor and the 25-seat majority were just about what all those with three-figure IQs expected. It was the night Labor was accepted by a majority of Australians; it was the night when those who considered themselves born to rule were humbled and humiliated. Having endured too many wakes when yet another electoral hiding had been dished out to us, we were happy to know that Labor people everywhere were rejoicing.

When Hawke entered the tally room towards the end of the night, the roar from the crowd was as great as any I had ever heard. Only a few hundred people can fit into the tally room, but what they lacked in numbers they made up for in volume. Bob and Hazel, with Geoff Walsh bringing up the rear, got the deafening reception they deserved, and people stood and cheered in a million homes across the country.

In the movie *The Candidate*, Robert Redford's character—a political novice managed by a shrewd operator who defeats an older, more experienced incumbent—asks the moment his victory is declared: 'What do I do now?' There was no way Bob Hawke would have the same doubts. We had waited a long time. We were ready.

CHAPTER 2

Dividing the Spoils

Whoever said winning isn't everything can't have won very often.

The 1983 election result was the one we had waited for all our lives. We savoured the glorious moment when Hawke claimed victory, and from thousands of homes and hundreds of victory parties we cheered as we had never cheered before. But the highlight was provided not by Hawke, but by Malcolm Fraser. The quivering lips of the Prime Minister when he conceded defeat from Melbourne's Southern Cross Hotel got an even bigger cheer. The Labor Party had not forgotten the events of 1975, and if vengeance could not be wreaked on Kerr, it certainly had been on his henchmen. There was no residual goodwill for Fraser. This cold, unfeeling patrician had long been an object of scorn and hatred for us all. For those lucky enough to have videos, those quivering lips were recorded for posterity, replayed again and again on the night and dragged out for years afterwards whenever Labor people gathered.

The reception given to Hawke when he entered the Caucus room on his first day as prime minister defined what winning means to everyone. Those who only months earlier had sworn to oppose him with every breath they took stood and applauded just as enthusiastically as those who had been with him. Winning heals and nurtures, forgives and forgets, encourages and emboldens. God, it's good!

This was my first Caucus meeting. I had just been elected a senator, largely because I didn't have anywhere else to go. I couldn't stay in the ALP office forever, I fancied myself as a speaker, I was closer to Hawke than probably anyone else so it seemed like the thing to do at the time. When you've done everything you can do in one job, you look for a change. I changed. I went to the Senate with no plans for a long-term career and an earnest hope that this job would keep me interested and off the streets.

The division of the spoils was the first task, and it was never going to be as difficult as some might have imagined. The euphoria of victory for the historic losers had been enough to cut through the ageless hatreds of the worst of the factional warriors, and those already ensconced had an obvious advantage. The shadow ministry expected to emerge from the shadow. There was some incongruity in this, since Hayden had managed to have many of his closest supporters elected over the previous few years and a hard core of Hawke opponents, who came on board only when they could fight no longer, found themselves with a walk-up start for jobs that few Labor representatives could claim ever to have occupied.

As the shadow ministry was to be elected en masse, there was never likely to be any discord from their point of view. For the most part, this was not such a bad thing. Unlike those elected in 1972 after the Whitlam win, time servers were few and far between. Most were unaffected by too many years in frustration at the impotence of Opposition and were still fresh enough to perform. Hayden's term as Opposition leader had been good for policy development and shadow ministers were accustomed to hard work. Most had demonstrated sufficient competence: they wouldn't let the party down.

The factions were not fully organised in the Caucus, except for the Left, though the others had been battling it out in the state branch structures for decades. The Hayden–Hawke battles had created a de facto Centre grouping and the New South Wales and Victorian Right, having co-operated closely for the previous couple of years, were a much more cohesive force than before. The Left were able to overcome their worst suspicions of a Hawke government dominated by the Right because they were getting something: Brian Howe, then seen as the new leader of the Left, was included as a new minister.

Returned to a Labor ministry after eight years was that warrior of the Left Tom Uren. Oddly enough this created little angst: Uren had never engendered personal hatred in the federal Caucus and the only time I can recall him making a thorough bastard of himself was away from any Caucus frolics. Some years earlier he had fought the construction of Parramatta stadium and its chief proponent, his colleague and federal Member for Parramatta John Brown. The building of the stadium was an issue of little consequence: an overwhelming majority of residents in Sydney's western suburbs supported the building of this much-needed facility. But New South Wales state council and conference meetings of the party were subjected to some pretty torrid debates on this seemingly unimportant issue because Tom wouldn't let go. That he would have allowed such a minor issue to be beaten up into a major Left/Right brawl is both a measure of his commitment to urban environmental issues and his inability to understand when to fight to the death and when an honourable defeat is more than sufficient to prove to yourself and your constituency that you tried. John Brown and Neville Wran had their way: the stadium was built and is now an accepted part of life in Sydney's west.

It took me some time to understand what was special about Tom Uren. He was supposed to be the Right's great foe and yet both Keating and Leo McLeay, our hardest men, had an affection for him they had for no one else on the Left. Tom Uren was an honourable opponent—quite unlike some of those with whom he associated.

Arthur Gietzelt, having served the Left for years as the hardest of the Cold War warriors, was finally to become a minister. My, what the gumshoes at ASIO would have thought about this! I bet apoplexy was the order of the day, and for many days thereafter. I've never had the opportunity of asking anyone from this august organisation exactly what they did think of this and some other ministerial appointments; perhaps my question is better left unasked.

John Dawkins, Peter Walsh, Neal Blewett, John Button and Don Grimes had been the heart and soul of the pro-Hayden forces. Perhaps because a ballot had been averted by Hayden's decision to resign as leader, perhaps also because in the aftermath of victory any move against them would have been considered small-minded, there was no attempt to remove the loyal shadows. Those Hayden supporters in the shadow ministry, combined with the Hawke team such as Keating, Evans and Young (I never did work out how to categorise Bowen) went on to form the nucleus of successive Cabinets for the next decade.

For the Right there were a few opportunities as well. Clyde Holding, the long-suffering Leader of the Opposition in the Victorian Parliament through all the years the Victorian branch was dominated by George Crawford and Bill Hartley, made a successful transition to the national stage. Having been a passionate advocate for Hawke during the leadership struggles of the previous few years, Holding was an obvious candidate for higher honours. I don't know what goes on at Melbourne's Richmond Town Hall but I do know that, whatever is taught, the school produces graduates who are tough, resourceful and utterly ruthless.

Kim Beazley would be promoted to follow in his father's footsteps, keeping a family tradition alive. Beazley lives for politics: aside from his obsessive interest in the American Civil War, it is practically his only interest in life. Had he been defeated in the 1993 election, a seat would have been found for him somewhere in Australia. Just how many of us are 'institutionalised' by political life I don't know: now I suppose I have the opportunity to discover this for myself.

The New South Wales Right now saw the promotion of some of its most favoured sons. Although John Brown was disliked and disparaged by many in the Hayden camp and the Left, his close friendship with Hawke made his elevation a certainty. But generally there wasn't a great deal of discipline in the New South Wales Right team just after the election.

Michael Maher, the quietly spoken victor of the Lowe by-election in 1982, thought it was his turn. Barry Cohen, the jovial survivor of several close electoral calls since he was first elected in 1969, fancied himself and his chances. Bill Morrison who, like Uren, had been a minister in the Whitlam government, had been re-elected in St George after five years in the wilderness and had certainly not returned to be a backbencher. In trying to reach a consensus about who should be on the how-to-vote card to be supported by a big majority of the Caucus, a choice had to be made between Cohen and Morrison.

The Hayden forces didn't much like either, but decided that the decision should be left with New South Wales. Keating, whom Morrison had beaten to a ministry by one vote in 1972, forcing Keating to wait almost three years until a very brief stint as a minister just before the sacking in 1975, understandably preferred Cohen. I canvassed most of my colleagues and discovered little enthusiasm for either. Although I had just been elected myself, I was in a position to decide. I liked Cohen, he had a sense of humour and it didn't seem fair that he should be dumped for someone who had been out of the parliament for some time. I conveyed my view to the relevant parties and so ensured Cohen's victory.

Morrison and Maher both insisted on running in the ballot, and I made sure they received sufficient votes to avoid being totally humiliated, though it was obvious they would poll badly. (I doubt the same thing would happen today: contrary to popular opinion in the press gallery, threatening or heavying anyone is not necessary. Just pointing out how silly people look when they get a single-figure number of supporters from more than a hundred votes cast is usually enough.) I knew Morrison wouldn't stay round on the backbench for long, but simply hoped that we could persuade him to remain until the next election. We just managed to do this.

Barry Cohen learned nothing from these events. In circumstances I will explain later, he ran against the ticket in 1987 and received only seven votes. Over the years, several people have tried to break the factional control of Caucus ballots and have failed. In 1983, even before the Centre and the Right had set up formal factions, the defiance of a few individuals didn't matter once arrangements had been entered into.

The day of the ministerial ballot produced few surprises, though the choice of Speaker was not particularly edifying. The Left were successful in getting Harry Jenkins elected, defeating Les Johnson, a former Whitlam Minister for Housing. This was not a good decision, largely made because Hayden and some of his supporters were paying back someone they detested. The Left happily joined in because Jenkins was one of theirs and Johnson had been one of theirs but had dared to change sides. Jenkins brought little to the office. I never understood why, if the Left were to get the job, they didn't pick someone better or, if Hayden's team wanted someone, they didn't opt for Gordon Scholes, the last Speaker of the Whitlam government. Still, it was a case of anyone but Johnson, and anyone but Johnson won.

In the ballot Ralph Willis topped the poll. This surprised nobody; Ralph had offended fewer people than anyone else during his time in the parliament. Keating, whose tongue had too freely lashed the untalented (defined as anybody with whom he disagreed) was always likely to lose a few. Bob Brown, MP for Hunter, who went on to become a Centre Left minister at the 1987 election, had stood against the ticket and achieved the ultimate rejection—he got only one vote out of one hundred and ten. If that wasn't bad enough for him, our scrutineers examined every vote, even those discounted early in the count. Assuming he voted for himself, Brown had failed to include Keating in the list of the twenty-three ministers to be elected. Whatever anyone's opinion of Keating, that Brown considered him unworthy of being among the first twenty-three was something he should have kept quiet. You would have to wonder how anyone could fail to recognise Keating's worth, and we all wondered about Bob for years after this. It was no surprise that Bob Brown stuck with Hawke till his bitter end eight years later.

I felt a little uneasy about the whole ballot process. If anyone had even suggested to me at any time in the previous decade that I would be supporting Arthur Gietzelt in my first Caucus vote, I would have worked out a way of removing this unstable crazy person from the premises. Yet here I was, voting not just for Arthur Gietzelt, but for Uren and Stewart West, not to mention Hayden, Dawkins, Button, Walsh and all those I had been fighting for the previous two years in some cases and for a lifetime in others.

Given that I had to make sure Bill Morrison was not humiliated,

I decided to vote for him instead of Brian Howe, the only time in my life that I didn't vote for the 'ticket'. My excuse was of course that there was no Right vote for any ticket, so I wasn't bound. I can remember trying to persuade John Ducker to get a job for a party official in 1977, a man who had been working for the party, full-time, for twenty-five years. Ducker simply responded: 'He ratted in '56.' Voting against the ticket is a serious business.

Caucus gets very powerful when Labor is in Opposition, and the new Prime Minister did not challenge its power at that initial Caucus meeting. He attempted to play by the rules as established over time, and had little influence on the makeup of the ministry. While he had no love for many of those who became his ministers, he simply went with the flow.

His first task was to allocate the portfolios and choose a Cabinet. This was all done with the minimum of fuss, and there seemed to be only one portfolio with which he had a problem. Within days of the election, he told Peter Barron, by then his principal adviser, that he was worried about making Paul Keating his Treasurer. Barron's response was very quickly to make him understand that if Keating were denied the Treasury portfolio, the New South Wales platform, upon which Hawke's leadership had been built, would explode. Barron told me about the conversation, but I couldn't believe it would be a real problem.

Keating was uncertain in the job of Treasurer, which was understandable given that he had been in the shadow portfolio for only a few months before the election and Treasury was the most complex of them all. Nobody could be expected to master its intricacies quickly after such a long period in Opposition without access to the data that is the prerequisite of competence.

However, within a month of the victory, I was called to Kirribilli House—a venue that seems to have assumed a special place in the Hawke–Keating relationship—to be informed by Hawke in person that Keating just wasn't up to the job. My message to the new Prime Minister was quite simple: any attempt to remove Keating would be treated as a declaration of war. Hawke let the matter rest for the moment, but for the best part of another full year he continued to raise this doubt about Keating. By Christmas of 1983 he was still questioning Keating's capacity, claiming to me that Keating just couldn't contribute to the debate about the floating of the dollar. I wasn't privy to the Cabinet debates or to the private discussion between Hawke and Keating, so I can't comment on the accuracy of the Hawke assertion.

It is worth noting that for the first six months of government, both Keating and Hawke were full of praise for the then Treasury secretary and later National Party senator John Stone. There is no doubt that Stone enjoyed their confidence and had considerable influence on economic policy in the early days of the government, certainly in the framing of the first Budget. At the traditional post-Budget party in 1983, John Stone wasn't simply present by virtue of his position, but an honoured guest who spent much of the evening in the company of Hawke and Keating. It has become fashionable to suggest that Stone was suspect from day one, but both the public and private utterances of the PM and the Treasurer for the first six months indicated nothing but praise.

Over time, Caucus was to find that its power would be substantially eroded by the need to be in power. As most in the parliamentary party came to realise, the only power that mattered was the power to run the country. For the next decade, and certainly for some time into the future, the sanctity of party policy, the conscience of the individual and the power of Caucus were all subordinated to the need for power. Power had been pursued and captured: it would not be given up without a fight. It is of course never difficult to justify any of this: we all fervently believe that Labor is so much better for Australia than the alternative. This kind of imperative carried with it enough absolution for the sins we were about to commit.

CHAPTER 3

Combe, Ivanov and John Le Carré

A new government with a big majority doesn't really expect trouble. But trouble finds governments with frightening regularity, and it is never far away. For Hawke and his ministers, particularly those who served on Cabinet's Security Committee, trouble came within weeks. And for ministers with no experience of running an administration as large as the Commonwealth of Australia, crisis management could be learned only the hard way. In April, only a month or so into our first term, Hawke's authority was severely tested.

The Combe–Ivanov affair, as it became known, had all the ingredients of a novel by John Le Carré. The cast of characters were Mick Young, a former shearer who had gone on to be Labor's national secretary and was now a Cabinet minister; former Whitlam staffer Eric Walsh, who had become Canberra's best known lobbyist; David Combe, a former national secretary who wanted to become Canberra's best known lobbyist; and Laurie Matheson, a shadowy businessman responsible for a big chunk of Australia's trade with the Soviet Union. And there was also, of course, a KGB agent named Ivanov, who was being watched by the Australian Security and Intelligence Organisation—ASIO, Australia's premier spy organisation that had devoted so much of its time in the past thirty years to spying on the Labor Party. David Combe had met Ivanov on more than one occasion: his phone had been tapped for some time and his meetings with Ivanov had been filmed.

On 20 April 1983, ASIO informed the new government that Valery Ivanov and David Combe had formed a relationship which could pose a danger to Australia's security—a proposition I would have regarded as a joke had it been put to me. On the following day, the National Intelligence Sub-Committee of Cabinet met to consider ASIO's information.

That night, in the car park of The 19th Hole restaurant in suburban Canberra, Mick Young told his old mate Eric Walsh that Walsh's client Laurie Matheson had been referred to at a meeting with the Prime Minister, that 'a Russian' was to be expelled from Australia and that David Combe had been mentioned in connection with said Russian. Eric Walsh met Laurie Matheson in Melbourne a few days later and gave him the news. Nobody could have expected Eric Walsh to realise that Matheson was an ASIO agent, who eagerly reported all this to his case officer.

To this day the thought of David Combe's phone being tapped seems bizarre. And because Mick Young and Eric Walsh had been great mates for years, the image of Mick telling Eric details of the security committee while standing in the car park of The 19th Hole restaurant in Canberra always seemed to me to be relatively harmless. Certainly many Caucus members agreed. Most of us would have preferred to see Mick Young slapped on the wrist, severely reprimanded and left alone to resume his ministerial career. This may seem a rather laid-back attitude, but when you have spent most of your professional life being sceptical at best about ASIO and the way it did business, when the irritation of the Cabinet leak had not yet penetrated, when the gravity of security breaches was not fully appreciated, everybody was looking for an easy way out. The problem this gave Bob Hawke would have been much easier to solve if it had come after five years in government, but at the time it was a nightmare, harassing and annoying him for six months.

Old loyalty and friendship were at the root of the trouble. Mick Young was closer to Hawke than anyone in government. They had shared a flat in Sydney's Park Regis apartments during the hectic months of 1972 leading up to the election in December, they had been allies on the national executive for more than a decade, they ate and drank together, laughed together, went to the football together and rang the SP bookie together. They were mates.

In the weeks after the election, as Hawke was briefed on the seriousness of the Combe–Ivanov situation, his sources of advice were pretty limited. The only person on his staff whom he consulted was Graham Evans, a career public servant whom Hawke had appointed principal private secretary and the only member of Hawke's senior staff who had a security clearance. Peter Barron, Bob Hogg and Geoff Walsh, who were to provide the political advice, had not been told of the ASIO surveillance. When the Security Committee took the decision to expel Ivanov, the only people who knew what had been going on were those on the committee and Graham Evans. Barron, Hogg and Walsh, who did not have security clearances, were told by Hawke, while they all had lunch at George's Fish Cafe in Adelaide, that 'we are expelling a Russian today'. They still knew nothing of David Combe's involvement.

Even at this stage, however, Hawke was issuing warnings for people to stay away from David Combe. He couldn't tell his Cabinet colleagues to avoid talking to someone as prominent in Labor circles as David Combe without some serious rumours flying round the parliamentary corridors. It was impossible to call Richard Farmer, an old friend, journalist and adviser in election campaigns, and tell him to avoid going into business with his close friend David Combe, without the odd alarm bell ringing through the cool Canberra autumn.

Having therefore given out warnings that could certainly be interpreted by his political opponents as breaches of security in themselves, Hawke was then confronted with the news that Mick Young had told Eric Walsh about the problem, and Eric had passed it on. Hawke's natural instinct was to look after Mick Young and avoid the necessity of taking on a close friend. Hawke and Young took only a few minutes to decide upon an exchange of letters in which the Prime Minister could express his dismay and disappointment while the hapless minister could express his sorrow and promise never to transgress again. The bureaucracy approved this plan and Hawke no doubt believed that a crisis could be avoided.

Asked his opinion, Barron came up with the bombshell question: 'What about the Crimes Act?' Given that Michael McHugh, QC, had already warned Hawke that one of his ministers was in serious strife, that Hawke or Young could have considered this exchange of letters enough to solve the problem just demonstrates how inexperienced Labor was when it came to the exercise of power and responsibility. After Geoffrey Yeend, the secretary of the Department of Prime Minister and Cabinet had been consulted, the Commonwealth Crown Solicitor was asked for advice. It was found that no breach of the Crimes Act had been committed, but the gravity of just how close the government had come to such a breach made the deal between Hawke and Young redundant. The deal had to come unstuck.

Mick Young was forced to resign, and the Hope Royal Commission, which had already been set up to examine the relationship between Combe and Ivanov, examined the whole fiasco. These events deeply wounded Mick Young. He left Canberra accepting the need to resign after his discussions with Hawke, but it was a different story once he got to Adelaide and spoke to Clyde Cameron, one of the most persuasive people we ever produced. Clyde and a few of Mick's other cronies convinced him that he was being dudded by Hawke and he sought to have the decision turned around. While there was no chance that this would happen—the Senate, the Opposition and the press gallery were likely to give the government a hard time if Mick didn't stay out of the ministry for a long period—Mick's state of mind grew even worse. Having Mick Young out of the tent was a sure recipe for more trouble.

Stories began to appear in the press that Mick would be out of the ministry for a long time. Mick Young's staffer Wayne Swan (now the federal Member for Lilley) discovered that the sources for these stories were Peter Barron and Geoff Walsh. Mick's anger knew no bounds. Barron was placed on his hate list—so was I, as a close friend of Peter's—and it took years to regain the friendship.

For Hawke, the Royal Commission presented some very real difficulties. One slip of the tongue could have meant the end of his political career. Days in conference were required with QCs Michael McHugh (now a High Court judge) and Neil Young. While we were able to hold summits and prepare a Budget that included old-style boosts for the economy such as the community employment program, the business of government was slowed down by the amount of time Hawke had to invest in making sure that his appearance before the Royal Commission did not produce any surprises.

For virtually the whole of this period, Hawke did not ask my opinion. I was not cleared for such information, and he never breached any rules by telling me. So I could observe the effect the episode had on the relationship between Hawke and Young, and on Mick himself. The affair gnawed away at Mick's confidence, and I don't believe he was ever as sharp again. He could still use his wit and humour to devastating effect in the parliament, but in the Cabinet and the Caucus at large he never achieved the influence and power that he should have. It took him years to forgive Hawke and, while he and the Prime Minister did become friendly again, by 1991 Young was canvassing on behalf of Paul Keating.

CHAPTER 4

Changing the Rules

Entering the Senate at the time a Labor government came to office was a bit unusual. Labor had been in power for only three of the previous thirty-three years. While Hawke, Keating and the galaxy of stars who made up the Cabinet set about the tasks of government (that is, the jobs you have to do when you are in power), Robert Ray and I concentrated on making more certain that Labor could embrace power as a right and make the task of anyone trying to take it from us as difficult as we could.

For three decades, conservative governments had written and rewritten the electoral laws to suit themselves. A joint committee of the parliament (the Electoral Reform Committee) was set up under the chairmanship of Dick Klugman, a member of the New South Wales Right with an independent point of view—a sort of Peter Walsh with a sense of humour. Robert Ray and I represented Labor and the veteran senator Sir John Carrick represented the Liberals. Carrick was a wily old performer who knew how much the Liberals stood to lose from fair electoral laws. Senator Michael Macklin, a Queensland teacher, represented the Democrats and he too was obsessed by the mechanics of elections and voting systems. The committee had virtually made a living out of knowing everything there was to know about elections, and we knew much more than the experts who gave us the benefit of their wisdom.

The committee worked solidly through the Canberra winter in 1983 and took six months to complete its report. The reforms that the parliament later adopted as a result of this report stand up pretty well eleven years after their enactment. Public funding and the disclosure of election donations were common in most comparable democracies, but were reforms that the conservatives fought tooth and nail. Fair electoral boundaries were guaranteed, and a system was introduced to ensure that neither side could rig those boundaries. Since then there has not been one complaint of political bias in a federal redistribution in any part of the country. Members who might losc their seats as a result of changes still complain, but the system that brings them undone does not do so because of their political colour.

List ticket voting was brought in to overcome the massive number of informal votes recorded at a number of Senate elections. Trying to number candidates consecutively from 1 to 73 (one Senate ballot paper in New South Wales actually had seventy-three candidates listed) was a task far too daunting for the elderly, the visually impaired and many people of ethnic origin. No one would seriously challenge this reform now, but the Liberals knew that a lower informal vote would advantage Labor, so they wouldn't have a bar of it.

These reforms and a number of others made our efforts worthy, even noble. The decision taken to expand the parliament by adding twenty-four seats to the House of Representatives and giving Australia twelve extra senators did nothing to harm the fabric of Australian politics, though it is hard to argue that we have a better country for it. What it did create, though, was a certainty that Labor would be the big winner. The Caucus worked this out in about a minute flat, and while some ministers might not have liked it much this was a very popular plan in Labor circles.

The real problem we faced was how to get the plan up. We did not have the numbers in the Senate, so we would need some help. It was hard to imagine that the conservatives would support the idea, because it lessened their chances of winning an election.

While this has logic behind it, logic and the National Party have never been inseparable, and they had a very different view. Ralph Hunt, a genial, nice man who was the National Party representative on the committee, secretly approached Dick Klugman with the idea that the parliament should be expanded. He and Ian Sinclair could see how much their party was in decline and they knew that the only losers from the proposal would be the Liberal Party. Coalition partners or not, the self-interest of the National Party would see them willing to sell out their Liberal cousins to ensure their own survival.

Dick Klugman explained to poor old Ralph Hunt that it would be very difficult for him to persuade those bastards Ray and Richardson to go along with the idea. To have any hope, he would have to offer us some concessions. Many concessions later, Ralph was able to report to the National Party leadership that he had won the vital battle in ensuring their survival. Sure he had been forced to make some concessions, but Labor had reluctantly agreed to go along with him and expand the parliament.

Mick Young who, as Special Minister of State, had carriage of electoral matters, had never liked the idea but he did learn to live with it. He attended the Caucus committee which was examining what Robert and I were proposing (the Legal and Constitutional Reform Committee). Mick was never slow in sniffing the Caucus breeze, and when he saw that twenty-five marginal seat holders were attending that meeting to show support for our plan, he got the message.

By the time it went to Cabinet, the Combe–Ivanov affair had interrupted Mick's ministerial career and Kim Beazley had carriage of the proposal. In spite of Kim's eloquence, he was the only one of thirteen Cabinet ministers to support an expanded parliament. Bob Hawke summoned Robert Ray and me to the Cabinet room and told his colleagues that they should listen to us before rejecting the plan. It was quite an honour for us to be invited to a Cabinet meeting, but neither Robert nor I was the type to be overawed by the occasion. For forty minutes we gave the Cabinet an unassailable case (couched in terms, of course, of militant self-interest) and as we got up to leave, Hawke summarised the proceedings by saying, 'Well, we've heard from the boys. I take it that it's unanimous that we support the proposal now.'

With our own party locked in behind us, the last hurdle was to get the Senate to agree. With the Democrats and the Liberals vehemently opposed, we would need a few National Party votes to win. I have it on reliable authority that Sinclair and Hunt corralled Senator Ron Boswell, the Queensland National Party senator, in his room for two hours before the vote. They prevented any Liberals from talking to him and then escorted him to the chamber to make sure no one had a chance of turning him around.

That Boswell voted for our proposition was remarkable. He owed his position to Joh Bjelke-Petersen, who did not support expansion, and we knew that if Joh had ever been kicked up the arse, Ron Boswell would have suffered from concussion.

CHAPTER 5

Under a Mushroom Cloud

We all knew there was only one plank of the platform that was likely to give Labor a real problem, just one timebomb ticking away and destined to explode, mushroom cloud and all—uranium mining.

The 1982 conference decision as drafted by Bob Hogg and carried with so much acrimony had at least signalled to the banks that the uranium mines they stood behind would continue to exist. But the question of the new mine, Roxby Downs, the biggest uranium mine in the world, still had to be answered, and fast. The mine was always going to be a problem. The long, convoluted and internally inconsistent resolution that Bob Hogg had crafted to enable this issue to be dealt with at the 1982 conference had enabled Labor to get through a South Australian and a national election, but it could not be sustained over time. Eventually Hawke had to confront the question of whether the Roxby Downs joint venturers would have the capacity to write export contracts. The Bannon government was under pressure in the South Australian Parliament for the mine to go ahead because of its job-creating potential in that state, and Hawke needed no convincing that a go-ahead had to be given. The Left, predictably, were utterly committed to phasing out the uranium industry and preventing Roxby Downs from getting started. But Hawke knew that the failure of the mine to proceed would do the government irreparable damage in the business and financial sectors both here and overseas, and he threw himself into the debate with gusto.

The months went by and the issue headed inexorably for a bloody conclusion. By 1983, it had become politically correct to oppose uranium mining. Every party unit had an opinion, and most conveyed to the government were against any start for Roxby Downs. Hundreds of party branches passed the obligatory anti-uranium motion, used by the Left to justify its stance as the guardian and defender of the rank and file's point of view.

Anyone who visits branches and electorate councils regularly, as I have done as party secretary and a New South Wales-based senator, can always tell when an issue really worries the rank and file. They never stop telling you about it: not just the hard-line activist cadres in the branches, but everybody. In 1979, when rank-and-file preselections were seen to be under threat in New South Wales, everyone wanted to complain about it. When the argument was reduced to a simple alteration, involving the Upper House being included in the state Caucus, we had a hell of a fight on our hands, though not one that was destined to worry us for long.

Uranium was always going to be that kind of issue. While anti-uranium resolutions were carried in branches all over Australia, the venom from the cadres wasn't any worse than usual. Some of these cadres, of course, had to have a cause that would enable them to oppose the government. While every genuine Labor person should be upset about the large losses of party members during the last decade, the blessing is that many of the boring Stalinists who could never get used to Labor being in government have gone in the exodus. They were the ones who told us that to allow Roxby Downs to export uranium was to undermine the fabric of the party and destroy its chances of further electoral success. But there was simply no comparison between 1979 and the Rules arguments and 1983 and the uranium issue. No matter how many tears were shed by Jeannette McHugh or how much anger was shown by Gerry Hand or Stewart West, the anti-uranium feeling from the rank and file simply wasn't there.

But the Left were determined to fight to the death, and Hawke was also determined to take the issue to the wire, so I could see the first real Caucus fight of my parliamentary career. I had remained close to Hawke and was yet to have a serious falling-out with Keating, so when the battle loomed I was called upon to assist in making sure that Hawke prevailed.

This was not going to be easy. Very early the Victorian Left made it abundantly clear that any Victorian Right MP or senator who voted to allow Roxby Downs to go ahead would be in preselection trouble. The hysteria that the uranium issue always generated in Victoria had fed the paranoia that most of the Left felt about us anyway. At a committee meeting about a month before the final Caucus debate on the issue Lewis Kent, a member of the Victorian Left elected to a marginal seat in 1980, in discussing the Right's view on uranium referred to 'those drug pushers from New South Wales'. In our first few years of government, when the old hatreds still meant something, such remarks were not uncommon.

Hawke knew the government would be very lucky to survive a defeat on such a motion as this. A victory for the Left would have been seized on by the press and the Opposition and Australia's reputation as a reliable supplier of commodities could have been seriously undermined. He needed to know whether he would win if he chanced his arm.

This was the first time I acted as a real numbers man for Hawke in the Caucus. I felt a real charge, a surge of adrenalin. This was better than sex and almost as exciting as a good feed.

My first port of call, not surprisingly, was Robert Ray. The giant-sized Victorian senator was known to many of us as 'the fat Indian'. In fact when Keating called him this during the Hawke–Keating challenges of 1991, he was only quoting a nickname we commonly used for many years—except in Ray's presence. I don't believe I ever had a real argument with Ray—partly because I feared him so much. In an interview for the ABC TV series 'Labor in Power', I said John Dawkins 'scared the shit out of me' when he chose to attack me in Cabinet. This was true, though Dawkins could only ever damage my ego. But like Keating, Robert Ray went straight for the jugular or the genitals, and any blow he intended for those regions always found its mark.

Robert was fearsome in private as well as in public, and had a way of sounding really menacing. So when he told me that he and his colleagues in the Victorian Right could not support a resolution in favour of Roxby Downs and export for its uranium, I was really shaken. Such pressure was coming from the Victorian branch that the Right wouldn't support the resolution, and without the help of the Right, victory was going to be very difficult. The Left always had about one-third of the Caucus, and the Right between 40 and 45 per cent if united. To cobble together a majority we needed every Right vote we could find—and here I was being told that we were starting to lose them. Robert was quite prepared to participate in helping to get votes, but not those of his Victorian colleagues. No amount of lobbying from the Prime Minister could shift anyone from the Victorian Right except for Barry Cunningham, whose loyalty to Hawke was always the fiercest. If Robert Ray was going in one direction for the political survival of his faction, his Victorian colleagues would stick with him.

In the days that followed, I either spoke to or had someone speak to every Caucus member who might vote for us. We would need the Hayden supporters, Mick Young's South Australian friends, the junior ministry, the old guard from Queensland, and any other poor bastard with a heart larger than a split pea. By asking a whole heap of Caucus members not aligned to the Right about their intentions in the forthcoming vote, there is no doubt that I created a fair degree of resentment. When the Centre Left was formed a few months later, my role in speaking to quite a few who were not among my closest friends created a problem that would cause me grief in the not-too-distant future.

I determined that some of the Queensland old guard would desert ship, though that faction had a long-held belief on the issue, so some forgiveness was possible for them. Hawke sought to influence his junior ministers, with mixed results. While he could not get Peter Morris, then Minister for Transport, to commit himself, he must have had a powerful effect. Morris, still a member of the Left, eventually put his hand up to support uranium exports. The Left never forgave him and within a few months Morris signed up with the soon-to-be-formed Centre Left.

Barry Jones was another whom Hawke lobbied continuously. The newspapers kept listing him as a waverer, and Hawke fancied his chances of getting Jones's vote. I don't know what it is about Barry Jones that makes people on the Right think he will ever support them. In the Hawke challenge to Hayden in 1982 Hawke had hoped for Jones's vote, and Keating was adamant that Jones was never a possibility. Keating was right again. On this uranium vote, I could see absolutely no hope that Jones would vote against his Victorian Left masters. Sure enough, when the big day came, Jones was against us, as he has been on every major factional vote as long as I've known him. As national president of the party, his voting record remains unblemished.

Quite a few Caucus members were overseas and the word got out that the Left had summoned its members home from all parts of the globe. We immediately issued the same instructions, and Hawke found himself calling his ministers in London and various European capitals. Not everybody rallied to the call. For whatever reasons the New South Wales Right MP John Mountford and Nick Bolkus, a Left senator from South Australia (later the Minister for Immigration), were allowed to continue their travels in Spain. Presumably an informal pair arrangement had been agreed to and, at great personal cost, they continued to serve Australia abroad. Rick Charlesworth was with the Australian hockey team in Pakistan at the time, and he probably didn't know the vote was on.

Pressure was the order of the day during this period, and it wasn't just pressure from the Right. I have been accused of political thuggery for most of my career, but the extent of the threats by the Victorian and Queensland Left were extraordinary. Our Victorian Right colleagues had no doubt at all about their futures as MPs if they dared to support uranium exports and Roxby Downs. And Queensland party president Ian Maclean even took to threatening preselections publicly during uranium debates.

When Stewart West resigned from Cabinet prior to the debate because he could not abide by the principle of Cabinet solidarity, Brian Howe, then the Junior Minister for Defence Support, actually declared that he thought there had been 'intimidation of ministers and backbenchers by the Prime Minister and the right wing of the party'. Considering how his own Victorian Left had been threatening preselections, this hypocrisy was majestic. It was, however, dwarfed by the stupidity of his next statement: 'I think that on a significant issue such as uranium, that if we are to retain an inner Cabinet, Cabinet solidarity should not be enforced or alternatively the full ministry should be involved.'

As Deputy Prime Minister, Howe became a staunch defender of the principle of Cabinet solidarity. Without the knowledge that all of the Cabinet will support every Cabinet decision, a prime minister will be permanently vulnerable to the charge that he cannot lead the party. Howe's statement was either a measure of the depth of Left feeling on the issue (that is, that uranium mining was such an important issue that any other principle could be jettisoned) or maybe just a cry of defiance for the benefit of the troops back home. Perhaps it was a combination of both.

On my final count of the fors, againsts and doubtfuls—and I'd be a millionaire if I had a quid for every page of counts I've done with F, A and D at the top of the page and all the Caucus names divided underneath them—I was frustrated when Ray kept insisting that Dean Wells, a pretty sensible bloke, would vote against the resolution. Wells, now the Queensland attorney-general, was then a newly elected MP. Finally Robert let me know the reason: 'He was born in Hiroshima,' he said. At least I didn't have to waste my time trying to convince him.

The debate itself was something of an anticlimax, particularly given the charged atmosphere of the previous year's debate at the national conference. It would be impossible for any future discussion on the subject of uranium to capture the same atmosphere. The Left were armed and ready: Gerry Hand was bitter, Jeannette McHugh emotional, with Tom Uren and Stewart West bringing up the rear. But some aspects of their case were terribly weak. Their line that Labor would lose votes by betraying its earlier promise was pretty shallow; polls had consistently shown a majority in favour of uranium mining, and the electoral damage caused by the defeat of Hawke and his Cabinet would have been much, much greater than that caused by alienating those who would vote against Labor solely on the issue of uranium mining. They actually argued that this decision would cost us Senate seats. Subsequent election results made a mockery of these assertions. The suggestions that nuclear weapons would proliferate if we exported more uranium was even sillier. With a glut of uranium on the world market then, as well as now, warmongers have had any number of suppliers. The Left amendment went down by 62 votes to 37 and the substantive motion was carried by 55 votes to 46.

The real argument was about the primacy of Labor's platform. Certainly many party members resigned over this issue, but the long-term future of the party is better served by those who believe in the full breadth of Labor's credo rather than those who are interested only in one policy.

And now, who remembers all of this? The fact that the banning of uranium mining has completely disappeared from the political agenda in no way dampened the ardour of the occasion. The issue that could well have split the party is now no longer an issue at all. It is never raised at any party meeting by anyone. The dogs barked loudly, but this caravan passed on.

At its 1979 conference the trade union movement had made the decision to oppose uranium mining, but they never even paid it lip service. In my speech to the 1982 ALP conference (as I have already stated in this book) I said that no matter what the conference decided: 'Miscellaneous Workers Union members will still dig it up, Transport Union members will transport it to the port, Waterside Workers Union members will load it onto ships.' That was certainly the truth, as Nabarlek and Ranger continued to operate and export.

When Caucus made its decision Cliff Dolan, Hawke's successor as ACTU president, made a few perfunctory noises about the ACTU looking at ways 'in which we can implement our policy in an attempt to stop Roxby Downs, whether it has been given the parliamentary okay or not'. Following Bob Hawke was always difficult for Dolan, who was no orator, no genius and carried little real authority in the union movement.

Ray Gietzelt, the federal secretary of the Miscellaneous Workers Union and the brother of Arthur, was a different kettle of fish entirely. He had sponsored the young Bob Hawke into the ACTU presidency thirteen years earlier, and led the largest left-wing union, which was highly politicised. But he also represented his members, and they worked at Nabarlek and Ranger, the two working uranium mines in Australia. When asked whether he expected any effective opposition by other unions to new contracts for those mines or for Roxby Downs, he replied: 'I don't anticipate any, because not one single affiliated union has implemented the ACTU policy since it was laid down in 1979.' Herein lay the reason for my confidence that this debate would eventually wither and die on the vine. The Miscellaneous Workers Union was too big and too important in the Left to be ignored forever. In fact, by the time of the 1984 national conference, when this issue was to be debated again, Bob Hawke talked to his old friend Ray Gietzelt and secured promises that two delegates who were members of the MSU would cross the floor and vote with the Right.

It was finally decided that the government would allow uranium produced from the mine at Roxby Downs to be exported, subject to whatever safeguards applied generally to uranium exports at the time. No new uranium mines would be developed, and all future exports of our uranium under existing and future contracts should be made subject to the most stringent supply conditions. These would be determined after an inquiry into our role in the nuclear fuel cycle, which would be conducted by the Australian Science and Technology Council and report no later than mid May 1984. This inquiry would look at our nuclear safeguard arrangements, waste disposal methods and the opportunities for Australia to advance the cause of nuclear non-proliferation. A permanent commission was to be set up to look at issues relating to the nuclear fuel cycle, and no contracts for the export of uranium from existing mines should be approved until after the enquiry had reported, except for two already negotiated. Last of all, the suspension on uranium exports to France would stay, to be examined further in the light of the inquiry's report or any progress towards the cessation of French nuclear testing in the Pacific.

So Hawke had been able to achieve a relatively sensible policy by pushing as hard as he could against the Left. He was utterly contemptuous of them, and it showed. If the Left as a group, or indeed the Left leadership, knew what Hawke had said about them as individuals, it is hard to imagine that they would have become his main support base when Keating challenged him eight years later.

The Left, of course, were pretty liberal with the colourful language themselves. They threatened a special national conference of their own, which fell apart because they couldn't get four states to support the resolution. New South Wales, South Australia and Queensland resisted any such call. However, the Victorian branch went ahead with a conference of their own, in which genius after genius predicted that the uranium decision would be the beginning of the end for the Hawke government. At this conference the Right took on the Left, providing a full slate of speakers: Holding, Crean, Willis, Ray, Evans and Duffy. The Left, which had threatened to sit until midnight, pleaded to have a ballot by 1pm. They'd had enough of the debate by then.

Far from sealing the fate of the government, what happened was probably the exact reverse. The decision proved to the business community that this was an economically responsible government in deadly earnest about maintaining Australia's image internationally as a reliable supplier of commodities. In fact, after this the business community completely altered the pattern of behaviour they had laid down over aeons. They kept their heads down during the next decade (with the exception of the 1993 election) and while the Liberals might have been relatively well funded by them, the enthusiasm and consistency of business support for their traditional allies just faded away.

For all that, the policy result still lacked complete logic. We managed to approve the biggest uranium mine in the world to assist a state Labor government in South Australia, while refusing to permit Jabiluka and Koongarra in the Northern Territory, or Yeelirrie in Western Australia. While there might have been a legitimate argument about the mine at Jabiluka because of its location in the most environmentally sensitive areas of Kakadu, Pancontinental never had an opportunity to put forward a plan. Unlike Jabiluka, Koongarra and Yeelirrie would have been very hard to stop on any grounds, but they never got a look in either. While Koongarra was in an area excised from Kakadu by the Fraser government in the 1970s, it is a long way from any watercourse and presents no obvious environmental difficulties. And any environmental arguments that could be put against mining future uranium discoveries won't be needed—our policy still prevents any new mine outside of Roxby Downs.

Between the writing and publication of this book, another Labor conference will have the opportunity to debate uranium policy. It is to be hoped that a sensible outcome can finally be achieved.

CHAPTER 6

Left, Right and Centre

In February 1984, a coalition of the long since dispossessed, the recently dispossessed and the afraid they might be dispossessed gathered in Adelaide to form a faction separate from the Right and the Left. Bill Hayden, still smarting from losing his big chance in Australian politics, Mick Young, still smarting from being kept out of the ministry for much longer than he thought appropriate, and Peter Walsh, a fundamentally cantankerous personality who was always smarting over something, were three of the prime movers. The others were Chris Schacht and Michael Beahan, now senators but then party secretaries in South Australia and Western Australia respectively, and Senator Peter Cook. He was a bit of a surprise entry, having come to prominence as a vice-president of the ACTU, to which he had been elected on the Left ticket.

Their idea was to form an alternative to all the nasty types (for that read me or anyone remotely like me) who were too concerned with power plays and pragmatism and who paid insufficient attention to policy development and more cerebral pursuits. The idea was attractive in several states: the non-Left forces did need to organise and in Western Australia a number of sensible people, who had been uncomfortable even being seen as left-wingers, needed a home. Outside those two states, it was more difficult. Tasmania was a complete muddle with as many factions as it had members (this is still true) and a Centre group was going to have some attraction. Bill Hayden was a Queenslander who had some following there, including the state secretary. Also on side were Susan Ryan, who had apologised for her inability to attend, Neal Blewett and John Dawkins, who was there in spirit, even if his body was in Europe at the time. Great predictions were made of expansion in the Caucus as well as in the machines of New South Wales and Victoria.

Press reports were full of the rhetoric of the really bright people in the party wanting to form their own faction, where freedom of thought and action would be the order of the day. Policy development would flourish and a cushion would be formed between warring Left and Right factions. In fact, the formation of the faction merely formalised a loose grouping that had existed in Caucus for years. All the newspaper articles of the period predicted a big comeback for Bill Hayden and said Lionel Bowen's position as Deputy Prime Minister was in danger. I don't believe Bill Hayden had any intention of challenging Bowen; at that stage I am sure he envisaged other possibilities for seeing out his career.

Saying that the Centre Left would be a buffer between the Right and the Left sounded reassuring, but it ignored every political reality of the time. To be effective any faction has to be disciplined, and within a few months the Centre Left had become yet another group enforcing rigid factional discipline by adherence to a show-and-tell voting system (voting in pairs to make certain of members' loyalty and presumably to eliminate any possibility for freedom of thought or action). But to last the distance, any faction has to have union support. At that time, every ALP state conference had more than 50 per cent of its delegates elected directly by the unions. The Centre Left had limited union support in Western Australia and Tasmania, none in New South Wales, Victoria and Queensland, the Northern Territory and the ACT. Only in South Australia did the Centre Left have a really formidable union base, and therefore only in South Australia do they have a guaranteed long-term future.

The Victorian Independent faction (a group formed by John

Button, John Cain and Michael Duffy to oppose the hardline Hartley machine of the late 1960s and early 1970s) were logical bedfellows, and the new faction flew to Melbourne to court them. Bill Hayden, Neal Blewett and Senator Rosemary Crowley addressed a meeting of the independents at the Lincoln Hotel in Carlton. According to press reports at the time, a Hayden crack about me 'produced great merriment'. While the Left was attacked to some extent, the clear message painted by these three apostles was the need for a third group to limit the influence of the Right. Neal Blewett apparently told the assembled multitude that the Centre Left would 'split off some unions from the Right and the Left'. Anyone with an ounce of nous would have regarded this as the most foolish kind of optimism, usually the sole possession of those who will never achieve their goals. Rosemary Crowley said she 'felt less isolated' by the formation of the group. She felt a bit differently a few years later when she realised that the Centre Left would never elect her to the ministry above one of the blokes. She eventually got there when a right-wing prime minister anointed her after some hefty persuasion from me.

The faction didn't exactly have a spectacular debut in Victoria. John Button, who seemed quite ambivalent about the Centre Left, eventually joined it, as did Barry Jones. Neal O'Keefe joined for a while before leaving for the greener pastures of the non-aligned or non-faction, depending on your point of view. Michael Duffy, one of the more entertaining people I have ever known, wouldn't have a bar of them, and told them so in no uncertain terms. People like Gordon Scholes, the former Speaker and then minister in the Hawke government, and John Mildren, the Member for Ballarat, just stayed away.

But dismal though this record was, the faction's real failure was in New South Wales. On 29 February, the ABC TV current affairs program 'Nationwide' was introduced by Geraldine Doogue with these words: 'Tonight Bill Hayden brought his new Centre Left faction into enemy territory. At this moment, Mr Hayden is sitting down with twenty-five [state] Labor MPs in the Macquarie Street parliamentary dining room.' The self-elected spokespersons for the meeting, along with Hayden himself, were Paul Whelan, displaced as a minister in the Wran government a few months later, and Kevin Ryan, who could never muster the numbers to win a Caucus ballot, and who blamed me in particular and the Right in general for that failure. In my experience, failure is never the fault of the person who has failed. (I said at the time of the 1984 state election: 'We've got the perfect result—the government's been returned and Kevin Ryan hasn't.')

Their interview with Geraldine Doogue was a classic. Whelan declared: 'It's going to encourage philosophical discussion of our party's platform and our policies . . . as far as I'm concerned the philosophical blending of minds and members of the ALP, both federal and state.'

Doogue's response was: 'That all sounds terrifically wishy-washy.'

In the event, the twenty-five MPs never signed up, the faction could never muster six votes in a state conference of 850 delegates and only recruited two federal MPs in Bob Brown and Peter Morris from the Newcastle–Hunter region. Fortress New South Wales remained intact. No unions even thought about crossing over.

Even in his home state of Queensland, Bill Hayden couldn't take a trick in setting up the faction. Here union power continued to elude the Centre Left, and there were other problems. Of the early Centre Left Caucus members who signed up, David Beddall and Senator Mal Colston were always ours and known to be so, and the replacements for Manfred Cross and Len Keogh were never going to be Centre Left.

The faction does not exist in Queensland any more: indeed, it is fading everywhere. The early predictions of forty to fifty Caucus members were hopelessly overstated. The faction once boasted thirty members; in ten years, it has been reduced to sixteen members. In 1983 and 1984, due to the re-election of the shadow ministry that Hayden had assembled during his period as leader, the Centre Left had a majority of Cabinet, and it is now down to one out of seventeen.

Despite the rhetoric at the time of the Centre Left's formation, my relations with the Centre Left remained cordial. But if it had been founded to curb my power and that of the Right, as Bill Hayden told Bob Hawke, it had little success in either. In the longer term, the Centre were on side with the Right on every major policy issue, and in the short term the Right's hold on

Hawke was unshakeable. Some reports even suggested that Keating's long-term leadership ambitions would be upset by this new grouping. In fact, the Centre Left were aboard the Keating leadership cart before any of the rest of us. By 1988 John Dawkins and Peter Walsh would be telling anyone who wanted to listen that Hawke's time had run out and that it was Keating's turn.

CHAPTER 7

Election '84

After the uranium decision the government was riding high. Hawke was on top, Keating on the rise, unemployment and inflation were falling and the Left was in decline. It would have been difficult to imagine a better scenario for an election.

Eight months into a three-year term was obviously ridiculously early, but our minds turned to when it might be possible. The fact that Fraser's election in 1983 had been a double dissolution made things much simpler, giving us the perfect excuse to go early. The terms of some senators in the new parliament would expire on 30 June 1985, so a half-Senate election had to be held before then. The usual practice, of course, is to hold elections for the Senate and the House of Representatives at the same time. The plan to have an early election towards the end of 1984 was hatched a year in advance. So we entered 1984 knowing that we would go to the polls at the end of the year.

One might reasonably expect that every step taken during that year would have been carefully programmed in order to win electoral support. I certainly expected it: I was wrong again. To my surprise, the Hawke government began to show its commitment to policy above votes. This was certainly courageous—using the word in the damning Sir Humphrey Appleby *Yes Minister* sense—and this courage was looked upon with great suspicion Right, Left and Centre.

The 1984 Budget had several centrepieces—the introduction of an assets test on the pension, an incomes test on the pension for people over seventy (which affected only those with a large private income) and a tax on lump sum superannuation. The assets test was finely calibrated to terrify every actual or hopeful holder of a marginal seat. Certainly the taxes on pensions abolished some middle-class welfare, tightening pension eligibility and helping direct payments to the needy. So some pension dollars were taken off a few hundred thousand older people with a few million relatives and friends, all of whom were likely to be influenced by a shameless Opposition scare campaign. It was very risky, and I came from a school that did not believe in risk. Picking on old ladies had never been in the instruction manual for good politics.

I had a problem with the ethics of the decision, too. As a fairly traditional Labor Party member, I couldn't bring myself to look at the need to shave government expenditure by cutting welfare spending in any way. Only evil conservative governments, I had been led to believe, could do such a thing. The economic rationalist arguments I doubted: like most of my colleagues, I considered economics an inexact science whose importance had been greatly exaggerated. My view was that pensions were not generous: they should be increased whenever possible, certainly not means tested.

The politics of the assets test were dubious as well. About 20 per cent of Australians relied on pensions of various kinds (age, disability, sole parent, carers' and so on) and they and their families represented a huge voting bloc. Even if our policies were right, we could be brought undone if the Opposition could scare these people more effectively than we could reassure them.

Hawke and Keating, however, were absolutely determined on this issue, and they began to pull out all stops to ensure its passage through Caucus. That meant making sure that Robert Ray and I kept the troops in line. This wasn't easy: this time the troops, especially those from marginal seats, were very jittery indeed. Gary Punch, the MP for Barton—a seat we always had to win and hold to be in government—was then only twenty-seven years old and something of a firebrand. He never shrank from attacking proposals he didn't like and his political instincts (and not many people have better ones) told him that in Barton the pension proposals would be very hard to sell. He wasn't alone. Plenty of his colleagues, Left, Right and Centre, had come to a similar conclusion.

(It's worth commenting that the electorate of Barton was frequently used as the litmus test for the sales potential of many a government policy. This led Peter Steedman, a real character from the Victorian Left who represented the electorate of Casey for that first term of government only, to say that the government would go only as far as the electors of Barton would let them.)

As if alienating the pensioners and our own people wasn't bad enough, we decided to alienate the trade unions as well, with our proposed 30 per cent tax on lump sum superannuation. Public sector unions had been growing while private sector unionism had declined—a trend that has continued to this day—and virtually all these members had some form of lump sum superannuation scheme. They were bound to rebel.

I was worried about the superannuation question on the grounds of politics and equity. There is always a dilemma in the party, at least among its electoral strategists, about Labor's relationship with the union movement. Some will claim that, as the percentage of the workforce in trade unions declines, it may sometimes be good politics to fight the unions or at least be seen to do so. I have never accepted this. If a Labor government, any Labor government, fights too often with the trade unions, it will be undermined by internal division. The unions have 60–40 dominance of most state conferences and enough pull on the national executive and national conference to cause real trouble if they are so minded. It is sensible, then, to make peace when peace is possible and to fight only when there is no alternative.

For most of this century, the unions had fought on conditions such as superannuation, and they guarded their gains jealously. I cared about the low-paid workers in particular: the ticket collectors at the railway stations, the street sweepers at the local council and all the other workers whose only real joy in the job was a modest super cheque at the end of their working lives. They could pay off the house and the car, take a decent holiday and then, having spent the super, retire to a pension. I just couldn't see how taking that joy away from them made us better economic managers and neither, I suspect, could a fairly large majority of the Caucus.

The Hawke–Keating argument for changing the rules was that smaller government with a more equitable base meant a tighter welfare budget, which meant a needs-based welfare policy. The assets test wouldn't actually take benefits away from the people I was worried about, just those with greater assets. As the party with a greater belief in welfare equity than the Liberals, we were prepared to terminate some middle-class welfare. Courageous this might have been in the Sir Humphrey Appleby sense, and it was also courageous in the ordinary sense.

So the majority in Caucus, including me, were wrong. Those first tentative steps on the road to rational economic management were critically important to Labor. They did require visionary leadership and a ton of courage—and the knowledge that a few of us had enough faith in them to make sure that a restless Caucus didn't get in the road. So, after putting my own views as strongly as I could in private, I went out to do the bidding of the leadership in public. I spoke to those who doubted the wisdom of the Cabinet decision, asking them to reconsider: I knew the Cabinet would not be defeated, but I wanted to make sure that those who had serious criticisms were listened to.

Hawke needed to listen to those who were worried and to give them a good hearing. Unfortunately, it is always hard to get leaders to listen. After one Caucus meeting, where Gary Punch had led the charge of those whom Hawke called the 'nervous nellies', Hawke savaged Punch, calling into question both his courage and his judgment. Punch stormed out of the Caucus in high dudgeon, closely followed by David Beddall (a Queensland MP who, along with Punch, later became a minister) and myself. David and I set about calming Gary down outside the Caucus room, where Hawke, having finished his report to Caucus, walked right into us. My recollection of what happened next can never be perfect but, though I swore much more than this, I basically screamed at Hawke: 'That better be the last fucking time you single out one of ours for an attack like that!' A bemused Hawke shuffled off to his office, and I sent Beddall off to buy Punch a cup of coffee. Half an hour later, Hawke rang Punch and apologised. Yes, it's hard to get leaders to listen—but it's not impossible.

It's worth remembering that the pensions and superannuation decisions were the first of the 'rational' economic decisions we took and kept taking for another ten years. Regardless of the difficulties in persuading other Caucus members, I was still concerned that the assets test in particular was being badly launched and badly sold. With the Opposition doing its level best to scare the elderly, the easiest group to scare in our community, our duty—if the policy was right—was to get out and sell it properly. But in a pattern we were to set on too many issues, we came out of the boxes slowly and didn't really start selling the tests, particularly the assets test, until the election campaign was on in earnest about three months after the Budget.

If all this wasn't the best lead-up to an election campaign, we didn't have too much to worry about. Hawke was still the most popular living Australian, Andrew Peacock and the Liberals had made little or no impact, and the electorate always gives a government a second term. Besides, for the first time ever, Labor was confidently looking at a majority of forty in the House. We—and our leader—became just a bit cocky.

Hawke decided to have a long campaign, lasting just under eight weeks. We didn't need to fear this, he said. In fact, we were going so well that the old tried and tested rule—that election campaigns should be as short as possible—could be discarded. We would write new rules, we were invincible. It all sounds so stupid now, and for some of us at least it didn't sound all that brilliant even then. There is always the fear that, the longer a campaign lasts, the more time there is for a mistake to bring you undone. The frenzied activity usually obvious in the PM's office and the Labor machine around the country just wasn't there. We couldn't lose and we knew it. We were right about that, but our complacency and Hawke's personal difficulties robbed us of a great deal.

The effect that the discovery of his daughter Rosslyn's drug addiction had on Bob Hawke was devastating. He found out when his wife Hazel interrupted him just prior to a meeting with

Malaysia's Prime Minister Dr Mahathir, and such was his shock that he walked straight into his meeting with Mahathir and promptly told him. What Mahathir thought about this episode can only be the subject of speculation, but it couldn't have helped. Hawke was still so distressed that a few days later, on 20 September, he broke down and cried at a Canberra press conference broadcast on national television. This shocked and startled a fair number of people, but Hawke's tears were never a real political problem: Hawke had cried before and would cry again, and he was the kind of character people wanted to make allowances for, and usually did. The real problem lay with what caused the tears: at first a great shock, followed by a fair degree of guilt and depression—and, most importantly, a mind so dominated by the enormity of the personal problem that it was unable fully to concentrate on an election campaign.

The night I saw Hawke's tears on television I rang to wish him and his family well. But in the weeks that followed, like so many of those who were close to Hawke, I sensed detachment, distance. Hawke wasn't firing. The star campaigner of 1983 was a real dud in 1984, and nothing we did could shake him out of it. His staff were mortified, his mates worried. And his Treasurer was stunned.

Keating was appalled at Hawke's lack of discipline in telling Mahathir what had happened, and he couldn't make the allowances that other Australians had permitted. Keating's disdain for his leader started to build; later he said that at this point Hawke stopped being prime minister. From that moment onwards, Keating thought of Hawke as inferior, and from this moment the Treasurer began to assert himself. He reasoned that his knowledge had increased, he knew about economics and the economy. Paul Keating began to think he was ready. Meanwhile, Bob Hawke was finding difficulty in deciding anything.

With an emotionally disabled leader, the long election campaign he had wanted turned out to be a very bad decision. Peacock displayed great tenacity. Written off by the pundits, most of his own party and all of ours, he battled on to the last moment, never showing the slightest sign of defeatism. He whittled away Hawke's lead with good old-fashioned 'promise them what they want to hear' politics. He would abolish the assets test and the tax on lump sum superannuation. The Liberals would introduce nothing that might upset anybody in Australia, except for a union official. And in the classic Liberal tradition, Peacock hammered the question of tax. This could have done us huge damage—we had been considering introducing a capital gains tax but we dealt with it by announcing a tax summit for the following year, at which our decisions would be made. When you have a problem in our business, you announce a review, add a summit if necessary and hence dispose of the issue.

Despite his well-worn rhetoric and a pretty ordinary performance, Peacock's tactics worked. Bob McMullan, Labor's national secretary, reckoned that Labor's vote declined by as much as 1.5 per cent during that campaign. The facts were inescapable: considering Hawke's popularity, a lacklustre Opposition, the improving economy, increased employment—this was our big chance and we blew it. The respective policy speeches, the advertising, even the well-publicised 'great debate' between Hawke and Peacock were all pretty dull. That Hawke didn't outdo Peacock in the debate just confirmed the way the campaign had gone since that day in September when Hawke found out about his daughter. Prime ministers are expected to win these debates, and a draw is counted as a loss.

The final election result showed a 1.4 per cent two-party preferred swing from Labor towards the Coalition. The forty-seat majority of our dreams went down to sixteen. We lost at least three backbenchers who looked to have a bright future. In politics, you can count on nothing except what you can control for yourself and for most of the backbench, this was precious little.

No change was made to the ministry in the aftermath of this election; the factions simply agreed to re-elect the lot. From the Right's point of view, this wasn't such a bad deal. The only person in danger from our side was Barry Cohen, and the newly formed Centre Left would have struggled to keep Barry Jones in place. The most sensible course was to go for what we had and to promote Brian Howe to the Cabinet in order to make the Left more a part of central decision-making, and Robert Ray and I arranged this deal on behalf of the Right. I can assure everyone that, no matter how much Barry Cohen complained about the rigidity of the faction system when it displaced a really talented bloke like him in 1987, on this occasion he was delighted to avoid the test of Caucus democracy.

The Right, which had been getting more harmonious ever since the 1983 election, held an historic national meeting of the faction to endorse this position. The pro-Hawke coalition, as we had styled ourselves, met at the Camperdown Travelodge in Sydney and bonhomie and friendship were the order of the day. The New South Wales and Victorian Right were working ever more closely together and, with members and senators from other states, it was a pretty impressive gathering. The resolution to re-elect the ministry was carried unanimously. All those with batons in their knapsacks thought better of nominating against 'the ticket'.

So as we headed for the Christmas break, we had every reason to be hopeful, despite the election result. Our majority was not large enough to guarantee the next election result, but the gods were still being kind to us. The Liberal camp was a mess, the antipathy between John Howard and Andrew Peacock as deep and bitter as ever. There was nothing more certain than that Peacock's relatively good result in the election—a 1.4 per cent two-party preferred swing from us towards the Coalition—would give him no more than a temporary reprieve from a Howard challenge. Howard's expression of loyalty and support for Peacock after the election was meaningless: when two contenders really hate each other, such pledges mean nothing. Leadership contenders have to lie, and do so publicly. It is not always possible to tell Australia what you are doing in order to undermine the leader of your party, but anyone who is serious about continuing a challenge can keep the public informed by means of background briefings and judicious leaks. The story doesn't need a first-person quote in it: the message is out and about. And the Howard camp had their message out very early. If the chance ever came, Howard would take it.

For our part, we didn't care who would triumph. Just as long as they belted hell out of each other along the way.

It is doubtful that Bob Hawke could ever have regained his personal equilibrium had his daughter Rosslyn not overcome her drug problem. The percentage of those who recover from drug addiction is tiny. To be counted among that group is a recognition of phenomenal personal effort by Rosslyn and her mother Hazel. In the families of our leading male politicians, the children are brought up by their mothers, and it is their mothers to whom they turn in times of crisis. Hazel met every challenge and managed to encourage and nurture her daughter through what must have been the worst of times.

CHAPTER 8

The MX Missile Crisis

Shortly after the 1984 election it was time for me to take my first overseas trip as a senator. Having been the referee between fiercely competing MPs for these trips, it was time to sample one myself. Robert Ray and I decided to go away together, on what was known as the 'leader's trip' to Japan. The PM nominated four members to go as guests of the Japanese government. I didn't know whether the Japanese government realised that Robert and I nominated who would go on these particular trips, and the PM never interfered, but I felt no real need to burden them with this information. So Robert and I nominated ourselves, David Beddall and David Simmons (the New South Wales Right Member for Calare).

This was, we thought, a pretty good delegation. We were mates, we had never been to Japan, we were interested in industry policy and we were going to the country with the most advanced technology in the world. I mentioned our trip to my friend Laurie Brereton, then the New South Wales minister responsible for building Darling Harbour, that huge tourist development adjacent to Sydney's business district. The Japanese government had also invited Laurie to go to Japan to look at an aquarium that might be a model for the one to be built in Sydney. A few phone calls to the ambassador later, we had a delegation of five.

The Japanese proved courteous and generous hosts. We were treated to a series of incredibly expensive banquets, as well as some fascinating glimpses of Japanese efficiency. My most enduring memory of the business side of this trip was a visit to the Mazda works in Hiroshima. The factory was built right on the docks, and a state-of-the-art robotic assembly line churned out classy cars which were then driven fifty metres to the waiting, open holds of custom-built ships. At a meeting with Mazda management, I asked a pretty simple question: 'When was the last time you had a strike?' The assembled managers went into a huddle for five minutes before answering that there had been no strikes for something like ten years. The Australian delegation exchanged heavy sighs and heavenward glances. No need for us to verbalise that this kind of managerial huddle wouldn't have been necessary for us to nominate when the last industrial stoppage had occurred at a car plant in Australia.

Robert Ray, the senior senator, led the delegation. I will always treasure the memory of this quite large person trying to sit on the floor to eat in traditional Japanese restaurants. We had further briefings on trade and industry, all of which we greatly enjoyed, and we saw the ancient capital of Kyoto and the beautiful resort town of Nara. Then we arrived in Tokyo for our last few days in Japan, staying at the magnificent Imperial Hotel. It had been a great trip.

While we were there I had a call from Kim Beazley. As soon as I answered the phone, I knew we had a problem: Kim is a well-known worrier and his already high-pitched voice had gone up a couple of octaves. He told me that Bob Hawke and the Cabinet Security Committee had agreed to allow the US government to test fire the MX missile off the Australian coast. When word of this leaked out, the Labor Party naturally went berserk. The art of taking the party further than it wants to go always involves a degree of consultation; for those of us responsible for delivering the numbers at conference or in Caucus, a little bit of consultation is a minimum requirement. On the MX missile decision no formal consultation had been possible, but on any practical level this was a decision that should never have been taken without first determining whether it was possible to make it stick.

Now things were really getting out of control. Hawke was in Europe, the party was in revolt and even some in our own faction, such as Alan Griffiths, were going public. The Left were threatening to hold special conferences and some of the Victorian hardliners were having a field day.

'What are we going to do?' Kim asked me.

My definitive response was: 'Fucked if I know.' I said I would make some enquiries.

Robert Ray and I hit the phones and we didn't take long to discover that our range of options was pretty limited. Holding the line in Caucus was going to be very difficult; we were unlikely to hold all our own people, let alone all of the Centre. Holding the line at a special conference would have been impossible; the Left was rampant. To have any hope of winning, Hawke would have to put his leadership and reputation on the line, and even then victory could not have been guaranteed. It was time for him to back off, to withdraw approval for US missile testing near Australia.

It will surprise nobody to learn that Paul Keating didn't see the issue like this. As far as he was concerned, any backdown was a sign of weakness. When he rang to give me the benefit of his wisdom on this question, I still hadn't spoken to Hawke but Paul instinctively knew what my response would be and wanted to talk me out of it. He failed to change my view; even the all-conquering Keating couldn't have won this one.

Great decisions are not always taken in the most glorious of circumstances. When Hawke finally called from Brussels, I was in my room at the Imperial. I was in fact sitting on the toilet; this excellent hotel had a telephone installed next to it for just such emergencies. For twenty minutes, then, I sat on the throne and accomplished two major tasks: satisfying my own immediate and urgent personal demands and those of the national interest. It took little time to convince Hawke that the MX missile was one decision he should let go. Peter Barron, who was with him, naturally backed me up, and between us we convinced Hawke that this was not the issue to stake his leadership on.

The issue damaged Hawke in the polls, but those who interpreted his decision to cancel the MX test as a sign of weak leadership had no understanding of politics in general or Labor politics in particular. Hawke was a wise enough leader to listen to sensible advice. Sure if he had decided to fight, the personal effects of his daughter's drug addiction would have hindered him, but this fight was beyond Hawke at his best. This was a time to walk away and survive. Fortunately the Hawke relationship with US President Ronald Reagan and Secretary of State George Schultz was so strong that the US were prepared to release him from his and the Australian government's obligations without rancour or resentment.

We celebrated our last day in Japan in the Fontainebleau restaurant atop the Imperial Hotel, an expensive dinner to end an expensive trip. I don't know whether this was simply coincidence, but from then on the Japanese government reduced from four to three the number of Caucus members who would represent the leader.

But as we flew back to Australia, my mind was not on the MX crisis, the wonder of Japanese industrial efficiency or even the sight of Robert Ray trying to sit cross-legged on the floor to eat. We had all visited the Hiroshima memorial and nobody who has ever had the opportunity to do this can ever forget it. The destructive power of the atomic bomb dropped on the city in August 1945 was awesome, the images of what happened to the people who were there are horrific: too horrible to want to remember, too dreadful to allow anyone to forget.

CHAPTER 9

In and Out of the Tax Cart

In a nation with only three years between elections, the first year is the one in which a government can really do things. The 1984 campaign had produced Labor's promise of a tax summit, preceded by a review of taxation. Both Treasury and Keating believed passionately that the existing system, with its fragmented tax base and potential for rorting, had to be changed: it was costing the country money. At the same time, the principles outlined for the review included that no welfare beneficiary would be disadvantaged, nor would direct taxation be increased. In fact, as ever, personal income tax cuts were desirable. But the same amount of revenue had to be raised and the obvious solution was to increase indirect taxation—in effect, to bring in a consumption tax.

Paul Keating and his Treasury colleagues had made up their minds about this long before the review even started. For twenty years, Treasury had waited for the chance to bring in a consumption tax, and now they had a powerful Treasurer whose success record in Cabinet was second to none. Bernie Fraser, Ted Evans and David Morgan, the most senior Treasury officials, who worked on the nine options considered during the review, had been captured by Keating. The Keating presence can be awesome. When he turns on the charm (he never has to turn on the persuasive powers nor the best use of the English language I have yet heard; these things never leave him) he can be irresistible.

However, these Treasury officers were not just serving the government: they had real closeness with Keating. Some ministers enjoy this kind of relationship with their public servants, and indeed if you are unable to inspire their loyalty you will eventually be their victim. A department that doesn't like its minister often starts the process of bringing him down, and public servants know where too many of the bodies are buried. Furthermore, there are thousands of them and one minister. I never liked those odds, and neither did Paul Keating. But his intellect, wit and charm ensured that he never had these worries.

Arraigned against them was practically every other department, minister and adviser. The Hawke advisers, with Peter Barron and economist Dr Ross Garnaut (later Australia's ambassador to China) in the forefront, bucketed the consumption tax from day one. As the option was put to the task force set up to examine our taxation policy and word of this spread around Parliament House, Keating and his advisers looked desperately alone. The ministers of the newly formed Centre Left—Dawkins, Button, Hayden and Walsh in particular—became scathing critics. Peter Walsh was always a dangerous opponent. He had a sharp mind, an acid tongue and total disregard for political convention. As Finance Minister he had the opportunity to get across every area of government expenditure, and his capacity to master detail made him even more formidable.

Walsh never had time for the ordinary courtesies shown between colleagues as a matter of course. Disdain and disgust were etched on his face and there was menace in his tone whenever he spoke to someone of whom he did not approve. I first met him over dinner at the Cornwall Hotel in Launceston during the Bass by-election campaign in July 1975, and he made obvious his dislike of the New South Wales Right. By 1985 he was an occasional Keating ally in Cabinet, but his view of the New South Wales Right had not changed. This struck me as curious given that, time and time again, he proved himself to be one of the most conservative people in the party. Most of them were to the left of me, but not Peter Walsh. He was brilliant on one hand, stubborn as a mule on the other, and I always had the impression that he would fight to the last drop of every marginal candidate's blood to achieve everything he believed in.

It was quite a shock, then, to see Walsh oppose Keating on political grounds. He argued that a consumption tax was unsaleable and inequitable, that it would dramatically add to inflation and that compensating all those at the bottom end of the scale would be impossible. Keating was scathing about him in private, which suggests that Walsh must have been doing a pretty fair job of undermining the Keating package. In one of the very few examples of the Department of Finance frontally opposing Treasury on a fundamental issue, Walsh actually prepared his own taxation option.

The trade unions also refused to wear a consumption tax. This must surely have riled Keating the most; he had put more effort into winning ACTU secretary Bill Kelty than I ever saw him put in to win anyone else. Neither the Right nor the Left of the union movement would have a bar of what they saw as a regressive tax that would disadvantage their base. The welfare movement couldn't have been harder or harsher as they joined in this overwhelming chorus. In the wider Labor Party there was great scepticism; supporters of the consumption tax were harder to find than businessmen prepared to state publicly that Alexander Downer would last as Liberal leader.

Most of us would be daunted by this array of opponents, but not our Paul. Anyone with a modicum of political instinct knew how risky this proposal was. The size of the fight only increased the risk, and Keating was always a risk taker. The more strident the criticism of his preferred plan, the more determined he became to sell it. The stakes were therefore raised to a great height immediately: the credibility and authority of the Treasurer were on the line.

This put Hawke in a particularly dicey position. If he backed Keating, he alienated practically every section of the Labor movement and most of his Cabinet and Caucus. If he opposed Keating, he was alienating a very dangerous man. Even then, it was obvious that Keating would succeed Hawke. Keating had everything, except perhaps judgment—knowing when to take a backward step. This was to be the great test. He had staked so much on his package that I wondered how much of him would be left if he failed. That question would be answered by September 1985.

In this atmosphere, Keating rang and asked me to show him some public support. Having always admired Keating for his inexhaustible reserves of courage and remembering my father's dictum that loyalty means sticking by your friends even when you know they're wrong, I had little choice. I would support him, whether I was convinced that his case was correct or not. Keating's request was also highly complimentary: up to now, my public support of anything had been worth bugger all.

The opportunity for me to show my loyalty presented itself with an invitation to address the ACT Fabian Society. Like most branches of this society, it had very few members, little by way of resources and less influence. Their dinner, held at the Australian National University, was attended by a maximum of twenty-five people, ten of whom were journalists. I went as hard as I could on the basis of a fairly rudimentary briefing from Keating, and next day ABC Radio's 'AM', the current affairs program that gives a million political junkies their fix every morning, began with my opening words: 'The tax system is on its last legs, it's had it. To put it crudely, it's stuffed.'

Bullshit goes a long way in politics, especially when you're quick on your feet and practised in the art of answering criticism from the experience of a thousand party meetings in dingy, spartan masonic halls and schools of arts across the country—but it's no substitute for knowledge. In the audience was Ross Gittins, the economic commentator from the *Sydney Morning Herald*, and when he questioned me over dinner, my puny grip on the argument was soon exposed. Gittins is the kind of economist who should have been a senior adviser to the Treasurer or a senior officer in Treasury itself. He is less besotted with theory than the Treasury team has traditionally been, and he seems to have a far better idea of how policy works on the ground than any other economist I have ever met. Gittins wasn't completely antagonistic to the introduction of a consumption tax, but his doubts had a habit of becoming the doubts of whoever was listening to him.

Keating had no doubts and no display of opposition had any effect on him whatever. This left Hawke in a real bind. He knew the extent of Cabinet's opposition and could find no significant support for the proposal anywhere in Labor's constituency, apart from my lone effort. And the longer the debate went, the less support Keating was able to generate. As the days and weeks passed, Hawke stayed with Keating in public and mostly in private. He wanted a way out, one that would leave Keating with his reputation intact, and Hawke with his hard-won Labor constituency also intact.

Keating's concerns certainly weren't shown in public, but he was worried. He constantly whinged that he was forever having to shore Hawke up. The Hawke advisers, led by Garnaut, would have another go at undermining Hawke's support for the package, and Keating would race around to the PM's office and get him back 'in the cart'. In the months leading up to the summit, Keating was openly contemptuous of Hawke to anyone who wanted to listen. What made my life pretty tough was that Peter Barron never liked the consumption tax. Being pulled from pillar to post by Barron and by Keating wasn't much fun, but at least I did not have any critical role to play. I told Hawke and Keating that if they opted to go for the consumption tax, they would get it through Caucus, but narrowly. This was pretty courageous advice, and I'm not sure I ever convinced myself of its accuracy. Had I declared that Caucus wouldn't pass it, I suspect that Hawke would have dumped it very early indeed.

The tax summit, which began on 28 June and ran for three days was the last example of grand consensus Hawke style. All the potential players gathered under one roof, presided over by Hawke. But there was never any real hope that this gathering would deliver an agreed resolution by consensus. Like most people, I assumed that the business community would support Keating; like most of them I was wrong. When Bob White, then chairman of the Business Council of Australia (BCA), got up and bucketed Option C, Keating had lost the one area of support that should have been in the cart. White delivered the usual short-sighted business leader's speech citing as the reason for his opposition the imposts that would go up with the consumption tax.

This was typical of the BCA, all of whose members wanted a

consumption tax. They shot down Option C because they all wanted the up side and would brook no hint of a down side. Yet when John Hewson put forward his consumption tax proposals for the 1993 election, BCA members fought each other for the right to be first and loudest to proclaim its wonder. No hint of support for Keating's package in 1985, however, meant that the summit was over virtually as soon as it started.

In the 1980s and early 1990s, I often wished that business could produce a leader with authority, someone whom the others could follow. The entire period of Labor government hasn't yet seen a class performance from business as a lobby.

While Hawke and Keating had never been close, up to the time of the summit both had made a real effort to give at least the appearance of unity. Hawke's on-again, off-again support for Option C put paid to that forever. When you have as much riding on the outcome as Keating had, you are bound to stretch friendships and relationships beyond reasonable parameters. To have doubts, to question or to be cautious about his proposal was simply to acknowledge how big a change Keating was seeking. Change is never easy for the electorate, business, the trade unions or the party, and Hawke's reluctance to embrace it wholeheartedly was easy for anyone but Keating to understand. He sent 'jellyback' and other terms of derision for Hawke such as 'the silver bodgie' ringing through the corridors and offices of the parliament.

One event above all sealed the permanency of the Hawke–Keating rift. During the summit Hawke, unknown to Keating, visited Simon Crean and Bill Kelty in their hotel to bury the consumption tax and to drop his demands on the ACTU. I don't really believe he caved in to Kelty, just admitted the reality that nobody besides Keating and his advisers wanted the Keating package. While it is possible to argue, as Keating did, that Hawke should have pushed on with this huge reform irrespective of any amount of opposition, he would have been crazy to try it.

But visiting Kelty and agreeing with him to scrap Option C wasn't very smart either. Knowing Keating's depth of commitment to the reform, knowing his restlessness and insecurity about their relationship and knowing how fundamental that relationship was to Labor's future success, Hawke should have fronted Keating and laid on the line his reasons for abandoning the reform. To come to that agreement at a meeting to which Keating had not been invited and to allow it to leak out to the press gallery before Keating had even been told was a dreadful miscalculation. Later Hawke reflected that his daughter's traumas of the previous year had taken a heavy toll on him. It lasted a long time.

Both Hawke and Keating rang me on the morning after Hawke had agreed to abandon the consumption tax. I was sympathetic to both, but it was one of those occasions where some right was on both sides. Hawke was right to worry about the capacity to sell a tax that virtually nobody outside Keating's office supported and Keating was right to feel cheated, perhaps betrayed, by Hawke's late-night dash to Kelty's bedside. But the issue had been decided and it was time to get on with the job. No matter how angry Keating might have been, Hawke was impregnable to challenge. The only thing to do was to move forward—and nobody goes faster or better in that direction than Paul Keating.

Robbed of his prized consumption tax, publicly defeated as never before, Keating could have been excused for taking a reasonable period in which to sulk and to brood. Whether he knew it or not, his performance in the period immediately after this humiliation would be the making of him. Anyone who doubted him had to be in awe of this, the greatest of all comebacks, expressed in the famous phrase: 'I think it's a bit like Ben Hur. We have crossed the line with one wheel off, but we have crossed the line.' Out on the canvas for the compulsory count, feeling wounded, betrayed and frustrated, Keating somehow managed to climb back to his feet and start all over again.

Now every tax option previously rejected as too hard was back on the table for discussion: a tough capital gains tax with no grandfathering for assets already held, a crackdown on every form of fringe benefit, the Australia Card, the abolition of the double taxation of company dividends. Personal income tax rates would be cut, though not to the same extent as would have been possible if Option C had seen the light of day.

Anyone who thought Keating's original tax package was pretty scary hadn't thought about the second. It was ready by mid September; very few of us were ready for it. The Australia Card proposal frightened the Left, the hardline version of the capital gains tax frightened the Right, the crackdown on fringe benefits

In the Sydney campaign office with Bob McMullan, the national secretary, and Ken Bennett, assistant national secretary, during the 1983 election. There was no doubt in anyones mind that Bob Hawke and Labor were going to win.

This cartoon by Mark Knight shows that by 1987 my image needed a little softening.

In Tasmania in 1986 I was converted to wilderness protection. Dave Heatley (right) and almost invisible on the left, Geoff Law, both of the Tasmanian Wilderness Society.

The photographs taken on Dr Bob Brown's Box Brownie are poor but they give an idea of what I saw to convince me.

The Sun

MINISTER BASHED IN WILD PROTEST

SATURDAY, SEPTEMBER 5, 1987

My second visit to Ravenshoe in Queensland in 1987 to explain why logging should stop in the rainforests. My assurances of full compensation fell on deaf ears. They all turned their backs on me in protest, which was at least an improvement on my first visit, as the newspaper banner above shows. However it did convince many others I was serious about the environment.

At the national conference in 1987 with Robert Ray, the leader of the ALP Right in Victoria. He is the toughest politician I have ever met.

Another start to a federal election campaign. In 1987 we hoped to make up for the unnecessary losses we had made in 1984 as a result of being over confident and running with a preoccupied leader. From left to right: Brian Nugent, Electoral Comissioner for NSW, Michael Sexton, Sen. Arthur Gietzelt, Sen. Kerry Sibraa, John Morris, Sen. Bruce Childs and Sen. Sue West.

Climbing Uluru in 1988.
This item on the tour nearly killed me, but I have always been prepared to make sacrifices for the job.

Visiting Katherine Gorge, Northern Territory in 1988, during a tour to see the Territories tourist attractions when Minister for the Arts, Sport, Environment, Tourism and Territories.

How Patrick Cook of the Bulletin *saw me in 1988.*

With (left to right) John Kerin, David Simmons and John Johnson at the 1990 state conference.

Family life suffers when you have to be away for long periods at a time. When parliament breaks up in December there is finally an opportunity to spend real time with the family. In 1987 Cheryl, Kate, Matt and I all went to New York for Christmas.

Discussing the Year of Landcare with Bob Hawke at a trip to Renmark in 1990. Being green was good for votes but this view of the Murray River shows how little we have done to prevent environmental disaster in this country.

frightened anyone who received one (a big percentage of the country). And the prospect of fighting Keating on any part of it frightened the hell out of me.

The Australia Card was the new identity card system that would save hundreds of millions of dollars by helping to eliminate everything from tax evasion and avoidance to social welfare fraud. It eventually died in the Senate after a long campaign by the Opposition and civil liberties groups around the country. Everyone from Peter Garrett to Neville Wran to Chris Puplick (one of the few effective Liberal Senate performers during the 1980s) chimed in to arouse public feeling against what they claimed would be an intrusive new way for governments to interfere in the lives of ordinary citizens. But I think this is one proposal that should have been adopted, despite these concerns. Identity cards are quite common in Western democracies, and there is little to fear from them if their use is properly monitored by parliament. In this case Australia backed away from a sensible reform on the basis of a clever public campaign that turned early poll majorities in favour of it to minorities in the space of one year.

In fact, the use of tax file numbers has done most of what an Australia Card would have done. The gradual extension of their use has gone virtually unnoticed, and complaints about invasion of privacy now come only from the privacy industry (that is, academics who earn a living writing articles about it). If we are to be serious about cracking down on welfare fraud or putting the brakes on the black economy, we must allow some scrutiny of what citizens do. The amount of revenue lost by not having a tax file number system in place earlier would run into billions, and Australia could do a lot with those billions right now.

Whatever might have been effected in the electorate, however, the Keating tax package had an immediate effect on MPs and senators: for the first time their perks would be taxed. This was a stunning blow to many MPs, particularly those in marginal seats whose electoral allowances, which had always been tax-free, would now be taxed at the top marginal rate. As deductions such as entertainment (for example, the buying of a few beers in pubs or clubs as they went about entertaining or buying lunch for constituents or journalists who might help their cause) were no longer to be allowed, every Caucus member could see his or her financial position being seriously eroded.

The Left took the high road. Largely at the urging of Gerry Hand, they decided to insist that MPs and senators should be treated like everyone else in the community. This was politically sensible because nobody likes MPs getting any more than they already have, and it appealed to the Left base which was largely drawn from battlers to whom a parliamentary salary took on enormous proportions. High-minded though it might have been, it ignored the serious plight of quite a few MPs who were carrying big overdrafts after paying for their campaigns. Some were in desperate financial straits and so quite a few of us raised this matter in Caucus. It is worth noting that a number of Liberal MPs were giving us great encouragement to press forward.

After a somewhat acrimonious Caucus discussion, Hawke agreed that a delegation of backbenchers would meet with him, Paul Keating and Mick Young, who as Special Minister of State had direct responsibility for MPs' pay and conditions. That same Caucus meeting saw the defeat of the main left-wing motion of opposition to the Keating package.

Peter Baldwin and Peter Duncan had argued that the top marginal tax rate of 60 cents in the dollar should not be reduced to 49 cents. Keating won the day by arguing that the top income earners would be hit hardest by the fringe benefits tax crackdown and some relief would be given to all taxpayers. There is more than a little irony in successive Liberal governments raising tax levels to 60 cents in the dollar and Labor governments giving substantial relief by bringing those rates down.

The delegation of backbenchers included Robert Ray and myself, and our meeting with Hawke and his ministers was bound to be fiery. It was at this meeting that a rift occurred between Keating and me. I was pretty vocal in querying Paul's analysis of the tax package's effect on MPs. He drew his figures and diagrams on a blackboard and dazzled us with science as he explained how black was white and we had a bloody hide to suggest otherwise. I remember Keating saying: 'Look, fellas, the package won't cost you a cent.' He was right: it cost us $10 000. When you know you are being dudded, no amount of science will change your mind, and there was not enough sugar in north Queensland to make this sandwich taste like anything but what we knew it was.

I was unkind enough to say that I didn't believe a word of it, that other taxpayers around the country could negotiate with their employers to cushion the effects of the tax changes and that unless we got a deal better than the one Keating was offering, very serious financial pressure would be placed on a number of our colleagues. Keating grew hostile at this remark, and declared to the assembled gathering: 'Graham, you've got a PhD in greed.'

That remark really got to me; like most senators, my financial position was pretty reasonable and I had been on fairly high salaries for most of my working life. I cut him dead from that moment and didn't speak to him for nearly twelve months.

To be charitable to Keating, the end result proved much closer to the view put by the Caucus committee than to the response it got. To his credit, over the next few years he and Hawke found various ways and means for making up for what MPs were losing. Setting salaries for MPs will never be easy and no one will ever agree with any increase. That is why it is getting so hard to recruit successful business people or professionals to run as candidates. There is not much joy for a top lawyer earning $250 000 or more in running for parliament earning $90 000 per year which is all taxed, hoping the party of his or her choice wins government and then waiting in the queue for five to ten years for a possible chance at becoming a minister.

At the time there were MPs who couldn't pay their parliamentary dining room bills, whose bank managers were constantly harassing them about the overdrafts that serviced their last campaigns, and who were still contemplating how they would pay for the next campaign. While bagging politicians is always good for a laugh and will always be popular, if Australia won't pay for the best, it won't get them. It should be remembered that all who do this job are away from their families during the week and get home on Fridays too tired to listen or to participate properly in ordinary family life. The quality of life as a parliamentarian isn't all it's cracked up to be.

Hawke was still handicapped by his family's tragedy, and he had pretty well abdicated responsibility for policy by now. Keating was infuriated by Hawke's insistence that the full ministry, not just the Cabinet, would debate the final tax package from

14–16 September—a radical departure from the normal procedure. Then, on the second day of the debate, Hawke left to attend Papua New Guinea's tenth anniversary celebrations, leaving Keating to face a fractious ministry where virtually every part of his package would meet opposition from someone. If there was a moment when Keating's disdain and lack of respect for Hawke turned to open contempt, that weekend in September was pivotal. Keating felt his abandonment acutely—he spoke of it for years afterwards—but he pushed the package through in classic Keating style. He got almost everything he wanted, and could reasonably claim to have delivered real change. To salvage this from the wrecked tax cart of a few months previously was Keating's finest hour.

Fringe benefits of all kinds were being attacked, even staff canteens. This meant that the conditions of millions were put into doubt, and many of these were Labor voters. Keating was prepared to opt for honesty with the electorate: if what they had wasn't good for the country, he would tell them. Resilience is an essential component of toughness: Keating not only demonstrated this, but he came up with a bold and ultimately successful result.

Good policy was mixed with an uncompromising attitude to doing what had hitherto been politically impossible. What Keating did was to present us with the basis of our approach over the next few years. Unpalatable medicine was credible for the first time in my political life: if times were tough, we didn't have to promise rose gardens. The rules of the game underwent fundamental change, and Australia actually began to see that promising a big bag of lollies every election wasn't the only way for political leaders to behave.

Yet again, this left the Liberals in a terrible pickle. They were very much wedded to old politics and for them change was well-nigh impossible.

Throughout my observations of this period, I have barely referred to the Liberals or the National Party. Between 1983 and 1986 they had been irrelevant: they just didn't matter. While Peacock had done better than expected in 1984, we still had a big majority and the Peacock–Howard tussle had that right feel of permanency about it. In September 1985 there had been a changing of the guard, a baton change between Peacock and

Howard, but I'm not sure that anyone, apart from the participants, really cared. On the day of the announcement that there was a new Liberal leader, I was staying in a motel on the south coast of New South Wales. The news neither frightened nor excited me. I can remember sitting on the bed that night and thinking it didn't matter who led the Liberals. Australia had never shown much love for either. Peacock was always that little bit too smooth, Howard never smooth enough.

John Howard has been by far the best Liberal performer in the parliament for all the 1980s and 1990s. He is the one with the capacity to hurt the government in debate. He can master a brief and make the best use of it, and if you can't master the parliament you are in a lot of trouble. The parliament is not just the workplace of parliamentarians—it is the workplace of the press gallery who present how MPs perform to the nation. If you perform badly often enough, they will write you off. If that happens, you cannot win an election.

The problem is that being good in parliament is but one of several prerequisites, all of which are necessary for electoral success. You have to be a good media performer. When Australians are sitting in their lounge rooms, they have to feel comfortable about you being in there with them. John Howard always was a lousy television performer and a particularly boring radio performer as well. He is a formal, conservative man who gets more formal and conservative in front of a camera. His incapacity to be the same in front of a camera as he is at other times was his undoing. Australia just wouldn't, and still doesn't, warm to him. It's tough to know that God made you a good No 2 but never gave you the right stuff to be a No 1. I think Howard knows it, but can't quite accept it still.

Andrew Peacock on the other hand was smooth. Nothing else, just smooth. He never had the substance and he never overcame Keating's devastating remark about souffles not rising twice. That so summed up the overwhelming feeling of most Australians that many of us could not look at Peacock without thinking of a souffle. Andrew's destiny was never clear to me. The only thing that was clear was what his destiny was not—to be our prime minister.

The rest of the Liberals and Nationals barely rated a mention in the media of the mid 1980s, and the situation is much the same today. Fred Chaney made a reasonable fist of Opposition leader in the Senate and could put in solid if unspectacular performances. Mind you, he was up against John Button and Gareth Evans, so spectacular performances were necessary. Peter Baume was a man of honour and very, very capable, but he was a 'wet' who wouldn't toe the line, so he languished on the backbench and then departed. Chris Puplick, who became my shadow in the Environment portfolio from 1987 to 1990, was a very good performer who was booted out of the Senate by Bronwyn Bishop. The rest of them—Jim Carlton, Michael Mackellar, Wal Fife, Phillip Ruddock and a host of others—never could cut the mustard. Many were nice decent people who mixed well with the residents of Sydney's North Shore or Melbourne's Toorak but who never understood the masses of people who could not afford to live there—that is, most of the country.

So Howard won the leadership after Peacock resigned because Howard had defeated John Moore, Peacock's candidate for the deputy leadership. Only the Liberal Party could have staged a fiasco like this one: a leader trying to unseat a deputy and not telling anyone that if he didn't get his man up he intended to resign the leadership. It was so well organised that the Peacock supporters at first moved that the leadership be vacated before they got the message that only the deputy's job was supposed to be on the line. Not even Howard had expected to win, so astray was the counting on both sides. But Peacock would never give up on Howard, just as he wouldn't give up on Fraser.

It is heartening to know that your opponents will spend all their time on each other and have no time left for you.

CHAPTER 10

A Bit of the National Spotlight

In 1986 I emerged from the fabled smoke-filled back rooms and started to see a bit of the spotlight. Up to this point I had been mentioned in the national press and on TV on the odd occasion—usually negatively, to do with party brawling or the like—but I had remained a New South Wales figure who was very difficult to export. Now all this began to change.

At the time, our fortunes were starting to decline; after three years of dominating the Opposition, our ascendancy was beginning to sink. The fallout from the tax package was considerable: workers felt short-changed by the taxing of staff canteens and employer-provided motor cars, employers were angered by the extra taxes they were having to pay to keep their workers happy. Virtually everybody ignored the benefits that flowed from the tax package, such as lower tax rates for all and the raising of the lowest tax threshold which meant that 100 000 people no longer had to pay any tax at all.

I felt we were failing to explain what we were doing, and I wished to make my feelings known. If you want to send a message to the Prime Minister and the Treasurer that they will not heed in private, you do it in public. My opportunity to do this took place in fairly humble circumstances: I was the guest speaker on 9 November 1986 at the annual dinner for delegates to the party's New South Wales rural conference. That year the conference was held in the Singleton Workers Club northwest of Sydney. While the country conference is a fascinating meeting with enthralling debates about rural policy, it attracts very little media coverage. If you want coverage, you have to organise it: I told Laurie Oakes to make sure he got a Channel Nine camera crew to cover the speech.

I flew to Singleton in a chartered light plane with Michael Lee, later a Cabinet minister, and a number of colleagues. During the flight I told Michael I was concerned that my speech was bound to get me into trouble. Something told me Hawke and Keating might be less than excited about what I intended to say.

I stood up in front of that rural audience in Singleton and for thirty minutes I gave the government a free analysis of where we were going wrong. I criticised Hawke and Keating for using economic language that nobody could understand, I nominated group after group in the Australian community, components of the constituency Labor had built over the years, who had now been alienated or who saw little reason to support it. The party audience in Singleton lapped up every word of it; my speech summed up the feelings of party members all over the country. This was heady stuff. I can remember watching Al Grassby talking to an audience at the Windsor theatre on the western outskirts of Sydney in 1972 and being in awe of his capacity to play them for laughs or to make them angry and resentful towards our opponents. I thought then: *If he can do this, so can I.* Years of practice were now paying off.

When Laurie Oakes ran the story on Channel Nine the following day, a wave of publicity washed over me as it had never done before. Newspapers editorialised; Paul Kelly had the whole speech reprinted in the *Australian*. Because I was a prominent member of the government, any speech I made critical of it was bound to get some publicity. But I knew that if you want people to listen to speeches, what you say must have some credibility. I wasn't entirely critical of government policy, but defences of every decision a government has made impress nobody unless there is some acknowledgment that mistakes have been made. If humour and passion can be injected along the way, impact is not too difficult to achieve. One thing was for sure—I had made an impact.

That one speech hardly changed the course of history, but it did make a contribution. True to what I had expected, Hawke was pretty angry and he made his views known to me in blunt terms when I next saw him in Canberra. But the general message did get through. The Caucus, whose almost unanimous sentiments had been summarised in the speech, kept making their feelings known to ministers and to the party, and the trade union movement did likewise. For a time I think we had been asleep but, now awakened, the government put more effort into selling its policies. This was made easier because the pall of lethargy that had hung over Bob Hawke for almost two years had begun to lift. The old Hawke was coming back and just in time, too.

CHAPTER 11

What's Red and Flies at 140mph?

The 1986 national conference was approaching, and with it the perennial problem of changing New South Wales's preselection system away from a panel totally run by the rank and file to a system where a centrally elected body would get 50 per cent of the votes. This would never be solved except by the adoption of national Rules; at a New South Wales conference the emotion behind the traditional preselection method would always be hard to beat. At a conference where the Right has 60 per cent or more of the delegates in most ballots, I don't believe we could have carried a resolution to change the system and if I had tried the damage done to the Right would have been incalculable. Mass ethnic branch stacking will eventually undermine the system and it is interesting that the Left, the great defenders of the rank-and-file system in New South Wales, have successfully opposed the introduction of this preselection system in every other state.

I organised a meeting between the Right and the Centre Left in a suite at the Inter-Continental Hotel in Sydney a couple of weeks before the July national conference which was to be held in Hobart. The secretaries of the South Australian, Western

Australian and Queensland branches—Chris Schacht, Michael Beahan and Peter Beattie—flew into town. The national convenor of the faction, Senator Peter Cook, came as well. The Right were represented by Robert Ray, Stephen Loosley and myself.

The venue was a far cry from a back room at the Trades Hall, being a beautiful suite with sweeping views of the Botanic Gardens and Sydney Harbour. We served a good lunch, trying to create the perfect atmosphere for doing a deal to line up a majority of votes for this Rule change. We would ambush the Left and score one of our greatest victories. This was to be my finest moment as a factional boss.

I started to evaluate the Centre Left. From the Right's point of view, Peter Beattie was the least reliable—he would have to be watched. Chris Schacht was from South Australia, the Centre Left state closest to the Right, but he was probably much farther distant from us personally. Michael Beahan was a stranger to us and Western Australian Labor Premier Brian Burke had some concerns about his reliability. Peter Cook we just didn't like, feeling that his heart had remained with the Left even if his body had moved to the Centre. No doubt if the Centre Left members had been asked for a free character assessment of myself, Robert Ray or Stephen Loosley, their response would have been equally frank.

We started talking, circling each other like wary boxers in the ring, probing for weaknesses, assessing strengths and working out the odds on what would happen if either side had to throw a punch. The argument from our side was fairly simple: the addition of a central component to the local rank and file would no longer mean that the candidate with the greatest number of friends and relatives in the local branches, or the best branch stacker, would always be elected. The Centre Left's argument was that, as this central panel would always favour the Right, we would use this advantage to take more and more parliamentary seats over time.

We were indignant: fancy the bastards thinking we'd do such a thing! But there were two real arguments against this happening. Firstly, the Right wouldn't be stupid enough to try and take everything. We were promising to leave untouched the percentages of factional representation in state and federal parliaments. Therefore over time both Left and Right would have the opportunity of improving the quality of their representatives. And secondly, the national executive, where the Centre Left could always combine with the Left against the Right if we were making pigs of ourselves, would sit in judgment from the lofty heights of Canberra. Here was a way of eradicating the problem identified by the Centre Left that some seats in New South Wales needed to be filled by better people.

Our discussions were not heated: they were calm, rational and at times even friendly. As the day drew to a close, I could see light at the end of the tunnel. National Rules were a bit frightening for South Australia and Western Australia, who wanted to keep their own quaint undemocratic systems, but to achieve our objective we were more than prepared to make compromises.

Finally we had a deal and I was on top of the world. All human beings are flawed, me more than most. My greatest fault is trusting too many people too often, and I was on top of the world because I believed what I had been told. Now, Robert Ray can perhaps be accused of having a few faults, but nobody would accuse him of being too trusting. He was far from convinced. Three times he repeated to our Centre Left co-conspirators this warning: if this deal isn't a deal, we should not proceed with this debate at the conference. While this was said with a smile (and sometimes Robert's smile is indistinguishable from a smirk) he left the very clear impression that he would find difficulty in trusting this lot out of sight on a dark night. But we received their absolute assurances that this was a deal that would stick, and so we headed off to Hobart a few weeks later with our hopes high and our confidence up.

In those days we had national executive meetings with long agendas. Traditionally the Thursday and the Friday before the conference were for the executive meeting, the weekend was for serious plotting, and the conference, which runs for five days and four nights, would reflect these efforts. The executive went peacefully enough, although I could see the beginnings of discussion between the Left and the Centre. The Left knew a debate was scheduled to take place on the question of national Rules, and their antennae were good enough to record the unmistakable signs of trouble ahead. Lobbying began in earnest and the lifts, corridors and the rooms of the Wrest Point Casino came alive.

For the next few days they saw much more action than the gambling tables as the mad scramble for a majority of votes got under way in earnest.

I was ensconced in Room 1002, which quickly became the meeting place for the Right and the Right's meetings with the Centre Left. It saw a lot of action; the smell of smoke, beer, spirits and bad breath hung in the air for a week. The Centre Left were meeting with the Left, where Gerry Hand and John Faulkner were wooing them with tales of horror that no left-winger from New South Wales would ever again be elected to parliament if the Rule changes went through. The Centre Left—who, like the Left, loved meetings—would then go back to report to their delegates' meetings. They seemed to come at us in relays, with different deal makers and breakers every time.

Soon we knew our deal was in deep trouble. There were plenty of spies in the Centre Left, and we learned that their national delegates' caucus, augmented by assorted parliamentarians, had baulked at supporting us. The Left worked hard on their more obvious marks, and for us to win we had to hold at least those with whom we had made the deal in the first place.

But the Left had more powerful magic than we did, and we knew we were losing. For us, the real problem proved to be the Tasmanian Centre Left. At many of the meetings in Room 1002, the Tasmanian representative was Alan Evans (later chief of the Premier's Department in Tasmania and a senior adviser to John Dawkins when he was Treasurer). Formerly from New South Wales, where he had sided with the Left, Evans would never agree to change the preselection rules in New South Wales. Nick Sherry, his colleague from Tasmania (then a union official but now a senator) had similar thoughts. The Centre Left could not afford to split, and the Tasmanians were playing for keeps. If they hadn't all voted as a bloc, the faction would have looked like a joke, and they knew it: Cook, Schacht, Crowley, Beattie, Beahan, Evans, Uncle Tom Cobleigh and all. We lost count of the number of people who came in to represent them, but it didn't matter who turned up: they were turning against us.

As the big day of the Rules debate approached, the meetings became more and more acrimonious. It was difficult to believe that we had ever been to the Inter-Continental or that any agreement between the Right and Centre Left had ever been reached. Robert Ray could only look at me and say: 'I told you so.'

At the last meeting with the Centre Left, we really got stuck into them. We told them that if they wanted to survive in the party, they couldn't rat on arrangements solemnly entered into. They expressed their regrets and used the excuse that the leaders of the Left always trotted out when entering into a deal: We agree, but we have to put it to a general meeting, and we can't guarantee the outcome. That might have had some validity had we not known from our friends who were attending Centre Left meetings that the people who had done the deal with us were no longer supporting it.

As the meeting was breaking up, Robert Ray looked at Peter Cook, whom we considered the chief villain, and said: 'What's red all over and flies through the air at 140 miles an hour?'

'I don't know,' said Cook.

Robert's reply was one of those lines you can never forget: 'You, you bastard, when I throw you out that fucking window!'

On that happy note, the Right was faced with determining how to handle the debate. There were several possibilities. To save ourselves the embarrassment of public defeat, we could put up little or just token opposition, we could back off, thereby saving the party from the public division that had been an all-too-familiar feature of the 1950s, or we could stand and fight with scant regard for the consequences. It went back to a rather basic philosophy of mine: never let the enemy have a free kick, because if they can hurt you without penalty they may make a habit out of it. We had been betrayed, we believed we were right about the Rules change. We decided to go down with all guns blazing.

Since the Thursday executive meeting we had been arguing day and night, and by the time the Rules debate began on the following Tuesday afternoon there were many frayed tempers and not a few tired and emotional people as well. By the end of the week we had drunk $2000 worth of beer in Room 1002 alone. Fortunately there were plenty of willing wallets to share the burden. Deeply impressed was Johnno Johnson, that great character of the New South Wales branch who so typifies the

Catholic Labor working-class sentiment that gave rise to the Right in that state; he doesn't drink alcohol and he marvelled at the capacity of those who did. We were still standing, looking no more the worse for wear than he.

The debate began on Tuesday evening at 7.30. We decided that I would lead off for the losers, a role to which I could never have become accustomed. To cover up my deep sense of betrayal, I decided to use some humour. 'Everyone knows my room number—I think the whole world does—it's 1002 and I think you've all been there,' I said.

Mick Young interjected: 'Gerry (referring to Gerry Hand) hasn't.'

'I have got some standards, Mr Chairman,' I replied.

We were off to a good start: pretty well all the delegates were laughing. While I now hesitate to use too many quotes from my speech because this would look too much like Alan Ramsey's Saturday column in the *Sydney Morning Herald*, a few of my lines summed up the debate and all that led up to it.

I continued: 'We have met for four and five hours a day, to one or two in the morning, to look at the question of national Rules. The first difficulty you have when you do that is that every time you open the door, they've got new leaders. They've got more leaders than members of the faction, but I learned to live with that. I learned to know that every time I opened the door, somebody else would be there with a new plan. Someone else who could explain why they had ratted on the last one.

'The Centre Left are of course these men of principle, the men of policy, the men about all things good and holy. But in my room I've got to tell you, delegates, they committed a few sins. Because in my room we discovered that what they were really about was jobs, power and what the rest of us have been about all the time anyway. What we discovered was that at last the three factions had something in common—self-interest.'

I continued in this vein for ten minutes, and had the Centre Left laughing at themselves. The Left were laughing too, and why not: they'd never had it so good. It has always been my view that the Left dislike the Centre Left more than they dislike the Right, so the Left were combining with them and enjoying the bath I was giving them. The only reference I made to the Left in the speech was to say that 'they only came to Hobart to do us. I understand that. I've been in that sort of deal myself on occasions.' I was interested to see that later that night delegate after delegate from the Left came up to congratulate me.

Then it was Robert Ray's turn to speak. He didn't use humour so much as direct, cold, hard threats, proving again that when wronged he is probably the most menacing person I have ever known. He described the Centre Left as 'a group of mendacious, irresponsible and unstable individuals who meet consistently, who backstab each other and who in some way get the support of another group to backstab themselves. I can live with these proposals, but the memories of how they were achieved will be a bit harder to live with.' You don't make such statements unless you have retribution on your mind, and our minds were full of it.

Nothing spectacular occurred during the rest of the conference. All this bitterness was forgotten as we combined with the Centre Left to defeat Left amendments in debates on the economy, foreign affairs and industry policy. Cursory formalities were observed when we met Centre Left delegates in the corridors.

But the thirst for vengeance had to be quenched. Over the next few years, the Centre Left representation in the ministry was cut back; while their overall numbers had declined anyway, there was no need for us to try and help them, for any desire of that kind was wiped out on a cold Tuesday evening in Hobart in July 1986. Peter Cook took six to eight months longer to become a minister than he otherwise might have done. The Left got slightly better treatment for a while, but after twelve months all was forgotten, or at best almost forgotten.

Eight years on all this is only a memory. We have come a long way since those days. The relations between Peter Cook and myself have been more than normalised, and are now very friendly. I supported Chris Schacht becoming a minister, and both Robert Ray and I supported Michael Beahan becoming president of the Senate. If you hate forever, you become bitter and twisted, boring and useless. I have seen a few colleagues consumed by hatred, and I have maintained an absolute determination not to become like them.

CHAPTER 12

The Stuff of Labor Dreams

By mid 1986, Hawke was climbing back to form after his personal crisis. We needed him, too: we were facing a rather difficult time for several reasons.

By May Keating was really worried by our growing balance of payments deficit. It was no use trying to explain it away yet again—as we had done—by declaring that Qantas had bought another plane (they had already bought an awful lot). Keating needed to issue a shock warning to Australia and to overseas investors. On Sydney's John Laws show, he told the radio audience that Australia was importing about $12 billion more than we were exporting every year, and that if the government couldn't get manufacturing going again and keep sensible and moderate wage and economic policies we were basically done for, and would end up being a third-rate economy. He said: 'The only thing to do is slow the growth down to a canter. Once you slow the growth under 3 per cent, unemployment starts to rise again . . . then you are gone. You are a banana republic.'

This hit the public and the markets with cataclysmic force. The dollar immediately dropped three cents and the voters couldn't understand why the Treasurer, who had been boasting about economic growth, was suddenly saying Australia might be overtaken by Brazil. He modified what he had said, he produced new figures, he said the economy wasn't sick, it was too strong. But for the rest of his time as Treasurer, Keating had to live with the 'banana republic' tag.

His remarks came as a complete shock to his Prime Minister. Hawke was on a tour of Asia at the time, and he railed from Beijing to Tokyo that we were *not* facing a crisis. He was furious with Keating, not least because the Treasurer had seized the initiative, if only temporarily. The Hawke–Keating rivalry was already showing, and neither could see what an ideal partnership they were. The Prime Minister was out there being loved and loving it, the Treasurer was guiding the hard but necessary policy shifts that kept us in business. To the credit of both of them, they were usually prepared to put enough bandaids over the wounds to keep the public satisfied. Given what Hawke and Keating think of each other these days, it's hard to remember that they were the best vote-winning duo we ever had.

Keating, the agent of change, powered through a lot of other economic reforms that year, many accompanied by screams of protest from both the Left and the Right. He persuaded the ACTU to accept another wage discount, he persuaded the government to sanction further savage cuts in expenditure. He even convinced us all that a partial deregulation of home loan interest rates would not be political suicide. He had begun by demanding full deregulation, which certainly would have been suicide, but eventually he compromised, getting I suspect exactly what he wanted: everybody who already had a home loan would keep their 13.5 per cent ceiling, all new loans would be at market rates.

All this cost-cutting, all these dire warnings of banana republics were doing us no good at all in the polls. As 1987 began, the Liberals began to look alarmingly as if they might stand some sort of chance in the election that had to be called that year. But when luck, or God, is on your side, something always turns up to save you, and on this occasion our salvation came from the most unexpected source—Queensland Premier Joh Bjelke-Petersen.

In January 1987, backed by a strange informal coalition that included Gold Coast entrepreneur Mike Gore and Andrew Peacock and supported by several influential businessmen and journalists, he launched his campaign to become Prime Minister of Australia. The original idea was that he would resign as Queensland premier and enter federal politics at a by-election, taking the leadership of the National Party from Ian Sinclair. Andrew Peacock, rolled as leader of the Liberal Party in 1985 and now deputy to his replacement John Howard, would resign and recontest his safe Liberal seat of Kooyong as a National Party candidate. Howard would continue to lead the Liberal Party; the National–Liberal coalition, led by Bjelke-Petersen and Peacock, would win the federal election, so Joh Bjelke-Petersen would be Prime Minister. Peacock would later replace him, with the Nationals being the majority party. What made this absurd scenario even more captivating for us was that Joh had exactly one policy—a 25 per cent flat rate of tax—and he could barely string one coherent sentence together.

But I had other things on my mind at the time. While Joh was launching his campaign, my family and I headed for a six-week sojourn driving around Europe. As each term of parliament ends, every MP and senator is provided with a round-the-world, first-class ticket. This can be converted to two economy-class tickets, then you need only provide half fares for the kids and away you go. In the United Kingdom, France, Germany and Italy I met politicians and party officials. In Germany an election was in progress, and I attended a Socialist Party rally in Munich. This was held in a massive beer hall with bands of all types, singers and dancers, political speeches and most of all millions of gallons of beer. That night I drank six pints with my German hosts and enjoyed the rally as much as anyone there, even though I didn't understand a single word that was said. The rest of the audience had similar feelings: it's impossible for speeches to be boring when people are as pissed as those two thousand were that night. In the election the Socialist Party was trounced, but I'm sure they didn't notice.

Refreshed, I returned to Australia to find the Joh bandwagon rolling on. Lots more people were climbing aboard: new Queensland millionaires, redneck entrepreneurs, aggressive businessmen who were disillusioned with the Coalition's leadership team of John Howard and Ian Sinclair, others who hated Keating's capital gains and fringe benefits taxes, members of extreme right-wing fringe groups. In rural centres all over the country there were rallies of the faithful coming to see the new messiah whose message was so dangerously simple: elect me and you will pay less tax. Audiences looked upon him as some kind of prophet and they hung on every word, despite the fact that rural incomes were so low that many would have actually paid *more* tax. I wish we could make Labor Party audiences as compliant and unquestioning.

The main assistance Joh gave us, however, wasn't just his candidature which, linked as it was with Peacock, undermined John Howard by its very existence. It was his cavalier attacks on Howard and Sinclair; he spent more time getting stuck into them than he did 'the socialists'. I assumed that we were 'the socialists', spearheaded by Hawke and Keating, whose names were interwoven into every speech. The Left are not famous for recognising irony, but even they must have seen some in anyone attacking Hawke and Keating for being socialists by 1987.

Fatally flawed by the lack of interest in anything Bjelke-Petersen had to say in the big cities, the Joh for Canberra push undermined Howard from day one. It was crude, rude and utterly hopeless, the stuff of which Labor dreams are made. That people with the reputation of Sir Robert Sparkes, president of the Queensland National Party, could have taken it seriously still stung my delicate sensibilities. But with the Gold Coast white shoe brigade putting up the big bucks, we knew the push wouldn't go away or wither on the vine. Joh was playing for keeps, but playing out of his class. He said he was ready for an election at any time, and according to his hopeful deputy Peacock, his campaign was 'a God-driven and abiding duty to drive the Hawke government from power'. Bill Hayden suggested that when Joh did make it to Canberra, he might consider appointing his horse to the Senate.

With the conservatives in a complete shambles and Hawke showing renewed signs of vigour, the fact that we trailed in some of the polls wasn't too big a worry. We didn't seriously doubt that we would win the next election, but we knew we were in for a real fight. By now there was some changing of the guard at the palace, which can be pretty significant if key personnel are involved. Peter Barron had resigned on 30 June 1986 and gone on to Kerry Packer's greener pastures. With an election due within twelve months, the right person had to be found, and pronto. I recommended Bob Sorby, a journalist turned lawyer who had worked on Paul Keating's meagre staff in the bad old days of Opposition. Hawke never said so, but after Barron's success and his own reliance on the New South Wales Right as the core of his support base, he would never rule out my nominee for the job of his chief political adviser. Sorby was bright, tough, experienced and loyal—not a bad combination, I thought. He quickly formed a very good relationship with Hawke and like Barron was never overawed by working for the prime minister and not afraid to put his views, even when Caesar didn't like them.

In May 1987, I left on another overseas tour of duty. This time I was a member of the Australian delegation to the Commonwealth Parliamentary Association. We were based in London but visited Wales, Oxford and Guernsey in a hectic three-week merry-go-round of meetings, dinners, dinners and dinners. Before I left I had several discussions with Hawke and Sorby about the timing of the next election. They were thinking of going early instead of waiting till the end of the year, a concept to which I was opposed. They gave me their word that if anything serious were about to happen about this proposal, I would be contacted in London and consulted. Knowing that I would get a final shot at talking them out of it was enough to send me off happily.

When my official engagements were over Cheryl flew to London to join me, and we went to Ireland for five days of soaking up that beautiful country at a particularly nice time of year. Before leaving London, I rang Sorby to check on developments and was told that no decision had been made but discussions were on in earnest.

We headed for Shannon airport with nary a care in the world. We hired a car and drove to a pub just near the famous racecourse known as the Curragh. The Irish Department of Foreign Affairs had assigned one Michael Geoghegan to meet and greet us. Michael bought us lunch at the pub and then took us to the racecourse, the only genuinely undulating track I have ever seen.

Michael Geoghegan knew a bit about horses; I had four bets on his advice and won more than 400 Irish pounds. This effort paid for our drive around Ireland and if you haven't seen the Ring of Kerry, you haven't lived. I don't know what has happened to Michael Geoghegan, but I know who will look after him if he ever visits Australia.

Our last two days were spent in Dublin as I met a number of politicians from the main political parties. We stayed at the Boswell Hotel in central Dublin and after breakfast on Wednesday 27 May we rang home to talk to our children. Now, by this stage of my career, I definitely fancied myself. After all, I was the confidant of the Prime Minister, I ran the faction, I read about my importance in the papers and I was in the know about all decisions affecting the nation.

Imagine how stupid I felt, then, when my thirteen-year-old son informed me that Hawke had called an early election for Saturday 11 July. I recall sitting on the bed very quietly and wondering how this could have happened without me. The answer was pretty simple—you should never start believing your own bullshit. (When I resigned from parliament Gareth Evans, in addressing the faction meeting that farewelled me, said: 'You're getting out at the right time. You only believe *some* of your own bullshit.')

Cheryl and I flew out of Heathrow for Australia two days later. I did not know then that this was the campaign that would put me in the public eye, not to mention the ministry. This was the one that mattered.

In the 1983 and 1984 campaigns, one of my roles had been to fly to campaign committee meetings with the leader. Typically these were attended by the Prime Minister and his staff with at least Bob McMullan, the party's pollster Rod Cameron and myself. From the Hawke staff, Barron (now replaced by Sorby), Bob Hogg and Geoff Walsh would always be there.

This was a very professional team who were never beaten, but by the time 1987 came around some of the good personal relations that had developed among the group had fallen apart. Rod Cameron and Bob Hawke had no basis of trust, somewhat surprisingly given that Cameron's polling had been a handy weapon immediately before Hawke's assumption of the leadership in 1983. By 1987 Cameron had little time for Hawke and he wasn't keeping it a secret; he told me and probably many others that this would be his last campaign with Hawke.

Even though Robert Ray doubted much of his research, I still believe Cameron to have been the best pollster of the past two decades. He worked for many campaigns both state and federal and, while not infallible, he was usually right in his quantitative and qualitative work. My experiences with him had all been positive; for Neville Wran he had been very good indeed.

However, pollsters should be trusted only to prepare the figures. How they are interpreted and what solutions should be adopted to the problems the figures have highlighted should not be allowed to become the pollster's domain. By 1987 Rod Cameron had almost become a player in the game. He considered himself the equal of or better than pretty well all the politicians and party officials with whom he worked. The problem this caused was demonstrated in the New South Wales state campaign of 1988, when Barry Unsworth was running against Nick Greiner. Cameron took it upon himself to bucket Greiner's wife Kathryn on the front pages of Sydney's newspapers. This was a solo, wilful act, unsanctioned by Unsworth or New South Wales branch secretary Stephen Loosley, who referred to it at the time as 'inspired unilateralism'. Far from being a clever ploy, it backfired on Labor and did us no good at all.

It was also Rod Cameron who advised Barrie Unsworth to make an issue of gun ownership during that campaign, based on the misconception that an anti-firearms policy was overwhelmingly popular. Unfortunately, 85 per cent of people believed that the rules on gun ownership should be tightened, but very few would change their votes because of it. The 15 per cent who owned guns or approved of others owning them were in a very different category. Almost all of them were prepared to change their vote on the issue, and up to this point enough of them had been Labor voters for this one decision to go down as the greatest political blunder in a long time.

All that aside, Cameron was a great pollster, and I wish he were still working for the Labor Party. Provided he knew what limits had been set for him, his polling work was second to none; far superior to anything being done for the Liberals, and we were always better prepared. But Cameron had decided that there was much more to Paul Keating than to Bob Hawke and given that his views were no secret, relations between him and the Prime Minister were poisonous.

The 1987 election was the first time the party used John Singleton to prepare its advertising campaign. 'Singo' is consistently the best, and he still draws on people like Alan Morris (the 'Mo' of MoJo), probably the best hand Australia has ever seen at political advertising. This was a questionable move in party terms. Singleton had previously done advertising for the Liberal Party. Many of us remembered the 'Estonian woman' ads of fifteen years before, when an eastern European refugee compared Labor to a bunch of communists, like those she had fought in her own country. Singleton was a thorough professional. He and Hawke got on very well and the campaign meetings were much more productive than some have since claimed. Singleton is a great character who can charm just about anyone. The journalist Alan Ramsey once warned broadcaster Mike Carlton that I could 'charm the flies off a turd'—Singleton does even better.

For us, Singleton produced the famous Wendy Wood commercial. Wendy was a member of the Erskineville branch of the ALP and the wife of the ex-Newtown Jets footballer Barry Wood, one of Singo's closest friends. Barry and Wendy first came to prominence when our slick new advertising agency needed a family to walk around doing whatever families do in political commercials, while our new jingle 'Let's stick together, let's see it through' was being unleashed on a public no doubt breathless with anticipation. The commercial had to be made in a hurry, on a Saturday, so Singo rang his friends Wendy and Barry, who obliged.

Then, when it was decided that a hard-hitting ad was needed to undermine the Howard tax bribe, Wendy became a star. Her reiterated: 'Where's the money coming from, Mr Howard?' might not have been a purist's dream, but it worked. Her strong working-class accent was just what was needed at the time and when she asked whether John Howard would cut Meals on Wheels, he was forced to respond. Wendy, a long-term ALP member, was on the march. She appeared on 'A Current Affair' and at one point even challenged John Howard to a debate. She was articulate enough to carry off some very good interviews.

Since 1983, Labor's advertising has been consistently superior to the Coalition's. In every campaign we sit anxiously looking for the new Liberal commercials, then realise that our anxiety has been wasted. If the Liberals ever discover a good pollster or one slick advertising agency with real creativity and quick response times, they will be dangerous. But to find these, you need a smart machine and an experienced, aware leader. I think Labor is safe for now.

In those days Keating rarely attended campaign meetings, preferring to run his own race. In this campaign it proved to be just as well, for it was Keating who delivered the knockout blow to Howard and the Liberals.

John Howard was ten years behind in knowing how to campaign, and even further in understanding the electorate. He produced a tax package which had been cobbled together under great pressure and which had as its main theme a huge tax bribe. Individual and business taxes would be reduced by more than $7 billion and he would pay for this largesse by cutting government expenditure. Reducing expenditure by that much would have been impossible without laying waste to social security beneficiaries, hospitals, schools and virtually every service provided by the government.

Under any circumstances this would have been impossible to sell. Politicians are not trusted at the best of times; years of being disappointed by promises on taxation had resulted in a cynical electorate which would need hard evidence of good faith. In this case, the only evidence they could find was Howard's promise to cut everything they held dear.

The whole idea of the tax bribe was hopeless. It became much worse when Keating's people—either Treasury officials working in Treasury or those on his staff—found a critical error in the Coalition's arithmetic. Keating said they had underestimated the cost of their tax package by nothing less than $1.6 billion, and he came up with a classy detailed analysis to prove it. The Liberals took four days to find a response, which was basically: 'Really, this isn't too bad, we're not one and a half billion wrong, we're only half a billion wrong.' The efforts of shadow treasurer Jim Carlton to make Howard carry the can elevated the episode from high farce to fiasco, and the fact that the Liberals had to admit a $500 million error was a killer blow to their campaign. The election was only a few weeks away, and the whole thing proved that you can't wait until an election is announced to develop a policy. Policy development has to be ongoing, so at least there is time to run figures through a calculator before an announcement is made.

Whatever was left of the Liberals and their coalition partners the National Party after this tax debacle, Joh was destroying as fast as he could. He wandered around the countryside campaigning for the prime ministership while not bothering to stand as a candidate: a spoiler who was determined to wreck his party if he couldn't get his way, an aged spoiled brat with a mean-spirited approach to anyone who refused his request for yet another lolly.

Most backbenchers from safe seats or the Senate are doomed to pretty boring election campaigns; they get to help out in the seats that can't be won, and their destiny is to tour bush towns and hamlets trying to lift the Labor vote from 30 per cent to 32 per cent. My break from this drudgery came when I flew to Brisbane's Sheraton Hotel to attend a campaign meeting, but otherwise I did what most of the others do or are supposed to do. My campaign diary for 1987 shows me addressing small dinners of the faithful in Armidale, Tamworth, Taree and Port Macquarie—it can be hard work, but you do get the odd laugh from them. To be a party member in some of those areas takes a good deal of courage, and the least you can do for them is turn up and put on a good show.

The lunch I addressed at a restaurant at Port Macquarie was a step up on some of them. One hundred and twenty of Port Macquarie's finest turned up to hear my words of hope and inspiration. Our candidate, however, had other ideas. He was new to all this and when put in front of a crowd, with a microphone, this mild-mannered pharmacist took on a whole new persona. He proclaimed to the crowd his disgust at the way in which the Labor government had treated the safe National Party seat of Cowper (Port Macquarie has since been redistributed into the seat of Lyne). Roads, bridges, schools and hospitals had never materialised because the electorate had been misguided enough not to vote Labor. This poor treatment had continued in the campaign because Bob Hawke, Paul Keating and John Button had not deigned to turn up . . . 'and look who we got!' he cried.

Just try giving the words of hope and inspiration after that.

Being better known now, I was starting to get some better invitations, and in this campaign Ros Kelly did me a great honour, though she may not realise it. She invited me to address her main fundraising dinner at the Peking Restaurant in the Canberra suburb of Phillip. Three hundred people attended, it went very well, and it was then I really started to feel I could make it with the public and not just be the king of the smoke-filled rooms. I then spoke at a dinner for Ted Grace (Deputy Whip in the Caucus) in his safe western Sydney seat of Fowler. This also went well, and it turned out to be the beginning of years of being asked to do Labor Party fundraisers. I spoke all over the country, in some draughty country halls and suburban bowling clubs, and by the time I resigned I had done more fundraisers than anyone else. I am the victim of a thousand party barbecues in every corner of our nation.

One of the disappointing aspects of reading some accounts of the 1987 election is the criticism of Hawke's performance. It is true that he made one of the biggest errors of his career at the official campaign opening on 23 June at the Sydney Opera House. Here he uttered the not-so-immortal words: 'By 1990 no Australian child will be living in poverty.' His text was that 'no child will need to live in poverty' after Labor's promised social security measures had been put in place. Whether the mistake came from feeling the exuberance of a big crowd on the biggest day of the campaign or from a simple misreading of the text, I have never been certain. But the phrase haunted him for years. It was a simple error, but a big one, and as one who has made plenty of them, I cannot cast the first stone.

That having been acknowledged, I thought Hawke was in great form. I saw him at meetings and dinners in several cities around the country, I listened to him on radio and saw him on television. I thought he was back to his best, and the crowd reaction was as good as it had ever been.

By the time 11 July—election day—rolled around, we knew we couldn't lose. For the third time in a row, we were going to win. As soon as I walked into the tally room as part of the Channel Nine commentary team, I could tell from the demeanour of the Liberal camp that they knew the third loss on the trot was only a few hours away. Australians doubted Howard, knew his tax package didn't add up, feared where he would find the money, and still had enough residual goodwill to keep us in business.

And so it proved, but it was a fairly close result nonetheless. Our two-party-preferred winning margin was 1.6 per cent, with a national swing to the Opposition of 1 per cent. But we still increased our majority from 16 to 24 seats. The huge swings against Labor in the safe seats were offset by a good performance in those that were more marginal. Labor's dominance in all aspects of campaigning, from central advertising to the production of literature for the letterboxes, was never more evident.

We won on preferences, with regional issues being prominent, and for the first time we had some real assistance from the environmental movement. They had urged a vote for Labor and, while the environment vote was not as large in 1987 as it would be three years later, they were worth between half a per cent and 1 per cent of the vote to us. The only disappointment for me in that election was seeing the big swings against Labor in its safest seats, such as Fowler, Prospect in western Sydney and Cunningham in Wollongong. We had shaken the faith of the hard core, and that faith would take a further battering over the next few years.

Selecting the ministry after the election presented only minor difficulties. The real task was to find room for Robert Ray, who had to be accommodated. Not many phone calls were necessary to sort out a position for him; Chris Hurford, a South Australian MP who had served in parliament for many years and was then Minister for Immigration would become consul-general in New York, and a vacancy was created. While that part of the operation went smoothly, we lost his seat of Adelaide in the resultant by-election by a fairly large margin. Hurford did not leave immediately, and we were able to wait a few months before any announcement, but the people of Adelaide thought they had elected Hurford for three years and resented his early departure.

It was a high price to pay for getting Robert Ray into the ministry, but worth every ounce of discomfort. I told Hawke that this guy's turn had come and a vacancy had to be found. He had power, intellect and ability, and he had been there nearly two years longer than I had.

Despite the image promoted by jaundiced pundits in the press over the years, in the Right consensus usually proved to be the best method. I would check with my colleagues by telephone and discover what the general mood was. There was sympathy for giving John Brown and Clyde Holding one more term—and one more term only—and virtually unanimous support for myself. Gerry Hand, the factional organiser of the Left, also made it in 1987: it was a big year. When the faction gathered at the Hyatt Kingsgate Hotel in Sydney a week after the election, there was no argument about who was going to become a minister.

There was little support for Barry Cohen, Minister for the Environment and the Arts for the past four years. Contrary to his protests later, I never asked one Caucus member to turn him down. From his point of view, it was pretty hard to say—it always is—'Nobody wants me, I've had four years and they think it's enough'. It's much easier to say that backroom deals have been done to force the Caucus into voting for faction heavies of whom the Caucus are in fear of their lives. Those less talented buffoons, the story went, were replacing really talented people like Barry by unfair means. When Franca Arena complained after the faction failed to support her for Senate selection upon my resignation, she was saying the same thing. What both of them really meant to say, I'm sure, was that the system of faction heavies recommending support for people was fine, even admirable—until it finally failed to recommend them. Neither of them thought the system was so terrible when they were its beneficiaries.

Hawke had asked me what portfolio I would like, and I jumped at the opportunity to plead for the Environment and the Arts. While the Arts wasn't ever a big issue in the public arena, it did represent a significant interest group that had been strongly pro-Labor since Whitlam's run in the early 1970s. There was a degree of selfishness involved here, too. My image needed softening, and this combination of interests was a pretty good start.

The great thrill, though, was becoming a minister. We were sworn in at Government House by the Governor-General Sir Ninian Stephen, and Hawke took all the ministers and their spouses to the Lodge for lunch. Cheryl and I were seated at the right hand of God. I had not had a lifelong ambition to become a federal minister, but becoming one gave me a thrill to remember forever, particularly as Hawke had given me the portfolio of my choice. The environment was a challenge. I could tell it would be at the centre of the action for the next few years: if not, I could put it there.

CHAPTER 13

Out of the Smoke-filled Rooms and into the Forests

More than a year before the 1987 election, I travelled to Tasmania at the invitation of the forestry industry in that state. Some industry representatives took me on a tour of the forests, though fog made helicopter travel very difficult and the trip was therefore limited to the distances that four-wheel-drive vehicles could take us on any one day. I was taken to regenerated areas of varying age, I saw plantations and presumably the best the industry could find. While the character of one valley looked to me to have been permanently altered by the logging, I was basically satisfied with what I saw and said something to that effect in the Tasmanian media.

Shortly afterwards, the Tasmanian Wilderness Society asked me to do another forest tour under their auspices. Having accepted the industry's invitation, it seemed pretty reasonable to give the environmental movement a similar opportunity.

God obviously supports the environment cause: the sun shone

brightly that morning and the helicopter had no problems. I travelled with Dr Bob Brown, internationally known as the saviour of the Franklin, Geoff Law and David Heatley. On the morning of Thursday 3 April 1986, we flew over some of the world's most beautiful forests and stopped for a lunch of soggy sandwiches near a small mountain lake called Lake Sydney.

We walked around some of the area, sat by the lake and talked. Bob Brown wanted chunks of forest, or preferably the whole area, put into World Heritage classification and protected forever. So utterly convinced of his cause, Bob can be utterly convincing; his passion and sincerity are very difficult to overcome and by the time we arrived back in Hobart I was a convert. Having been shown the awesome forests and streams he wanted protected, I wanted to become a warrior for his cause. That was a bad day for the logging industry in Australia but a very good one for me, the environmental movement and the Labor Party. It didn't take too long to work out that we had a perfect convergence: what was right was also popular.

The main environmental group in the country was the Australian Conservation Foundation (ACF) and its director Phillip Toyne was another character whom I found difficult to refuse. Like Brown, Toyne had the sort of commitment to the cause that would never let him give up and admit defeat. He was slightly quicker than Brown in knowing when to compromise—not difficult because Brown never compromised in his life. The omens for bringing the environmental movement to government notice were good; working with Toyne was the ACF publicity officer Simon Balderstone, a former journalist who was already on good personal terms with Hawke and who went on to work for me, Hawke and Keating. 'Baldo' made it much easier for me to bring Toyne (to whom Hawke warmed over time) and Brown (to whom Hawke never warmed) into the halls of power and decision-making.

Brown and Toyne had become frustrated by the reluctance of Barry Cohen, then Minister for the Environment, to deal with two of the most controversial issues of the day—the World Heritage listing of the wet tropical rainforests of north Queensland and firmly setting the expanded boundaries of Kakadu National Park, with its vast mineral wealth. Cohen's view was that the intransigence of the Queensland government made nomination of the rainforests too difficult, and there had been bickering with Gareth Evans and his Department of Resources and Energy over Kakadu.

I organised for Brown to see Hawke and to put his case on these two issues, as well as his request for action on Tasmanian forests. Toyne and Balderstone attended the meeting, and so did Barry Cohen. It was close to the 1987 election and Hawke wanted the environmental movement on side. He told Cohen to get on with the job of nominating the wet tropics for the World Heritage listing and to prepare a statement and course of action to implement this, and also told him to try to settle the boundaries for Stage III of Kakadu. Hawke knew instinctively that the ACF and the Tasmanian Wilderness Society were natural allies of the government who had to be brought into the tent. He had embarked on a green course that would do him no end of electoral good in the next few years.

Cohen announced the government's promise to list the wet tropics just before the election date was announced. However, he had given up on the quest to have Stage III of Kakadu declared before the election. Toyne and Balderstone met with Gareth Evans and the three of them agreed on a course of action and a set of words for a decision. Soon afterwards, the 4479-square-kilometre Stage III of the Kakadu National Park was declared, though an area half that size that could still be explored for minerals, including Coronation Hill, was left out as a so-called conservation zone to be further considered after the election. This decision was bound to go down well with the electorate, though the mining industry lobby wasn't too thrilled. Perhaps, like the conservative side of politics, they never realised the breadth of Kakadu's appeal. Looking after Kakadu was popular not just with hard-core green activists, but with millions of Australians who had either visited it over the years or knew someone who had. If you were not in favour of preserving Kakadu, you would always battle to get a majority of Australians to agree with you.

The Kakadu announcement was the icing on the cake for us. The green movement could do little else than advocate a vote for Labor, and while it could not be said that this won the election for us, it certainly did no harm. The friendships and trust I had established by helping to achieve these victories for the conservationists became hugely important to me as Minister for the Environment.

On Sunday 26 July 1987, a couple of days after I had been sworn in as a minister, I flew to Melbourne to attend the ACF conference. There was considerable scepticism in the ACF ranks as to my bona fides, so it seemed sensible to march in and get the introductions, and any unpleasantness, over with. The meeting took place at the ACF's Melbourne headquarters and was presided over by Hal Wootton, a distinguished lawyer who I think was meant to provide a contrast to the hairy, radical look the environment movement still possessed.

If you want to convince people to believe in you or at least to give you the benefit of the doubt, an open frontal approach is the only way to go. I promised to fight on every issue, an approach different from what the environmental movement was accustomed to seeing from their minister. The Environment portfolio, I said, would have as strong a voice as any other department. I told the ACF I believed in most of the things they did. I would fight to save old growth forests, though I could give no guarantee that forests in the National Estate would not be logged. (National Estate listing acknowledged the importance of a forest area, but it did not place obligations on state or local governments. Under Section 30, only the Commonwealth was bound to recognise and protect it, and the Commonwealth owned or controlled precious little of our land mass. Federal heritage legislation provided for the Commonwealth to override the states on National Estate matters, but legal advice had suggested that this provision would be struck down by the High Court.)

I told them I was more than willing to use World Heritage legislation to protect forests of sufficient quality. I promised to maximise the area of Kakadu that would be protected. And so that there could be no misunderstanding, I told them about the one real difference between us—I supported the mining and export of uranium. Out of all the hundreds of issues on which they sought to influence government, I would be offside on just one. The uranium argument was as well known to them as it was to me, so there was no point in arguing about it. I wasn't going to budge and neither were they, so the sensible thing to do was to respect each other's point of view and not let the difference cause too much friction. That very early effort did much to take the wind out of the sails of those determined to oppose this New South Wales Right ring-in who had been given the job of protecting the environment.

That Sunday meeting also exposed the tendency in the environment movement which I have found extreme difficulty in accommodating—they love to eat vegetarian food. Having flown in early from Sydney, having spoken and answered questions at the meeting for a couple of hours and being a meat-eater of massive proportions for many years, I was ready for a feed. What was dished up by these kind, dedicated, gentle people of the ACF was a sensational meal—if you like lentils. I scoured the room for something to sate my hunger for real food, but alas, lentils, lentils everywhere and not a thing to eat. Amazingly enough, nobody else was complaining. At countless functions attended by the green people of our nation over the next few years, similar fare was served again and again. As soon as I left these cholesterol-free gatherings, McDonald's got a good workout. Mind you, I won't sell out for a feed. The mountain cattlemen of Tasmania gave me a great barbecue, but it didn't change any plans for World Heritage listings there.

After my first exposure to the movement, it was time to get down to business. Trees have always been popular, so saving trees was bound to be even more popular than the trees themselves. In the public mind there are grades of forest, even if these categories are not scientifically based. At the top of the list will always be rainforests, and most citizens know that around the world the rainforests are vanishing fast. They evoke images of lost civilisations, Indian tribes under siege from developers, medical breakthroughs being made on a regular basis, but most of all images of real beauty, unspoiled and untouched. Tropical rainforests were therefore the highest priority. Some other temperate rainforests had already been protected in World Heritage areas of northern New South Wales and Tasmania, but no tropical rainforests had been protected, and Australia would get only one chance.

Australia had ratified the World Heritage Convention in 1974, and the use of the Commonwealth's foreign affairs power to sign international treaties that Australia was bound to honour had been the key to saving Tasmania's Franklin River. Because the convention requires Australia to take all necessary steps to protect any listed property, the Commonwealth can override the land use power of the states. It should not have been necessary to use the foreign affairs powers in this way, but Joh Bjelke-Petersen's government had no intention of saving any rainforest: indeed, they intended to make a virtue of its destruction.

Opponents of the World Heritage listing for the rainforests had two main criticisms. First and foremost, they cried out for the protection of those who logged the forests or treated the timber brought out of them. The claim that thousands of jobs would be lost by a decision to ban logging was made all too frequently. At the time of the 1987 election, the rainforests of north Queensland probably supported between five and six hundred workers in sawmilling, veneermilling, plywood and mouldings manufacture and truss manufacture from local and imported timber, as well as retailing and wholesaling.

Many of these workers were employed part-time in the timber industry, but the culture was well and truly ingrained. They were determined to fight for their way of life, not just their jobs, and in timber towns such as Ravenshoe on the Atherton Tableland, the feelings ran very high indeed. Despite the often abysmal wages they were paid, the almost total lack of superannuation and the appalling standards of safety and training, these people had lived the same lives for generations. Whether I thought they lived well or not hardly mattered; they liked their lives and they would contemplate no change.

Their concerns about their future, however, had been building for years, despite the so-called support of the Queensland government. The logging industry always talks about 'sustainable forestry', but the industry itself was regularly changing the definition of 'sustainable'. This was bad enough in any old-growth forest, but it was a damning weakness in their case for logging rainforests. On Friday 18 July 1986, a year before I became a minister and announced the Commonwealth's intention to go for World Heritage listing, Ravenshoe's local paper, the *Millstream Times*, carried a report that 100 people attended a protest meeting in the Ravenshoe Town Hall because the Queensland government had cut the quota that north Queensland mills were permitted to take from the rainforests by more than half, from 130 000 cubic metres to 60 000 cubic metres. Even Bjelke-Petersen's people were admitting that the forests would be permanently damaged if the previously 'sustainable' level of logging were allowed to continue. Quota reductions had been occurring for some years and the mills in the towns of Millaa-Millaa and Mt Malloy had already closed. Hundreds of jobs had already been lost and not one penny in compensation had been offered by the Queensland government.

The second main line of argument against World Heritage listing was that control of part of Australia would be ceded to UNESCO and diplomats from countries all around the globe would exercise sovereignty over Australian territory. This argument was peddled by the League of Rights, that sick organisation of lunatics that still holds meetings and attracts some support in rural Australia. It was an argument just too good for Joh to ignore, so he threw up the prospect of Colonel Gaddafi pitching his tents on the Atherton Tableland. The fact that other areas of Australia on the World Heritage list at the time (Lord Howe Island, Kakadu, Uluru, the Franklin River, and so on) had witnessed no loss of sovereignty made the stupidity of this argument blindingly obvious—but when the contrary to his argument was obvious, Joh just became more stubborn and determined.

The League of Rights chimed in with a conspiracy theory that had Fabian socialists combined with Jewish bankers and communists to establish a one-world government. World Heritage was proof of this conspiracy and all over the country appeared leaflets proclaiming the imminent destruction of civilisation as we know it. It's like those predictions of the end of the world that at least three times during my lifetime have made a lot of poor bastards turn up at Sydney's North Head on a specific date predicted by the latest prophet: the prophecies never come true but they're still trotted out.

I only ever met one genuine one-world government whacko, and that was in 1989 at Shark Bay in Western Australia. I had suggested that Shark Bay should be listed for World Heritage and all the old arguments got a run—the underground tunnel linking Parliament House to the American Embassy, the Deakin telephone exchange as the conspiracy headquarters. Debating this whacko outside the Denham Town Hall was like debating Brian Wilshire, Sydney's late-night radio talk show host who writes books about these theories. Hard evidence is apt to be greeted by blank looks and claims of bigger and better plots and conspiracies.

To their credit, some people in the National Party rejected any form of alliance with the League of Rights. While maintaining staunch opposition to World Heritage listing for the rainforests, Senator Ron Boswell campaigned publicly to make sure that his party never succumbed to the more sinister forces of the lunatic Right.

For conservationists, no definition of sustainable forestry could ever apply to rainforests. Their argument, which I found irresistible, was that as soon as you log one big tree and open the canopy you change the ecology of the rainforest. Only natural disturbances from cyclones cause trees to fall over, and that kind of disturbance amounts to very little compared with logging. These rainforests are millions of years old and until the last two centuries natural regeneration seems to have worked very well. Some loggers' claims that opening up the canopy and letting the sunlight in actually helps the forests to regenerate ignores the fact that without the sun these forests have grown perfectly well, in pristine condition, for millions of years. Logging changes the arboreal homes of the birdlife and furry creatures, and as logging tracks are built and the big trucks rumble through, introduced species of vegetation, including weeds, are inevitable.

In any event, the sustainable forestry argument fell down because of the way the industry had structured itself. The first cut in any new virgin area was always for the biggest and oldest trees, which provided the industry with the easiest and richest dollar rewards. Once those trees have been taken and are not available in the second cut, new areas to log are constantly needed. No effort had been put into value-adding industries or to reafforestation. The industry depended upon virgin rainforest, and I was about to take that resource away from them permanently.

We did, of course, need to establish boundaries for the World Heritage area for the benefit of private landholders and so the logging industry would know what resources were available to it. I called for submissions on the extent of the boundaries and decided that, while the argument raged, the least I could do was to go to north Queensland regularly and face the opposition. In August I went to Cairns twice to talk to timber industry representatives and the Australian Workers Union which represented the unionised minority of timberworkers in the region. I met with local government authorities and state MPs, and found that very few people in Queensland public life were prepared to support World Heritage listing. The federal Member for the area, Cairns solicitor John Gayler who had been elected in 1983, was pretty supportive, which showed courage in the face of his state colleagues' attitude. The local Member was Bill Eaton, the state ALP spokesman on forestry, and he was never on side. This made the position of the state ALP pretty interesting, with its environment spokesman Pat Comben (now a minister in the Goss government) calling on Mr Eaton to resign.

On my second visit to north Queensland on 20 August, I announced the indicative boundaries on which I sought comment from the public, the forestry industry, conservationists and the Queensland government. I also took a quick peek at some rainforest near Ravenshoe and got an early taste of the local feeling. After I had inspected an area of forest that had been logged, my exit was blocked by fifty or sixty local citizens. They expressed their anger and prevented my car from leaving for a short time while I explained my position and promised to return within a few weeks. When the crowd began to disperse and I was allowed to leave, a woman claimed that she heard me say to my driver: 'Get me away from this rabble.' This became folklore in the district, and was all the evidence the locals needed to be convinced that I was another southerner with an attitude problem. The fact that these words were not uttered at any stage—confirmed by the driver and by my staff who were in the back seat at the time—was of no interest to anyone in north Queensland. I was condemned by words I had not spoken.

I arranged to return two weeks later to address a public meeting in the Ravenshoe Town Hall. During that fortnight I kept working on the boundaries of the area to be listed. Being a busy new Minister for the Arts as well as the Environment, I visited Film Australia, the National Gallery, the Australian Opera, the Australian Film Television and Radio School, had appointments galore and lunched with broadcasters John Laws and Mike Carlton. I knew that I would face a hostile reception in Ravenshoe, but I did not believe I had cause to be afraid. It was business as usual and as a new minister with two great portfolios, I thought business was pretty good.

Meanwhile, old Joh was busily upping the ante, calling on the people of north Queensland to 'wage war' on me. The claims about World Heritage listing became even more bizarre—electricity supply to the area would be interrupted because all telegraph poles would have to be removed from the World Heritage area, all local beekeepers would be out of business as bees would be banned from the area (how we were going to put the world's biggest net over and around the rainforests was never explained), traditional Aboriginal rights such as hunting and foraging in the forests would be banned. Private landholders would be forced from their homes, huge buffer zones outside the area would be declared and all rights over this extra property would cease (although just what my power was to enforce such a rule was never explained either). Hysteria was breaking out all over, and I was rather naively walking into it.

On Friday 4 September I returned to Ravenshoe. It was a fine day and I travelled to the Atherton Tableland by helicopter, as I also had commitments down on the coast. The flight over those magnificent forests was an experience I couldn't forget. Helicopter rides over beautiful rainforests on balmy north Queensland days late in the dry season are uplifting. The trees, the streams, the waterfalls are all awe-inspiring in their own way. I didn't know that what was about to happen would be even more unforgettable.

By the time we landed in Ravenshoe, I was feeling just about as good as I have ever felt. There was no disturbance at the local golf course where the helicopter landed, just a few interested spectators. I was accompanied by three members of my ministerial staff and one departmental official, as well as federal member John Gayler. We climbed into a taxi and headed into town. Virtually every house we passed had a protest sign displayed somewhere on the fence or in the yard, but there was still no sign of trouble. Then the taxi entered the main drag about half a kilometre from the town hall.

A large crowd was spread out over the road, and as soon as

they saw us they surrounded the taxi. The driver tried her best to drive down the street, but she couldn't. The crowd started rocking the taxi and the ringleader (there is always one of those) informed me that I wasn't going to the town hall. I was to address the crowd from a truck they had parked in the middle of the very wide avenue that is Ravenshoe's main street.

The ringleader, who had bussed in workers from mills in other areas, was the brutish member of a family with decades of involvement in the timber industry of the region. Apart from his rather obvious numerical superiority, he had another ace up his sleeve. The police contingent in Ravenshoe that day showed very little interest in protecting me or my staff. When the taxi approached and 500 people started yelling and screaming, they did nothing. When I was forced from the cab and marched to the back of the truck, they did nothing. They simply stood around a police car parked a few metres away and talked amongst themselves. During the next ninety minutes or so, all but one of them stood riveted to the same spot, completely ignoring the commotion going on around them. I suppose it shouldn't have been too great a shock for me to learn that these policemen merely reflected the community they represented, and from which they themselves had come. Old loyalties die the hardest.

I was forced to leave the taxi and to climb onto the back of the truck, with John Gayler and the others, and the public meeting began. Trying to address an overwhelmingly hostile crowd is a futile exercise: every time I opened my mouth to speak or to answer any questions, I was drowned out by chanting. The verbal battle raged for more than an hour, during which two young girls, who were no more than fourteen or fifteen, kept up a continuous barrage of bad language. Some of the organisers moved about the crowd, making sure the truck was well and truly surrounded. This was a well organised fiasco: the only people who benefited from the ongoing dialogue were the journalists, who were getting a real bonanza.

I had climbed onto the back of the truck at about 11.45, and as one o'clock approached I indicated to the crowd that I would have to leave, as I had a meeting to attend in Tully on the coast. The chief thug and his henchmen made it abundantly clear that my exit would be prevented. One of my staff slipped away and at least could arrange for the police car and taxi to be parked as close to the truck as possible, to give us some sort of chance to get out. After more than an hour, not one policeman had bothered even to wander over to the truck.

It is difficult to know what makes ordinary decent people—and with one or two exceptions, those were precisely the people in that crowd—behave in that manner. Fear is a powerful motivating force, and the fear of an unknown and uncertain future was creating this mayhem. Fear was having a powerful effect on me as well: after about an hour I was about as terrified as it is possible to get. This was the only time in my political career when I really began to fear for my safety. Trying to remain calm, to sound as if the panic building up inside me was nothing more than firm resolve, continuing to answer questions while showing some grasp of the subject matter was almost impossible. I had to stand my ground, I had to state my case, I had to remain as impassive as possible while they expressed their fear and frustration: I owed them at least that. No matter how threatening the situation became, I had to keep remembering that these were everyday Australian men and women who were driven beyond breaking point by a decision I was taking. Even if the decision was right, these people were being displaced, and I couldn't even bring myself to dislike them. It's not hard for a couple of provocateurs to incite an angry mob; it's a story as old as humankind.

Nobody would accept any of my assurances that the Commonwealth would provide significant sums to help generate employment and to make termination payments to those who lost their jobs. Worker after worker made plea after plea to allow rainforest logging to continue. They pointed to their children, they spoke of their homes and their way of life, and for them I had no answers. If you believe that logging stops a rainforest from being what it has been for millions of years, let alone if your Prime Minister has announced the decision to stop logging, there is no compromise to offer. I couldn't say there would be a little logging here and there; logging was going to be banned in the World Heritage listed area. Some would continue on private land, certainly, but this would never amount to much, and it would certainly not employ many of the three hundred or so workers who were about to lose their jobs.

Finally, at about one o'clock, I informed the crowd that I was going to leave. My staff and I leapt off the truck and headed for the police car and the taxi. They were only twenty metres away, but on that day the distance might as well have been twenty miles. As soon as we began our long march, the mob became very angry indeed. Plenty of kicks and punches were thrown, most of them intercepted by my two staffers, Simon Balderstone and David Tierney. A few got through to me and our progress was painfully slow, or at least it seemed so at the time. Someone grabbed my hair and started pulling me backwards, forcing me off balance. At that crucial moment, a flying wedge of twenty or so in the crowd came straight at us. If I had lost my footing, I would certainly have been trampled. Using a technique common in that code of football they play in Melbourne, Simon convinced the guy holding my hair to let go: he elbowed the bastard in the ribs.

John Gayler, a big man by any standards, was leading the way, showing considerable courage. He walked straight into a local with a build remarkably like his own and I had a momentary vision of two sumo wrestlers about to join in combat. Then, surprisingly, one lone policeman waded into the fray and placed himself between John Gayler and his opponent, yelling at the crowd that if all this continued, someone was going to get hurt, and it would be the other sumo. His performance was convincing enough to stop the crowd for a few moments, restoring my faith in human nature and the Queensland police force. I had regained my footing, if not my dignity and composure, and his action gave us just enough time to reach our taxi.

The short drive to the helicopter was accomplished in relative silence: we were all too stunned to speak much, except to enquire about each other's well being. I profusely thanked our taxi driver Mrs Bailey; she was a brave woman who, through no fault of her own, had been placed in some danger. I later found out the name of the policeman who had saved the day and thanked him too. He deserved the highest commendation. I didn't thank anyone else in Ravenshoe. As far as the other police are concerned, to use my father's favourite expression, I hope their fowls die.

It was a great moment when the choppers lifted off. They raced us to the coast where we set down on a beach, ate some sandwiches and drank coffee. The tranquillity of that glorious coastline was just about perfect for calming our fractured nerves.

The ringleader of the demonstration was a real hero that day, but a month later I got to see how good he was when he didn't have 500 of his mates to back him up. On that occasion, he and four of his mates marched into a Cairns hotel in an attempt to crash my meeting with some local government representatives. One Commonwealth policeman stood at the top of the stairs with his arms folded. He wasn't the biggest policeman I had ever seen, about five feet seven inches and weighing perhaps 80 to 85 kilograms, but he had that look in the eyes that suggests complete calmness in the face of danger, the expression of a man who either knows no fear or has a way of completely overcoming it. Our hero raced up the stairs and halted a few steps from him, and there were a few agonising moments when he and his colleagues looked at the policeman and at each other. Then, without a word being spoken, they went back down again.

Later I asked that policeman whether he had expected trouble. He told me he knew there would be none when he looked into the 'hero's' eyes. He had the same way of detecting courage as I have of detecting truth: it's in the eyes, and in the eyes of the 'hero' in those few moments, the policeman saw cowardice. I wish I could have seen it on that day in Ravenshoe, but surrounded by his supporters our hero knew no fear.

On the day after the Ravenshoe incident, the Melbourne *Sun*'s banner headline was 'Minister Bashed in Wild Protest'. This exaggerated the events: a few punches and kicks that did little or no damage, and losing a few hairs to the guy who grabbed my greying locks do not constitute a bashing. It had been wild, though, and it did receive enormous publicity, even scoring a run in the British newspapers and the BBC news. In Australia, television, radio and newspaper reports gave everyone some kind of glimpse of a few minutes that I'm sure a few of the protesters hoped to forget.

If Joh Bjelke-Petersen and the organisers of the protest believed that this disturbance would help their cause, they had made a massive mistake. Having been cast so often as the villain, I became an instant hero. To the green movement all around the country, all doubts about my commitment to their cause were swept aside as they heard, read or saw the media reports. Outside the movement, the protest and its aftermath did me no end of good and the loggers' cause no end of harm. Even in Queensland, World Heritage for the rainforests became a very popular cause. On 18 September the Channel Seven news in Brisbane conducted a poll showing 58 per cent in favour, 21 per cent against and 21 per cent without an opinion.

The irony of this ugly incident doing my career a power of good has not been lost on me. Coming so soon after being given a portfolio that caused concern among the green movement and the Labor Party, it would have been the perfect political manoeuvre and if I'd planned it I would have been a political genius. In truth, I went to Ravenshoe for the right reason—to face my accusers—and got lucky: lucky that a demonstration occurred with cameras whirring and lucky that, when all turned ugly, I could get out with body and soul intact.

I did return to Ravenshoe a few weeks later for another protest meeting. This one took place at the theatre and a strong police presence ensured there would be no trouble.

The Ravenshoe incident was the beginning of the end for Bjelke-Petersen and his government, heralding the close of that era in Queensland where the interests of developers were considered to be paramount, regardless of the merits of the case. Subtlety was never Joh's forte, nor was grace under pressure.

The Police Complaints Tribunal in Queensland conducted an investigation into the Ravenshoe debacle. They did this without interviewing me, my staff, departmental officials or the taxi driver who had been right in the thick of the action. The tribunal, under Justice Pratt, concluded that allegations 'that there may have been some neglect of duty on the part of police officers who were present in Ravenshoe that day by not providing proper security for the senator . . . were totally unfounded'. This was justice Queensland style: hold an inquiry, don't talk to the victims, and then conclude that one of the victims was responsible for the problem.

Some of the statements in the report of the tribunal would do justice to a comedy script. Deputy Premier of Queensland Bill Gunn claimed that I had been 'a victim of my own ministerial inexperience'. At the heart of that claim was the statement that

I had failed to liaise with the Queensland police prior to the visit and that had I done so, the incident could have been avoided. Even allowing for the state of Queensland justice at the time, this was a real shocker. Neither my staff nor I had even been contacted by the tribunal, and there had been no attempt to discover the truth—a commodity in short supply in Bjelke-Petersen's world.

In fact, my office had told the Protective Services Co-ordination Centre of the Attorney-General's Department of my visit, and they had informed the Queensland police. A telex containing a complete itinerary of my visit was sent to a senior officer of the Special Branch at Queensland police headquarters on 1 September, with a follow-up call from the Attorney-General's Department the next day. Apparently nobody bothered to enquire why Special Branch had not fully informed the local Ravenshoe police. In fact, they met two helicopters that landed prior to my arrival but, as they contained media crews, the police returned to the main street. To drive from our landing place to the main street takes a couple of minutes, and anyone would have to wonder why my helicopter wasn't similarly met after it had made two circuits of the town prior to landing.

Mr Gunn said that the police had maintained 'a low-key approach', and I certainly agreed with him about that. But then he congratulated the police on showing 'considerable initiative and resourcefulness in protecting the senator while shepherding him to a police car'. Commending the police after they failed to clear the way for my car, failed to clear the way for me to walk to the town hall, failed to move in when I jumped off the truck to leave is a bit rich. I could never have delivered such bullshit with a straight face, but in Joh's Queensland bullshit was trumps. The tribunal report was a sham: I can't imagine any state government of any political persuasion trying this sort of stunt again.

The last gasp for Bjelke-Petersen on this issue was to send two of his ministers to the World Heritage convention in Brasilia in 1988 in order to lobby delegates against the listing of the rainforest. This must have been a very expensive exercise in futility: they had no standing to address the convention and were generally regarded as redneck invaders. One of them said all that needed saying about the Bjelke-Petersen government when he invited the Muslim delegate from Yemen to come up to his room that night for a few beers.

That conference was very interesting for me. Gough Whitlam accompanied me to Brasilia and proved a real hit with delegates from the richest to the poorest countries; on that evidence, his time in Paris at UNESCO must have been spectacularly successful. Brasilia is a good example of how these conventions can be subverted by a bit of well placed pressure. However it was meant to be when the Brazilian government built this city in the middle of nowhere as a grand showcase for a rapidly developing nation, the reality was very different indeed. The city is full of half-finished eyesores, empty monuments to an era of faded dreams. Nonetheless, it was added to the World Heritage list with little formal argument, achieved by a consensus forming around the need to keep happy the emerging nations of the world. Offending the national pride of Brazil was a price they would not pay for maintaining real quality in that list of the world's most special places.

Similarly, poorer nations are not always kept up to the mark in protecting areas already on the list. Particularly in Africa, some magnificent areas are being degraded due to lack of funds and effective planning. It may be that, if we want the best places in the world preserved, we will have to pay for the privilege. Those nations whose main priorities are feeding starving people cannot be expected to spend much on conservation. At a conference in the Netherlands about setting targets for greenhouse gas emissions, the delegates argued about the amount that electricity generation contributed to greenhouse problems. The delegate from Tanzania grabbed the microphone and said: 'In my country the only time our people see electricity is in the lightning of a storm.' Debates about preserving what is aesthetically beautiful mean more in countries such as ours than they do in those places where the main question is the preservation of life itself.

When I became Minister for the Environment, I knew that the whole question of logging in Tasmania would be one of my biggest headaches. This was a problem determined to happen, and happen it did.

The arguments about which forest areas should be logged and what should be preserved had been going on for a long, long time. In order to try and resolve the conflict, in February 1987 the Commonwealth had introduced a bill seeking to establish an inquiry into some of the most controversial areas, to recommend those that might be suitable for World Heritage listing. The bill became law in May, and on the eighth Barry Cohen announced the Inquiry into the Lemonthyme and Southern Forests. The commissioners were Mr Justice Helsham, a retired judge from New South Wales, resource economist Robert Wallace and former forester Peter Hitchcock, and the inquiry was given one year to report.

It was charged with investigating an area totalling 283 000 hectares. The Lemonthyme area of 14 300 hectares was arguably the hottest issue to be settled, certainly in terms of the struggles in that area over time. The Southern Forests area was 269 000 hectares. Tasmanians knew all about World Heritage: listing the area to the west of this inquiry area had resulted in the saving of the Franklin after the customary long-drawn-out battles between the Tasmanian government and Bob Brown's hairy warriors.

Brown never liked the idea of an inquiry. He wanted the areas preserved and could never bring himself to believe that an inquiry with a highly legalistic approach and batteries of high-priced QCs grilling witnesses and making submissions would ever reach the right decision. His scepticism had some foundation: though the accepted truism in politics is that you never set up an inquiry unless you know its result in advance, the real truth is that you never know what inquiries will find. Commissioners with broad powers and huge resources do what they like, and prime ministers and premiers have little control. Just ask Nick Greiner how much he had over Ian Temby.

The Commonwealth never attempted any 'fix' with the Helsham inquiry: Helsham was an independent man with an impressive judicial career behind him. Nobody was going to demand or even suggest to him what he should find; he would do the job himself and lob the resultant grenade into Hawke's lap. But long before the commission released its report in 1988, Bob Brown was sounding warnings about the way it was doing its job.

On ABC Radio's 'The World Today' on 19 April 1988, he

claimed that the inquiry had manifested great unfairness to the environmental point of view, adding: 'The results it's going to come up with, I believe, are not going to be as creditable as they would have been had it been conducted with an even hand.' It was smart of him to cry foul early and to create the climate of a biased referee. Brown claimed that environmental consultants to the inquiry had been 'grilled by forestry industry barristers', but that pro-industry lawyers representing environment groups did not give the same treatment to consultants examining the maintenance of forest resources.

On 6 May 1988, the Helsham Report was handed to me as the responsible minister. Brown was right: by a two-to-one split decision, the commissioners recommended that only 8 per cent of the area be listed for World Heritage. For the government this was the worst possible result. Any decision to give 92 per cent of the argument to one side was bound to send the other side berserk, and that is precisely what happened. Nine of the environmental and cultural consultants to the inquiry wrote to me immediately to complain about the way in which their advice had been trivialised and ignored by the commissioners. A number went public and the pressure was on me to overturn the umpire. I doubt whether I had ever been given a tougher task.

The first thing I did was to let the environment movement know that this was a battle I would not or could not fight alone: I encouraged them to make 'a deafening roar' about the decision that could be heard all the way to Canberra. Unfortunately, ministers such as John Button, John Kerin, John Dawkins and Peter Walsh, who were pro-development, thought this was tantamount to calling on the people to revolt. There was much greater disagreement in Cabinet about the environment than about the economy: the economic ministers and I were in constant conflict, much of it public from the moment the Helsham Report became an issue, and we had some really bitter encounters over the next few years.

When this problem arose, I had been a Cabinet minister for three or four months. My elevation after John Brown's resignation early in 1988 had been achieved with little difficulty. Putting me into the Cabinet was a good move for Hawke; he didn't have a stronger supporter at that time and our friendship was close. I had factional clout, was a high-profile minister and was bound to be his ally in Cabinet. I argued successfully for Michael Duffy to be put into Cabinet as well. Duffy had no factional clout at all and was in the ministry using a position that would normally have been claimed by the Right. But he was good: witty, affable and wise. Hawke put us both into Cabinet at the same time.

There was no way I could do anything but to take a submission to Cabinet and try to overturn Helsham's recommendations. If I didn't, the green vote was gone, and I had already put a considerable amount of energy into that strategy. But more importantly, every piece of available evidence showed that virtually the whole of the Lemonthyme and Southern Forests area would qualify for World Heritage listing. I had no doubt that an international jury of scientists would pass it with flying colours. It was that happy confluence of good politics and good policy again, but could I convince the Cabinet?

I thought the omens were good. My submissions on the wet tropics rainforests, including a $75 million package to assist those who suffered unemployment as a result of the decision, had not met serious opposition when I presented them the previous year as a junior minister. So I was stunned to see the extent of Cabinet opposition to this.

The Cabinet debated competing submissions from myself and Resources Minister Peter Cook in three separate meetings lasting more than fourteen hours. No one could dream of a more rigorous examination. With complex issues before us, we found it difficult to present a case in less than an hour and a half. During the course of the other meetings, Tasmanian forestry official Evan Rowley and Professor Lindsay Pryor, a botanist, gave the Cabinet the direct benefit of their specialist knowledge. The use of outsiders to address Cabinet is unusual but not unprecedented, and I was not opposed to Peter Cook's using them. I chose to do all the rebuttal myself and I didn't ask for any outside assistance. I did talk to a few colleagues when possible between Cabinet meetings, but mainly I encouraged those who doubted what I had to say to allow Peter Hitchcock, the minority Helsham commissioner, to brief them on the issues.

Few Cabinet members were deeply committed on any green issue, and as Peter Cook and I argued on, it became apparent that the Cabinet was fairly evenly divided. Peter Walsh made much of two theories, one of which had been pushed by Lindsay Pryor. The first was the so-called 'hot fire paradox', postulating that in some forests the most common form of disturbance (that is, fire) must be intense enough to bring on the germination of new seedlings of some eucalypt species (such as *Eucalyptus regnans* or mountain ash), even though it appears to kill the forest. Not many people doubt the truth of this and the argument that some eucalypts are particularly sensitive to fire, but I argued very strongly that this in no way provided a reason to allow logging of these areas. In fact, I argued, it added to their significance and value and in any case, logging would not provide the conditions for germination, since in many ways it differed in its impact from severe bushfires. Walsh also reckoned that all these old trees were about to die. No matter how hard I tried, I never managed to visualise thousands of centuries-old trees all deciding to fall over together in some form of mass suicide.

After the first meeting, Michael Duffy and Kim Beazley (both of whom eventually came down on my side) told me I was behind and suggested that I should shore up some weak edges to my case. If anything, some Cabinet ministers would be quite happy to help line up my case for me. What I needed after the first meeting was an indication from Hawke that he supported me. He was a smart enough politician to know that there were plenty of votes in this, and he was committed to environment protection anyway. Support from Hawke would give an air of inevitability to the result and we could then debate the extent of my victory.

Try as I did, however, I couldn't budge him. His adviser Craig Emerson and Simon Balderstone from my office, who were both personally very close to him, couldn't budge him either. I think this reluctance had nothing to do with a lack of belief or faith in what I was trying to do and everything to do with the way he saw his role as Prime Minister and chairman of Cabinet meetings. Hawke knew how much his early intervention would annoy and upset the majority of his ministers who were on the Expenditure Review Committee (ERC). And if I hadn't been holding my own, or even if I was losing, Hawke might just have let me go down to defeat.

Knowing that I needed some heavyweight support, I asked

Keating to enter the fray. All those with a green bent should take note that he offered no resistance to this proposition at all. Keating was not quite an avid 'greenie', but his record of supporting environmental causes in government was often put to the test, and it was a test he rarely failed. Even though he was the chief economic minister, I can only think of one time when he opposed me on an environment argument, and that was the first time I raised the prospect of setting goals and targets for the emission of greenhouse gases. Keating was concerned about the effects on Australian industries if we acted unilaterally, leaving our competitors with a real advantage.

At the second meeting, despite strenuous opposition, fuelled by real anger, from his ERC colleagues, Keating went in hard. He rubbished industry claims about job losses, stressed the conservation cause and told the Cabinet that even after we had preserved a majority of the areas in question, there would still be plenty of resource left for sawloggers and woodchippers. He believed we could cut a deal with Robin Gray's government in Tasmania. That intervention did me a power of good.

Finally, during the third Cabinet meeting, our Prime Minister indicated his preference for preserving as much as possible of the area. He was prepared to reject the Helsham Report recommendation to save only 8 per cent of the area in question. When I heard him say this, I knew the meaning of elation. This was a very big win.

The Cabinet decided to nominate 70 per cent of the area for World Heritage. After the meeting was over, I didn't even have time to gloat, but went straight to the airport to fly to Brisbane to address a party fundraiser. When I told the audience about the decision, I got all the applause I expected. You never upset the party rank and file by announcing a pro-environment decision. My staff and departmental officers were all delighted as well, and the Caucus was happy. There was some bitterness in the Cabinet; though Peter Cook took the decision pretty well, some of my colleagues regarded me as the enemy within from that moment. But basically these were great moments because everybody was happy—except the environment movement. Bob Brown and his mates hadn't got enough.

Having achieved an increase in the area to be listed for World

Heritage from 8 to 70 per cent, I had expected a little gratitude, but Bob Brown was never very good at compromise. Peter Hitchcock had recommended that the whole of the area under investigation should be listed, and some other adjacent areas as well: this was the kind of decision that the Tasmanian Wilderness Society wanted, and they were saying so all over the media.

Over the next few months, Peter Cook and I paid numerous visits to Tasmania, talking to the forest industries representatives or the greens, negotiating with the government and the Opposition. Bob Hawke was keen to follow every development, and when we came close to an agreement with the Gray government, Hawke gave us all a glimpse of the real power that a confident, popular Prime Minister can wield.

On 29 November 1988 he announced an historic agreement that nominated vast areas for World Heritage, with the Tasmanian government being a joint sponsor of the nomination. Instead of the 70 per cent of the Lemonthyme and Southern Forests area that Cabinet had agreed to nominate, 80 per cent of the area was now agreed to. What was more, two adjacent areas, the Walls of Jerusalem National Park and the Central Plateau Conservation Area, were added. This meant that the total additional protected area was 378 000 hectares, and that is a whole lot of Tasmania.

The Cabinet had never agreed to this. It was Hawke, acting on advice but acting alone as a leader, who negotiated with Tasmania without any Cabinet approval. His actions were not challenged: he knew they wouldn't be. The Tasmanians also agreed to declare a national park covering the area known as the Hole in the Doughnut, more formally the Denison Spires.

This was enough to soothe the greens, and it really was a terrific result. The rest of the agreement, however, contained some clauses that made their hair (and many of them had plenty of that) stand on end. The Commonwealth undertook 'not to initiate any further inquiries into forestry in Tasmania or to propose any other areas of Tasmania for World Heritage listing without the concurrence of the Tasmanian government'. The last part of that agreement contains the clause that ensures that forestry arguments in Tasmania will go on and on: 'The Commonwealth agrees that logging can continue in the National Estate areas subject to the consultative arrangements at present in place or those agreed from time to time, such as the proposed Tasmanian Forests Agreement.' I had been careful never to promise that the Commonwealth would halt all logging in the National Estate, but the hard core of the Tasmanian Wilderness Society could never really accept it.

The rest of the agreement was a $50 million package to help the Tasmanian government and its forest industry to adjust to the resource loss. Also included was a resource guarantee to the proposed Huon Forest Products mill. While this was hated by the greens, I never bothered about it much because I couldn't imagine the mill ever being built, and it never was. While any resource guarantee was going to upset some of the activists, forest industry workers had rights too, and their industry needed secure guarantees of its future.

Despite the efforts of some, you couldn't categorise this as anything but a big win for the environment. The Tasmanian greens would find great difficulty in opposing Labor in a federal election after this decision. More importantly, the environment movement right around the country was watching to see how far the Commonwealth was prepared to go. From the moment this decision was announced, the Green preference strategy for the 1990 election was a fact of life, even if the Labor Party didn't know it yet.

The tests any Minister for the Environment had to pass were tougher in Tasmania; in forest arguments, they always set the bar higher. Maybe the tall trees are tallest, the old trees oldest or the forests more beautiful, but I was expected to work miracles in the island state. Fortunately, having won an important battle with Helsham, I had a head start in confronting the next test.

In February 1988, the officials of North Broken Hill (NBH) informed a number of federal ministers that they planned to build a pulp mill at Wesley Vale, a few kilometres from Devonport in northwest Tasmania. By May 1988, when the Helsham Report was released, NBH had found a partner with sufficient financial resources to turn its dream into a plan. The Canadian company Noranda were on board and, with that kind of clout behind them, NBH could push a bit harder for support.

In Minister for Industry John Button these joint venturers had the perfect ally. As a senior respected minister he couldn't be ignored, and in an era when new investment was desperately needed (when has this not been the case?) his support for this project had unanimous Cabinet endorsement. In using the word 'unanimous' I am of course including myself, and I am not ashamed to concede that I was in the cart. I would support any shift from woodchip production into pulp and paper production, as I took the view—and still do—that woodchipping is a scandalous waste of forest resources. We export both the resources and the jobs to Japan and we are paid precious little. But I parted company with some of my allies in the Tasmanian Wilderness Society and the Australian Conservation Foundation in my willingness to support any pulp mill with environmentally acceptable technology.

The Commonwealth had to support the concept with a financial incentives package just to get it past the feasibility stage: the infrastructure costs were massive and the Tasmanian government was given Commonwealth approval to borrow extra loan funds to pay for the roads and railways. To help the joint venturers, special accelerated depreciation allowances worth millions of dollars were extended. All this happened before I had seen any plan of exactly the kind of pulp mill the companies were proposing.

Having supported a considerable incentives package, it was only natural that I would agree to the environmental impact statement (EIS) being studied under Tasmanian law: Hawke instructed me to agree to it in any case because this would achieve a positive result in a much shorter time. The Commonwealth retained the right to a last look at the process after the Tasmanians had finished their work. It was just as well we were given that opportunity.

A team of locals opposed to the mill visited me in my Parliament House office. They were led by a young schoolteacher who was all fired up about the issue but still showed the special kind of nervousness that belongs to the activist who has all the passion and commitment necessary without the practical political experience. Her name was Christine Milne, now a member of the Tasmanian Parliament and, since the retirement of Bob Brown, arguably the best known Green in the state. Her reticence is no longer there: it has been replaced by confidence and she is one tough lady.

In October 1988 I visited the site for the first time. While I knew Wesley Vale was going to be a big deal, until then I hadn't quite understood how much it meant to the locals. I was confronted by those who wanted the mill to go ahead and those who would oppose it at any cost. On that day I spoke to practically anyone who had a point of view: company executives, workers, local environmental activists, fishermen, farmers (normally a pro-development group but very much opposed here). All I could do was reassure the worried residents of the very pretty farming area of Wesley Vale that the Commonwealth would take a very close look at the environmental impact statement, and that if I wasn't satisfied with it, I would oppose the mill.

Thank God I visited Wesley Vale when I did. Three days after my visit, the EIS was released to the public. It precipitated a real outcry: not even the Tasmanian government could accept its inadequacies. After studying it for a month, my department raised eighty-five problems with our Tasmanian counterparts. The Tasmanians wrote to the joint venturers, referring to every one of these eighty-five matters as either inadequately addressed or not addressed at all in the EIS. While some of these were relatively minor, a few were absolutely critical. The bleaching process used in most of the world's pulp mills is known as chlorine bleaching, which has unavoidable by-products called organochlorines. These are particularly nasty chemicals and, while our knowledge of how bad they are is not yet complete, scientists from all over the world were at least prepared to say that their release into the marine environment had to be very strictly monitored to ensure that there was minimum opportunity for them to enter the food chain.

The bare minimum requirement for the joint venturers was to conduct a baseline study of the immediate surrounds of the ocean outfall from the mill. The letter sent to the company by the Tasmanian government had stated that 'a thorough study of the physical, biological and oceanographic characteristics of the area around the outfall will be required before the final location of the outfall can be approved. The Addendum [the next phase of the EIS process in which the company was required to answer the unanswered questions] must acknowledge that such studies are necessary to determine the final design and location of the outfall.' This was as strong a statement as you could get from the Tasmanian government; the company also knew that the Commonwealth had been consulted about the sending of the letter.

Early in January the company replied, providing a chilling example of how some foreign companies want to treat our country. They wrote: 'The oceanographic work, which will cost tens and possibly hundreds of thousands of dollars, cannot be justified until the project approval is secured.'

They might just as well have said 'up yours'. They didn't care what federal or state governments wanted by way of environmental standards: they considered themselves above the law. The sum total of their reply to the stipulation that the studies necessary to determine the final design and location of the outfall must be outlined was that 'the assumed depth is about 20 metres'. In relation to the effluent and the government's desire that its dilution and subsequent dispersal had to be predicted, the reply was if possible even worse: 'We completely disagree with this assessment, which misconstrues the nature of the EIS. This is not surprising since it has its origins in the submission from the Department of Sea Fisheries, which is notable for its misconstructions.' That this joint venture was a problem was now apparent to the Tasmanians as well as to the Commonwealth.

In December 1988 I attended the World Heritage convention in Brasilia and went on to the United States. While in America I addressed an environment seminar attended by a host of big companies, including Noranda, the Canadian joint venturer with an interest in Wesley Vale. In the blunt terms for which I am known, I told the seminar that Noranda would not be able to do to Australia what had allegedly been done to the areas surrounding the pulp mills they run in Canada. The president of the company Mr Zimmerman threatened to sue me, and high dudgeon was expressed by his representatives. The suit never happened but the threat showed the company's sensitivity about their position in Canada—fine feelings never shown about their position in Australia. The emission standards for pulp mills in Canada were under review at the time and Noranda was afraid that the acceptance of high standards in Australia would inevitably lead to similar expectations in Canada, where they had more mills and a huge investment. Wesley Vale was important for Noranda but Canada was home, where most of the money was.

However, when I got home I began to believe that perhaps this project could go ahead with reasonable—that is, reasonably tough—environmental safeguards. On 3 January the Tasmanians announced their environmental controls, and they were good. Peter Hodgman the Tasmanian Minister for the Environment (and brother of former federal Member Michael) defended them, and when they were introduced into State Parliament one week later, my complete lack of faith in Tasmania's commitment to a genuine environmental safeguard process was beginning to look harsh.

Noranda had claimed that some of the guidelines would be technically impossible to meet; on 1 February Premier Robin Gray announced that this was not the case. He queried the intentions of the joint venturers, saying that perhaps they were not serious in their commitment to the project. His tough words were echoed by Deputy Premier Ray Groom: 'I sense they are not particularly keen to get a result,' he said. He added that Noranda representatives had privately assured the Tasmanian Cabinet that the guidelines could be met. With Gray and Groom going hard publicly, uttering rhetoric that left no room for a change of heart, the Tasmanian public were entitled to believe that their government would remain firm and that Wesley Vale would not go ahead.

But you can't trust the conservatives on environmental issues: when the crunch comes they will always take the pro-development option. When, on 31 January, Noranda threatened to shelve the project if the government's guidelines were not changed by 3 February, the acid test for Robin Gray was in place. The speed with which he failed the test surprised everyone; on 3 February, I witnessed the most breathtaking backdown I have ever seen in politics. On North Broken Hill letterhead, a letter announced that in ten days the Tasmanian Parliament would be recalled to 'approve legislation designed to clear the way for the project to proceed'. Furthermore, this legislation would be 'jointly agreed to by the companies and the government'. In what Bob Brown described as 'an unparalleled display of company power over government', a new pulp mill agreement was signed by the end of February, incorporating more than forty changes to the original 'principles and interpretations' of the environmental guidelines.

The company had simply ignored a letter from my department seeking to clarify a range of important issues such as dioxin emissions, chlorine dioxide substitution levels and the emission of odours. Noranda weren't about to change their modus operandi: Mr Zimmerman announced that the project would be cancelled if the guidelines were altered in any way.

Having achieved a world record in retreat from sense and sensibility, the Tasmanian government now threw the ball straight into the Commonwealth's lap. We were told that if we could persuade Noranda to agree to changes in the guidelines, Tasmania would be happy to comply. How's that for leadership?

For what it's worth, if I had changed as Robin Gray did, Bob Katter MP and his mates would have been demanding that I face a Royal Commission. People of that ilk always have to look for base motives in their enemies. In the case of Wesley Vale, the baseness of the motive was in the eye of the beholder. Robin Gray wanted the jobs the mill would provide directly and indirectly. His mistake was being prepared to pay any price in terms of environmental degradation. Australia cannot be treated like a Third World country when it comes to environmental standards; if companies want to do business here, they have to be prepared to keep it clean.

The media were having a field day with all this. Peter Hodgman and I debated each other on a special edition of 'A Current Affair'; Jana Wendt presided over a debate attended by hundreds of pro- and anti-development supporters in the Wrest Point Casino (in the room used for federal Labor conferences). While the issue was polarising the community, this was probably the first time that the Tasmanian electorate had not sided with the developers. You couldn't get an audience with a pro-mill majority in Hobart.

By the time federal Cabinet came to discuss the matter in mid March, the CSIRO and the Bureau of Rural Resources had assessed the information provided by the joint venture company and were singularly unimpressed. I went into Cabinet fairly confident that, at the least, I would win an argument about the necessity for insisting on tougher environmental conditions. But John Kerin opened the meeting by saying: 'The EIS is ratshit and the guidelines are a joke.' There was no argument; with those words real debate was over, and even the leading proponent of forest industries had walked away from the Gray sellout. The most avid pro-development ministers knew that the issue wouldn't go away and that nobody would be thanked for allowing a multinational to bully them out of the right environmental decision.

The Tasmanian backdown did me a great favour. Only John Button still thought the project worth defending under the new Tasmanian arrangements. He and his department had worked for a long time to bring to fruition a project worth billions, and I could hardly blame him for trying. The decision was made to grant Foreign Investment Review Board approval to the project provided tougher guidelines were drawn up by my department and John Kerin's Department of Primary Industry. Further environmental studies were also requested, with strict monitoring by the federal and Tasmanian governments.

With John Button and Paul Keating, I met with representatives of the joint venturers to tell them about the Cabinet decision. They disliked being forced to do the biological and chemical baseline study of the area likely to be affected by liquid effluent discharge, and they were not delighted about having to do an oceanographic study either. What they did was confirm what the exercise was really about. When it came down to determining standards for the quantities of organochlorines and other nasties permitted to be discharged, they said they could do better than the Tasmanian government requested, but that they would not accept guidelines to make that better performance mandatory. They would not accept tough environmental standards that other governments—such as Canada's—might latch onto. And they refused to agree to modify their production processes if at a later date the level of damage being caused to the environment was unacceptable to us.

As a sovereign nation and developed country, Australia must set high standards and ensure that these are followed. While the Tasmanians would not insist on changes to production processes, serious damage could have occurred, and there was no way the national government could fail to take a stand. That there was so little disagreement about this in an Australian Cabinet is something of which every Australian should be proud.

I hope we do see a world standard pulp mill in Australia with the world's best technology, adding value without increasing damage to an already stressed marine environment. We need this kind of investment, and I hope there are business people with vision and banks with courage to make it happen. I will not hang by the neck waiting.

CHAPTER 14

The Old Bull and the Young Bull

During the whole of 1988, the party began to see that the Hawke–Keating relationship could not remain as it was. It was a case of the old bull and the young bull, the oldest game in town.

Keating had been Treasurer for the whole of Hawke's prime ministership. He had waited and served with distinction, but now his patience was running out. Keating was definitely thinking about leaving politics. If Hawke showed signs of staying on for another five years as Prime Minister and Keating was unable to defeat him in a ballot, Keating said he would take the 'Paris option' (a highly paid bank or finance position in Paris).

Keating had entered Parliament in 1969, Hawke in 1980, and Keating often said that 'twenty years of top performance' should have its rewards. However Hawke, who had indicated in 1983 that he would not try to break Robert Menzies' record of sixteen years as Prime Minister, was going well. He still rated highly in opinion polls, he believed that his destiny was to be in that job. The fact was that no amount of persuasion would get Hawke to leave, and Keating's level of frustration was rising all the time.

In June, the *Bulletin* carried a story concluding that according to the Morgan Gallup poll, Hawke was the most popular Prime Minister in twenty years. Since becoming Prime Minister his lowest approval rating had been 44 per cent, compared to the lows of 28 per cent for Malcolm Fraser, 27 per cent for Gough Whitlam and 25 per cent for Sir William McMahon. After five years as Prime Minister, Hawke's approval rating was still 54 per cent, with John Howard, his opposite number, languishing with 28 per cent. The Morgan poll also suggested that Labor would win an election held at that time.

This kind of article was not lost on Hawke. His confidence was at an all-time high (it never had many lows), a confidence shared by most members of the Cabinet, the Caucus and the party at large. Just a couple of days before the *Bulletin* article appeared, I had said on Channel Nine's 'Sunday' program that Bob Hawke would 'lead us into the next election, so I'd imagine that means you've got another four or five years of Bob Hawke as Prime Minister'. While I had nominated Keating as a 'certainty' to replace Hawke, I had delivered a public message to Keating that as far as I was concerned—and that meant practically the whole of the Right—any challenge to Hawke's leadership would not be supported.

That all this should have been necessary was sad but inevitable. When a brilliant successor consistently outperforms an incumbent in public, eventually there is leadership speculation. At the 1988 federal conference, Keating had given one of his virtuoso performances in the economic debate: on issues ranging from privatisation to financial contributions for higher education, he had sparkled. By now Hawke had developed the hectoring style of a parson giving a sermon, and this was very much in evidence when he addressed the conference.

Of course, ability in speaking and performing in public is critically important, but it is not the only criterion by which a prime minister should be judged. The strength of the Hawke phenomenon was in what the masses thought of him. Their love affair with Hawke had developed over almost twenty years, and his capacity for making speeches had little to do with it. It was built on television and personal appearances, and above all an almost inexhaustible capacity to talk to every person at every function he attended. There had been thousands of functions over the years and hundreds of thousands of people had experienced the Hawke personality, even if only for a few seconds.

At the time, Keating was not particularly popular for all the wrong reasons: the years of cutting costs in Budgets and mini Budgets had seen him deliver far too much bad news for that. He was of course aware of this, but I doubt whether at that point personal popularity bothered him at all. What did bother him was how likely Hawke would be to hand him the reins after winning his fourth election.

For Hawke's successor, the task of winning a fifth election seemed insurmountable. While the idea of replacing Hawke was legitimate in terms of Paul's personal ambition, it failed to acknowledge the real question in the minds of those who thought keeping Labor in government was worth almost any sacrifice. Why replace a man who would be almost impossible to defeat in the next election with a relatively unpopular challenger who, at best, might win the election after that if everything went perfectly for the next two years? Nonetheless, Keating felt he was being robbed of his future. All he had worked for would come to nothing if Hawke hung on too long to give him a real shot at the title.

For those who hold marginal seats the only test is electoral; for the rest who are ministers or who want to be (that is, all of them) the niceties of succession timetables mean nothing measured against the party's electoral success. As far as I was concerned—and I was not alone—Hawke was still a winner, and Keating took a long time to forgive me for not recognising that his time had come. However, a few Cabinet members were letting every journalist with an interest, and a few without one, know that they believed there should be a change of leadership well before the next election so a rejuvenated government could seek a fourth term. This meant studiously ignoring the polls that had us well in front with Hawke dominating Howard as preferred PM.

John Button was the most talkative on this question, but he was always talkative about something. John Dawkins made known to all who crossed his path that he had become a committed Keating disciple, and Peter Walsh would support anyone who wasn't Hawke. Keating and Dawkins even claimed at the time that Brian Howe was making noises of support. Some others might have been in the push, but they were more circumspect, prepared to let Button and Dawkins lead the charge.

On the backbench all was quiet. Throughout 1988 I can recall only two backbenchers from the Right who showed any support for Paul Keating. David Beddall, later Minister for Resources, and Michael Lee, later Minister for Communications and the Arts, both proclaimed their view that the leadership should be changed earlier rather than later—a piece of forward thinking that did their subsequent careers no harm.

Gary Punch, who became the main bomb thrower for Keating in 1991, actually went to see him at my request to tell him that the majority of the Right were not on his side. This caused Keating to refuse to attend Right Caucus meetings for quite some time. The faction still called itself the pro-Hawke coalition (so named when first formed in the early months of government) and he found it hard to rally to that banner with any enthusiasm. He told me that if the New South Wales Right, let alone the rest of them, wouldn't stick with him after all his years of loyalty, he could no longer stick with them. When Keating loses his temper he often goes over the top, and those of us who have known him for a long time have learned to discern the idle threat from the promise that may take a generation to carry out. We knew Paul would come home when the time was right because, as sure as God made little apples, whenever he decided to seek the top job he would need the support of the New South Wales Right. He knew it, too. For the next couple of years, while he didn't attend faction meetings, he continued to vote for the faction in all the Caucus ballots. It was a case of not having your cake and eating it anyway.

With the Hawke–Keating relationship obviously fracturing, there was considerable concern among the troops. Most wanted to say to Keating: Soon, but not yet. Keating cannot hide disappointment, so his private rhetoric on Hawke got worse and worse, and he tried out that rhetoric on anyone from the Caucus who wandered into his peripheral vision, as well as quite a few press gallery members who were lucky enough to strike him in the right frame of mind.

As word of this spread to Hawke himself, he too hardened his position, and towards the end of August this rather pathetic quarrel boiled over. Hawke appeared on the '7.30 Report' and put the view that the government could live without Keating. I watched this with some trepidation, because I knew the kind of reaction this would get from Keating.

I gave Hawke a piece of my mind about this indulgence. Generally speaking, Hawke was above this kind of response, and keeping Keating going was worth putting up with a bit of the Treasurer's spleen. Hawke would have to right this wrong, and the next night he appeared on 'A Current Affair' telling the world that Keating would be Prime Minister one day and that 'he is undoubtedly the best Treasurer this country has had and, I repeat, the best Treasurer in the world and I really mean that'. Oh, really.

On the way out to dinner, I rang Keating from my ministerial car to tell him that Hawke had gone public in trying to heal the breach and that the two of them should get together to bring this nonsense to an end. Keating proceeded to tell me exactly what he thought of his leader. I can't remember all of the choice language he used, but 'envious little turd' does spring to mind. After paying out on Hawke for about five minutes, Keating discovered that I was using a car phone. For a while his invective was directed not at Hawke but at me.

Murphy's Law applies far more often than many people realise. The only thing that could go wrong was that some bored radio fanatic would be getting his jollies by scanning car phone traffic, singling out our conversation for special attention. Sure enough, out there was just such a dickhead, who taped the conversation we were determined not to admit had ever taken place. The tape was obviously a very valuable piece of property and its owner was ringing the press gallery, the Opposition and anyone who would answer him, offering to sell it.

Some months earlier, we had quite properly passed a law making the recording of such conversations illegal, and their sale illegal as well. So far, so good. But when Murphy's Law is operating, there is always something else wrong. Unfortunately we had never proclaimed the law, so for a few days there was a danger that this tape could legally see the light of day. We had to pretend it was illegal and rush to get the relevant provisions proclaimed. We got lucky on this occasion, and the media and

Opposition never did buy it because they thought it was illegal. In any event, the dickhead went to ground when he thought he might get into strife.

Nonetheless, word of the tape spread like wildfire and neither Hawke nor Keating was terribly impressed. Hawke rang me at the Old Tai Yuen restaurant in Sydney, where my family and I were having dinner. I didn't get too many words in while Hawke told me how stupid I was. There was no defence, so I entered a plea of guilty to get it all over with quickly.

The next week in both Houses of the Parliament, the Opposition tried to get Hawke (whom Wilson Tuckey branded as a wimp for failing to take action against his Treasurer over the car phone conversation), Keating or me to comment. In the House of Representatives, Joan Child ruled a question to Hawke on this matter out of order. It was a pretty hot ruling, but in the circumstances a useful one. Senator Puplick asked me a question in the Senate and all I would do was say I didn't believe I had to answer questions about alleged conversations taped by anonymous persons. It was weak, but it beat the hell out of admitting that the conversation had taken place.

As happens with all these minor dramas, Australians wrapped their fish and chips in this a few days later and the world moved on. However, speculation about Keating continued almost unabated. Button and Dawkins made a few statements about the need for a firm timetable on the succession to be sorted out between Hawke and Keating. Dawkins had met with Hawke and told him he should resign: a pretty gutsy thing for any minister to say to a very popular Prime Minister. Not only did Joe do that, but he leaked the conversation to Paul Kelly, who splashed it in the *Australian*.

This was no ordinary campaign to destabilise the leader. Keating was throwing out the challenge even though he had no more than three or four Cabinet ministers and a handful of backbenchers on his side—10 votes if he was lucky. But he has never understood the concept of being in a position of weakness; he just keeps going and expects his position to improve by virtue of its inherent correctness; if it's his position, it must be right. On this occasion, he misjudged the mood. If I wouldn't get the New South Wales Right to go with him, he couldn't build momentum. With a mere handful of votes and with the rest of the Caucus committed to Hawke, failure was certain. (While I didn't find out about this for a few more years, he did get the Kirribilli meeting and a definite promise on a time for the Hawke resignation—not that this meant very much when the time came for the promise to be kept.)

The sniping and publicity continued for a few more months. John Edwards, who went on to become a Keating staffer, wrote a very long article in the *Sydney Morning Herald* late in September entitled 'A Lust for Power'. It was all about what made Keating tick, a mini-biography that gives as good an insight into Keating as any of the books subsequently written about him or the period. A month later Craig McGregor in the same newspaper went even further. His piece entitled 'Borrowed Time: The Last Days of Bob Hawke' was instantly recognisable as being in print what Keating had been saying in private for months, if not years. It contained ridiculous statements such as: 'Disaffection with Hawke spreads right through the Labor Cabinet.' Keating had three or four supporters there, but anyone who read this article could have believed that Brian Howe and the Left were just about to pledge allegiance. To realise how difficult it was to keep Hawke calm during this period, one need only look at this extract: 'Button and the other ALP powerbrokers engineered Hawke's accession to the Labor leadership knowing full well he had few ideas and that his main appeal was as an election winner. He's done just that: won an unprecedented series of elections for the ALP. Now they want a real leader, and Hawke won't go.'

While our two antagonists were able to get their act together and private promises given by Hawke might have mollified Keating to some extent, this period of tension changed the atmosphere of Cabinet. Leaks became increasingly common, camaraderie much shakier. Many Caucus members were disillusioned with Keating after this; they shared the view that he had been blackmailing all of them by threatening to resign from politics if he failed to get the top job. This didn't matter; Keating knew that whatever disillusion was felt couldn't last. When inspiration was needed in the Parliament, when the Opposition looked like scoring a few points against us, there was only one saviour, only one who would deliver us from evil. While some of us couldn't live with him, almost everyone couldn't live without him.

CHAPTER 15

From Micro to Macro

By March 1989 the Hawke–Keating alliance, though fragile, was strong enough to do me over in the name of microeconomic reform.

This useful phrase was discovered only after we came to government. The wharves and coastal shipping, our railways and transport systems in general (indeed, the whole economy) were bristling with rorts and featherbedding when Malcolm Fraser was Prime Minister, but nobody asked him to do anything about them. When a Labor government came to office we had to fix all the problems by yesterday. And one of the most pressing issues for microeconomic reform was the third runway for Sydney airport.

The conflict was between alienating thousands of voters who lived around the airport (many in houses that had not been underneath any flight paths when they bought them) and improving the air links to the country's major city at a time when tourism was becoming a major earner of export dollars. Another element in the debate was the timing of a new airport at Badgery's Creek on Sydney's western outskirts.

Two Labor-held seats were in danger over the decision to build the runway; to be realistic, probably only one. St George, held by Steve Dubois, had a big enough majority to survive, but Gary Punch's Barton stood out as a real electoral casualty. I worried about this; with a worsening economy and interest rates going ever higher, I do not apologise for being concerned with issues of electoral wisdom. However, Keating, Leo McLeay and Peter Baldwin, among others, considered the problem of threatened seats only one of several factors: their electoral bases were safe. Labor had cancelled Malcolm Fraser's decision to build the runway, and had promised to reject the runway again and again. Hawke himself had made the promise many times.

Cabinet was evenly split between the economic ministers led by Keating and the political pragmatists led by Robert Ray and me. We argued the case on cost grounds, on Labor not being seen to make worthless promises, on the hardship caused to hundreds of thousands of people and on the timing of Badgery's Creek. The government had originally intended to pay for the homes of those badly affected to be insulated and their windows double glazed to cut down the noise problem; that idea was scrapped when we found out how many millions it would cost. I have always believed that Labor voters especially, but all voters when it comes to the crunch, deserve better than that.

I was suspicious of the studies suggesting that relatively low numbers of people would be affected; more recent research put those numbers very much higher than the original estimates. And many of the figures quoted in Cabinet from the Department of Transport were rubbery. Every estimate for Badgery's Creek was put at its utmost top edge, every one for the third runway shaved for effect. Certainly there was a case for a third runway, but in my view not at the expense of a start for Badgery's Creek.

Contrary to the impression now abroad, the Cabinet debate went on and on because those of us opposed to the third runway did have a case. The Cabinet was divided: had the question been pushed to a vote, we would have been defeated by nine votes to eight. This was a vote Hawke and Keating wished to avoid at all costs. A kind of consensus decision-making had existed in Cabinet since 1983, but this time we were angry. Only a matter of days before the first Cabinet discussion, Hawke and Keating had given assurances that they were opposed to a third runway and we were entitled to believe them. When Gary Punch and I held a press conference to dispel rumours that the government would consider building a third runway, we did so after seeking yet another assurance from Hawke. Keating was making the same noises, so we went into these Cabinet discussions feeling pretty confident. But a funny thing happened on the way to the forum, and to this day I have no idea what it was.

The day of the final Cabinet meeting began with my being called into the Oval Office to be greeted by a united duo of Hawke and Keating. I was told that it was time to give up the fight, lie down and not force a vote. I was annoyed by all that had occurred on this issue, but not so moved as to wish to upset the very foundation of government. My colleagues and I continued the fight at the last meeting, but with all the grace we could muster we had to accept defeat.

Gary Punch, for whom this decision had been a knockout political blow, showed that some in this business still have some integrity. After this loss he couldn't face his electors in Barton, so he resigned from the ministry and campaigned from the backbench. He won his seat with an increased majority, so the electoral pain this decision could have brought us was saved by Punch's integrity and guts.

Punch blamed Hawke entirely for the debacle: somehow he considered Keating, who had supported Hawke, to be blameless. During the next two and a half years, Punch became the most bitter enemy Hawke had. He became the bomb-thrower for Keating, briefing journalists, haranguing Caucus colleagues, never missing a chance to do Hawke a disservice. Punch is a great friend and a terrible enemy. While not everything he did was constructive in helping the Keating cause, the sheer ferocity and consistency of his attacks on Hawke helped keep the cause alive when it occasionally ran out of puff. Hate is a wonderful motivator, and there never was a better hater than Gary Punch.

Paul Keating had his own moments of personal difficulty over the runway decision. His old friend Laurie Brereton was running for the seat of Kingsford Smith, which bordered the airport, and large sections of the Botany end of his electorate were among those most affected. Like Punch and myself, Brereton had campaigned hard against the runway and, like us, he believed that Keating would oppose the proposition. He regarded Keating's support for the runway as an act of betrayal and announced that he would never speak to him again, despite the friendship they had enjoyed for twenty-five years. Those of us who knew Laurie well could not take this announcement too seriously. Like Leo McLeay, Laurie Brereton could, would and did forgive Keating this indiscretion, as both were passionately committed to seeing Paul Keating become Prime Minister. Laurie's anger lasted about six months, long enough to show how much he was hurt and short enough to enable the friendship to continue.

I didn't let the process affect any relationship of mine. There was a case for the third runway and I couldn't blame anyone for supporting it. I just wished their intentions could have been made known to me a little earlier. The media greeted the decision very positively, so the government did well out of it. Meanwhile, interest rates continued to rise and the boom continued to get out of control. Interest rates were hurting us too badly for microeconomic reform to have made any real political impact.

Sydney is now getting a runway that will just about see its capacity exhausted in another ten years. A decade is a significant period of time, but the cost is high. The decision to build the third runway put off for some considerable time even the possibility of real work beginning at Badgery's Creek. While few of us who uses airports regularly likes to think of going right to Sydney's outskirts to get a plane, it will happen. Delaying the start of Sydney's new gateway can't be smart. And the third runway can't take jumbos—another triumph for microeconomic reform.

CHAPTER 16

Election '90 and the Wooing of the Greens

In the twelve months still to go before we had to hold an election in 1990, Labor had to wrestle with ever-increasing interest rates, designed to slow the economy down without delivering a recession. The amount of faith in a soft landing was fading every day: by the end of the calendar year 1989 every set of figures, from balance of payments to employment and debt, was going badly for us.

While Button, Dawkins, Walsh and Kerin continued to rail against me over the environment, some of them had doubts about the orthodox policies the government was pursuing. Button thought the 1988 Budget had not been tight enough, Walsh thought interest rate hikes would hurt too many little people. While they continued to hold the view that Hawke should go in favour of Keating, they didn't believe Keating had all the answers.

At one point Walsh came very close to resigning. I'm glad he didn't go through with it. I didn't like him all that much and had bitterly disagreed with him over the environment, and I considered his political judgment weak at best and non-existent at worst—but he was brilliant. He mastered his briefs as Finance Minister and on the rare occasions when we debated the economy, what he said had to be listened to. There is a difference between being brilliant and being smart. The best are both, but most have some claims to one and fancy themselves on the other. That Walsh would consider resignation in early 1989 suggests that he picked the recession and its causes earlier than most. Maybe I underestimated him!

Keating wasn't about to change any aspects of economic policy and he kept interest rates high, accusing of cowardice anyone who expressed doubts. In private chats with Hawke, I was able to get him to agree that something had to be done about housing and business interest rate concessions. But private chats and private understandings mattered nothing once Keating got hold of Hawke. The Prime Minister was in a genuine quandary; economic decisions can often be close calls, and it is possible to argue either way. Keating was in no doubt about his own position, and became less compromising as every economic indicator worsened.

With the economy looking pretty ordinary and Paul Keating as popular as a pork chop in a synagogue, the only thing we had going for us was our environment policy.

In July 1989, Hawke delivered a comprehensive environment statement in the New South Wales town of Wentworth, at the confluence of the Murray and Darling rivers. In this beautiful environment, Hawke listed all the government's achievements in the area of environmental policy and committed us to a land care program, the planting of a billion trees in a decade and a save the bush program to protect remnant vegetation around the country. There was historic co-operation between the Australian Conservation Foundation and the National Farmers Federation, but most importantly there were two busloads of journalists who followed us from Renmark in South Australia to Wentworth. They saw the salination occurring in the Murray–Darling system, the dead trees, the desolation that most Australians never see or read about.

The whole idea for this statement (which those of us in the

know were calling WGES for World's Greatest Environment Statement) had come from Simon Balderstone in my office and Craig Emerson (who now heads Queensland's Environment Department) in Hawke's office. The WGES was not a big-ticket item for the money ministers to worry about. At a cost of $520 million over ten years, it was more of an opportunity to focus attention on the government's environment record and its future plans. Once again, here was an opportunity to contrast Labor's record with that of the Opposition.

I was delighted that about 60 per cent of the money was promised to combat land degradation. Our loss of vegetation and topsoil, increasing salinity, declining water quality, and so on, are issues that have never gripped the vast majority of the citizens who live in our cities. Chop down a tree in a forest and a horde of protesters will descend in a matter of minutes; if a few million tonnes of topsoil blow away from a property that has been overcleared, nobody bothers about it much. There were good programs in the WGES that have continued, and significant money for research into the crown of thorns starfish, endangered species and a new virus to wipe out our ongoing rabbit plague. While Toyne and a few of his cohorts later criticised the statement for not setting real goals and targets on greenhouse gas emissions, what it helped to do was keep the environment on the front page. It helped that the press gallery were there and could go on and report it to the nation. By the banks of the Murray and Darling rivers, Hawke took a giant step towards re-election.

If I did anything to help this cause during my three years as Minister for the Environment, it was to elevate it to page one and keep it there. When I left that ministry, the environment left the front page, and it has seldom returned. The environment groups themselves have not managed to keep their issues in a high-profile position, though obviously in a recession people will concentrate more on survival than on extras such as being kind to the environment. But in the next few decades the environment will return as an issue, because it has to.

At a seminar for campaign directors and electorate staff held at University House at the Australian National University in October 1989, I outlined for the first time to a major party gathering the need to chase preference votes from the greens and the Democrats. I pointed out that according to surveys conducted over the past two years, the environment had come from twelfth to second place as an issue of public importance. Our surveys were consistent with all the others, and my message was that we could drag reluctant voters to our side by a preference strategy that stressed our impressive record on the environment.

I urged our local campaigners not to campaign against green candidates but to pursue them for preferences which, overwhelmingly, they would want to give us. I pointed out that if Andrew Peacock had been Prime Minister, the Franklin would have been dammed, logging in the wet tropics rainforests would still be going on, Wesley Vale would be under construction and the bulldozers would be moving into Kakadu (later we used this same line against Hewson, and it will be used against other Opposition leaders again and again). This was a powerful message to sell to a growing constituency who worried about the environment and didn't particularly like either candidate for Prime Minister or either party manifesto. The widespread and very public dislike for Keating's economic measures and the perception that we were slipping into a recession were doing nothing for our popularity.

Given the number of people who have since claimed responsibility for the idea of having a preference strategy at a time when our primary vote was going to be very small, I can be forgiven for claiming just this one as mine. Others might have made decisions during the election campaign to run particular advertisements on this theme, but my staff and I came up with what was at that time a radical departure from normal campaign thinking, labelled as 'off' strategy by many in the party hierarchy. I was able to present the strategy so forcefully because, only a couple of weeks earlier, Labor had made the last decision necessary to guarantee green support.

The Kakadu National Park had more symbolic value than any forest, lake, reef or mountain range; it was the benchmark by which our commitment to the environment would be judged. No matter how many good decisions we made—and we had made many—if we allowed substantial mining activity in Kakadu there could be no political gain. If we failed to make the right decision, the greens would punish us.

I proposed delaying approval for the Coronation Hill gold and platinum mine and adding to the park most of the area set aside for mineral exploration, reducing the exploration zone from roughly 2200 square kilometres to less than fifty. I also proposed a new environmental impact statement on the mineral-rich area to supersede that on the Coronation Hill mine.

The plan to shrink the exploration zone so boldly, in defiance of written undertakings given by Hawke at the time of the 1987 election, was not mine. The idea came from the Left's Stewart West, Minister for Administrative Services at the time, with carriage of the granting of leases or permissions to explore. He brought the plan to me and convinced me that it was a worthwhile exercise. The myth that I created it myself did not come about because I tried to steal West's thunder: it occurred because the task of convincing a majority in Cabinet fell to me. So did the task of creating the political climate in which to make it all possible, and the task of selling the decision once it had been made. While I could not have pride of authorship, I adopted this cause with single-minded zeal.

Failure to use federal power to stop the Franklin dam had cost Malcolm Fraser dearly, though he had made some good environmental decisions about Kakadu, the Great Barrier Reef and Fraser Island. Kakadu was for us what the Franklin had been for Fraser: failure here would undo all our good work. I never hid from the Toynes or the Garretts my view that BHP's mining of gold and platinum at Coronation Hill should be allowed to proceed (I voted that way when a majority of Cabinet supported the mining in May 1991 and was overruled by Bob Hawke) but I was sure that if mining proceeded willy-nilly through the conservation zone, untold damage could be done to the headwaters of the South Alligator, the river that gives Kakadu so much of its special quality.

Since Hawke had previously given undertakings to BHP in fairly unambiguous terms, his support for any change was necessary. Justification that went well beyond political expediency would be necessary to convince him. The fragility of the environment in the conservation zone was pretty obvious: this was either a cause for worry or it wasn't. Either the economic considerations outweighed the environmental ones or they didn't. We gave Hawke plenty of briefings on the environment in the area and on the kind of damage that would be done if mining and exploration were permitted. When you added the polls' showing that Kakadu was an icon in the hearts and minds of ordinary Australians, there was only one sensible way to go.

But the economic ministers, with the exception of Paul Keating, were really angry about this proposal. With BHP, they argued that government commitments should be honoured, and they said that investor confidence would be destroyed if we were seen to pander to special interest groups. The balance of payments situation was scarcely healthy enough to place at risk the potential for billions of dollars in mining investment. Button, Dawkins, Cook and Walsh provided some of the most heated Cabinet opposition, as did Bob Collins, then a backbench senator for the Northern Territory who had worked in Kakadu for years.

As I have already said, Keating usually followed his instincts on the big environmental questions, and he was on side. He told me that, for the sake of keeping faith with his colleagues on the Expenditure Review Committee, he would have to oppose me. But he indicated he would make a very short speech, then disappear. This spelled the end of any possibility that I would be defeated in Cabinet.

When I told Hawke about my conversation with Keating, the Prime Minister readily agreed to open Cabinet discussion with a very strong declaration of his own support. Whenever Hawke chose to do this, the result was guaranteed (this is now also pretty much the case for Paul Keating). When the authority of the Prime Minister is put on the line, a Cabinet has no choice but to follow: most ministers would never push to defeat him under these circumstances. This was one time when I went into a Cabinet meeting with the deck stacked in my favour.

True to his word, Keating spoke for five minutes against the proposal, then left the meeting to keep an urgent appointment. The debate didn't take very long and Hawke duly carried the day. But the dire predictions from Button, Dawkins and Walsh in particular had a real edge to them. They doubted the political strategy and believed we were sacrificing the economic future of Australia for all the wrong reasons. However, to their great credit, their commitment to Cabinet solidarity meant that they kept their disappointment to themselves in public. John Kerin, who had been out of the country for the Cabinet meeting, did let fly with public criticism of the decision, earning a rebuke from Hawke. Frankly, after this decision the only thing that surprised me was that more ministers did not break Cabinet solidarity: this was the decision that pushed Cabinet about as far as it could be pushed.

The decision got no support in the media, who made great play of the fact that Hawke had capitulated to green pressure. (While it is true that Phillip Toyne spoke to him for ninety minutes on the night before the Cabinet decision was made, he was merely reinforcing the environmental case I had been putting.) But the public loved it: not only did the polls get better for us, with environment being the growth issue of the time, but 75 per cent supported the Kakadu decision. We were on a winner, and I knew it.

We were now ready and the decks were cleared: within six months or so after the October decision there had to be an election, and the environment was going to win it for us. Whether the greens would have advocated support for us without the Kakadu decision will always be a matter for conjecture, but I doubt whether the preferences from rank-and-file Democrat voters, as well as green voters, would ever have been so high without it.

To even attempt to counteract our success in the environment movement was very difficult for the Opposition. Their shadow minister, Senator Chris Puplick, was a committed conservationist who had been forced to take positions he quite obviously didn't like (such as opposing World Heritage listing for the wet tropics rainforests). The real crux of his dilemma lay in the dividing line between state and federal power. There were many conservative Liberals in the state organisations, as well as the Federal Parliament, and the National Party was even worse. These two groups were able to thwart all Puplick's efforts to forge a policy that held open the tiniest hope that a Peacock government would ever overrule a state on a major environmental issue.

In the years I was Minister for the Environment I made a mess of Puplick's shadow ministry. In saying this I am not giving myself a pat on the back: he was a talented performer, but it was never a fair fight. When he was beaten by Bronwyn Bishop and pushed down to the number three spot on the Senate ticket, the Labor Party were pleased. Their two best in the Senate while I was there were Peter Baume and Chris Puplick, and the Liberals seemed to know only how to kick them.

The environment cause began to suffer a few years later, after the decision to refuse permission to mine Coronation Hill in May 1992. The lines blurred between the good and the bad guys, and the issues were no longer top of the pops in the polls. A lengthy and deep recession had a great deal to do with this, but I suspect that our success in Kakadu was also a contributing factor. While our decision was absolutely right on environmental grounds, it was exploited by the mining industry as proof that Labor's power had been usurped by the conservation movement, and the business community was outraged by it.

That we could approach an election towards the end of 1990 with some degree of confidence was more a measure of the Liberals' failures than of our successes.

Business and commercial interest rates were running at more than 20 per cent. But interest rates were not our only problem; the failures (dare I say the historically unprecedented failures) of state Labor administrations were beginning to catch up with us. While the full tale of disaster wasn't yet fully understood, the Cain government in Victoria was really on the nose. Revelations were just becoming public that because of its merchant banking arm Tricontinental, the State Bank of Victoria had lost billions of dollars. It was a colossal disaster, and Cain seemed utterly unable to deal with it, refusing to sack either the chief economic adviser Peter Sheehan or the Treasurer Rob Jolly. Nobody, apparently, had done any wrong, so no one would pay a penalty. Again and again Bob Hogg tried to convince Cain to do something—anything—about the problem, but to no avail. The Victorian public were angry and during a prolonged transport strike in Melbourne during January 1990, the party's morale was suffering. The only strategy for Labor was to hope and pray that the loss in Victoria would be only five or six seats. There is little you can do under these circumstances and while Labor's main campaigners spent a lot of time in Victoria, the task was hopeless: nobody was listening.

Western Australia was in danger of becoming a similar problem. The WA Inc scandal was also just beginning to attract attention.

In a classic machine operation, the Premier Peter Dowding was deposed and replaced by Carmen Lawrence early in February. The sheer cruelty of politics is that in spite of a lengthy Royal Commission investigation, Dowding has never been charged with any offence. Despite this, for the Western Australian Labor Party to recover in a state or a federal election a sacrifice was necessary, and Dowding became an unwilling lamb to the slaughter. Having won an election for Labor, he was dumped unceremoniously. That it was necessary for him to pay such a price is a matter of regret as much as it was a matter of fact. When you enter this game, you should realise that gratitude from the party is not endless. You help it and you let it help you, but when the party says your number's up, then up it shall be.

The bright spot on the horizon was Queensland. In December 1989 the intolerably long rule of the National Party was brought to an inglorious end. Wayne Goss won in a landslide and, no matter what was happening in Victoria or Western Australia, the Fitzgerald Royal Commission had revealed a great deal about the Queensland National Party that Queenslanders would not forget. Just like Cain's Labor Party in the south, in the north the National Party were going to be punished, and federally we were quietly confident that a few seats could be won.

For the Liberals, all was not rosy either. Labor's major health policy initiative of the 1980s, Medicare, was still popular as the 1990s began. The Liberals had been promising a new health policy for twelve months, but nothing had been announced. The reason for this became clear late in January 1990 when they were forced to abandon the policy that their shadow minister Peter Shack had been working on for a long time. Any attempt to get rid of Medicare runs a grave political risk, and Peter Shack had produced a policy that would cost significant sums of money to hundreds of thousands of people. With an election due at any moment, Peacock was in all sorts of strife. He had the choice of adopting a policy that the hard Right would love and the electorate would hate, or abandoning that policy and going into an election with a 'trust me' promise on a basic issue that affected each and every Australian.

Peacock chose the 'trust me' option, a real problem for any politician whom not enough voters trusted. This amounted to the perfect campaign start for Hawke and the Labor Party. By 1990 the electorate had no faith in politicians or political parties. They would be choosing whomever they believed to be the lesser of two evils, and the fewer promises made, the more likely the success. The health policy failure was an unmitigated disaster for Peacock, from which he never recovered. It meant that Hawke, no longer everyone's hero but still with enough residual goodwill to get by, was in the box seat. If the losses in Victoria could be kept to a minimum, if Western Australia could return a relatively neutral result and we could gain a few in Queensland, in spite of the growing evidence of a recession induced by high interest rate policies, Labor would win.

In early February I headed off to New Zealand to spend a few pleasant days at the Commonwealth Games. One of the best jobs in government is Minister for Sport (with Tourism and Territories, this had been added to my existing portfolio of Arts and the Environment). You get to meet your heroes and watch them in action. I had been fortunate enough to go to the Olympic Games in Seoul and see the Duncan Armstrong gold medal, the Ben Johnson–Carl Lewis race and much, much more. The Auckland Commonwealth Games couldn't compete with that, but it was still a terrific way to spend a few days before what I knew would be an exhausting campaign. As Minister for Sport I had worked hard to win very big funding increases for Australian sport, and this visit was the fun part of the job.

Before leaving for Auckland, I had been briefed on all of Labor's research. If we believed what our research was telling us, we would have gone off to slit our wrists as soon as possible. It showed very big swings in Victoria and Western Australia and fairly slim pickings anywhere else. My impression from reading this material was that it accurately picked up serious dissatisfaction with our government but failed to register properly what voters felt about the alternative. I am not sure what the Liberals' research was showing but after that election a Liberal frontbencher told me there had been profound shock in the party at losing because their research had led them to believe it wasn't possible. In both 1987 and 1990, the Opposition really thought they would win. This was good training for 1993, when even we thought they would win.

I never doubted that we would campaign better than our opponents. Bob Hogg was the most experienced machine politician of either party still in the game and John Singleton was an advertising man of flair and speed. In virtually every state, the machines were well oiled and ready to roll. Devising a strategy wasn't all that difficult; we had to talk about the economy as little as possible, focus attention on Peacock as much as we could and use the environment preference strategy to help push us over the line. If the campaign could become a personal contest between Hawke and Peacock, we held an advantage. The health policy debacle weakened Peacock at a critical time, and I was confident. Medicare would again be central to Labor's campaign (as it always seemed to be) and with the environmental string added to the bow, I didn't worry too much about the research. The campaign would therefore do the trick and the punters would not tick Peacock's box on polling day.

Professionalism is of real value when the going gets tough. Hawke and Keating were proven winners, Geoff Walsh, then Hawke's chief adviser and now occupying the same position in the Keating office, was a real pro. His combination with Bob Hogg was important because by the time of the 1990 election the relationship between Hawke and his national secretary had soured badly. With his main researcher Rod Cameron (who had been persuaded to give us one more try), Hawke's relationship was even worse. These problems could have seriously disrupted a Labor campaign and surely would have done at practically any other time in the party's history, but this time around professionalism prevailed. The differences were papered over and they all got down to the business of winning.

The election was announced at the end of the second week of February. The week's news was good and bad for Labor: a deficit of $1.3 billion for Tricontinental was now public knowledge, which meant that every Victorian knew that the incompetence of a Labor government had cost them plenty and would cost them plenty more as taxes were raised to pay for it. By this stage every senior person in the party believed we would lose at least six seats in Victoria. John Cain had still not admitted wrongdoing by himself or by any member of his administration. Apparently no policy or its implementation was wrong, so he just kept doing nothing about it. I didn't like John Cain much, but up till then I had had some admiration for his political skills. This cock-up was so huge in its dimensions that he just couldn't accept that it had happened, let alone that he and some members of his government might have to bear some responsibility for it.

The news wasn't all bad, though. Peter Dowding went on 11 February and so did his deputy, David Parker. Carmen Lawrence's accession to the premiership assured her of a honeymoon and gave the federal party real hope that a disaster could be averted. The morale of candidates in marginal seats went up straight away, with Ron Edwards in Stirling and Caroline Jacobsen in Cowan now thinking they had a chance. Stephen Smith, another bright young machine operator who later became the MP for Perth and who is definitely ministerial material, had delivered a stunning and fairly bloodless coup. Dowding, after testing his Cabinet support and finding it wanting, did the right thing and resigned. No bloody party room brawl was necessary and the whole affair couldn't have gone better if we had scripted it. By resigning with dignity and avoiding an embarrassing party room defeat, Dowding showed the grace that in other leaders has been conspicuously absent.

Sometimes your best gifts come from your opponents. Deputy Leader of the Liberals in the Senate was Senator Austin Lewis, a reasonable bloke if ever there was one. On the Wednesday night 14 February, good old Austin gave an interview to Paul Lyneham that could at best be described as expansive and more accurately as suicidal. This was an opportunity to give John Howard his umpteenth kicking, and Austin did not miss him. Why he would have sought to reopen the old wound of the Howard–Peacock rivalry, by then a dead issue, remains a mystery. He followed up this promising performance by warning his leader Peacock to pull up his socks, and proclaimed that the Liberals had been unable to convince Australians of their fitness to govern. While Peacock sacked him as soon as he could get to a telephone, the horse had bolted. One of the four most senior Liberals had been guilty of an appalling breach of discipline. Maybe it was a succession of polls showing a Labor victory, or maybe Lewis knew what the Liberals' private polling was showing, but gifts such as these on the eve of election campaigns are rare indeed.

Lewis's effort gave Hawke what turned out to be the most effective line of the campaign. From that moment on, in every speech and interview and in many of the paid campaign advertisements, Hawke taunted the Opposition with the thought that if they couldn't govern their own party in Opposition, they couldn't run the country. This was a great diversion from interest rates and the economy, which we didn't want to debate at all. Paul Keating, who by this stage was sinking into a mire of unpopularity that would last for nearly two years, kept a low profile; if you don't want to debate the economy, you don't put your Treasurer up too often for all the world to see. We still had to calm Hawke down and make sure that his temper was under complete control. An enormous amount of good could be undone by a few seconds of indiscipline.

Both sides knew that the by now traditional televised debate between the two leaders would be all-important for their chances of victory. In the 1984 campaign, Hawke had clearly been surprised by Peacock and had not performed well. His capacity to get aggressive at the drop of the proverbial hat was the main negative he had to overcome. Hawke had much more knowledge than Peacock and a better grasp of the issues, but Peacock was smoother and if he had been coached well enough, he could still present himself as a formidable opponent. The two were allowed to ask each other questions, so there was a real need to keep Hawke as calm as possible.

The Hawke staff, Peter Barron, who was called out of retirement for the occasion, Geoff Walsh, Bob Hogg and the national secretariat and advertising agency team all urged on Hawke the need to remain calm no matter what the provocation. On the day of the debate I gave him the same message myself. I did have some worries about the outcome, but given that I had been one of those responsible for the decision to debate the Leader of the Opposition in the first place, I had to accept this as a risk worth taking. There is a school of orthodoxy in campaigning that says you should never debate your opponent. Normally I would have agreed with that view, but this time the debate was something we needed, not something we should have sought to avoid. Labor was making leadership an issue, so Labor had to show enough confidence in its leader to be prepared to expose him to a debate with his opponent.

I don't know how Hawke's nerves were before the debate, but I have rarely been as edgy. This was a high-stakes game that could well decide the election outcome. Hawke's opening remarks convinced me the gamble would pay off. He was so quiet as to be almost inaudible. Tonight there would be no cocky Prime Minister abusing or mocking his opponent. He was the statesman we had been praying for.

I have few recollections of the debate itself, just a memory of great relief when it was all over. The two impressions I carried away with me, however, were reflected in the research over the following days. Much discussion and negotiation had taken place about the format of the debate and Hawke prepared himself thoroughly on the basis that neither he nor Peacock would have notes. On the night Peacock was allowed to use notes and lost out by comparison to a Prime Minister who appeared to have no need for them because he knew his stuff so well. The inability of Peacock to think quickly enough on his feet to ask his opponent tough questions contrasted badly with Hawke, who never missed a chance.

Most importantly, the environment gave Hawke the perfect opportunity to attack without the need for aggression. As soon as the issues were discussed, he was able to point out how differently things would have gone had Peacock been Prime Minister over the previous seven years. All the big pluses for Labor got a run: the World Heritage listings that saved the Franklin, the wet tropics and the great forest areas of Tasmania; the Wesley Vale mill that wasn't spewing tonnes of organochlorines into Bass Strait every single day; the bulldozers that were not moving into Kakadu. These were the points on which Hawke had been rehearsed time and time again, and he delivered them perfectly.

The debate had a huge audience and the polls confirmed my view that Hawke was a big winner. In this business you have to back your judgment, and the main thing was what the millions of people at home in their lounge rooms thought about it all. The atmospherics of the debate were such that voters would have been in no doubt about who won. So many people have been critical of Hawke on the basis of inadequate intellect, ineffectual policy contribution and failing to instil sufficient spirit into his government. Those four election wins didn't happen by accident. He was a great campaigner, and you can't be that without a whole range of skills.

Our policy launch in Brisbane was a deliberately lacklustre affair, shamelessly poll-driven. Australians were not about to believe a great wad of promises, so it was decided to keep them to a minimum. In the weeks just before the election was announced, Paul Keating had produced yet another economic statement that included some tax promises, so the big-ticket items were already dealt with. Hawke promised a swag of high-tech, clever scientific research centres around the country; our research had shown good reaction to the 'clever country' concept, so the speech went for it. Similarly, much to Peter Walsh's chagrin, there was another large commitment to child care. The number of places in child care was increased by hundreds of thousands. Women rarely vote Labor as often as men, so promises of this kind are often designed to try and raise our support levels among women and to keep them higher.

The Liberals' campaign launch, which had preceded Labor's, was a demonstration of poll-driven fear. Peacock wasn't polling well and in their documentary-style televised opening, John Hewson featured just as much as his leader. The only time Labor had found the need to do this was in 1980 when Bill Hayden wasn't polling well and Bowen, Wran and Hawke had been given some prominence. Peacock promised to fix all of Australia's ills by the following Friday, and by so doing he reinforced the negatives he had been carrying all his political life. The view of him as a lightweight pollie with no depth, who would say almost anything to get a vote, wasn't going to be shed by that kind of performance.

Along with the rest of the Cabinet, I attended the Brisbane policy launch, but that was about the only time I saw Hawke during the whole campaign. I embarked upon the campaign trail with all the fervour of a zealot. I didn't have a day off and spent five weeks campaigning in every state as hard as I could. The government allocated me my own Falcon VIP jet, which meant the travel was a bit easier, but it only made matters worse because I travelled more and worked harder. On one day I started in Hobart, moved on to Melbourne and finished up in Perth. There wouldn't have been a single talkback radio program or a current affairs television show that I didn't appear on: I worked for eighteen and sometimes twenty hours a day, seven days a week. On one visit to Perth I woke up in the morning to do my first interview of the day and couldn't remember what city or hotel I was in. I visited virtually every marginal seat from one end of the country to the other and flogged the environment message during every waking moment.

Since the Ravenshoe incident I had been the subject of a few threats, so I was allocated a federal police guard for the duration of the campaign. Whenever I travelled, my police guard was with me. There were no incidents of violence, but the policeman was a terrific bloke whose wife worked for Andrew Peacock. Small world, isn't it! I doubt there was an environment group in a marginal seat whom I didn't see. Sporting groups didn't miss out either, given that I had come up with the scheme that finally brought Ros Kelly undone, albeit a smaller version thereof.

I debated a Liberal Senate candidate in Perth and campaigned heavily in both Stirling and Cowan, our two most marginal seats. Ron Edwards, who finally lost his seat at the 1993 election after four heroic victories, was working frantically in 1990. Like the rest of us, he must have been driven to the depths of despair by the 12 March decision of the Democrats in Western Australia to direct preferences against sitting members. Given that the marginal seats in the West were all held by us, this would have been a devastating blow for Labor, one that could have cost us the election. We put enough pressure on the Democrats nationally and on former Democrats leader Janine Haines (then more concerned with winning the South Australian seat of Kingston for which she had nominated after resigning from the Senate) to have this decision changed to fall in with most of Australia, where a split ticket between the major parties was offered.

While many people explained this away as a typically silly thing to do which could easily be forgiven, I have always suspected that it was much more sinister than that. The national Democrat organisation had quite a deal of trouble with some people in their Western Australian division. The Democrats in Western Australia at that time would probably have had between fifty and a hundred active members. With a stacking operation about the size of three men and a dog they could have been taken over, and probably had been. Not even the most stupid Democrat—and that's pretty stupid—wouldn't have known that this preference decision was a huge plus for Peacock, which Stephen Smith as ALP state secretary had immediately branded it.

In the radio business they tell you to be wary of program directors who conduct a survey of one, usually themselves. In politics this too can be a problem, but you have to be some sort of judge of public opinion. Election campaigns are even worse than preselections for trying to judge how someone will vote because most people want to be nice to you. Mostly when you are going well they cross the street to say hello; when you are not going so well, they tend to ignore you. If you ignore all gatherings of the faithful, big and small, and note only how the public are reacting, you are halfway home. In the West they were crossing the streets to say hello, and I rang Hawke to tell him that I thought we had a real chance of holding all our seats against both the odds and the polls. This came as a huge relief to several people, including Kim Beazley who, as usual, was panicking about holding his seat. This always meant he worked even harder to hold it.

In Victoria, there was no chance of any pedestrians being killed in their rush across the streets to greet us. At meetings to discuss the environment I was drawing reasonable crowds, but the general public wore that stony look of insolence they get when they are about to hand out punishment. I was continually asked to go back to Melbourne when I campaigned in the marginals of McEwen, Dunkley, Corinella and La Trobe. I had a feeling we weren't going too well, but when we lost all the seats I had campaigned in I had that 1974 Northern Territory feeling all over again.

But New South Wales and Queensland were bright spots for us, and every visit to either state built up my hopes. At the beginning of the campaign I told Bob Hawke and Bob Hogg that the seat of Page in northern New South Wales, based on the city of Grafton, would be a real chance for a surprise win. There is always one big surprise in a campaign and I picked out Page because there had been a terrific local issue (a proposed pulp mill that the National Party had supported but were now running from) which I helped to exploit. Our candidate was Harry Woods, a popular local publican, and his opponent was a tired old National Party member who had long since lost the capacity to blow out a candle. There was a strong green candidate, whose preferences would flow overwhelmingly to Labor. Harry Woods won, of course, so I picked it.

It's good to get one right, particularly when you get the one next door so completely wrong. The electorate of Richmond on the border between New South Wales and Queensland has been the subject of my appalling judgment at the last two federal elections. In 1990 I announced on the Channel Nine election coverage that we couldn't win the seat, and here we set records that may never be broken. The primary vote for Labor declined by almost 9 per cent in a seat where we needed a big swing in the first place, and we *still* won. Victory was achieved because Dr Helen Caldicott, the independent of anti-nuclear fame, achieved more than 23 per cent of the primary vote and delivered almost 80 per cent of her preferences to Labor. Not content with one failure, during Channel Nine's 1993 election coverage I fearlessly predicted that Neville Newell, Labor's 1990 winner, could not possibly do it again. That he did so by a fairly comfortable margin is now a matter of history.

This was the last election where we got a reasonable result in South Australia. John Bannon had just survived a state election with the help of a couple of independent Labor members and the signs of decline were there for all to see. Bob Catley won back the seat of Adelaide, lost in the by-election following Chris Hurford's departure for New York. Hawker was lost, a disappointment as its member, Liz Harvey, was very talented. Elections are cruel tests: often the best are casualties and the ordinary survive. Fortunately, in the seat of Kingston which I also visited during the campaign, Gordon Bilney comfortably held off Janine Haines, whose loss to the Democrats in the Senate would be felt for the three years it took to give the job to Cheryl Kernot. Eventually when the Savings Bank of South Australia announced its multi-billion-dollar loss, much worse per head of population than that suffered by Victoria, yet another state Labor government was swept away and a federal electoral penalty paid.

My three years in the Environment portfolio had been the most hectic years of a hectic life. I was buggered. I had come to realise that I needed a job that got me home occasionally and that did not involve a flight to somewhere every day. Environment had done a great deal for my public life, but had not been real flash for my private life.

While in Adelaide, I made an irrevocable decision to vacate the Environment portfolio after the election. I attended a meeting with conservation groups and came across one of those wide-eyed single-issue fanatics who has no idea what is going on. She asked me a question about a World Heritage nomination for some area in the backblocks of South Australia and was highly critical of the fact that I had failed to visit her cherished spot, declaring that this brought into question my commitment to the environment. Normally I would have shrugged this criticism off with humour, oozed a bit of charm over the audience and moved on—but not this time. I gave this woman a piece of my mind, pointing out how little time I had been able to take off during the previous three years and why I could make no apology for failing to visit whatever lake or forest was the subject of her intense interest.

During that campaign, everywhere that Hawke went the pilots were sure to go. After considerable government resources had been used to break the pilots' strike in 1989, the pilots saw him as the villain. They heckled him at the Brisbane campaign launch and harassed all of us. Whoever went on talkback radio could be absolutely certain that at least one pilot would ring. When I walked out of the 6PR studio in Perth following an interview with Howard Sattler, I bumped into the leader of the pilots' union, Captain Brian McCarthy. This guy had convinced the pilots to go out on a limb and continue to cheer while the limb was lopped off. He still didn't understand that against the resources of the ACTU, the Arbitration Commission and the domestic airlines, the pilots could not possibly win. It is dangerous for those in positions of leadership to be so ignorant of strikes, their consequences and the finer points of when to attack and when to pull back. He couldn't be blamed because there was democracy in the pilots' union and, if anything, the rank and file seemed to be urging him on. When the inevitable debacle occurred and all the pilots lost their jobs, quite a few of them approached me, asking me to help them get their jobs back. I am still occasionally approached and I try to explain to these people that the airlines made it crystal clear to each one of them the consequences of continuing the strike, so there was no possibility of re-employment.

Early in the campaign I appeared on the Steve Vizard show, which was new and very popular at the time, predicting a Labor victory by eight to twelve seats. This turned out to be an accurate early prediction, though Bob Hogg phoned to tell me not to make confident predictions of victory. He and Wayne Swan held the view that when Labor is doing well, a reverse bandwagon effect takes place which weakens the Labor vote. I do not subscribe to this theory and, while I was delighted to find something that Swan and Hogg could agree on, I take the view that Labor supporters must be given nourishment in the form of genuine hope for victory and I don't accept that people flock to losing causes.

By election day on 24 March I was confident enough to have quite a few thousand dollars resting on the result. That night I did the Channel Nine election coverage with the Liberals' Fred Chaney. His team had a few telephones underneath the studio, as did mine, and once again the shortcomings of the modern Liberal Party were in evidence. After a few hours it was obvious that the Labor scrutineers with whom my staff were in contact had a far more accurate picture of what was happening than their Liberal counterparts. Chaney's team stopped bothering even to check on the National Party; they had even fewer clues than their Liberal colleagues.

Election night 1990 produced my predicted result of a fairly narrow Labor victory: 78 seats to us, 69 to the Coalition and 1 Independent in the House of Representatives. In the Senate (it had been a half-Senate election), Labor ended up with 32 seats, the Liberals won 29, the National Party 5, the Democrats 8, and there were 2 Independents. In Victoria and Western Australia, there were substantial swings against us: nearly 5 per cent in Victoria and almost 4 per cent in Western Australia (where we still managed to retain all our seats), with swings of less than 1 per cent in Tasmania and South Australia. Our notional majority was reduced from 18 to 8.

Our victory cannot be put down to any particular decision, policy or issue: a whole range of factors contributed to the win.

Hawke was a very big plus; he campaigned hard and well, and the comparison with Peacock worked effectively for Labor. Our advertising was consistently better than theirs. The first Liberal advertisements contained their slogan: 'The Answer is Liberal'. Keating's immediate response was: 'If the Answer's Liberal, it must have been a helluva question.' I quipped that 'the poor bastard [Peacock] doesn't know what the question was'. We couldn't believe our luck that they had a slogan so totally wrong for its time. Their answer was something nobody believed, and in five weeks there was no hope of voters changing perceptions to that extent.

The debate and policy launches also went well for Labor. The arrival of Carmen Lawrence and her electoral honeymoon came just in time for Labor to hang onto all of its seats in Western Australia, where even three months earlier a loss of three or four seats had looked certain. On the negative side, the debacle over Liberal health policy and the Austin Lewis sacking did a great deal to undermine Peacock's credibility as a leader. The Liberal campaign was lacklustre centrally and at ground level; the National Party got its worst result for many years and lost its leader, Charles Blunt, into the bargain.

All that having been said, there were two other very significant factors. The first is that by 1990 Labor had marginal seat campaigning down to a fine art. Down in the trenches there is much more to the war than just putting up a few signs in your supporters' front yards, sticking two pamphlets in the letterboxes and handing out how to votes on election day. For example, if your computer work is good enough, direct mail to different interest groups is a cheap but effective method of campaigning. Our candidates could mail particular interest groups (teachers, nurses, doctors and so on) letters of special interest to them. Doorknocking was co-ordinated over very long periods, and Labor does this much better than its opposition. Fund raising locally has also become much better; by 1990, many of our candidates spent as much as their opponents or even outspent them. Identifying the key opinion leaders in local interest groups had been going on for so long on the Labor side that more and more local groups identified with us on the hustings. The likes of Gary Punch, Ron Edwards, David Simmons and David Beddall have won their seats time and time again by being far superior to their opponents. Labor's rank and file outfights the blue rinse set (to which much of the Liberal Party's rank and file has been reduced) every time. To suffer a 4 per cent swing against the party in Western Australia and yet retain marginal seats where the Liberals needed less than 2 per cent to win, is irrefutable proof of this assertion.

It has to be stressed, however, that to win an election with 39.4 per cent of the primary vote is extraordinary. This occurred because we received an unbelievable preference drift, and there is no doubt that the environment was the issue that delivered us the preference share. Some people in the party, especially in the Cabinet, could not accept that view because they had opposed the green direction at every turn. Their arguments are shallow, unworthy and mostly sour grapes. The ten seats we won, after being behind on primary votes, were all won because of the overwhelming percentage of green candidate preferences and the two-to-one majority of Democrat preferences, the highest we have ever achieved. It is no accident that our percentage of preferences has never been higher. Our green preference strategy, building on all the other factors I have mentioned, dragged us over the line. The Democrat vote had nearly doubled between 1987 and 1990, so by getting a greatly increased percentage of a greatly increased vote we were able to come from way behind and still get there.

Our marginal candidates were in no doubt whatever about the significance of the environment preference strategy. We ran advertisements pleading for Labor preferences over the last week of the campaign, after Bob Hogg had convinced some reluctant state administrations of their value. These were the culmination of three years' hard yakka convincing the conservation movement of our bona fides, shepherding through Cabinet a series of hotly contested and controversial pro-environment decisions and promoting the issue at every opportunity. This was not the only factor—there never is only one—but it was a very big one in a great Labor victory.

As their defeat became more obvious, the Liberals in the national tally room on election night were finding it difficult to accept gracefully. The normally friendly Fred Chaney referred to me as 'the most dangerous man in Australia'. My crime was not just to have harnessed an issue that had helped to drive the last nails into their electoral coffin, but because I had supposedly risked Australia's economic future by stopping logging or mining in a few key areas. I was surprised by those words, but took them as an accolade. The Liberals knew that the environment issue had been a major factor in their defeat. If a few people in my own party couldn't accept it, our opponents knew exactly what had happened to them.

CHAPTER 17

Whatever It Takes

The 1990 election victory was a good one, but I was too exhausted to get really elated. After a few days' rest I was back in Canberra, ready, I thought, to help Hawke choose the kind of ministry he wanted and to see what he had in mind for me.

Peter Smark had written in the *Sydney Morning Herald* that this was no longer a Hawke–Keating government, but a Hawke–Keating–Richardson government because of my contribution to the victory. I suspect that articles of this kind never did me any good, but whether for that reason or not, Hawke's reception of me was very different from any I had received from him over the previous twenty years. My great friend whom I had served so loyally for so long, who had repeatedly acknowledged all I had done for him, was cool towards me for the first time, treating me like just another minister waiting in a very long queue. This took a while to sink in because, not unnaturally, I had thought I would be king of the kids for at least a week or two.

There are always problems for a Prime Minister when a new ministry is elected. Very often the Caucus does not wish to select all those whom the Prime Minister believes to be worthy. March

1990 was no exception. The first problem for Hawke was his old friend Ralph Willis, with whom he had worked at the ACTU in the 1960s. Ralph was widely considered a less than brilliant performer in Transport and Communications; there was no organised movement against him, but I could find very few who were prepared to support him.

Robert Ray agreed with my assessment, and we jointly put to Hawke that Willis would be a casualty, though neither of us argued that this should be the case. We did not support the dumping of Ralph Willis, but we did report on how the numbers in Caucus were going. The Prime Minister could not accept such an ignominious end to Ralph's ministerial career, and asked for us to ensure the Right's agreement that he could stay on for another twelve months. In the meantime, Hawke said he would talk to Ralph and make sure that he accepted an appointment such as High Commissioner to London at the appropriate time.

Hawke's requests did not end there. He wanted Bob Collins and Simon Crean included in the Right's list of nominees for the ministry. There were no places for either and finding room would present enormous difficulties. Still, my leader's wish was my command, so I took aside Alan Griffiths and Ross Free, who were close friends, telling them that Hawke was entitled to have Bob Collins if he wanted him, and that one of them would have to step aside on the understanding that the next vacancy would be his. Both knew that they would beat Bob Collins in a ballot of the Right faction—Collins had been there only since 1987 while Free and Griffiths had been there since 1980 and 1983 respectively—so stepping aside was a real measure of selfless commitment to a cause. I had rung Collins at the beginning of that crazy day to tell him he was 'fucked'. I rang him at the end of the day to tell him he was 'unfucked' because of Hawke's support and the generosity of Ross Free, who had decided to make the sacrifice. The next vacancy was definitely his.

That still left Simon Crean without a spot. Simon had only just been elected to parliament, and nobody in the Right was about to make way for him. Hawke graphically demonstrated the power that a Prime Minister has after four election wins in a row when he delivered something impossible—he convinced the Left to give up one of their spots. This was staggering for a faction that had repeatedly and bitterly complained of being under-represented in the ministry. Hawke spent a few hours with them, promised them the next vacancy (the difficulties with Ross Free could be sorted out later) and stitched up a deal to put Simon Crean straight into the ministry.

This manoeuvring caused some concerns within our faction. Queensland and New South Wales were aggrieved that they had not been given extra representation, considering that Victoria was grossly over-represented. This was true in numerical terms, though with the likes of Evans, Ray, Griffiths, Crean and Willis, as well as Hawke, the Victorian Right could argue greater talent. At the faction meeting called to discuss our nominees for the ministry, I had to do a fair bit of talking before sanity prevailed.

Oddly enough, the greatest resentment was about Ralph Willis. Many felt he had been in the ministry long enough, and I agreed with them. We were all wrong, of course. Sometimes a particular portfolio is more suited to a person's talents than another, and from the moment he was appointed Finance Minister Willis never looked back. Nobody reads Cabinet briefs more thoroughly, nobody asks better questions. Since his promotion to Treasurer in more recent times, Ralph has become such an integral part of the government's core that most people in the Caucus will be pleading with him to stay if and when he decides to move on.

There was also consternation in the Centre Left as there was no room for Peter Morris and Barry Jones. The faction had been reduced in ministerial numbers, but was still over-represented as a percentage of the Caucus. Peter Morris has apparently blamed me for his demise, but I had precious little to do with it. The Centre Left were (and still are) over-represented, but even so Peter and Barry had to take their chances with other members of their faction in a ballot. And however aggrieved they might have felt, very few Labor parliamentarians have ever served seven years as a minister.

As always, the Left had their problems too. Peter Duncan, always a controversial figure in his own faction, was defeated after serving only three years in the ministry, a defeat that caused deep and persistent schisms in the Left. Still, Peter Duncan has always played it hard, and those who do this sometimes get hurt. The Left in the federal Caucus still have an in group and an out group and one day, unless the politics of inclusion are practised, the out group will grow tired of being good only for providing the in group with the numbers to gain office.

Once the Caucus met and endorsed the factional tickets, Hawke had only to allocate portfolios. Like all the other ministers, though probably a little earlier than most, I trooped into the Oval Office to stake my claim. I told Hawke that after the contribution I had made during the election campaign I was entitled to a promotion, and the job I wanted was Transport and Communications. This claim was summarily dismissed: the job had been promised to Kim Beazley. The only job left, I was told, was Social Security, and it was to be mine. I was told that this would be the making of me, and because it came with an appointment to the Expenditure Review Committee of Cabinet, I would learn all the workings of government, enabling me to get another portfolio at some indeterminate time down the track.

It wasn't the refusal that upset me, it was the manner of it. I was being put in my place, and I couldn't—and still don't—understand why. Paul Keating was called in during the discussion as an ally of Hawke to convince me to accept the honour that was being bestowed on me; the rapprochement between Hawke and Keating was obviously going pretty well. I didn't indulge in a screaming row with Hawke, but I said enough to let him know I was a very, very unhappy little Vegemite.

Somewhat stunned, I returned to Sydney. I was unprepared for the far greater indignities that were to follow. That night as I watched television with my family and tried to forget the day's events, the telephone rang, and the Prime Minister was on the line. He did not report a change of heart, however, but rather a job offer that shocked me more than almost anything that has ever happened to me.

During our earlier discussions about Ralph Willis's future, Hawke had indicated that Ralph might well reject the offer of being High Commissioner to London. I had responded in jocular fashion, saying that if Ralph didn't want the job, any other minister who was offered it would accept in a flash, including myself. Now here was the Prime Minister actually offering me the London job.

Perhaps Hawke was just doing the right thing in offering a

really good job to a really good friend, but that was certainly not how I saw it at the time. I was appalled, hurt, furious. Without taking any time to think about it, I just said: 'No.'

That night I made two phone calls that stay in my memory to this day. First, I rang Peter Barron to tell him of the day's events. I said to him: 'I'll get this bastard, I'll do whatever it takes, but I'll get him.'

In my next call, to Paul Keating, I used very similar language. In reference to the London offer, Paul told me that though he and I had shared plenty of tense moments, he would never have tried to remove me from the equation. He still tried to sell me the Social Security portfolio as a prize, but he must have felt elated. That was a very good day for Paul Keating and a very bad one for Bob Hawke.

On the day the portfolios were to be announced, I had arranged to have breakfast with Ros Kelly, Hawke's certain nominee for the Environment portfolio, and Phillip Toyne. They had not met and I wanted their relationship to start off on the right foot. While we were chatting over the meal, a breathless waitress hurried over to tell me that the Prime Minister was on the phone. There, in the Pavilion Hotel, Hawke told me he had had second thoughts in the shower that morning and was now considering making me Minister for Defence, which had never been suggested before. I was asked to come in urgently for another meeting.

I abandoned Toyne and Kelly and headed for Hawke's office. He told me he was concerned about the legendary temper of Robert Ray, who had been told the previous day that Defence was his. Defence ministers engage in highly sensitive negotiations with foreign governments, and Hawke said he was worried about how Ray would perform under these circumstances. If I was prepared to accept the offer, the Ministry of Defence was mine. I had never shown the slightest interest in the portfolio, so had never given this job a moment's thought. We talked it through and I accepted his offer.

After the morning's events, I wandered back to my office in something of a daze. Word travels fast in Parliament House and as I walked past Hawke's media chief Colin Parks, he saluted and addressed me as 'Admiral'.

While I was busily breaking the news of my new job to my

staff, Hawke called Robert Ray to his office to tell him he was going to get Social Security in a swap with me. There was no contest. Ray refused even to consider the offer. He told Hawke that meeting the masses, being on public display and displaying warmth and compassion in public were much more up my alley than his.

Even though Hawke had absolute power in handing out portfolios, he caved in. Without knowing anything about the results of this discussion, I was once more summoned to appear before him. The Prime Minister told me of Robert's reaction, apologised for the way he had handled the events of the morning and informed me that I was back in Social Security. The job that someone else wouldn't take was handed back to me because I would take anything.

Nothing in politics, or indeed in any facet of my life, has ever made me as angry as I was that morning. All the years of serving Hawke, of doing so much of the dirty work, taking so much flak for bringing down anyone who stood in his way, then delivering the extra votes that gave him his fourth election, had come to nothing. Nobody else had been treated so badly. All I could think of was revenge.

Perhaps a bigger, better person than I would have been more understanding and accepted Hawke's explanation and apology, but I have never pretended to be Mother Teresa. Having lived by the principle that nobody ever took a free kick at me without massive retaliation, I was now completely won over to Keating's side. In fact, Paul Keating now had a convert to his prime ministerial cause who would make St Paul look like a piker. Keating, aghast at this development, naturally did nothing to discourage my anger.

It was inevitable, anyway, that I would eventually join forces with Paul Keating. The tribal loyalty of two mates from New South Wales would one day overcome both our differences and Hawke's friendship with me. But had this personal relations disaster not occurred, the process might well have taken longer. No matter how unpopular Keating became over the next couple of years as the promised 'soft landing' turned hard and the recession officially arrived with all its misery and human cost, Keating now had an ally who could bring some numbers to his side.

On that morning, the close friendship I had enjoyed with Hawke was terminated, never to be reborn. I didn't call around for a chat, and he didn't call either. I mourned the loss of a friendship as much as I hated what had been done to me. Perhaps giving me Social Security was a big help to me, and being on the Expenditure Review Committee would certainly round off my knowledge of other portfolios, making me worthy of a better job, but from that moment the Hawke prime ministership was doomed.

Over the next couple of months, word leaked to the press that Hawke and I had fallen out, that the London job had been offered to me and that I had been in and out of Defence within the space of a few hours. Telling the truth about it all was impossible, so we all went into denial mode. I loudly proclaimed my love for the Social Security portfolio, Hawke's office denied the London offer and naturally I concurred with Hawke's denial. In politics you never tell the truth about division in the upper echelons of your own party unless you are declaring public war on your leader. I had told Hawke that I could not forgive him for what he had done, and he knew exactly what that meant. But there was no public declaration of war, not even a private one. Before declaring war, preparations have to be made. Time to build and time to plot are needed—and the clock was now ticking.

Whether I liked it or not I was Minister for Social Security, and I immersed myself in the mechanics of efficiently spending thirty-odd billion dollars a year. This was a totally different experience from Environment and Sport, and having to bear responsibility for it certainly did broaden my ministerial experience. I don't accept that this was the only portfolio in which my experience could have been broadened, but it did involve a big commitment in reading the thousands of pages of briefs that went with the job and even more commitment in attending meetings of the Expenditure Review Committee.

Most of the necessary social reforms had been carried out during Brian Howe's period in the portfolio. He had ushered in the new family payment arrangements that remain one of the Hawke government's greatest achievements, and there was plenty to administer. When Budget time came around, I proposed several measures encouraging pensioners to maximise their income.

Many pensioners were keeping large sums of money in savings accounts, earning 1 or 2 per cent interest at a time when rates of 12 per cent were easy to find. My idea was that any interest on pensions for amounts over $2000 would be assessed at 10 per cent, or the actual rate of return if higher, thus preventing the banks from ripping off those in the Australian community who could ill afford it. Australia's banks had mercilessly preyed upon too many older people who lacked access to good advice, and the Department of Social Security was told of many cases of elderly pensioners having up to $200 000 in passbook accounts earning practically no interest on the advice of their friendly bank manager. By deeming pensioners a rate of more than 8 per cent, the banks would be forced to offer special arrangements to the very people who had been exploited for so long. Pensioners would now be offered better interest rates than anyone in the community.

All pensions are subject to income and assets tests, and by minimising their income many pensioners thought they would be better off because the government would be unable to reduce their pensions. Any effort at all with calculator, abacus or toes and fingers demonstrated that even after tax, greatly increased interest income would more than compensate for any decrease in the amount of the pension. We also agreed to allow pensioners to give away up to $10 000 a year without it affecting their pension.

The problem, of course, was that nobody wanted to believe a politician who was saying: 'Trust me, you'll be better off.' There is also the fact that when anything is changed for pensioners, some will be confused and many will be frightened. Many older people are quite isolated from information and change can be really worrying. For those who found getting around difficult and who had no younger family members to transport them around town, the prospect of being forced to go through the drama of opening and closing bank accounts was terrifying.

Just in case there was a pensioner somewhere whom we had failed to terrify, in the same Budget the government proposed to introduce a co-payment for pensioners and cardholders (the unemployed, sole parents, and so on) for the purchase of pharmaceuticals. Even though the co-payment was $2.50 and the pension was increased by $2.50 a week to compensate, allowing for fifty-two prescriptions per year, way above pensioners' average use, with all this change around fear and loathing were everywhere.

I supported both decisions because I thought they were right. No pensioners would be disadvantaged by those decisions and justice would be done. But I knew that in proposing the deeming provisions there would be a huge negative reaction, and I told the Cabinet that it would take at least twelve months to sell this issue to Australia's pensioners. Prior to the Budget announcements I made sure, as I did with all the ministries I occupied, that I spent plenty of time with all the lobby groups trying to get in the door. I spoke to the various pensioner groups, some of whom were fairly strong Labor Party supporters, the Australian Council of Social Services, sole parent organisations, charities like the Brotherhood of St Laurence, the St Vincent de Paul Society and virtually any other group who was interested. No matter how well I succeeded in getting along with them and making sure the dialogue was meaningful, when the decision was announced it was universally condemned.

So was I. On the Friday after the Budget, I attended a protest rally at the Lower Town Hall in Sydney organised by the combined pensioner organisations. Estimates of attendance varied between two and three thousand, and not one of them was there to support me. I still remember this as the most difficult time I have ever spent in the Town Hall, tougher than some of the rowdy Labor conferences I have attended there, where my enemies tried to drown out whatever I said. At least at party conferences I knew my opponents, many of whom I didn't much like anyway. Here I had to face lots of older Australians, overwhelmingly decent people whom I had frightened and annoyed enough for them to get together to tell me what they thought.

I couldn't respond by getting stuck into them, as I did to my opposition at party conferences. I had to wear the solemn arguments against me, the inevitably overdone rhetoric of local, state and national organisations trying to outdo each other in condemning the government. But most difficult of all, I had to listen to a bunch of my fellow countrymen telling me what a bastard I really was. I knew the decisions were right but it was a pretty tall order, when the numbers were several thousand to one, to tell the several thousand they were wrong and I was right. However, that is exactly what I did.

No matter how right you think you are, if someone presents an unanswerable argument and you are halfway fair dinkum, you must acknowledge your error and promise to try and sort out the problem. An old lady suffering from emphysema pointed out that she would go through her fifty-two annual prescriptions in a few months, that she had practically no money in the bank and at great personal risk she would be forced to forgo some of her medication if we went ahead with the decision as announced. I told the crowd at the Town Hall that I would seek to amend the decision to help the chronically ill who had little money. This calmed them only a little: at that stage, they considered deeming to be the greater evil.

Whatever I was in government for, it wasn't to be responsible for the murder of little old ladies. It had simply not occurred to me that chronically ill elderly pensioners might use fifty or so scripts in just a few months. Hawke's view was that I should immediately try and find a way out, and I agreed. He indicated that he would be prepared to support a change to the original Cabinet Budget decision if this meant that people in the same category as the woman with emphysema would have to worry no more. I knew Hawke would react like this because, irrespective of any argument I might have been having with him, he was one of the most compassionate men I had ever met.

For reasons I could not understand, some of the staff in Brian Howe's office opposed making any change to the pharmaceutical co-payment arrangements, arguing that this would show some kind of weakness in the face of pressure. Fortunately Brian Howe himself, with whom I had breakfast prior to lodging a Cabinet submission that would ease the burden of the chronically ill, could see the need for change and supported that position in the Cabinet. Pensioners with high pharmaceutical usage and with few financial resources were given the added protection of a safety net that guaranteed free pharmaceuticals once the fifty-two prescriptions were filled. If this number of prescriptions was to be filled very quickly, then those affected could apply for and receive a three-monthly advance of their pharmaceutical allowance in a lump sum. While I could rest safely in my bed knowing that

I had saved the poorest, sickest pensioners from hardship, very few of them ever took advantage of the change. Despite the publicity that the criticism of me had been given, and the efforts of my department to publicise this concession, the number of takers was minuscule.

As for deeming, I attended meetings with pensioners in every state over the next few months and got tired of hearing myself on talkback radio. My claim that nobody could be disadvantaged by this new regulation was demonstrated by Christmas 1990. None of my critics could actually find anyone who lost because of it, and the criticism faded much more quickly than I had thought possible. Within six months it had disappeared completely. One of life's little ironies occurred in 1991. The banks begged the government to abolish deeming, and the Combined Pensioners Association was begging the government to retain it. Sometimes doing what is right is not popular, but if the truth of your position can be demonstrated quickly, you might as well have a go.

The other decision that caused me some grief was a Cabinet resolution to reduce or abolish the pensions received by women living overseas. Australian law allowed some people who had visited Australia for very short periods, sometimes only a matter of days, to be paid Australian pensions. While the decision applied to all countries with whom Australia did not have social security agreements, the real effect was felt by a couple of thousand women in Greece and Turkey. Some of the women who would have their pensions reduced or abolished would suffer considerable hardship. While the pension might not be worth a great deal here, in Turkey it represented more than average weekly earnings, and in Greece it didn't represent poverty either.

The mass meetings of Greeks and Turks that I attended in Sydney and Melbourne were more like community events than serious political meetings. The community leaders all had to outdo each other, so the meetings went on for hours. I did not discourage these big protest rallies; our hope was to pressure the Greek and Turkish governments into paying their pensions to Australian residents who were entitled to receive them. The politics of taking pensions away from these women was terrific because many had little or no connection with Australia and there was considerable community resentment about them receiving the benefit of Australian largesse. On the other hand, publicity about the harshness of the decision helped me to get the Cabinet to compromise: Greeks and Turks vote Labor in droves. Once more I had to turn up, be abused, allow all that pent-up spleen to be vented against me and give some ground and proceed to what was clearly a good decision in such a way that none of our supporters really believed they had been abandoned.

As Minister for Social Security, I made several trips overseas in pursuit of social security agreements. Ministers are always open to criticism for taking overseas trips but, as usual, I was more heavily criticised than anybody else, even though other ministers had spent much more on their trips than I did on mine. As Minister for Social Security, my trips resulted in the signing of agreements with countries such as Germany and the Netherlands, raising tens of millions of dollars for Australia at a cost of a few hundred thousand, a pretty good bargain by any standards.

In Greece I found out why I could never quite understand the politics played out in the Greek community here. I met with Dr Gianoukou, the new Minister for Social Security, one of the very few ministers in the Greek government who did not belong to the parliament. She had a long career as a medical specialist and had been chosen on merit alone. I knew our meeting was going well when she asked the officials from both sides to leave the room, allowing us to have a private conversation. Senior public servants don't approve of ministers speaking privately without them; this can be positively dangerous.

The Greek Minister had very little political experience, and was finding real difficulty in following the official line. She knew it was unreasonable for Australia to keep paying pensions into Greece when the reverse happened only in a handful of cases, and readily agreed that Greece should sign an agreement with Australia. We called the officials back into the room to announce the decision, which shocked the Greek social security officials; open-mouthed and silent, they filed from the room. I wanted to extract a similar promise from Turkey, but their minister, a wily and experienced politician named Mrs Aykut, merely promised to consider the matter.

When I returned to Australia, I announced the results of my conversation with the Greek minister as a real breakthrough, telling the Greek press that a new agreement might be signed within a few months. I was in no position to know that the Greek minister took her proposal to the Cabinet and was rolled. When such things happen in Australia, the minister concerned admits failure, the fuss lasts five minutes, and life goes on. Not so in Greece: the government and the minister both publicly stated that no undertaking had ever been given to me. I didn't believe it possible that democratic governments could lie to other governments like this. Foreign Affairs had never been my abiding interest and perhaps it was the only area of policy about which I could claim naivety. No admission of the truth ever came. Beware of Greek ministers bearing gifts.

Part 4

THE HAWKE–KEATING CHALLENGE

CHAPTER 1

Hawke

From March to November 1990, I thought very little about a challenge to Hawke's leadership: it's difficult to stay angry when you are busy, and learning a new portfolio takes time and effort. Meeting welfare groups, pensioners and homeless kids in every city of Australia took time, and time does heal all wounds. However, the healing process does leave a scar. While revenge was a commodity I had no time to invest in, extra effort might be called for if a chance came. For Paul Keating, that chance could come only if there was a widespread belief that Hawke could not win an election in 1993 and if Keating were not seen as an even worse prospect.

The year 1990 had started so well. An historic fourth consecutive election win had boosted everybody's spirits to the point of euphoria. But this disappeared as the unemployment numbers began their big surge, the recession had to be officially conceded and the government's standing slid alarmingly.

For Paul Keating 1990 was not a good year. The election had been held just ahead of the official confirmation that we were in a recession (that is, two successive quarters of negative growth).

But official confirmation meant very little to the couple of hundred thousand who had joined the dole queues in the previous twelve months. The 'soft landing' promised by Keating had not been delivered, and Australia was laying much of the blame on him personally. Keating's cause had not been helped by some of the phrases he used to describe the Budgets he brought down to promote the soft landing and prevent the recession. People remembered 'bringing home the bacon', but it didn't smell like bacon by the time they had brought it home. His failure to lodge a tax return had the terrible stamp of hypocrisy on it: lecturing people about tax avoidance and tax evasion while failing to lodge a tax return was not calculated to endear him to anyone. There was no hypocrisy, just a busy man forgetting to do what every citizen has to do, but how things look is often more important than how they are.

Keating's penchant for the headline phrase had landed him in trouble before, but mostly his choice of language had a purpose behind it that justified the result. While I didn't like his 'banana republic' warning at the time, it was exactly what Australians needed to make them understand the necessity for the government to severely cut its outlays. But 1990 was the year in which the headline phrase drew all the wrong headlines, which could only enhance the Keating reputation for arrogance.

The words 'this was the recession we had to have' did Keating serious damage. No Australian, me included, would accept that a recession was necessary. So much damage could have been avoided if he had explained that slowing down the economy was necessary to prevent our debt becoming unmanageable or inflation getting out of hand. He should have said he was sorry that the sought-after slowdown had meant hardship for many people, that he felt deep personal regret that the slowdown had become a recession. If he had asked for some understanding and forgiveness for this result when decisions on interest rates made years before had effects so much later, and added that only the Almighty could be certain of results, his standing could have gone up instead of plummeting. But not for the first time, the Keating failure ever to acknowledge error had led him into strife. By insisting on an interest rate policy that would obviously bring on a recession and claiming all the time that no recession would occur, he left

PRYOR
PRIVATE RICHARDSON
GENERAL HAWKE
GUESS WHO?

In 1991 Keating was set on challenging Hawke for the leadership. The launch of 'Mates' in April 1991, a book about the NSW Labor Right, was an appropriate time to reflect on the past and consider the future.

Interviewing Bob Hawke for radio station 2KY in September 1991. Keeping an image of unity was becoming almost impossible as the party was going through one of its most bitter leadership struggles ever.

In Cabinet with Bob Hawke within days of the final leadership challenge.

After the swearing in of Keating's new ministry in 1992, with Ros Kelly and Bill Hayden, the Governor-General. I had no idea my biggest political setback was just around the corner.

As part of my new role as Minister for Transport and Communication I met with Vice Premier Ghu Rongji who holds the finance and economy portfolio in China.

After the Marshall Islands Affair in 1992 they said I could not come back from the dead.

Being sworn in as Minister for Health by the Governor-General, after Paul Keating and Labor won the 1993 election.

I won my first debate when I was twelve. For the 1993 ABC World Series Debating I wrote my own speech. In the vanquished opposition were Andrew Denton, Bronwyn Bishop MP, *and Paul Lyneham political commentator for the ABC in Canberra.*

My last day in parliament.

Leaving the Sydney Town Hall with Kate and Cheryl in 1994 to a standing ovation after my final appearance at a NSW Labor Party conference.

himself with too few options when the arrival of recession could no longer be denied.

That Australia's most unpopular politician could still be in the leadership race was more a tribute to his single-minded tenacity and to the continuing decline in the government's fortunes, to which he was contributing, than it ever was to his judgments as Treasurer. The polls were showing an alarming downhill slide for Labor generally and for Bob Hawke in particular. This plunge was helped by Keating's recession blunder. It is the supreme irony that Keating's chances of becoming Prime Minister ran in inverse proportion to the party's decrease in popularity.

By the end of 1990 most of the Labor Party, whether in the branches, the Caucus or the Cabinet, believed that the government was in terminal decline. Unfortunately, there was no unanimity about how that decline should be arrested. Hawke wandered all over the nation, telling everybody that he and only he could win the next election. Keating wandered the nation less and less, seeing fewer people, but making sure that those whom he did see were left with a view of a Prime Minister who had run out of puff and a Treasurer who had run out of patience. And towards the end of that year, Keating finally told me about the famous agreement he and Hawke had reached at Kirribilli House.

Unlike many others in politics—some may say too many others—I have never kept a regular diary. However, at the time I made full notes of what Paul Keating said to me about the Kirribilli agreement.

Wednesday 28 November 1990

Met with Paul Keating on leadership. After the 1988 abortive challenge, he had gone to Europe depressed and ready to leave politics. Upon his return Paul had a private meeting with Hawke where they had a discussion about succession. It was suggested by Hawke and agreed by Keating that a meeting should be held with Peter Abeles, a friend of both, at which undertakings could be given in front of a trusted witness. When Paul returned to his office he had some misgivings about this arrangement as Abeles, while a friend of his, was undoubtedly someone whose loyalties would lie with Hawke. Paul telephoned Hawke to suggest that a fourth person also attend this meeting—namely Bill Kelty. Hawke agreed without argument.

The meeting duly took place and Hawke naturally assumed the role (if not the posture) of good guy. He agreed to leave after the next election and in plenty of time to allow Paul to recover popularity and establish an ascendancy over the Liberal leader. Hawke's last words at the meeting were that if word of the meeting leaked to anyone the deal would be off. The meeting took place at Kirribilli House.

I was the first person Paul had ever told about the meeting and he had done so now because he believed Hawke would go back on his word. He had not raised the leadership issue with Hawke for six weeks. Paul agreed to meet with Kelty and Abeles on Monday 3 December as a prelude to a second meeting with Hawke.

Thursday 29 November

Beazley phoned. Wanted to know if anything was happening about the leadership. I told him to remain calm and that he would be among the first to know if anything was on the boil. He told me that Dawkins had told a group of people at a dinner on the previous Friday that 'we are getting rid of Hawke by March'. Whoever 'we' were was never explained.

Paul Kelly called in. He was convinced there would be no challenge as the resultant damage would cripple whoever won. That is probably my view. I told him that even if I were to support Keating, that we would get fifty votes and just fail. This is not necessarily true as I think we could just about get there or be within one or two votes. Dawkins, sadly, has obviously been talking again.

Nick Bolkus had afternoon tea. He and Hand had met with Keating who had told them the Left would be crazy to say anything to Hawke which could be interpreted as a promise of long-lasting support. While Bolkus and Hand had been unwilling to go too far in front of Keating (let alone in front of each other) Bolkus conceded to me that he thought

Hawke would go and that he would talk to colleagues about keeping the Left's options open. The prospect of Howe being deputy PM was an attractive carrot.

Friday 30 November

Geoff Walsh told me that Carmen Lawrence had informed Hawke of the Dawkins performance (same incident as Beazley described). I told him I was sick and tired of hosing journos down while Dawkins poured petrol on the fire. Hawke was going to talk to Dawkins and threaten to sack him and take the matter to Caucus. Judging by Hawke's past performances, I couldn't imagine him having the guts to do it.

Monday 3 December

Geoff Walsh had rung on Saturday to tell me that Hawke had got stuck into Ross Free over comments Free had made about him. He now told me what he wouldn't tell me over the phone—that a Hawke staffer had received information to this effect from John Scott. Fancy believing anything Scott said! I told Ross about it and said not to worry, I'd talk to Hawke and smooth over the problem. It just shows how edgy Hawke has become.

Tuesday 4 December

I had another talk to Keating after Caucus. Kelty, Abeles and Keating had met in Sydney on Monday night. Kelty had been adamant that Hawke had to go, while Abeles as expected was obviously preparing the way for Hawke to rat on the agreement. The three had agreed that Hawke should meet with them by Friday. Paul will tell Hawke at that meeting that if Hawke isn't gone by March, Paul will resign by June. He will also tell Hawke that given the arrangement has not been honoured, he will tell me about it. I have agreed to go and see Hawke and respond appropriately. We live in interesting times!

Walsh reported that Hawke hadn't spoken to Dawkins. Big surprise!

Friday 7 December

Saw Keating at 4.15. He had Tom Mockridge with him. Mockridge asked me why I wouldn't tell Hawke to go. I told him we needed the morally superior position of Hawke breaking his agreement and me being told. Obviously I wasn't the fifth man to know about this agreement, but the sixth.

Saturday 8 December

Simon Balderstone rang early to tell me Paul had made some comments during a speech the previous night which amounted to an attack on Hawke [this was the famous 'Placido Domingo' speech, so called because at one point Keating said: 'I walk on that stage, some performances might be better than others, but they will all be up there trying to stream the economics and the politics together. Out there on the stage doing the Placido Domingo.']. Keating had said Australia had never had a great leader and that leadership was more than just strolling around shopping centres tripping over camera cords.

Sunday 9 December

The papers led with Paul's speech, interpreting this as a challenge to Hawke's leadership. I went to Adelaide for Bob Catley's Christmas barbecue [Catley was the newly elected Member for Adelaide]. The ALP members informed me that Keating was a total disaster, and they were almost unanimous.

I then went to Nick Bolkus's place for the annual good guy Left barbecue. I was treated pretty well which shows that big changes have occurred during the last few years.

Nick remains open on the question of Hawke v Keating. Hawke rang me during the Catley function. He was pretty angry about Keating's speech, citing his attack on Curtin as an example of Paul's incredible ego and his reliance on Jack Lang's views of the major party figures of his time. I told him not to comment until we had both talked to Keating.

Keating could not be reached during the day as he was in outback Queensland.

Monday 10 December

I got off the plane in Canberra having had only four hours' sleep, dressed casually and wearing sunglasses. I had intended to do a doorstop at Parliament House after going to the flat for a shower and a change of clothes. The media turned up at the airport and I looked like an ailing gangster. It was not my finest hour. I said if Keating was the Placido Domingo of Australian politics, as he had claimed, then Hawke was the Pavarotti. My last words were: 'I'm innocent.'

Hawke and Keating arranged to meet at 4.30 or 5pm and I spoke to both of them prior to the meeting. Keating was, as usual, unrepentant. He maintained that he had scribbled out some notes while he was being introduced. He managed to say in the [Placido Domingo] speech that Australia 'had never had a great leader', leadership was more than just strolling around shopping centres, Curtin was 'just a trier' and Chifley was ordinary. By the time I finished with him, I think he understood that his outburst had lost him the high ground in trying to get Hawke to stick to the '88 agreement.

I told him to apologise as soon as he got into the room. When I said to him that all he needed to have done was to say that up to '83 Australia had never had a great leader and we wouldn't have any problem, he replied: 'I won't praise him, Graham. I won't praise the bastard.'

Then I went around to Hawke's office and told him I had spoken to Paul, who was going to apologise for his remarks and undertake to give no repeat performance. I said it would be foolish to provoke a confrontation. I put to him strongly that he would need to promise to run for five more years and do so publicly very soon. His statement on Perth radio that he would retire some time after the next election was hopeless. It meant people would have to vote for Keating anyway, even though he hadn't been given the opportunity to be Leader. Hawke agreed to make the promise. He didn't realise how hopeless that promise was because absolutely no one would believe it.

I went to dinner with Paul Kelly. I told him I had looked in on the meeting on the monitor in Sandy Hollway's office and it looked peaceful. I told him they would patch up the problem for the moment but nobody would believe the problem had been solved for good.

Sure enough a short statement was issued at the end of the meeting declaring that everything was rosy in the garden—and no one believed it.

Finding out about the Kirribilli agreement two years after it happened was galling to say the least, particularly when it became obvious that the Keating staffers Tom Mockridge, Don Russell and Mark Ryan had all known about it since day one. Keating was close to his staff, closer than many ministers would dream of becoming with theirs, and in turn the Keating staff were fiercely loyal, even over-protective. It is remarkable that word never leaked out about such an historic gathering, and it speaks volumes for the discretion of the participants and those told later. At least some of Keating's intemperate behaviour could be excused once the secret of Hawke's promise became known.

Much of my anger had subsided in the eight months since I swore revenge on Hawke, but by telling me of the Kirribilli deal Keating had given the scars a good rub and I was back on track. I doubt that I would have bothered to start plotting in earnest if Labor's fortunes had been riding high, with Hawke in firm control. You need more than a desire for revenge, you need a reason.

Labor's headlong dive in the polls would have been a good enough reason in itself—I'll never know whether the correct word is 'excuse'—but Keating's revelation about the secret meeting produced the degree of righteousness that, while not essential, is nonetheless comforting. It is far better to be a knight in shining armour attempting to restore the party's honour and to defeat the evil enemy than to be another grubby politician obsessed by revenge to the point of trying to remove the most successful leader in the party's history. At this stage of the game, I was a bit of both. (By late 1991, no knight's armour could have been shinier.)

I was absolutely certain that Keating was seriously considering his own retirement if he failed to become Prime Minister very soon. For some years the party had been accustomed to being led by two men who were a great team: the popular Hawke and the devastating Keating who could demolish the Opposition on the floor of the House. While party members didn't know it yet, they were no longer able to enjoy this luxury. Keating's patience had run out; by November 1990 I thought that if he wasn't in the Lodge by June 1991, he would resign from the parliament. This was no idle threat. While I was confident that we could keep him in the parliament a bit longer, I knew he would not bring down the 1991 Budget as Treasurer.

I spoke to Hawke about retiring in the last parliamentary week of 1990, saying that while the Caucus did not want to take part in any exercise to have him removed, a majority would prefer him to go. This was not an over-estimation of the true position: I had spoken to a host of Caucus members without even suggesting to most of them that a challenge would ever be contemplated. I had a long chat to Hawke because I wanted him to understand that I agreed with this position. This wasn't an official warning that a challenge was on, but he knew we were coming, and he knew what that would mean in the end.

Trying to tell Hawke that it was time for him to go was one of my more difficult moments. He delivered his standard speech expressing his 'profound' belief that he was the only one who could lead Labor to victory; the conviction he had developed on this was total, and he was not open to argument. I didn't try to convince him that Keating was the answer, but rather that more and more Caucus members were coming to that conclusion. He wasn't convinced, which was pretty reasonable given that this was a slight exaggeration: for everyone convinced of the need for change, there was another convinced that Keating's bastardry (as they saw it) should not be rewarded.

My Christmas chat with Bob Hawke might have had marginally more than a snowflake's chance in hell of convincing him had Paul Keating not delivered the 'Placido Domingo' speech. Chris Higgins, the secretary to the Treasury and a close friend of Keating's, had died suddenly a few days earlier and Keating was terribly upset. The deadly combination of grief and unrequited ambition brought the press gallery, assembled to drink and share some Christmas cheer, an unexpected seasonal bonus—the biggest story of the year.

Keating's speech was stupid, intemperate and entirely understandable. His claim that Australia had never had a great leader (a crazy statement from a man who wanted to lead a party that still revered Curtin, Chifley and Whitlam), without even mentioning the incumbent, made it very clear that only he could lead Australia into the brave new world. It goes without saying that none of those associated with the push to make Paul Keating Prime Minister had any knowledge that this speech was to be made, and I suspect that when he got up Paul hadn't known how far he would go either.

Anyone who has been given a promise, its solemnity witnessed by agreed men of integrity, and who is sure that promise will not be honoured may surely be forgiven for feeling levels of frustration that will cause him to act unwisely. This is a very boring way of saying that Keating had been ratted on by Hawke and had decided to tell the world what he really thought. Given Keating's temperament and the view he has of himself as a brawler-statesman—a perception unique in Australia's political history—what surprises me in retrospect is that he didn't break out much earlier and tell the world how he felt about his leader. Keating's lack of discipline was and is his biggest problem.

When I went to Adelaide to speak at the fundraising barbecue for Bob Catley, the rank and file's reaction to the speech and the leadership struggle mirrored the dilemma that the Caucus would face. A majority wanted Hawke to stay as Leader, and practically all of them wanted Keating to remain as Treasurer.

While I was there, a furious Hawke rang. Hawke had idolised Curtin since he was a callow youth and to hear his hero dismissed as 'a trier' seemed to enrage him as much as anything else. Keating was not the only one who felt betrayed that day. Hawke never referred to the Kirribilli meeting or its promise, and I didn't raise it. He had no way of knowing that I was in on the secret and, since secrecy was a prerequisite to the deal being kept, it hardly seemed appropriate to ask why Hawke was showing no signs of honouring it. I was sure the promise would not be honoured; at no time during our conversations had I seen evidence of a man about to vacate office for any reason whatever. The 'Placido Domingo' speech was being worked on as an excuse for walking away from the deal.

When I spoke to Keating, I told him how crazy the speech had been. Even in private, he tried to argue, for a little while at least, that he had not meant it to be a direct challenge to Hawke's authority. Eventually he tried this line on Hawke himself, no doubt with similar success. As the leaks from the speech increased over the following days, his denials and pleas of innocence were expressed with less gusto. Keating and Hawke met for yet another patch-up effort which failed to solve any longer-term problem. A few bandaids were placed over the latest cuts, but the leadership was still under a cloud. That any relationship between two people at the centre of parliamentary power in our country could deteriorate, then disintegrate, was tragic. Maybe some of us who were aware of the disintegration should have moved to stop it much earlier, or perhaps it was inevitable. In any case, it was better for it to come to a head well before Australia and the party faced up to another election.

The real question was whether Hawke ever intended to keep the promise when he made it. Making a promise several years before the need to keep it is easy; reprehensible circumstances can always raise their ugly heads in the nick of time, relieving the promiser of that obligation. It is possible that Hawke had so convinced himself of Keating's unsuitability for the position that he figured Keating would be out of the running in two or three years. No one can ever be certain, and I'm not sure it matters anyway. If it was revealed at any time, Hawke would be seen as a liar, which meant Keating had a powerful weapon that could bestow on him a legitimacy he could not otherwise gain. All that was required was the proper use of the information at precisely the right moment, and that required the co-operation of the challenger.

CHAPTER 2

Hawke and Keating

Immediately after seeing Hawke, I headed overseas with my family. I had plenty to think about on that trip: with Keating's patience running out, the challenge would soon be on.

I knew we could expect little or no help from the Left. Keating had hoped that Brian Howe, seen for quite some time as the Left's leader in Canberra, would convince his colleagues to go with the challenger, since Howe had indicated both to Keating and to Bob Hogg his belief that the time had come for a Keating takeover. But Paul mistakenly believed that Howe led the Left and could carry them on an issue of this kind.

Leading a faction that inherently distrusts power (and being leader implies, of course, having power) must be incredibly difficult. The Left doesn't actually elect leaders, but by the end of 1990 Gerry Hand and Nick Bolkus were the leading figures, and they would not wear Keating at any price. I suspect that Bolkus, to whom I had spoken about the leadership on several occasions, might have had something of an open mind, but Hand, the senior figure, would not hear any argument for supporting Keating. From being Hawke's challenger for Wills in 1979, Hand had developed into a close Hawke ally. Hand had experienced some difficult periods as Minister for Aboriginal Affairs and whenever he had been in strife, Hawke was there for him, as solid as a rock. Keating's supporters on the Left were Frank Walker, Peter Duncan, Stewart West and Andrew Theophanous, but these people had no battalions. The Left army stayed firm for Hawke, who went on his Christmas vacation with the confidence a candidate always feels when he is in front.

Even after the treatment Hawke had handed out to me, being part of the Keating team wasn't exactly a bed of roses. Keating would hardly ever compromise on people or policies. Not long after the election he chose to give a public character assessment of John Button. While this would have been manageable if done by me or another of his supporters, the attack on Button demonstrated that Keating wanted to be Prime Minister, sure, but not desperately enough to suck up to those who were prepared to vote for him. Button had publicly endorsed Keating as Hawke's successor, making it abundantly clear that the change should take place as soon as possible. If Button stepped out of line, Keating would belt him as hard as he could. Friend or foe made no difference. Winning ballots is not easy when you insult your supporters and then try to humiliate them.

I incurred Keating's wrath over the Telecom debate from July to September 1990. Kim Beazley wanted to open up Telecom to competition but to retain it in government ownership. This was difficult to sell to the party, whose sensitivities had been raised by the partial privatisation of the Commonwealth Bank. The Centre Left, who determined whether any Right motion would get through a conference because they had the balance of power, were in turmoil about whether they could go this far. The South Australian Centre Left, that section of the faction more likely to support a Right proposition than any other, had as one of its most prominent members a fellow called Bob Pomeroy, an official of the union whose members all worked for Telecom. They were finding it hard to give any support to a proposal that opened up Telecom to competition and inevitably reduced the size of its workforce. The Left were implacably opposed: no amount of talking would shift them as much as a millimetre. The Telecom unions lobbied every MP, trade union and state ALP branch very effectively. The Right, whose base resided in the trade unions, were under real pressure to resist change. I flew to Queensland to address a meeting of old guard and Australian Workers Union–Shop Assistants officials, to convince them to go with us. It was a tough meeting, but I think I scored a victory, albeit a very narrow one. Even the New South Wales and Victorian Right groups were under pressure from their own unions. I was putting bushfires out all over the country for months, trying to force through a vital microeconomic reform.

This wimpish proposal did not satisfy Paul Keating, who wanted to go much further and sell off Telecom into the bargain. The sheer impossibility of convincing even the Right to vote for that proposition did not daunt him in the slightest. Selling Telecom was never on: I was having enough difficulty convincing the Right to support Beazley's much more moderate package, and problems with the Centre Left, who were vital to our success. Keating's view was that anybody who would not side with him was a pathetic coward. And if this was not bad enough, Keating also wanted to sell off Australian Airlines.

In September 1990 the cowards had the numbers, and Keating was alienating more and more of his mates; Chris Schacht, one of the strongest supporters Keating had, would not agree with him, which made Keating near hysterical. I arranged for Keating to talk to George Campbell, the Left union leader and ACTU vice-president to elicit his support, but again to no avail. Everybody who spoke to Keating would come away saying how clever he was and how they were still unable to vote for him.

A special conference was necessary to debate this because these privatisations directly contravened the platform. Here again there was no logic to the Keating push: anyone who cannot convince the Caucus has no hope of convincing the conference. As the direct links to government become more indirect, loyalty to any individual's concept of the party is just as important as loyalty to the government. The special conference to be held in September 1990 was preceded by a Cabinet meeting to establish the government's position.

When the majority in Cabinet refused to support Keating's hardline position on Telecom and backed Beazley, Keating did something I saw done only once in six years as a minister. He threw his papers onto the desk, abused Beazley, me and the Cabinet in turn and stormed out, Robert Ray's comment 'Spit the dummy' ringing in his ears. This was not a performance calculated to strengthen the resolve of his supporters or to win new converts to the ranks.

I was very angry indeed and almost as frustrated as Keating himself. Putting the party in the hands of someone who could behave like this was a risk that many could not justify. I called Laurie Brereton, Gary Punch and Leo McLeay around to my office and told them I could not continue to support anyone who behaved like this. Keating did not approve of me making sure that the Cabinet resolution prevailed at the conference, but had it been defeated the government would have been in terminal trouble, no matter who was leading it.

So my ardour for the cause was rising and falling with the day's or week's events. Throughout 1990 that was the problem, of course: Keating was brilliant one day and awful the next. Our hope was that, once in the leadership, the days of this inconsistency would be over.

In the early hours of a mid January morning in 1991, my family and I were occupying two rooms in a three-star hotel in Sorrento, Italy, when the telephone rang in the children's room. I stumbled through the dark to get to it and was greeted by the chirpy tones of our leader.

'It starts in ten minutes,' said Hawke.

I managed a really sharp reply such as, 'What are you talking about, Bob?'

'The fucking war, mate,' he said. 'It starts in ten minutes.'

Within twenty-four hours, I was on my way back to Australia to attend the special sitting of parliament that Hawke had called to approve Australia's involvement in the Gulf War. Hawke revelled in the drama of it all, and it must be said that Australia revelled in it with him. The cameras brought war into our lounge rooms as never before; it was eerie riding the radar-guided bombs all the way to their killing grounds. The rape of Kuwait and the deeds of Saddam Hussein, kept secret over the years but now revealed in graphic detail, justified every rocket, every bomb and every bombardment in the eyes of almost every Australian. Rarely has a war had so much support, rarely has a Prime Minister done so well from its prosecution.

Hawke's stocks rose with the disintegration of every Iraqi target shown on CNN. His love affair with the people showed every sign of being rekindled, his love of the job positively glowed through everything he did. The man who didn't want to go anyway knew that, no matter what Keating wanted or I wanted, the Caucus would not remove him at a time like this.

Keating could only brood over the cruel tricks fate was playing on him. Once again he tried out Hawke on the prospect of a peaceful changeover, but found no joy. He rang to inform me of Hawke's rigidity on the question of succession and resigned himself to waiting a few more months, but that was all. Whether a challenge was a good or a bad idea, it was bound to happen soon.

The Caucus believed the uneasy truce between their gods would stay in place for some time to come; while many were prepared to contemplate life without Hawke, very few wanted to see him forced out or humiliated. This is not to say that the Keating supporters were not active. Gary Punch, Leo McLeay, Laurie Brereton, Chris Schacht and George Gear, not to mention four or five Cabinet ministers, did not miss a chance to speak with a Caucus colleague or a press gallery journalist. However, from January to June the numbers remained much the same. When factional blocs decide to stick with one candidate, it is almost impossible to pick off individuals.

The battle was taking place in the Right, traditionally the most unified bloc of all. Very early in the piece, the passionately anti-Keating Robert Ray and I decided that we would not let the Right break up over the coming challenge. Over the previous three years Ray and Keating had disagreed several times, and at no stage had they been close. By the time the challenge finally came, the reasons for the antipathy were irrelevant. For both of us, the faction mattered more than either the champion or the challenger, and when the fireworks started we kept talking and a lasting split was avoided. Most of the New South Wales Right who were Keating supporters had no problem in maintaining good relations with a majority of the so-called pro-Hawke coalition, and most of the others voting for Hawke had a similar view.

This did not mean that lobbying did not take place within the

Right. In the months before the ballot Robert Ray, one of the best factional operators the party has seen or ever will see, worked on a number of people who were Keating supporters and not shy about saying so. Bob Catley, Senator Terry Aulich from Tasmania and Bob Collins all professed a belief that Keating should be the leader and finished up voting for Hawke. Whatever it took was provided. The Prime Minister had nothing to do with their conversion: the way to Damascus was pointed out by Robert Ray, and so was the transport to get them there.

As George Bush discovered, war-induced high ratings do not endure for long after the last shot has been fired in anger. Within a few months after the end of the Gulf War the polls were trending down again, Robert was shoring up the Hawke defences and I was doing very little. As the early part of 1991 slipped by without a Hawke gaffe to seize upon and use, the prospects of success for an early challenge were nil. But I knew we were moving towards a challenge because Keating could no longer work with Hawke and was unwilling to wait. I also knew that the first attempt was bound to fail: it would merely serve to set up the destabilisation period before a second challenge that would have a much greater chance of success. The only prerequisite was to be sure that Keating won enough votes to justify a second go.

Once the war was over, the Hawke parliamentary debating performance deteriorated rapidly. The House had never been an arena for demonstrating his greatest skills: where standing orders applied it was impossible to develop consensus, find solutions to disputes and merge diametrically opposing viewpoints. But parliament was where Keating shone, and the gulf between the two in terms of their debating ability was never wider than in April and May of 1991. Hawke bumbled his way through a botched defence against allegations that he received large sums of money from Western Australian entrepreneurs on behalf of the party while promising to defer a gold tax, and Keating routed the Opposition with one of his more spectacular performances. The gallery and the Caucus acknowledged his superior effort, but it didn't bring him any more Caucus votes.

John Button became very active with the press gallery on Keating's behalf during this period. He had the reputation of being a minister who would tell the truth, even if that meant moving away from the government line, with the courage to tell it like it was in public. If that was what he would say in public, the journalists reasoned, imagine what he would say in private! Quite a few of the gallery leaders, particularly Michelle Grattan of the *Age*, spent a great deal of time in Button's office. The Keating campaign had new life breathed into it each time the door closed and Button sat talking to journalists in his inner sanctum.

The role of the press gallery was critical. We all read what the gallery writes and hear what they say. What the gallery reports as fact is accepted by the great majority; what the gallery proffers as opinion is accepted by many. Even if it is not accepted it becomes the topic of conversation. A prime minister cannot survive a challenge over a twelve-month period if the gallery is hostile.

The pro-Keating pack was led by Paul Kelly, now editor-in-chief of the *Australian*, Laurie Oakes and Michelle Grattan. As his subsequent writings on these events have shown, Paul Kelly was an unabashed Keating supporter, and having someone like that on side does no harm at all. Alan Ramsey of the *Sydney Morning Herald* now had an opportunity to undo Hawke, whom he had hated for ten years and had been criticising almost permanently. I was horrified to learn that during 1991 Ramsey was an occasional visitor to the Keating home; not only did Keating brief him on what was happening, but he used him as a sounding board for ideas. Michelle Grattan got the Keating line from Button and the Hawke line from Michael Duffy. Any journalist who rang virtually any member of the Caucus could get an opinion one way or the other. Gary Punch and Chris Schacht worked the gallery tirelessly. Whether the challenge was going well or badly, it kept going.

I thought a June challenge was likely, but by May Keating decided he would not wait another moment. It was useless to warn him, as I had done occasionally, that if he won the job he might not like it and that whether he liked it or not it would take a heavy physical toll on him. When Keating is determined to do something—and the decision to challenge had been reached after months or years of thinking rather than being one of his instant reactions of anger to a real or perceived insult—he cannot be dissuaded. In this case, my choice was to go along with him or bail out of the challenge altogether.

My role in planning for this challenge and in the following six months has been misconstrued by most, including Keating himself. The challenge could not take place without me, as I carried enough support in New South Wales to make the vote too low for Keating if I was disinclined to support him. I could not control Keating—nobody could—but I always had to be listened to and at least occasionally agreed with.

Bob Hogg, the party's campaign director, not a great friend of Keating's but certainly a great supporter against Hawke, said he would urge upon Hawke the need to stand down in favour of Keating. Hogg knew that the numbers for Keating were not yet there, but he believed it was only a matter of time, and that uncertainty and division might irreparably damage our chances of re-election. He had spoken to Brian Howe, with whom he had been friends for many years, and Howe, who had openly advocated the Keating candidacy only twelve months before, told Hogg that the Left would stay with Hawke. Hogg reminded his old Left colleague about the views he had expressed earlier, but Howe refused to budge. Hand and Bolkus, who now ran the Left, had already secured a promise from Hawke that in the event of a failed Keating challenge, Howe would be Deputy Prime Minister.

Because Hogg was in fairly regular contact with Keating and occasional contact with me, he knew a challenge was getting very close. Accordingly, on 24 May he put the case to Hawke, as quite a few of us had done. He received the same response: Hawke had a special relationship with Australia, only Hawke had any hope of defeating the Liberals in the forthcoming election. Hogg responded that a second challenge almost always follows the first and that the anti-Hawke forces from the New South Wales Right and the Centre Left would not give up. Given such continuing destabilisation, Hawke could not possibly win an election.

His arguments were useless, and the relationship between Hogg and Hawke never recovered from this conversation. Hogg had joined the enemy, and I can only wonder at the possible progress of an election campaign in which the Oval Office and the party headquarters would barely have been on speaking terms. For my part, I had no reason to fear the fallout from a losing challenge after this: Hogg had confirmed just how much Hawke resented Keating, and that made a challenge imminent. Reports of the meeting served only to harden Keating's position. Mine as well: I could no longer see any hope for peace in our time.

Laurie Brereton occupies a stylish duplex in the Canberra suburb of Deakin. On the evening of Tuesday 28 May, the first day of the parliamentary sitting week, Keating and I joined him there for a takeaway Malaysian meal and a bottle of chardonnay. Not the least charming aspect of the Brereton style is that a good bottle of wine is never far away, and over it Keating informed us that he would challenge immediately.

This came as a shock: I had thought we had a few more weeks in which to work on the stragglers. Keating wanted me to approach Hawke immediately, serving him notice that I was aware of the Kirribilli pact and that its public revelation would do him terrible harm. I was also to tell him that Keating would challenge soon, without giving any date.

It has been said that I was playing both sides of the fence and could not be trusted by the Keating camp, even in the first challenge. Yet I attended all the meetings that mattered and in fact convened most of the planning meetings myself. On the night of the dinner at Laurie Brereton's place, I proposed a toast to the next Prime Minister, not because I thought Hawke would resign and not because I thought we could win a ballot. The counts we had done showed that we had close to fifty votes, a more-than-respectable number from which to launch a second challenge which we all thought we would win. Keating was uneasy about the toast, but we proceeded to drink and adjourned to prepare for battle.

The only change to his timetable I wanted was to delay for about two weeks, giving us a real chance to work on the doubtful votes in Caucus. Hawke was about to go overseas and I could sense that we would not do as well as we should in a ballot held now. The Left would insist on rigid factional discipline, so instead of getting three or four extra votes we would be down to West, Duncan and Walker. The Queensland Right were threatening preselections, and our support base there was weakening. We needed more time, but the tone of Keating's voice and the wild look in his eyes told me that any argument in favour of delay was wasted effort. I didn't push for the delay: I knew it would make no difference between winning and losing. We knew we were marching into a battle we would lose. The question was: Could we win the war?

We told very few supporters about the closeness of the challenge, and on the Wednesday I arranged to see Hawke, who had to be told that a challenge was coming. During the day I went over my lines and received some assistance that had not been requested. Paul Keating sent me a typed, unsigned note on plain paper, giving me the exact words I was supposed to say to Hawke on the Kirribilli matter. I kept the note, which will remain in a secure place for my grandchildren.

Late that evening I went to see Hawke. This was not a meeting about which I could get excited: I felt nothing but sadness at its necessity. The hunger for revenge had faded, and I really felt that I was just doing my job. Hawke's staff, particularly his senior adviser Colin Parks, was anxious to know why I had come. I'm told that many of them took the opportunity to check us out on the closed-circuit screen that senior advisers use to show them what the Prime Minister is doing.

They were probably disappointed, for there was no shouting or screaming: in fact, our meeting was mostly subdued. I told Hawke that I knew of his promise to make way for Keating, and I knew who had witnessed it. For a while the Prime Minister tried to suggest that the Kirribilli promise was nowhere near as definite as Keating was making out, but his heart clearly wasn't in it. Everything came back to his view that he alone could lead us to victory, that Keating was totally unsuited to being Prime Minister.

I really tried to convince him to leave as a conquering hero, not as the man who had stayed past his time, defeated either by Keating in a challenge or Hewson in an election. Knowing that most of humankind is susceptible to flattery and none more so than Hawke, I began with the words: 'You are a living legend.'

Unfortunately, this worked against me. Hawke claimed that only somebody described in these terms could lead Labor to a fifth electoral victory at a time when the recession was biting so deeply. Honour had dictated that this conversation take place, though its futility was depressing. He did offer a glimmer of hope by saying he was prepared to think about it while he was overseas, but I knew Keating would laugh at the prospect of delay for this reason. In the end I told him a challenge was coming, and soon, and made him as many promises as he made to me: none. Both of us lamented the death of our friendship.

When I left to return to the cool Canberra air, I felt old and tired. Hawke, on the other hand, looked bright as a new pin. Righteousness invigorates him, but it just makes me weary; it drives you forward beyond endurance and you don't win because of it. In contests like these, everyone claims to be on the side of the angels. My feeling is that there are far too many angels.

My report of the conversation to Keating the following morning did not surprise him in any way. When I told him of Hawke's promise to think about the succession while on his overseas trip and discuss it with us further on his return, Keating sneered that Hawke spent his whole life 'asking for another three months at a time', and said he wasn't going to give him three more weeks. We decided to announce the challenge that evening, Thursday 30 May, with me giving the story of the broken Kirribilli promise to Laurie Oakes in time for the six o'clock news.

Our plan was to have a ballot at the next regular Caucus meeting on the following Tuesday, using the story of the broken promise to justify the challenge in the short term but mainly to damage Hawke's credibility in the longer term. The point was that, whether we won or lost the challenge, Hawke would have to handle constant taunts about the lie. The Opposition and the media would never let go of a story as good as this, so we could rely on the problem lasting long after the challenge.

Paul Keating has a strange code of honour that guides his personal conduct. He had told Hawke that if he were going to challenge him, he would warn him first. At about four that afternoon, he interrupted a meeting Hawke was having with his hardest-line supporters: Queensland Premier Wayne Goss and Bill Ludwig, the national boss of the Australian Workers Union, to tell Hawke that the challenge was on. The meeting was brief and devoid of feigned politeness. While Hawke claimed he had never hated anyone because he wasn't capable of it, he gave every impression of hating Keating that day (a depth of feeling he has occasionally demonstrated since he left the parliament). Keating, of course, has never made any such claim.

Just after five o'clock on that Thursday afternoon, I told Laurie Oakes about the Kirribilli pact, and he raced away to put to air one of the best stories he had ever been given. Most commentators, including Paul Kelly in his book *The End of Certainty*, have written that the rushed release of the Kirribilli story plus the declaration of Keating's challenge was a strategic disaster. They fail to understand the nature of these contests. Sure it would have been good to have the time to exploit the Kirribilli pact more fully. This would have done Hawke more public damage but shifted very few votes our way. At our meeting I had told Hawke he would win a vote in the party room and I had wanted a few more weeks to improve our position by a few votes. But that was all delay would have achieved: a better-looking defeat.

That night was an extraordinary one, even for someone like myself who had been in the thick of things for so long. I rang almost all the members of the New South Wales Right to make sure they were on side with Keating. I didn't yell or argue with anybody. Our troops had wanted this moment for quite some time; even though they knew we would lose, the loyalty of the New South Wales Right came to the fore.

David Simmons, representing the New South Wales rural and provincial seat of Calare, was a close friend of Con Sciacca, the Queensland MP who had become the bomb-thrower for Bill Ludwig. Sciacca had made it clear to a number of Queenslanders that their preselections were in doubt if they supported Keating. David was a great admirer of Hawke's, and he clearly wanted to vote for him. I told him that we would be beaten and that the only way we could guarantee that retribution would not be taken against us was to go as close as possible. David, though quite emotional about this, undertook to stick with his New South Wales colleagues. It is sad that less than two years later when Keating was arranging his ministry he could find no room for David Simmons, who made no mistakes in his portfolios of Defence Science and Personnel, and the Arts, Tourism and Territories and worked very hard indeed. While it is true to say that being part of the New South Wales Right got him his ministerial guernseys in the first place, it is nonetheless sad that somebody who agonised about voting for Keating and eventually did so out of loyalty could not be supported for the ministry.

Roger Price MP rang to tell me he would support Bob Hawke. He shared a flat with Robert Ray, to whom he had become very close, and I did not try to talk him round. I liked Roger and was personally disappointed that he had decided to go against us, but it was very difficult to be angry with those who voted for Hawke. In May 1991 the Prime Minister was still relatively popular, even if his ratings were not as high as they had been in the halcyon days of the early 1980s. Our candidate was deeply unpopular and we were taking a very big risk.

Two Queenslanders came around to see me, and they were very upset. Michael Lavarch, now the Attorney-General, was nearly in tears, as was Les Scott, who had succeeded Bill Hayden as member for Oxley when Hayden became Governor-General in 1988. Their preselections had been threatened by Con Sciacca, acting on behalf of Bill Ludwig, and they had come to tell me that they would have to support Hawke. The Queensland Right had organised a complete 'show and tell' ballot, where every one of their pledged votes had been paired off so that no vote could slide away. The Left did this as a matter of course anyway, as did the Centre Left, but the Right had never gone down that path. If people do not want to vote for the person who will not only lead them but lead the nation as well, they should not be forced to. There was no way I could be angry with them and they left with my blessing, for whatever that was worth.

Then at about nine or ten o'clock Bill Ludwig himself turned up in my office. He was the national boss of one of Australia's biggest unions and the key figure in the Queensland Labor Party. That made him critical to the national Right, and he knew it. Whereas Robert Ray and I had a personal understanding about the challenge, no such arrangement existed with Bill Ludwig. He took the hardest anti-Keating position of anyone, including all of the Left and even Hawke himself. Bill Ludwig sat in my office for more than three hours, drinking Scotch, bagging Keating, expressing incredulity about my support for Keating, swearing death and destruction for any Queenslander who joined with Brian Courtice (MP for Hinkler, who was already under suspicion and who broke ranks with Ludwig on the following weekend, exposing the preselection threats).

But most of all, Ludwig kept me occupied: by the time he left it was one in the morning and most of the Caucus were tucked safely in their beds, well and truly out of my reach. For while I was listening to Ludwig, the Hawke office had announced that the vote would be held the following day, not the Tuesday we had planned. We were being robbed of a precious few extra days to round up further votes.

While I have never checked with Robert Ray or Bill Ludwig, I have no doubt that the intention had been to keep me busy, preventing me from persuading any doubtfuls to support Keating. If this was true, then it was a clever ploy indeed. Almost anyone who tried to waste my time that night would have been given very short shrift. But Bill Ludwig was too critical to the national faction I had spent half a lifetime building: I had to give him time.

The night had gone badly for us. Bob Collins, who had been with us and been turned around during the day, sat outside my office for two hours while Ludwig was inside. I'm not sure that I could have turned him back again, but I must have had some kind of chance. The Centre Left announced that they could not hold Michael Tate, Peter Morris or Nick Sherry from Tasmania, and John Button told us that we had no hope with Barry Jones (I never thought we did have). Harry Woods, a new member of the New South Wales Right from the seat of Page in northern New South Wales, had pledged himself to Hawke, and Terry Aulich from Tasmania had been persuaded to do so by Robert Ray. It didn't look good. We had lost quite a few, and were probably down to about 40 votes.

Bright and early next morning, a small group met in Keating's office. As well as Keating and myself, present were Chris Schacht, John Dawkins, Gary Punch, Laurie Brereton and Leo McLeay. Several of us had been told that Hawke would insist on Keating moving a resolution for Hawke to vacate his position, which meant a show of hands without even the pretence of a secret ballot. Given all the threats the pro-Hawke forces were making, this would have made a farce of proceedings. It appeared that Hawke wanted this course of action because it would force a debate between the two opponents and Hawke wanted to explain fully his reasons for dishonouring his pledge to vacate the Lodge for Paul Keating.

I strongly advised Keating to refuse to move the resolution if Hawke persisted with this view. We wanted Hawke to resign, allowing for both to nominate for the leadership, a vote taken by secret ballot. Hayden had declared his position vacant for Hawke in their first challenge: Keating should demand the same courtesy from Hawke. We all agreed on this strategy, and none of us expected Hawke to be so graceless. He held the numbers comfortably and we couldn't see that he would allow anything to stand in the way of taking advantage of that.

The meeting took place at eight that morning, and was as electric as was proper for a leadership challenge. Tension increases with lack of sleep and, like many in the Caucus, I had not been to sleep at all the previous night. In fact, for several days I had found sleep impossible, and even the adrenalin on which I relied was not pumping with much volume or regularity.

Hawke opened the meeting with the terse statement that Paul Keating had announced he was challenging for the position, so Paul should now move that the leader's position be declared vacant. Paul responded in subdued manner that Hayden had been more attuned to the gravity of these occasions by resigning, not forcing a show of hands, and allowing Hawke to contest a secret ballot. Hawke was adamant that he would not adopt that course. We couldn't believe our luck. Keating was adamant that he would not be moving any resolution.

The entire Caucus—Hawke and Keating supporters—was stunned. Ray and Beazley, much more experienced in Caucus machinations than Hawke, made their only mistake and it wasn't their fault. To have stood up and told their leader he was stupid, and that of course a secret ballot would take place after he resigned, would have been far too humiliating for Hawke. They were forced to remain silent.

I jumped up and said, 'Let's get out of here,' and signalled to our forces to leave. The forty Keating supporters ran from the room at full pace. We had escaped a hiding, we had been given a few days' grace to set the scene properly and to pick up some more votes. The faces of Robert Ray and Kim Beazley betrayed their feelings. A golden opportunity had been squandered, and the enemy was walking out to fight another day.

This was an important tactical victory. While it is difficult to make any judgment on whether a few days' delay had much impact on the final vote, I reckon we improved by three or four votes over the weekend. There is a world of difference between a scoreline of 70–40 and 66–44. A challenger has legitimacy with the support of 40 per cent of the Caucus.

The importance of our tactical triumph had not been lost on the chieftans of the Hawke camp, who held a crisis meeting in Hawke's office as soon as the shortest Caucus meeting in living memory had concluded. They knew what a disaster the morning had been for them, and decided to call another Caucus meeting for later that day. At about nine o'clock Robert Ray rang to tell me that it had been scheduled for ten o'clock. This time, he said, Hawke would resign and recontest to enable the secret ballot to take place. There was no rancour in this conversation, and we even shared a laugh. I told him there would be no Caucus, as our troops had already left the building or would immediately do so when I told them this. I don't believe Robert expected to hear anything else.

The next step was to page Gary Punch and Chris Schacht to tell them of the proposed Caucus meeting, and to urge those who had not left the building already to drop everything and go. Most members were in the dining room having a late breakfast. The bacon and eggs of the real men and the muesli of the sensible ones were abandoned to their fate as our fabulous forty fled. Ron Edwards the Deputy Speaker stood at the doors to the House of Representatives side of the building, arms akimbo, trying to stop members from leaving. There was no stopping this lot, however: they all knew how high the stakes were.

Hawke went to the Caucus room at ten o'clock surrounded by his own supporters and nobody else, and accompanied by the expected cries of 'foul'. Nobody thought Hawke would tell them he had been outmanoeuvred, though they all knew it. So a very short meeting was held while our troops busily ignored commands to return from the airport or their Canberra abodes. Hawke announced that the Tuesday Caucus meeting would be brought forward to Monday 3 June and the issue settled then. Therein lay the weakness of the Hawke position. There was not the slightest possibility that defeating Keating in a ballot on that Monday would settle anything.

Governing the country is supposed to proceed during times of internal crisis, and we made an effort to show the world that this was possible. Hawke and Keating had to discuss issues at a premier's conference; it is hard to believe that their minds were on the job. Prior to the Caucus, the Cabinet had actually convened to discuss Kakadu and the mining of Coronation Hill. Sanity prevailed and the Cabinet broke up after a few minutes.

Keating was disappointed and hurt at the level of support he received from the Cabinet. However, Willis, Evans et al had a reason to be unwilling to take a risk with Keating. When their backs are to the wall, when the polls are showing Labor's support crumbling, a special kind of courage is necessary to opt for an unpopular individual such as Keating—a kind of courage that does not necessarily have its roots in superior intellect.

The weekend was an endless round of telephone calls. People like Collins, Aulich and Catley, who had been so strong in support of Keating in earlier times, must have hated the sound of the phone ringing as we reminded them of their early commitments and the Hawke forces rang to remind them about their late ones. I reckoned we picked up three or four votes, but I couldn't get too excited about the numbers at this point. I was sure we had enough for a respectable result, which was all that mattered. A cheering note was provided by Brian Courtice, the Bundaberg backbencher who appeared on TV to announce he would defy Bill Ludwig and vote for Keating. And Keating himself appeared on the 'Sunday' program and put on a brilliant show. He conveyed enthusiasm and energy, the commodities that Hawke had been singularly unable to display since the election, promising that a government he headed would have 'direction, strategy, esprit de corps, enthusiasm and, dare I say it, where necessary, a touch of excitement'. While this might not have won any votes for the Monday ballot, it cemented the press gallery and their support, which would be critical when he entered the wilderness.

The Monday Caucus meeting displayed little of the drama of the previous Friday, and the only interest then was in the margin of the Hawke victory. Quite a few of the Keating voters showed their votes to me voluntarily: people like David Simmons and Steve Dubois wanted no possibility of being accused of doing the wrong thing. We went into the ballot on 48 promises that could be believed. On that basis I thought we would get 45, but I was always an optimist. The end result was 66–44, much better than the 70–40 which I was sure would have been the previous result. With the support of 40 per cent of the Caucus, a shift of only one vote in ten would be enough to change the leadership.

Still, Hawke was gracious in victory, Keating magnanimous in defeat, once again performing superbly at his post-defeat press conference. For some reason, losers seem to do well at press conferences. In this case it might have been post-stress euphoria—or perhaps the knowledge that the show wasn't over yet, not by a long shot.

CHAPTER 3

Keating

On the day of the challenge I went to see Hawke to tell him something that Keating later said to the press, that Keating had only one shot in the locker and had fired it. There would be no second challenge, I said, and I think Hawke wanted to believe it. What happened in the parliament would be crucial to his chances of remaining leader; we had only one big parliamentary weapon which we had just put into cold storage. Momentum was won and lost on the floor of the parliament, and I had no doubt that our capacity to generate that momentum had just been dramatically diminished.

The course of the next six months was made clear to me by the party held in Keating's office on the evening of his defeat. His party was not the function of a loser. Even though Keating was shortly to resign as Treasurer and retire to the back bench, even though he had been defeated, he was looking forward to success. By the end of the party Keating, who was suffering from one of his bad throats, even had a few drinks—which he rarely did—and was having trouble in making himself understood.

Shortly afterwards, our faction met to ratify a series of Hawke decisions that had not been shared with those who were voting for him. John Kerin, who had been nominated as Treasurer, fancied himself as Deputy Prime Minister and the Right troops wanted to elect their parliamentary secretaries. I had to tell them that Brian Howe was on a promise for the deputy's job, as he had been for some time, and Roger Price was being rewarded for his loyalty to Hawke with a parliamentary secretary's job. They were really impressed, especially about Howe.

Robert Ray and I met at his flat in Yarralumla, where I asked for lenient treatment for the troops who backed the loser, particularly the ministers who voted for Keating. There was no problem: Hawke could not afford to have the row that would have been created by demoting his opponents. Robert made sure that all the promises were kept and we settled down to see what would happen next.

The Cabinet meeting held after the leadership challenge dealt with Kakadu and the mining of Coronation Hill. At that meeting Hawke showed a number of ministers who had voted for him that they had made a mistake, and demonstrated even to his best supporters that the years and the pressures of office had seriously eroded his judgment.

Cabinet members were well aware of the arguments about Coronation Hill. The conservationists opposed mining because of fears that it would pollute the headwaters of the South Alligator River. As Minister for the Environment I had successfully prevented mining over a vast area of Kakadu, but had repeatedly told my green friends that the mine at Coronation Hill should go ahead. The area had been extensively mined in the 1950s, mainly for uranium, and the recent exploration had already disturbed fairly large areas of it. Local Aborigines opposed mining because Coronation Hill was the home of their sacred spirit Bula. We already knew that Hawke opposed mining there.

He surprised the meeting, however, not because of his objections—what he wanted the Cabinet to do had already been leaked—but because of the reasons he gave. He based his opposition to mining solely on the grounds of Aboriginal heritage. This was the argument least likely to sway the Cabinet, given that Aboriginal teaching had it that Bula left if the area were disturbed, which meant he had gone in the 1950s. And lest I hear the politically correct cries of 'racist', let me point out that protection for the Bula country had been a prime reason in determining that much of the conservation zone should not be exploited.

Even if the Aboriginal heritage argument were accepted, this was undoubtedly Hawke's worst Cabinet performance. Gareth Evans was particularly incensed and Bob Collins, whom we hoped to win over, was astounded. As the Cabinet ministers gave their views, it was apparent that Hawke did not have a majority—a point I could not help making because I knew it would be leaked. (Not by me, I hasten to add, but it was too good a line not to be reported by somebody.) Neal Blewett actually said he would support the Hawke position in order to avoid the Prime Minister having to look at Cabinet defeat.

The days when Hawke's word was enough to bring the Cabinet to heel were over. When this happens to a Prime Minister under siege, it is usually fatal: once lost, that authority is practically impossible to regain. Hawke was done over in Cabinet but solidarity prevailed, and we stopped short of voting Hawke down. Mining at Coronation Hill was banned, and the press fell savagely upon the news. It was too close to the ballot we had lost to take advantage of Hawke's woeful performance, but the dreadful hiding he took in Cabinet was nothing in comparison to the way in which the press received the news. The green cause had done too well in Kakadu up to then and by banning mining at Coronation Hill itself, the greens had been the victors once too often. The irony of this was that Hawke had not used any environmental argument against the mine. Nonetheless, the chances of keeping a pro-environment line going as popular politics, with me having left the portfolio, were just about zero.

Winter in Canberra is generally cold and miserable, but I cannot remember feeling much more miserable than I did during that winter. In fact, the period from May 1991 to December was the most difficult of all my time in politics. Living for revenge is a bitter thing, and by that time the events of the days after the 1990 election, while not forgotten, had dimmed in my memory. I still thought Hawke should be replaced, but now revenge was no factor at all. The government gave every sign of being asleep. We had no direction, we were leaderless.

Keating was quiet for a few months, as was appropriate under the circumstances, but he let those closest to his leadership campaign know that if victory failed to be achieved by the end of 1991, he would resign. This was no idle threat: a real time limit had been struck. Over those months, Keating used a number of media events and speeches to establish a real policy choice between sticking with Hawke or going for the new boy. Superannuation, Commonwealth–State relations and a more rapid lowering of interest rates were all used to create an argument between himself and John Kerin, his successor as Treasurer.

Keating was dismissive of Kerin, who had been a bit too cute during the weekend of the first challenge. Both Keating and I had spoken to him, and he promised both of us that he would speak to a number of regional members on Keating's behalf, though he did not quite promise to vote for Keating himself. There is no doubt that no pro-Keating phone calls were made. This did not bode well for the Kerin period in Treasury, with Keating seething in the background.

The atmosphere in Caucus was poisonous for the longest continuous period in all my experience in politics. Whenever Keating's comments from the backbench were construed as being too tough on Hawke my phone would not stop ringing as Caucus members, including some Keating supporters, registered their complaints. John Dawkins would break out now and again, Gary Punch and some of my other New South Wales colleagues never stopped. To bring the feeling to a head and still see Keating succeed was not getting easier as the weeks and months rolled by. It would require a failure from Hawke and the government, and Kerin was the most likely to provide this.

Kerin, who had neither killer instinct nor factional allies, might have been popular with the farm lobby, but his Cabinet approach was a problem. He is not by nature pushy or aggressive and he did not like the kind of confrontation that Cabinet debate frequently engenders, often withdrawing Cabinet submissions or retreating early when under attack. This lack of pushiness would not be a problem for any minister except for the Treasurer, who needs extra respect; Cabinet government cannot work when the Treasurer is just another voice. Lacking the ego and the confidence to stamp his own brand on Treasury, he put the departmental line all the time. The failings of Treasury in making economic predictions, which had grown worse during Keating's stewardship, came to haunt Kerin.

He did what Treasury wanted in the Budget; he seemed terrified of making mistakes and his lack of confidence could be seen by the number of excuses his staff manufactured to help him avoid giving press conferences. For a nation in deep recession, the Budget preparation left a great deal to be desired, and its initiatives were extremely modest, predicated on what he called 'sustainable longer-term policies' and a slow recovery the following year. Keating, who was promoting himself as the man to get Australia going again—to mixed reviews, it must be said—was urging a sharp drop in interest rates in order to promote greater economic activity and a faster recovery. Given that his decisions had helped cause the recession, perhaps this was Keating's way of saying 'sorry', since he couldn't utter the word under any circumstances. But it was pressure Kerin could not withstand.

His reputation as Treasurer was impeded by his Cabinet sponsorship of the failed wool reserve price scheme. Hawke had backed this scheme, and Keating had bitterly attacked it, saying it guaranteed only that the government would incur huge debts. He was correct to the tune of $3 billion, with a crippled wool industry thrown in. This, plus the Budget, was convincing a majority of Cabinet members that Hawke's choice of Kerin as Treasurer had been a very poor one.

One of the proposals in the Budget was a 'better cities' program, to cost $800 million over five years. It was proposed by Brian Howe and the only explanation for Hawke's supporting it was that he owed Howe and the Left for backing him in the leadership ballot. When it was discussed at the ERC, it had no support at all; hundreds of millions of dollars were sought with virtually no detail on how they should be spent, and John Dawkins and I sent it up mercilessly. Willis and Kerin could not be compelled to support it, no matter how many encouraging noises Hawke chose to make: Willis argued that some money should be agreed but that further work needed to be done before more was allocated.

One of the reasons why Labor governments have been so successful for so long is that the Budget proposals of Cabinet ministers are really put through the mincer. The 'better cities' program was the only time I witnessed the process breaking down. Kerin agreed with Willis' assessment, but he allowed his Prime Minister to pass the scheme on his own vote and Brian Howe's. There was none of the fight for Budget integrity that Treasurers need to show, and to have this demonstrated in front of the most senior ministers was inauspicious, to say the least. The fact that when he became Prime Minister Keating raided a reduced 'better cities' program to pay for a whole range of legitimate projects in no way changes the fact that when first proposed it should not have been ticked.

Brian Howe was a big contributor to breathing life into the Keating campaign, quite apart from proposing 'better cities'. The only time I thought taking a policy position really helped Keating was the Howe proposal in the 1991 Budget for a Medicare co-payment. This caused a real furore in Caucus. Keating's opposition to it was not just a clever move to embarrass Hawke, Howe or anybody else. Hardly any of Hawke's sixty-six supporters could agree with it, and Keating, who passionately believed that bulk-billing was sacrosanct and who fought the proposal tooth and nail, was putting a view upheld by almost every member of the party. For the Hawke forces the new proposal was a disaster. Once again phone calls were made to the Left, Right and Centre, telling them that if they did not support this one, it would look bad for Hawke. For once there could be no accusations of opportunism or hypocrisy: Hawke was forcing through a decision that in a free Caucus vote would not have attracted double figures.

From July, when some sort of effort to keep the Keating challenge alive resumed, all meetings to decide on the next step took place in my office. My dilemma was to keep the challenge going, while winning more Caucus votes than the process of keeping it alive was losing for us. The more difficult decision was to be prepared to call the whole thing off if we could not win. To continue a challenge forever when you cannot win is to destroy the party and the government, and if you have put a lifetime into assisting with those election victories, you can't let that destruction occur. You owe it not just to your parliamentary colleagues or the heavies who sit on national executives and state administrative committees, but to the hundreds of thousands of party members and supporters you will never meet.

To some people, however, my position was obviously seen as equivocal. One was obviously Paul Kelly in his book *The End of Certainty*. He wrote that my 'subsequent elevation as "the man who kingmade Keating" is a media myth. Richardson was adviser to both Hawke and Keating and, like everyone, was unsure of the outcome. So he took out insurance—and neither Hawke nor Keating fully trusted him'. In support of these words, Kelly goes on to chronicle an interview I conducted with Bob Hawke on Sydney's radio station 2KY (I occasionally acted as a talk show host for this station, which is owned by the Labour Council of New South Wales) in September 1991, when I said that no challenge would take place. He also mentions an occasion in early November, when I rang a number of media outlets to reinforce Keating's own efforts to hose down challenge talk. These examples are supposed to show that I was playing on both sides so that, no matter what happened, I would be a winner.

Paul Kelly's words have been eating away at me ever since his book was published. Paul Keating has denied to me that he was the source of these suggestions, as have Brereton, Punch, McLeay and anyone else I have now discussed this with. I point out here that dampening speculation about a challenge was absolutely necessary on several occasions: sometimes in public, often in private. When Caucus anger was boiling over and the temperature needed to be lowered, I had no hesitation in doing it or causing it to be done. This did not indicate treachery to Keating, but the difficulty I was having in helping him become Prime Minister without destroying the party. This sounds uncharacteristically noble, but having said that I have to add that to achieve that goal successfully I had to lie from time to time—which I did.

The Hawke interview on 2KY is a good example. Here I said publicly that no challenge was planned, which was true enough because the second time around there would not be one without my agreement. What I didn't say was that as soon as Hawke made a big mistake, we would be off like a shot. However, it would be equally true that if the end of the year was approaching and I could not count 56 sure votes for Paul Keating, the challenge would be called off in any case. It was disappointing that in five months of effort after the first challenge we had at best a six-vote gain and we needed twelve. I would not be in a challenge attempt that wasn't going to work, and I had enough support to stop a challenge being even a nuisance to Hawke.

I made these kinds of statements again and again at doorstops, during talkback appearances and television interviews: far from being treacherous to Keating, they kept his challenge alive. There were so many angry Caucus supporters who told me they could not vote for him again. There was just too much pressure from some of the unions, some state branches, and from their local rank and file. (Paul Kelly is currently revising *The End of Certainty*: it will be interesting to see what changes he makes.)

When Keating pushed for bigger drops in interest rates than the government was prepared to countenance, nobody could forget that he had been responsible for the savage increases over the previous few years, and he would be accused of hypocrisy. If he pushed the ACTU line on superannuation, it was often seen as Kelty and Keating getting together to undermine the government. The problem was in going far enough to undermine the credibility of the Prime Minister without giving the appearance of treachery. Whenever Keating attacked a government decision, Caucus members would not wish to be painted as traitors, and when they complained to me in numbers, I would say something to dampen speculation down.

Several times I thought we would never win; there were times when I despaired of getting a rock-solid Caucus majority. However, I was at pains to keep the core people from New South Wales and elsewhere with a touch of hope in the back of their hearts and minds. They were never assembled and told it was all off, they were never rung individually and told that either. If I had wanted to get Hawke on side and call off the challenge, giving Keating no hope by turning around some votes—a dozen would have been enough and had I been serious about it I could have turned around a lot more than that—I could have done it easily. But by late 1991 Australia needed Paul Keating, the Labor Party needed him to give us at least some hope by putting up a fight in the next election, and personally I was sure of a promotion if he won. Even if you rule out altruism as completely foreign to my nature, self-interest still had me on Keating's side. So whoever fed Paul Kelly the line about my ambivalence has rewritten history.

In November an incident occurred that produced damage to the party that would not have occurred if the drama of the challenge were not being played out. Tom Burns, Queensland's Deputy Premier and an old friend of Hawke's in a state where support for Hawke approached fanaticism, accused Keating of 'gross disloyalty' and said that the New South Wales Right was intent on destroying the government. I gave Tom Burns quite a verbal belting, using the forum of a Canberra branch dinner at which I had agreed to speak some months earlier.

Paul Kelly says that, in my alleged role as a player on both sides, I 'used this occasion to re-establish [my] Keating credentials with a personal attack upon Burns'. This is entirely untrue: in fact, at a meeting in my office, the usual suspects and I worked desperately to dissuade Keating from going out and really monstering him. Our view was that potential prime ministers don't get into slanging matches with Labor deputy premiers, and that people like me can do it because we have no aspirations for higher office.

Normally such an occasion would attract no media attention, but I told Laurie Oakes, Michelle Grattan and the ABC that I might say something interesting. I had to do a job on Burns, and at the Canberra dinner I said many things about him that I would never have said under any other circumstances. (The following morning Keating rang and said: 'Graham, you were magnificent.') I like Tom Burns. He represents a generation of Labor working-class people and he puts their views, whether they are fashionable or not. He is an electoral asset in Queensland. But Tom was wounded by what I said, and referred to me as a 'low slimy mongrel' in reply.

There wasn't much chance of a prolonged battle between Tom and me, although party president Stephen Loosley, who supported Keating, didn't help by saying, 'The party has come a long way since Tom Burns was its president' at a doorstop on the day the news broke. He had to do something to stop a real war breaking out, and he spoke to Keating, Burns and myself, asking us to pull our heads in. Though some of the things I said in my speech had outraged some Queenslanders, I had gone on to praise the Queensland branch for turning around its earlier poor results to become our most successful branch. This had not been publicised, so I had to get a transcript of the speech and make it available to Burns's friends and supporters. When a challenge is on, you become accustomed to walking on eggshells.

In the Catholic Mass there is a moment when the priest asks members of the congregation to offer the sign of peace to each other. When a Mass was held early in 1992 after the tragic death from cancer of Con Sciacca's young son, I attended with Laurie Brereton, Leo McLeay, the new Prime Minister Paul Keating, Wayne Goss and Tom Burns. When Tom turned to the person behind him to say 'Peace be with you', he was no doubt quite surprised that he had to say it to me. I meant my sign of peace, and I would like to think he meant his.

As I have said, the Tom Burns incident did the Keating cause no good at all. Party brawling on the front pages of the newspapers, particularly when the brawl is as unedifying as this one was, has all the hallmarks of damage. At yet another meeting in my office, Punch, Brereton and Keating all agreed that we were not adding to our tally of votes and that Paul himself should do some interviews and lower the temperature. I insisted that the leadership campaign should be abandoned until we had the numbers, and rang a few journalists to tell them that Keating was backing off. Keating and his core group were furious, and all of them let me know it, but I was as unrepentant about it then as I am now. The Opposition's Fightback proposal was about to be released, and with Hawke under enormous pressure to respond well, we could not be seen to undermine his effort.

On 21 November John Hewson delivered the Fightback package, with its central 15 per cent goods and services tax and a range of trade-offs around it. The media, particularly the financial press, gave it a fantastic reception. Fightback was a financial journalist's dream because it made a virtue out of hurting people. It often seems to me that the main qualification for becoming a commentator on the economy in this country is a passionate belief that ripping money from unemployed people, pensioners and single mothers is a really good idea.

On the night it was released I appeared on 'A Current Affair' and made the kinds of statements Labor supporters wanted to hear: 'Every time you put your hand in your pocket, John Hewson's hand will be in there with yours' wasn't a bad line, even if it wasn't original. Yet that afternoon I had been asked not to appear on TV and attack the package until Treasury officials had been given plenty of time to examine it and pull it apart.

This was a dreadful tactical decision. We should have made a fighting response immediately, not waited for a detailed analysis of Fightback's contents. Late in 1991, Australians hated Labor for giving them a recession, and we had to convince them that Fightback, with its consumption tax, would fundamentally change our society, taking money from a great majority and giving it to those who already had a dollar or two. On this occasion, then, silence wasn't golden: it was stupid. We had a huge task, we had to get moving on it and we were paralysed into inactivity. As we sat there mute and meek, the Caucus looked on with increasing dismay, and I could almost feel the shift we had waited so long to witness. It was Hawke's utter failure to lay a glove on Hewson and his Fightback package that put Paul Keating into the Lodge.

When an anti-Fightback strategy was finally in place, there were three press conferences that proved beyond doubt that a leadership change had to occur—and none of them involved the leader. Each portfolio planned its attack, spearheaded by Brian Howe, the Deputy Prime Minister and Minister for Health. He gave a wrong set of figures for which he later apologised, and ended his press conference by walking into a cupboard. I don't know what the rest of Australia thought about this debacle, but Colin Parks rang me about it in Adelaide, where I was talking to a team of Social Security officials whose job was to go out and knock on recipients' doors to find fraud. The call depressed me: whatever Howe's appearance did to harm Hawke or to help Keating, it must have done the Liberals' morale a power of good.

On 5 December John Kerin proceeded to demonstrate why he had developed such an aversion to press conferences. The September national accounts had shown that Australia was in its most prolonged slump since the 1930s: not the most cheerful news to deliver to a waiting nation anyway. But Kerin failed to remember that the initials GOS stood for gross operating surplus: hardly a slip to restore confidence in the economy or in himself. In isolation this might have been an error that we could have forgotten and forgiven, but in the climate of early December 1991, when he and the government were under intense pressure,

Kerin needed to perform well. The press gallery liked him and few among them would have enjoyed reporting his embarrassment, but report it they did.

Determined to maintain my reputation as someone who knew how to hurt Liberals, I spent days learning a brief demonstrating that Fightback was some hundreds of millions of dollars astray in its estimates on social security. I made a presentation to a press conference of which I was quite proud, and I answered every question about social security with ease. Then the leadership questions started, and the whole thing became a nightmare. Everybody knew Hawke had to go and that was all they wanted to talk about. I never once attacked Hawke in public and I did my best to field questions. No newspaper gave me much more than a line on my demolition of one section of Fightback.

About a year earlier, I had advised Hawke to tell people that he would stay for the rest of the current term and the whole of the next one—a total of five years—so that nobody could speculate that people would really be voting for the very unpopular Paul Keating, even if Hawke were still leader. This had made Hawke look really silly. He was the only person on the globe who thought he could or should last that long. Now I gave him some more advice that I knew would cause trouble. Robert Ray and I urged him to make a complete Cabinet reshuffle: to get some ministers to resign, to make wholesale changes that would give the government a new look, a new energy that would take it through to the next election.

Throughout his entire time as Prime Minister Hawke had resisted a major reshuffle, and I couldn't believe he would have one now: I figured he would take the easy way out and just dump Kerin. If that happened, it would be disastrous for Hawke. It was the job of two people to pull Fightback apart and they were doing it with no success at all. Sacking one of them would serve only to place the spotlight squarely on the survivor. Promoting Ralph Willis in Kerin's place would be good for the government—from the time of the 1990 election Ralph had steadily enhanced his reputation and had lifted himself out of the danger zone—but it was nowhere near enough to save Hawke. Had he chosen to go for the big change he might have saved his prime ministership, but the odds on his doing that were very, very long.

On Friday 6 December, the story of my advice to Hawke was reported in the *Sydney Morning Herald*, and once again Keating and his lieutenants decided I was up to no good. When I lunched with Laurie Brereton, Peter Barron and Rene Rivkin in the boardroom of Rivkin's sharebroking premises, Brereton opened proceedings by telling me that by advising Hawke to reshuffle I had 'saved Hawke's leadership'. Everybody reasonably assumed I had leaked the story (which indeed needed to be leaked), and everybody was wrong. I still don't know who did leak the story, but by then I was being blamed for all leaks and had given up denying my responsibility for them.

I told Brereton that, far from saving Hawke, a minor reshuffle—which I knew he would make—would destroy him. I knew the press gallery were going after him; they were in for the kill, and I predicted what the papers would do with the story. Even before this moment the Hawke backers Beazley, Ray and Duffy had been ever so slowly coming around: Hawke's failure on Fightback was a concern to everyone. This was our chance to go to the Hawke backers and tell them to tap their man on the shoulder.

Hawke announced his reshuffle: Kerin became Minister for Transport, Willis Treasurer and Beazley Minister for Finance, and the response in the weekend papers was as savage as I had anticipated. Almost without exception Hawke was portrayed as a desperate leader, one who had dumped Kerin in order to save himself. The situation was now so bad that even some Queensland old guard people were saying there had to be a change of leadership. I spoke to Beazley and Ray about how bad things had become and pleaded with them to see Hawke and tell him to go.

Michael Duffy had come to the same conclusion, and for the first time the Left were showing all the signs of knowing that the end was nigh. As talk of a challenge was the only conversation in town, both Gerry Hand and Nick Bolkus told me that the Left would not seek to bind their members, which was a real breakthrough: three or four additional Left votes were certain from the moment they said those words. Perhaps these hardy souls would have broken Left solidarity even without a dispensation (they privately indicated that they would support Keating this time, no matter what pressure was brought to bear on them) but I could tell Gerry Hand wanted an end to our party's public agony and the personal turmoil from which there had been no escape.

One by one Caucus members began to tell the press gallery that they had switched to Keating. Harry Woods was first out of the box and I made sure there was a steady flow to follow him. This was orchestrated because I still hoped that a ballot would not have to take place and that the transition would be peaceful and dignified. The Hawke ministers—Beazley, Ray, Evans, Duffy, Bolkus and Hand—met late on the night of Wednesday 11 December and agreed that the next day they would approach Hawke jointly to call it quits. My elation at hearing this news from Robert Ray was moderate: I could not get Robert to commit himself to my course of action if Hawke refused.

When these ministers, who had been the backbone of the Hawke forces, marched into his office to tell him he could not win a ballot and that he should resign, they knew they were sounding the death knell of his prime ministership. Hawke would only agree to consider the position they put to him and to meet him later in the day. That's enough, I thought. He has no choice now. He will resign.

At the second meeting, Hawke told them that he had thought about their proposal but after due consideration he had decided to fight any challenge that might take place. The delegation accepted this and added that they would support him in the ballot! That Hawke could reject their proposition was extraordinary; that these ministers could accept that rejection and pledge to vote for him was downright incredible. All of them were aware that the fatally wounded leadership that was Hawke's could not recover. They knew, and some of them at least desired, that Keating would be Prime Minister within days.

Perhaps the most embarrassing moment I have seen any minister endure was the press conference Kim Beazley gave to announce that Hawke would not resign and that those who had told him to go would now help him to stay. I was too stunned by what he was saying to feel sorry for him: that came later. I didn't waste my time being angry because the die was cast and the result was certain. That Keating would have to force Hawke out in the Caucus room was tragic, but we hadn't embarked on the journey to give it up before we reached our destination.

Bob McMullan drafted a petition for the requisite number of Caucus members to sign so that we could force a ballot if Hawke would not give us one. This effort to postpone a ballot till after the Christmas break was something I did not expect: if that happened, there would be no blood left in Labor's body. Even Hawke, I think, wanted the confrontation to be over. Beazley made several further attempts to persuade Hawke to stand down, but there was no hope of that. The date of the ballot was set for Thursday 19 December.

I was loath to share my concerns with too many colleagues, but I was worried. Hawke was not acting rationally, and if the PM is irrational more than one man should be concerned. He had been cheerful at the Lodge Christmas function for the Caucus on Wednesday 18 December, which I had had the good grace to avoid. And on the morning of the nineteenth, Stephen Loosley told me about a conversation he had just had with Robert Ray. The Defence Minister told Loosley that his great fear was that Hawke would simply walk out of the Oval Office, get into his car and drive out to Yarralumla to advise Bill Hayden to dissolve the parliament and call an election. Robert would not have told Stephen that story if he had not wanted him to repeat it to me. I told Loosley that Hawke was 'unhinged'—anything was possible. Robert and some of the others were working hard to get Hawke's numbers up and I could sense that they were doing very well—too well.

Keating and I had worked in tandem until almost three on the morning of the Thursday to dredge up our last few votes, and it was just as well we did. I rang Wendy Fatin and, after putting the case to her I asked whether she would mind Keating calling her at such a late hour. I told Paul to ring her and that I had just taken her name out of the 'Doubtful' column and put it in the 'Fors'. He rang back to say that she was in the cart, and I made another call: this time to Peter Baldwin, showing that time is a great healer. I cannot claim that he and I were close friends by the end of 1991, but I had come to respect his intellect. If anyone on the Left knew that Hawke was finished, it would be Peter Baldwin. When I went to bed at three in the morning, to toss and turn for a few uncomfortable hours before going back to Parliament House, I had Keating's confirmation that Baldwin could be moved across the page to join Wendy Fatin.

The meeting for the ballot was set for 6.30pm, and the phone calls continued all day, though the heat and passion of the June challenge were missing. This was much more subdued and sedate, though I had the shakes just the same.

As time went on I suspected that the Hawke forces, who had claimed they were only trying to make the result respectable, were doing much better than that. It was very, very tight. Con Sciacca, a Hawke supporter, had returned to Brisbane to be at his dying son's bedside, and I told Robert Ray that he could have a pair. Jim Snow, who supported Keating, rang to let me know that a family member had been in an accident. He offered to attend the meeting if necessary, but I was able to tell him that he would not be required.

I could see that a swing back towards Hawke was taking place. Later in the day, I decided to refuse a pair for Gareth Evans, who was overseas on official business. I have been criticised for this, and would advance two pieces of evidence in my defence. Firstly, on every other occasion I could remember where a vote was called for, from leadership challenges to uranium debates, ministers, like Caucus members, got on planes and came home: why should this be an exception? Secondly, this ballot was too bloody close for comfort, and there was nothing to be gained by giving away any votes. Giving Evans a pair would have been an act of madness. Mind you, it would have been fair and reasonable. This was the first visit to Indonesia by a senior Australian minister since the Dili massacre, and aborting it could have created a major diplomatic incident. But we were in it to win it, not to be fair.

Hawke kept calling people right up until the time the ballot began; he didn't lose heart, he kept right on going. At 5.30, an hour before the ballot was due to begin, a very worried Gary Punch entered my office. Without even bothering to sit down, he said solemnly: 'We can actually lose this challenge.' I stood up, took a deep breath and told him that, yes, we could lose because it was very close.

We walked into the Caucus room with 63 promises. This demonstrates why the telephone is such an inferior method of communication, in spite of being used so often in my trade. On the telephone you can't see people's eyes, and when you can't see their eyes you don't know whether they are telling the truth. Any halfway decent liar can learn to mask the voice, but only the super-gifted few can manage to lie without giving some sort of hint with their eyes. There was no way these 63 Caucus members could all be telling the truth. As the ballot began, I bet Laurie Brereton that we would get 56 votes: his count was 57.

The ballot took place. The returning officer, Senator Jim McKiernan from Western Australia, announced in his broad Irish brogue and with a tear in his eye that Paul Keating had been elected leader by 56 votes to 51.

That announcement released the tension in the party that had been building for at least three years. For the first time in a long time, we could again look outward, we could concentrate on defeating the real enemy.

Emotion in the room ran high. Caucus members swarmed round Hawke and Keating, and most of them had tears in their eyes. Even John Dawkins, who had been campaigning for Keating for years, was shedding a tear. It was the end of an era and the historic nature of the moment was lost on very few. Even if you didn't like Hawke personally, even if you had come to believe he had to go for the sake of the government, he was every bit the living legend I had told him he was six months earlier, even though that legend had been tarnished a little by the indignity of defeat in Caucus.

Hawke and Keating made the requisite speeches of the victor and the vanquished. I cannot remember a word they said because I was incapable of listening. I didn't shed a tear, I didn't rush to commiserate or congratulate. I felt no pleasure, no remorse. I felt nothing. I can only remember thinking that it would have been a better world and I a better person if none of this had happened.

Indeed, no triumph was visible on the face of any Keating supporter. Keating himself was quiet, thoughtful, apprehensive. He knew the height of the mountain he had to climb. He pledged to give the job everything he had, to be honest with the people and to fight the battle against unemployment with all the energy he could muster.

On the day before he became Prime Minister, a *Bulletin* poll measured Keating against Hewson. Keating was preferred as PM by 12 per cent; Hewson scored in excess of 80 per cent. While most of us suspected that the Opposition's GST would prove to be electorally unpopular, we were looking at a party trailing in the polls by more than 20 points, and a leader trailing by an unprecedented 70. Very few thought we had any hope of winning: Keating's job, as far as I was concerned, was to lift Labor and to put up a fight. If we were going to be beaten, at least we would go down fighting, our heads held high. I told Keating he could not win. Thankfully, and not for the first time, he completely ignored me.

The morning after his success, he rang me in the office to say he was coming round for a cup of tea. I told him that he was now the Prime Minister and that I would come to him. But with Hawke clearing out his office Keating had nowhere decent to go, so he drank his tea in my office. It was more than a social call, of course: he got right down to business about the allocation of portfolios.

Ministers who had supported Hawke were not demoted and most were happy. There were only a couple of exceptions. The first was Ralph Willis, who had been Treasurer for only a couple of weeks and was moved back to be Minister for Finance; John Dawkins, who had been there for Keating since 1988, wanted Treasury and there was no way Keating could refuse. John Kerin was given Trade, but he lost his Cabinet post. This was a sad end for his distinguished career as a Cabinet minister, but you are only as good as your last job and his stint as Treasurer had been disastrous. I asked for Transport and Communications and Keating immediately agreed.

The New Year promised excitement. I finally had the job I really wanted, I had the leader I thought the government should have. I could not know that out of clear blue skies, and without any warning, my biggest political setback was not far away.

EPILOGUE

The Price of Success

For someone like me, success has been as much a curse as it has been a blessing. In my own party, there were those who couldn't forgive the leadership campaigns and my role in them: in the Opposition too many saw me as the architect of too many Labor victories. In the press gallery, a flock of vultures were ready to pounce on me if I stumbled, some because they believed that, no matter how well I had done, I was not an appropriate person to occupy high office, and others because they just didn't like me.

The problem with that situation was that somebody like me was bound to stumble. I like to have mates and I like to help them. In fact during my career I have helped many people who couldn't be classed as friends, who were no more than acquaintances. Many were people who walked in off the street and asked whether I was in a position to help. I have rarely refused anyone.

So I couldn't contemplate refusing a reference to a friend I had known since I was in my teens. Throw in the fact that he was married to my first cousin and the thought of knocking back such a request did not enter my head. I signed a letter of introduction, informing the reader that I knew Greg Symons well and that he was a good bloke. I had signed many similar references over the years, not one of which had ever caused me to suffer the slightest discomfort. This one brought me undone.

In late April 1992, I addressed the conference of the Australian Telecommunications Users Group in Melbourne, and I told them I had the best job in the government and that I intended to hang onto it. The omens, as it turned out, were not good. That morning as I flew down to Melbourne I had complained to my staff that the *Australian* newspaper carried the story that Greg Symons—to whom they knew I had given a reference—had been arrested and charged with fraud in the Marshall Islands. I was whingeing that a story like this would not have made page 20 had it concerned any minister but myself. Some journalists at the conference questioned me about this, heralding the beginning of a saga that saw the Symons story stuck firmly to Australia's front pages for more than three weeks.

When Symons was arrested a week or two before the story broke I had been contacted for help by his family and friends. In the Marshall Islands, one man wields enormous power: Mr Kabua, the President. He has much more say in the running of every facet of government activity than would be conceivable in a country like ours. If Greg Symons were to be allowed to return to Australia, where all the necessary documents were kept, to prepare his defence, only one person had the clout to make it happen.

To ring Mr Kabua and ask for Symons' release on bail and the return of his passport to travel to Australia was obviously sensitive, so I rang Gareth Evans, the Minister for Foreign Affairs, and asked whether it would be improper. Gareth's response was that, provided I was asking only for Symons' passport to be returned to him, and provided I was sure as I could be that he would return to the Marshall Islands for his trial, I could make the call. He told me to stress that I was not calling in an official capacity.

It took me a few calls to reach Mr Kabua. I followed the script I had agreed upon with Gareth Evans, and the call lasted only a few minutes. The President listened, thanked me for calling and promised only to look into the matter. My request was never agreed to, I gave not the slightest hint of pressure to the President, and I had received the permission of our Minister for Foreign Affairs. Yet that one call, out of the many thousands I have made during my political career, just about sealed my fate.

When real publicity and pressure were generated over the following weeks, I had laid myself open to a charge of 'heavying' the president. That I had not done so and that there was no evidence that I had done so were of little consequence. My reputation, it seemed, was larger than I: everybody apparently wished to believe the worst. If there is one thing I hate being it is helpless, and for three weeks I helplessly watched the arrest of a friend in a group of islands whose location in the Pacific was a complete mystery to me.

At the same time, I stood accused of two other crimes. As a minister I had failed to declare on my pecuniary interests form that I was a member of the board of radio station 2HD in Newcastle. At the time, I was senior vice-president of the New South Wales Labor Party, the majority shareholder in the station. I had resigned as a director a few months earlier, not bothering to declare the directorship because I had received no remuneration for it, and it was a position I held by virtue of being an officer of the New South Wales Labor Party.

My failure to disclose the directorship was an error: even in retrospect it could hardly be described as a big deal. But apparently my apology for the omission wasn't good enough for the *Australian*, which took what might be described as a jaundiced view of my good self during this critical period. An editorial on 5 May summed up the perception problem pretty well:

> Yet in meekly accepting an apology from his Minister for Transport and Communications and refusing to take any other action, Mr Keating draws attention to the fact that Senator Richardson is not just any other Cabinet Minister. Senator Richardson's support for Mr Keating was a factor in his successful overthrow of Mr Hawke. Moreover the impression that Senator Richardson has often left is that he is a law unto himself within the government. That may be wrong, but it is only reinforced by the events of last week.

No Prime Minister would have treated any minister differently—

and the prospect of being sacked or asked to resign for a misdemeanour like mine is nil. The editorial did not get around to telling us what penalty would have been justified in the circumstances, but it well exemplifies the poisonous atmosphere in which I was trying to survive.

On Friday 8 May, Mike Seccombe in the *Sydney Morning Herald* wrote: 'Likewise [having just referred to the 2HD directorship] he neglected to reveal that he had the use of stockbroker Rene Rivkin's London flat and Rolls-Royce. Whoops. Bang.' In 1989 I had stayed overnight in Rene's flat. The Prime Minister's office had told me that because my stay had been so short there was no need to declare it. On the second occasion in February 1992, I had stayed for three nights, which I would have declared some months later when the register for the year was finally compiled. Inherent in Seccombe's piece was the view that my failure to reveal Rivkin's generosity was improper or a breach of the rules. That this was not the case was of no benefit to me in the climate that people like Seccombe had helped create.

Meanwhile, virtually every question in Senate Question Time was asked of me or about me. Having said that I had no knowledge of Mr Symons' business affairs, I admitted that I had been aware that Symons was involved in a business migration scheme. This was seized upon by the Opposition, the Democrats and the press gallery, and I was censured by the Senate for misleading it. Given that I knew no details of the scheme, I could not see how I had misled anyone: I know that BHP makes steel but I have no knowledge of the company's business. Misleading the parliament is a sackable offence, and it mattered little whether I had actually been guilty of it or not. By allowing even the slightest possibility that I had misled, I assisted in cutting my own throat.

On Saturday 9 May I rang Paul Keating and suggested that he should demand a report from me on the whole affair. Much of the attack from the media and the Opposition had centred on his failure to do something—anything—about me. I wanted him to be seen as seizing the initiative. On Sunday morning I waited in vain for the Prime Minister's announcement. His staff had talked him out of making one, and in so doing they did their boss a grave disservice.

Over the next few days a series of articles appeared, giving details of a number of failed business ventures in which Greg Symons had been involved. Various creditors were named who were allegedly owed $1.5 million. According to the newspapers a scheme of arrangement had been entered into between Symons and his creditors, where the latter accepted $25 000. With the exception of my cousin, Symons' sister-in-law, I did not know the creditors, and had never had so much as a conversation with any of them—yet I was deemed to know all about their business relations with Symons and their scheme of arrangement.

The Democrats lapped up this information and decided to find a way of 'gagging' me in the Senate. Their then leader, Senator John Coulter, said: 'How can you know someone for twenty years without some sense that he was involved in a string of business failures? This strains credibility to breaking point.' His colleague Senator Robert Bell was even better: 'He's asking us to believe he is Manuel on the one hand, and on the other he is the Svengali of Australian politics.' As well as being two foreign gentlemen, I was supposed to know what every move would be from every player in the game. Therefore, the story ran, I must have known a great deal more about Symons' business than I had been prepared to admit.

Finally on Thursday 14 May, five days after I had suggested Keating should ask me for a report on the matter, he announced that I would be required to produce just such a report. The Senate president Kerry Sibraa was also asked to prepare a report after it was revealed that at my request he had seen Greg Symons, who had asked him to facilitate some appointments with officials and politicians in the United States. As he knew Symons was my friend, Sibraa had complied with this request, and had asked staff at the Australian Embassy in Washington to assist Symons in these endeavours.

Sibraa was cleared very quickly: he produced evidence of correspondence from a number of Marshall Islands ministers that showed Symons was acting on behalf of their government. The fact that Symons did have some official status was virtually overlooked by the Opposition and the media as the pursuit of my good self continued to gather speed. Don Russell, Keating's senior adviser, gave me a copy of a memo that Symons had allegedly sent to me with a copy to an official in our US Embassy.

My office found no record of this memo being received, and I had no recollection of ever having seen it.

In May 1992, this was a pretty decisive nail in my coffin and denials were futile. I was too good a target, too many marksmen were taking aim and I was being hurt even when they missed. When the feeding frenzy is on there is no time for explanations and even if there is, nobody is prepared to listen.

A staff member found that memo in a Social Security file in December 1993. Ministers receive heaps of correspondence, most of which they do not see. Even if Greg Symons had put a document into my hands, I wouldn't have read it because I was too busy doing my job. On the other hand, I took time out to make some phone calls to help him in making contacts, because that's what I have always done.

In that feeding frenzy, Greg Symons' rights were never observed. Camera crews from all over Australia descended upon Majuro, the main island in the Marshall group, the London *Times* published an article about his arrest and every move he had ever made went under the microscope. People I had never heard of were interviewed and asked how often they thought I had met or spoken to Greg Symons.

When he was eventually sentenced in the Marshall Islands on charges of forgery and fraud relating to almost $2 million tied up in the business migration scheme, he served a few months' night-time detention and was returned to Australia. Just what role some officials in the Marshall Islands might have had in the affair was never explored. Symons was led up a dangerous and dodgy garden path by some people in that country and he never had a hope of defending himself.

What helped make this one of the most miserable periods of my life was the fact that I was suffering from my worst-ever bout of gout. This is a particularly painful ailment, as its sufferers will testify: my right foot was so swollen that I could not put a shoe on it for weeks. Despite medication, the pain was constant and soul-destroying, and the drugs prescribed were strong enough to cause vomiting and diarrhoea. On one classic occasion during the relentless Opposition questioning that went on for a fortnight I answered one question, hobbled out to the toilet to vomit while a government backbencher asked Gareth Evans a question, then returned in time to take the next question. This is a pretty good reason for a less than perfect Senate performance, though I could never have won this fight no matter how healthy I felt. To make matters worse, my family was under great strain, with the media camped outside my home for days—a habit I still despise.

Longevity in politics can bring forgiveness with it, and the loyalty my colleagues showed to me during this period came as a surprise. The Left, with whom I had fought for more than two decades, stuck like glue. Nick Bolkus rang Democrats to plead my case, John Faulkner argued my case in the Senate. Only one Labor MP displayed a lack of solidarity and that was John Scott, who had spent the best part of ten years turning Hindmarsh from a very safe seat into a marginal one. One place that actively undermined me in those weeks was the Prime Minister's office. Two of the staff consistently told journalists that Keating was about to ask me to resign, or that I should resign. These staffers were new to the Labor Party and had no concept of its traditions: for someone like me resignation, however painful, comes when it is required. To my great disappointment, Bob Hogg joined this chorus. He should have known better.

On Friday 15 May, I met with my advisers—Peter Barron, Laurie Brereton and Leo McLeay—and we agreed that I could not allow the government to bleed any longer. I discussed the matter with my family and we decided that I would resign on the Monday. I finished preparing my report to the Prime Minister and composed the letter of resignation to accompany it.

I saw Paul Keating at lunchtime on Monday 18 May. We had been at odds so many times, but none of those occasions had involved a time of crisis for either of us. Whenever I was in strife Paul Keating was always there for me, and this time was no exception. It took forty-five minutes to get him even to open the envelope with my resignation in it. He wanted to fight: the warrior in him did not wish to allow the bastards (the Opposition, the Democrats and the press gallery) to have a win. He did not accept that I had committed a sackable offence and he wanted to stare them down. He knew this attitude was damaging the government, but he told me that there were times when the principle was worth fighting for.

By this stage it was obvious that the Senate intended to set up an inquiry of some kind, which was likely to run for months. An election in late 1992 was still a live option, and I told Paul I couldn't bear being responsible in any way for a Labor defeat. Eventually he yielded and even canvassed the possibility that I could come back later in the year. This would have been a nice plan, but it ignored the reality that the issue needed to be killed off, and my burial had to last at least till the next election. We shook hands and I marched off to a press conference to make my announcement.

I told the press gallery what I had written here, but they didn't really listen. Alan Ramsey wrote that I would never come back, Margo Kingston wanted the Senate to pursue an inquiry despite my resignation. Marion Wilkinson produced a 'Four Corners' episode that appeared on the night of my resignation, and was frustrated that a two-year search had failed to turn up the millions she was so sure I had made during the boom of the mid 1980s. I told the press conference that I hadn't made enough to buy one of John Hewson's Ferraris. When I returned to the ministry less than twelve months later, none of the journalists took the slightest exception. The Marshall Islands affair wrapped up the fish and chips for many a family meal, and Australia moved on.

While I reject the tenor of the contribution made by Mike Seccombe in the *Sydney Morning Herald* of Tuesday 19 May 1992, it did sum up my problem: 'There is something about the way Graham Richardson speaks which always gives the impression of candour, no matter how implausible the words.' I could say nothing the gallery would believe. They needed a rest from me, I needed a break from them.

I was to spend ten months out of the ministry and because I couldn't imagine that Labor would win the next election, I thought I would never return. For the first time in many years I was able to work respectable hours (forty to fifty per week) and to rebuild my health and well being. I decided to write this book and embarked on it, continued to take a role in the Right faction and in planning for the election to come. I was no longer a big shot and I revelled in the lack of attention: a rest does the world of good. Not that I wanted this anonymity to last forever; temporary retirement can become permanent all too quickly.

As the whole affair faded in the minds of the press gallery (I don't think it was ever a big deal in the real world of voters), the government of Paul Keating set about trying to minimise the extent of the defeat they fully expected at the next election.

In February 1992, only two months after he became Prime Minister, Paul Keating announced the One Nation package to lift Australia out of recession. Full of heroic assumptions about the economy and the capacity of state government utilities to be able to move quickly, this statement was all about Labor being Labor. Building big infrastructure projects that could be seen as part of a microeconomic reform program—for example, a national railway grid would speed up the transport of goods around the country and make it cheaper, directly employing people at a time of record unemployment and spending government funds to achieve it—all this was music to Labor ears. The party loved One Nation, and for a time there were high hopes that this initiative would restore Labor's fortunes in the polls and point us towards victory.

Such hopes were the province of the desperate—a fair description of a government traumatised by two leadership ballots in six months and trailing its Opposition by 20 points in the polls. Australia didn't want this government or its leader, and there was an assumption that we would drift to an inevitable defeat.

This assumption reckoned without John Hewson and the Liberals. Fightback, launched with such fanfare in the last months of Bob Hawke's prime ministership, was still regarded as worthy of a first birthday party. John Hewson, Peter Reith and Tim Fischer beamed as they cut the cake and an adoring throng of parliamentary Liberal and National Party MPs, all of whom without exception declared later that they always knew Fightback was a dud, applauded with gusto.

Their enthusiasm was never shared by the rest of the nation. While no single knockout blow was targeted at Fightback during 1992, its weakness was in calling to Australia to trust its architects in government. No matter at what level a consumption tax (or any tax for that matter) begins its life, it can be increased at any time when a government needs extra revenue. Australia was in no mood to trust any politician and, while a vengeful nation wanted to get rid of Keating and his government, it bore no love for Hewson and his Opposition. Hewson could not be warm: nobody should have expected people to react to him warmly. He was not loved and only barely liked, which is hardly a basis for trust.

As 1992 drew to a close, Paul Keating contemplated a December election. Bob Hogg and I opposed this view on the grounds that every extra day people had to think about a consumption tax was a good day for Labor. News of the electorate's lack of enthusiasm for Fightback in all its glory had reached even the Liberals, and John Hewson's announcement that the consumption tax would no longer apply to food could have been a big plus for the Liberals had it been made in the first week of an election campaign.

Changing Fightback in December to remove its effect on food was an admission by the Liberals that there were problems in selling the package. Why it took the Liberal Party more than twelve months to work this out is the really intriguing question. It is too trite—as well as being incredible—to suggest that the entire parliamentary party and the organisation were mesmerised by the strength of John Hewson's convictions.

John Hewson had painted himself as a non-politician. He was telling us what was right, whether it was popular or not. By solemnly vowing that if Fightback was ever changed he would resign as leader, Hewson laid down a hurdle too big to jump. When the Liberals' polling showed that a change was needed, Hewson calmly announced it. Whatever gain might have come from removing the tax on food was lost when Hewson showed himself to be just another politician whose word meant little or nothing. Australia had not really loved him at any time, but might just have given him the job of Prime Minister if they didn't have to trust yet another politician.

Laying the blame for a dud policy entirely at the feet of John Hewson and his hapless deputy Peter Reith is convenient for the rest of the party, but it does not stand up to analysis. If any Liberals were opposed to Fightback during 1992, they were not sharing their views with anyone. Newspapers were not bristling with leaks expressing discontent and revolution because the whole party clearly believed that, with a minimum of fine tuning, they were on a winner.

The Fightback package—not just the goods and services tax but the savage cuts in government expenditure as well—suited their ideological bent. It was right up a good conservative's alley.

The business organisations praised its vision and all around Australia the Liberals repeated the errors that had so often been reflected in their inferior advertising during the 1980s: they are excellent at convincing each other that their policies are good, but they rarely find out whether the rest of the country agrees with them.

Mind you, Hewson had to accept his fair share of the blame. He was a man for whom listening came hard. Like so many self-made and successful men, he had a real conviction that his views were there to be accepted, not debated and, being He Who Must Be Obeyed, he resented those who challenged his policies.

Like so many of the modern Liberals—John Howard, Nick Greiner, Richard Court and the others—he was not a good mixer, an awkward man socially whose natural reticence and formality were hard to overcome in a country where easygoing mateship is prized as a virtue. On television he looked decidedly reluctant to enter Australia's lounge rooms, and no amount of photo opportunities showing him at sporting events helped. Once or twice an open-necked shirt would have looked okay, but the attempts to portray Hewson as just another informal guy was more difficult than simply getting him to remove his tie. It required a change in his state of mind and that, it seemed, was out of the question.

With the benefit of hindsight, it is easy to see the negatives for the Liberals. But we didn't see how they would help push us over the line. Well behind in the polls on preferred prime minister and voting intentions, Labor had no right to believe in victory. I gave us no chance at all. And as we headed home after Christmas, Labor's troops were still preparing for defeat.

When the campaign began in late January, there was a distinct lack of excitement and enthusiasm. On Channel Nine's 'Sunday' program I recorded a four-minute campaign review once a week, and there was precious little to report at the start. I suspect that, because all the candidates as well as the voters considered the result a foregone conclusion, the interest that election campaigns usually spark seemed to be missing. The campaign opening was a lacklustre affair at the Bankstown Town Hall, where Paul Keating seemed nervous and tentative. His speech was delivered haltingly and he occasionally stumbled. However, the Liberals did even worse, wiping out any cause for despondency. John

Hewson produced a parade of those said to have been injured by the recession. The press likened it to American evangelists seeking to heal the sick and the lame.

There were other straws in the wind. Jeff Kennett's industrial relations reforms were creating havoc in Victoria; for a time John Halfpenny looked as if he was on the side of the angels, with a real danger of becoming popular. We had lost a swag of seats in Victoria in 1990, and this was the state where we hoped a comeback might be possible. We hoped that Labor would gain because Kennett's policies were sufficiently unpopular to help Victorians quell their desire to inflict further punishment on the party that had given them John Cain and the worst of the recession.

In any campaign, the leader's staff play a critical role. The Keating office had very little campaign experience, and tensions between them and Bob Hogg's team were quick to surface. Having surfaced, however, they were even more quickly sunk. By the 1993 campaign, Bob Hogg was the most experienced party official in the country. This was his last campaign, and he gave it all he had.

On the ground, too, Labor was far better than the Opposition. Labor was nowhere near as well prepared as it should have been at the start of the campaign, but moved so fast that this was not noticed. In any event, a lack of funds dictated that the start of television advertising could be delayed and some more time for preparation was made available. I was sitting with John Singleton when the first Liberal advertisement was shown on television, depicting people targeted in the sights of a rifle and purporting to represent all the honest Australian workers struck down by Labor's policies. Singleton's observation was: 'Christ, I hope they stick with it,' which he repeated every time he saw a new advertisement. Bob Hogg, John Singleton and Alan Morris were far too good for their Liberal counterparts, whoever they were.

Prime ministers are on the road during the campaign, and they rarely see television. Nevertheless, every party member offers advice for the kinds of advertisements that should be run, and Keating was no exception. He and his staff sought to impose their view on the creative people. Keating was comfortable with Singleton and believed in Morris, so any tensions between his staff and the Hogg team never became serious. Fortunately for Labor, the professionals remained paramount in our thinking and very few problems were encountered.

The campaign did not spring to life until John Hewson appeared on the John Laws show on 17 February and was forced to answer questions about what parts of a birthday cake would be subject to the goods and services tax and how the tax would affect butchers and the price of meat. Hewson stumbled over the details of the tax, and too many people took the view that if Hewson couldn't understand it, then it was a bit rich to hope that everybody else could ever get up to speed.

The Laws program hurt Hewson badly and it was only then, two and a half weeks into the campaign, that the tide began to turn for the government. As soon as the focus was off unemployment (which was lead weight in Labor's saddlebags but not a huge negative, since by that stage Australia was familiar with high levels of unemployment) and onto the GST, Labor's poll ratings started to get better. The Liberals could not afford this kind of attention.

Keating also struck gold when Hewson denied that Medicare would be destroyed but maintained a policy that allowed for no other consequence. Shadow minister for health Dr Bob Woods managed to convince the Liberals to adopt what was virtually an Australian Medical Association policy; bulk billing was to go for most Australians, and those with private health insurance would be given tax breaks. Dismantling Medicare had brought the Liberals undone time and time again: they were determined to follow the same failed path in 1993.

As soon as Paul Keating saw that he was in with a chance, his performance started to improve. By the end of the third week of the campaign, Labor's private polls were showing substantial improvement. The Liberals' pollsters were clearly registering the same phenomenon. At Liberal rallies around the country, the faithful flocked to hear John Hewson take on student interjectors. His campaign team must have been asleep; it was difficult to believe that a potential Prime Minister would chant the banal phrase 'Labor's got to go' at rallies in all the major cities, but he did. To see Hewson, Howard and their ilk out there acting like a bunch of rowdy protesters was an unwelcome sight on our television screens every night. Rallies convince nobody, though they did give the Liberals another chance to convince each other.

The two Keating–Hewson debates shown on '60 Minutes' and ABC TV were the other main events. In the first debate on 18 February '60 Minutes' used a so-called 'people meter' with a studio audience to record the audience's reaction during the debates. A 'worm' graphed the progress of the contenders—and the worm turned for Paul Keating. He won both debates clearly and this was reflected in the polls. The worst moment for Hewson in terms of the 'worm' favouring Keating came with a defence of the AMA and his health policy. Any move on Medicare was still unpopular, yet the Liberals pressed on.

With two weeks to go, I started to believe that Labor could win. With one week to go I knew we would win. The polls showed a Labor resurgence but it wasn't until polling day itself that they got around to showing us that a close result was even possible. There was no shame in being wrong and the pollsters could simply have explained that, with neither side popular, it had been difficult for those interviewed to express a preference for anyone. It was the feeling against the goods and services tax that the polls never quite discovered. To explain this failure, it was suggested that there had been a late swing in the last twenty-four hours. I have never accepted the theory that the god of elections visited all of us in the early morn of Saturday 13 March and anointed us with pro-Labor intentions.

The second 'great debate' took place on 7 March, just six days before polling day. It was a slaughter. Whereas the first debate had been scored by both the people meter and the pundits as a narrow win to Keating, this one was scored by everyone as an overwhelming victory. Keating had peaked at the right time and a tentative Hewson gave every impression of struggling to last the distance.

My trip to Tasmania over the next few days was enough to convince me that we could make it. Tasmania had been a black hole for us for so long but even in Bass, held by shadow communications spokesperson Warwick Smith, one of the Opposition's better performers, I could sense a change. Bass had been the scene of a real debacle in 1975 but I had been there a few times in the previous twelve months and was beginning to understand the place. Tasmania makes up its own mind and mainland swings and opinions count for little. What's more, Tasmania tends to swing all over and I was able to ring Keating at the end of the week and tell him I thought we could win two or three in the island state. If we could, we were home.

By Friday 12 March, I knew we would win. When I'm sure I bet money, and this occasion was no different. On that Friday I ensured that by the Monday my cash resources would be considerably replenished. I have yet to place a losing bet on an election, but that is because I have had access to better information than those who thought they were experts. Given that my access to that information will be reduced over time, I think I will retire undefeated.

On the Friday evening I headed down to Canberra for the great day. I spent Saturday 13 March reading briefs on every electorate and every candidate so I could bring the right kind of specialist knowledge to the Channel Nine coverage.

My preparation was interrupted only once, when Paul Keating rang during the morning. While the weather improved later, it was raining as he drove along Parramatta Road in Leichhardt. Keating was depressed. He told me how hard he had fought the good fight, how much he had needed the extra time that Hawke's intransigence had cost him, and how tough it would be to see the Liberals win. He sounded tired, almost exhausted, and I was astounded. The polls in the newspapers that morning had Labor right back in the race and I had no doubts at all that this would be his greatest day. I told him to buck up, exude the confidence for which he was famed and prepare a victory speech.

The Channel Nine coverage was to begin at 6.30pm and I was supposed to be there early. I am always late and this was no exception. At 6.15pm I walked into the make-up room to endure yet another futile attempt to make me look good. The Liberals' Michael Kroger was sitting in the chair having the finishing touches applied to his handsome visage. 'Congratulations,' he said. 'I've seen enough of the Tasmanian results and we're fucked.' The vagaries of daylight saving, implemented differently by each state government, meant that voting in Tasmania had finished an hour earlier and the trends were already obvious. Even before the telecast had begun I knew we had won and so did Kroger.

He had to sit through another five hours of a telecast where he was forced to hold out hope when none existed. He was gracious in defeat, though he gives the impression that he doesn't like to lose.

It was a fantastic experience. Winning when you have been told for a couple of years you will lose is a great feeling. In New South Wales we won everything. You could drive from the Opera House to the town of Wellington in the bush and not leave a Labor electorate. In Victoria we won back most of the ground we had lost in 1990. In Tasmania we won three, including Bass. We dropped a few in the other states but had increased our majority, and governments have rarely done that since the Second World War.

John Hewson was supposed to celebrate at a black-tie dinner with the top end of town at Sydney's Inter-Continental Hotel. The sight of a host of well known businessmen staring incredulously at the television screens giving them the wrong message will take some forgetting. Some tried to skulk away into the night without being seen. The celebration didn't even turn into a wake—the guests just went home.

Hewson did not concede until far too late. When there is no hope you might as well make the concession, but not our John. When it finally came, he did not even have the grace to congratulate Keating. It seemed as if the defeat had not really dawned on him. He retreated to the Wentworth Hotel where the management, like so many Liberal supporters, had prepared a huge cake for the victory. It took the hotel's staff two days to finish it off.

Keating came out just after midnight to address his supporters at the Bankstown Sports Club. His speech was a classic, his depression of the morning completely forgotten. 'This is the sweetest victory of all. It is a victory for the true believers,' he said. The party was ecstatic, and the celebrations went on for months. The only other time I have witnessed such unrestrained joy in winning was Whitlam's victory in December 1972.

For me, the win meant a great deal. The events of 1991 had caused considerable angst among my colleagues, often directed at me. The victory ensured that the vanquished in the Hawke challenge would lose the resentment they had continued to harbour. For Keating it meant vindication. He was no longer the party operator who had usurped his leader's job by securing a majority of Caucus members. After a lifetime in politics, he was the people's choice.

A measure of the status that victory gave Paul Keating was the way in which the ministry was elected. For the first time in its history, the Labor Caucus simply endorsed a slate of candidates nominated by the Prime Minister. In keeping with his promises to promote new talent, Michael Lavarch and Michael Lee were catapulted into Cabinet. To the disgust of most of the Left faction Frank Walker got a guernsey, as did Rosemary Crowley. Neither could have won their faction's ballot, so prime ministerial intervention brought significant change.

After ten months on the back bench, I returned to Cabinet. On Monday 15 March, Keating rang me and said, 'I know I wouldn't have this job if it wasn't for you, so you can have any job you want.' He went on to suggest that I could have Industry if I insisted, but because he and I had never agreed on industry policy, he would prefer another choice. He reasoned that fighting with me would get more publicity than it deserved, and the government would suffer. I was in no position to argue, so I asked what else was available. He offered Health and I accepted immediately.

A few days later he offered me the post of Australian ambassador to the United States. The tone of the conversation was vastly different from the time three years earlier when Bob Hawke had offered me London. Keating just said: 'Mate, I know you don't want to stay much longer, and if you want a really important job after politics, have a think about this for a few days.' I am not certain that my family will ever forgive me for declining the offer.

These conversations sum up what many have never been able to understand about the bonds between mates. We fight and argue for as long as it doesn't matter. When it counts, we stick.

It is difficult to write about events that have occurred more recently than the 1993 election. Having resigned from the Cabinet and the parliament exactly one year after being sworn in as Minister for Health in 1993, it seems indecent to recount what happened yesterday. (Some in the Labor Party will chide me for writing about last week, as they see it, but I have prepared myself for that.)

While I was wrestling with various attempts to give this work a title, A. B. Facey's great book *A Fortunate Life* continually popped into my head. If his life was fortunate, mine has been even more so.

Probably nobody in post-war Australian politics has been in the right place at the right time as often as I was. Sometimes dumb luck had me in the right spot at the right time, sometimes it was careful planning or just an instinct for knowing where the right place will be and when to be there. To have been fortunate enough to work closely with the likes of John Ducker, Neville Wran, Bob Hawke and Paul Keating ensured that I had to amount to something. They did not teach me to lead because leadership cannot be taught. But from observing them I learned to recognise a leader when I saw one.

Neither Hawke nor Keating was as bad as his detractors thought, and neither was as good as his supporters wanted to believe. Whether you support the champion or the challenger, be assured that they are flawed. They have faults. They are weak at the same moment they are strong and ordinary when they are magnificent, because their faults don't go away for good, they just take a back seat when great deeds are being done. We support human beings and we make a judgment on who is best equipped at any given moment.

From my parents and from those at the thousands of party and faction meetings I have attended from my teens to my forties, I learned what makes people tick. I learned the right words to get someone on side and when to say them. If anger was needed or a hint of menace, I learned how to provide it. In short, I was a pretty good persuader, bloody good in fact. I was rarely defeated in the party or the Cabinet on any issue I fought for.

The real question, then, is whether these skills ever achieved anything worthwhile. In part this question should be answered by reference to the tenet held dear by party loyalists, that the worst Labor government will still be better than a Liberal alternative. The last decade, it must be admitted, has seen increasing doubt heaped on this principle. The performance of a few state Labor governments has certainly caused Labor diehards some anxious moments, but it stretches credibility to believe that governments led by Peacock, Howard or Hewson could have been better than those led by Hawke and Keating.

Historically, Australia has handed Labor governments the toughest of tasks. To Hawke and Keating fell the job of dismantling the protectionist walls that had created an inefficient internalised industrial machine. The change to a broad-based economy rather than one totally reliant on commodities will take a long, long time. Given that we began three or four decades too late, Hawke and Keating have made a brave start. While we made mistakes such as delivering a recession rather than the promised soft landing, the social safety net was extended to ensure there was at least something for the dispossessed.

This is neither the time nor the place to list Labor's achievements and to give a detailed defence of our record. That would rob some economic rationalists of the opportunity to bore the arse off anyone who reads the tomes they will surely write over the next few years. It should suffice to say that Australians have said yes to us (or at least no to our opponents) five times.

They compared our leaders and voted Labor. They compared our respective front benches and ticked our box again. Person by person, the Labor Cabinets of 1983–94 have been far superior to the shadows who opposed them. There are at present only seven people in the Australian Parliament who have all the intellectual equipment to lead our country, and six of them—Keating, Beazley, Crean, Evans, Lawrence and Lee—are Labor. On the Liberal side only Costello has this capacity, and his progress is stymied by a Jeff Kennett veto. Costello's close friend and even greater enemy of Kennett, Michael Kroger, is the only other Liberal I have met who could do it, and he isn't in the parliament. Kroger and Costello, though, are still unreconstructed hardline right-wing conservatives who would need to moderate before Australia could wear them.

Whatever our faults might have been, I am proud to have been involved and grateful to the Labor Party for giving me that opportunity.

This book has not been about the effectiveness or the results of government policies, but rather how government and party decisions were made. This has been an essay in the accumulation and exercise of power.

Above all else, I have valued loyalty. I have given it and expected it in return. Not every reader will approve of the way in which I have conducted myself over the last twenty years. Some may draw comfort from the knowledge that divine inspiration was behind it all:

> *No greater love can a man have than to lay down his life for his friends.*
> *You are my friends if you do what I command.*
>
> (John 15: 13–14)

Amen.

APPENDIX I

Ministerial Staff 1983–1993

Over my years in parliament I have had the assistance of many dedicated staff whom I would like to acknowledge and thank:

Simon Balderstone
Greg Borschmann
Alf Bardzys
Tony Barry
Mary Bourke
Tony Bourke
Margaret Carruthers
Michelle Camilleri
Michael Crawford
Paul Conn
Paddy Constanzo
Gerard Early
Helen Finlayson
Sarah Finlayson
Margaret Fisher
Tony Fleming
Dianne Ford
Jane Fowler
Brett Gale
Brian Geraghty
Susan Gibb
Marion Grace
Chris Gration
Julie Hatcher
Col Hush
Morris Iemma
Hank Jansen
Moya Kirkman
Annemaree Lavella
Michelle Macaulay
Jan Marangon
Anne McCaig
Bruce Meagher
Paul Mountford
Ewan Morrison
Anne O'Conner
Helen O'Neill
Heather Le Nevez
Anita Phillips
Martelle Pluis
Theresa de Smet
Ken Reed
Ruth Rutherford
Jane Ryan
Vic Smith
Bob Stevens
David Tierney
Patti Warn
Janet Willis

APPENDIX II

Selective List of Ministers and their Ministries 1983–1993

THE FIRST HAWKE MINISTRY, 11 MARCH 1983 TO 13 DECEMBER 1984

Prime Minister
Robert James Lee Hawke

Deputy Prime Minister
Lionel Frost Bowen

Treasurer
Paul John Keating

Minister for Industry and Commerce
John Norman Button*

Minister for Science and Technology
Barry Owen Jones

Minister for Foreign Affairs
William George Hayden

Minister for Trade
Lionel Frost Bowen

Minister for Finance
John Sydney Dawkins

Attorney-General
Gareth John Evans, QC*

Minister for Education and Youth Affairs
Susan Maree Ryan*

Minister for Aboriginal Affairs
Allan Clyde Holding

Minister for Transport
Peter Frederick Morris

Minister for Communications
Michael John Duffy

Minister for Aviation
Kim Christian Beazley

Minister for Primary Industry
John Charles Kerin

Minister for Resources and Energy
Peter Alexander Walsh*

* Senator

Minister for Health
Dr Neal Blewett

Minister for Veterans' Affairs
Arthur Thomas Gietzelt*

Minister for Social Security
Donald James Grimes*

Minister for Defence
Gordon Glen Denton Scholes

Minister for Defence Support
Brian Leslie Howe

Minister for Immigration and Ethnic Affairs
Stewart John West

Minister for Home Affairs and the Environment
Barry Cohen

Minister for Sport, Recreation and Tourism
John Joseph Brown

Minister for Territories and Local Government
Thomas Uren

Minister for Employment and Industrial Relations
Ralph Willis

Special Minister of State
Michael Jerome Young (to 14 July 1983)/Kim Christian Beazley (to 21 January 1984)/ Michael Jerome Young

THE SECOND HAWKE MINISTRY: 13 DECEMBER 1984 TO 24 JULY 1987

Prime Minister
Robert James Lee Hawke

Deputy Prime Minister
Lionel Frost Bowen

Treasurer
Paul John Keating

Minister for Industry, Technology and Commerce
John Norman Button*

Minister for Science
Barry Owen Jones

Minister for Foreign Affairs
William George Hayden

Minister for Trade
John Sydney Dawkins

Minister for Finance
Peter Alexander Walsh*

Attorney-General
Lionel Frost Bowen

Minister for Education
Susan Maree Ryan*

Minister for Transport
Peter Frederick Morris

Minister for Communications
Michael John Duffy

Minister for Social Security
Brian Leslie Howe

Minister for Primary Industry
John Charles Kerin

Minister for Resources and Energy
Gareth John Evans, QC*

Minister for Health
Dr Neal Blewett

Minister for Defence
Kim Christian Beazley

Minister for Immigration and Ethnic Affairs
Christopher John Hurford

Minister for the Arts, Heritage and the Environment
Barry Cohen

Minister for Sport, Recreation and Tourism
John Joseph Brown

Minister for Local Government and Administrative Services
Thomas Uren

Special Minister of State
Michael Jerome Young (to 16 February 1987)/Michael Carter Tate

THE THIRD HAWKE MINISTRY 24 JULY 1987 TO 4 APRIL 1990

Prime Minister
Robert James Lee Hawke

Deputy Prime Minister
Lionel Frost Bowen

Treasurer
Paul John Keating

Minister for Industry, Technology and Commerce
John Norman Button*

Minister for Science and Small Business
Barry Owen Jones

Minister for Foreign Affairs and Trade
William George Hayden (to 17 August 1988)/Gareth John Evans, QC*

Minister for Trade Negotiations
Michael John Duffy

Minister for Finance
Peter Alexander Walsh*

Attorney-General
Lionel Frost Bowen

Minister for Employment, Education and Training
John Sydney Dawkins

Minister for Aboriginal Affairs
Gerard Leslie Hand

Minister for Transport and Communications
Gareth John Evans, QC* (to 2 September 1988)/Ralph Willis

Minister for Primary Industries and Energy
John Charles Kerin

Minister for Resources
Peter Frederick Morris (to 19 January 1988)/Peter Francis Salmon Cook*

Minister for Community Services and Health
Dr Neal Blewett

Minister for Veterans' Affairs
Benjamin Charles Humphreys

Minister for Social Security
Brian Leslie Howe

Minister for Defence
Kim Christian Beazley

Minister for Immigration and Ethnic Affairs
Michael Jerome Young (to 12 February 1988)

Minister for Immigration, Local Government and Ethnic Affairs
Allan Clyde Holding (from 15 February 1988 to 2 September 1988)/Robert Francis Ray*

Minister for the Environment and the Arts
Graham Frederick Richardson* (to 19 January 1988)

Minister for the Arts, Sport, the Environment, Tourism and Territories
John Joseph Brown (to 19 January 1988)/Graham Frederick Richardson*

Minister for Industrial Relations
Peter Frederick Morris

Special Minister of State
Susan Maree Ryan* (to 19 January 1988)

THE FOURTH HAWKE MINISTRY: 4 APRIL 1990 TO 20 DECEMBER 1991

Prime Minister
Robert James Lee Hawke

Deputy Prime Minister
Paul John Keating (to 3 June 1991)/Brian Leslie Howe

Treasurer
Paul John Keating (to 3 June 1991)/Robert James Lee Hawke (to 4 June 1991)/John

Charles Kerin (to 9 December 1991)/Ralph Willis

Minister for Industry, Technology and Commerce
John Norman Button*

Minister for Science and Technology
Simon Findlay Crean (to 4 June 1991)/Ross Vincent Free

Minister for Foreign Affairs and Trade
Gareth John Evans, QC*

Minister for Trade Negotiations
Dr Neal Blewett (to 1 February 1991)

Minister for Trade and Overseas Development
Dr Neal Blewett (from 1 February 1991)

Minister for Finance
Ralph Willis (to 9 December 1991)/Kim Christian Beazley

Attorney-General
Michael John Duffy

Minister for Employment, Education and Training
John Sydney Dawkins

Minister for Aboriginal Affairs
Robert Edward Tickner

Minister for Transport and Communications
Kim Christian Beazley (to 9 December 1991)/John Charles Kerin

Minister for Primary Industries and Energy
John Charles Kerin (to 4 June 1991)/Simon Findlay Crean

Minister for Resources
Alan Gordon Griffiths

Minister for Community Services and Health
Brian Leslie Howe (to 7 June 1991)

Minister for Health, Housing and Community Services
Brian Leslie Howe (from 7 June 1991)

Minister for Veterans' Affairs
Benjamin Charles Humphreys

Minister for Social Security
Graham Frederick Richardson*

Minister for Defence
Robert Francis Ray*

Minister for Immigration, Local Government and Ethnic Affairs
Gerard Leslie Hand

Minister for the Arts, Sport, the Environment, Tourism and Territories
Roslyn Joan Kelly

Minister for Industrial Relations
Peter Francis Salmon Cook*

THE FIRST KEATING MINISTRY 20 DECEMBER 1991 TO 24 MARCH 1993

Prime Minister
Paul John Keating

Deputy Prime Minister
Brian Leslie Howe

Treasurer
John Sydney Dawkins

Minister for Health, Housing and Community Services
Brian Leslie Howe

Minister for Industry, Technology and Commerce
John Norman Button*

Minister for Foreign Affairs and Trade
Gareth John Evans, QC*

Minister for Finance
Ralph Willis

Attorney-General
Michael John Duffy

Minister for Employment, Education and Training
Kim Christian Beazley

Minister for Social Security
Dr Neal Blewett

Minister for Transport and Communications
Graham Frederick Richardson* (to 18 May 1992)/Robert Lindsay Collins* (from 27 May 1992)

Minister for Defence
Robert Francis Ray

Minister for Immigration and Ethnic Affairs
Nick Bolkus*

Minister for the Arts, Sport, the Environment, Tourism and Territories
Roslyn Joan Kelly

Minister for Industrial Relations
Peter Francis Salmon Cook

Minister for Primary Resources and Energy
Simon Findlay Crean

Minister for Trade and Overseas Development
John Charles Kerin

Minister for Justice and Consumer Affairs
Michael Carter Tate* (to 27 May 1992)

Minister for Justice
Michael Carter Tate* (from 27 May 1992)

Minister for Aboriginal and Torres Strait Islander Affairs
Robert Edward Tickner

Minister for Science and Technology
Ross Vincent Free

PHOTOGRAPH CREDITS

COVER
Arunas/Transworld Publishers

SECTION ONE
Pages 1–4: Graham Richardson
Page 5, above: Graham Richardson
Page 5, below: Mitchell Library, State Library of NSW/courtesy ALP, NSW Branch
Page 6, above left: Graham Richardson
Page 6, above right: Martin Brannan/Fairfax Photo Library
Page 6, below and pages 7 & 8: Mitchell Library, State Library of NSW/courtesy ALP, NSW Branch

SECTION TWO
Page 1, above: Martin Brannan/Fairfax Photo Library
Page 1, below: Mark Knight/Graham Richardson
Page 2: Dr Bob Brown/Graham Richardson
Page 3, above: Courtesy Sun Pictorial News
Page 3, below: Mirror Australian Telegraph Publications
Page 4, above: A. Porrit/Mirror Australian Telegraph Publications
Page 4, below: Courtesy ALP, NSW Branch
Page 5: Courtesy Simon Balderstone
Page 6: Graham Richardson
Page 7, above: Patrick Cook/Graham Richardson
Page 7, below: Courtesy ALP, NSW Branch
Page 8: David Bartho/Fairfax Photo Library

SECTION THREE
Page 1: Geoff Pryor/courtesy the *Canberra Times*
Page 2: Michael Jones/Mirror Australian Telegraph Publications
Page 3, above: Stephen Cooper/Mirror Australian Telegraph Publications
Page 3, below: Michael Jones/Mirror Australian Telegraph Publications
Page 4, above: David Gray/Mirror Australian Telegraph Publications
Page 4, below: Graham Richardson
Page 5, above: Bill Mitchell/Graham Richardson
Page 5, below: David Foote, Auspic/Graham Richardson
Page 6: ABC TV/Graham Richardson
Page 7: Courtesy Mike Bowers
Page 8: Courtesy ALP, NSW Branch/Graham Richardson

INDEX